Armies of the Nineteenth Century: Asia

Armies of the Nineteenth Century: Asia

5: Japan and Korea

Organisation, warfare, dress and weapons
135 figures, 57 illustrations

by Ian Heath

A Foundry Books Publication

First published in Great Britain in 2011
by Foundry Books
24–34 St. Mark's Street
Nottingham
NG3 1DE
United Kingdom
Tel 0115 8414141

Foundry Books is dedicated to furthering the study of all aspects of military history,
and is happy to consider suggestions for new books on
historical military subjects.
If you have an idea or project suitable for our list, please write to
Foundry Books Editorial Office
at the above address.

ISBN 978-1-901543-25-4

Typeset & digital manipulation by Kevin Dallimore.

Printed by C&C Offset Printing Co. Ltd.

Other books by the same author:

Armies and Enemies of the Crusades 1096–1291 (WRG 1978)
Byzantine Armies 886–1118 (Osprey 1979)
Armies of the Dark Ages 600–1066 2nd edition (WRG 1980)
A Wargamers' Guide to the Crusades (Patrick Stephens 1980)
Armies of the Middle Ages vol.1 (WRG 1982)
Armies of the Middle Ages vol.2 (WRG 1984)
The Vikings (Osprey 1985)
Armies of Feudal Europe 1066–1300 2nd edition (WRG 1989)
The Irish Wars 1485–1603 (Osprey 1993)
The Taiping Rebellion 1851–66 (Osprey 1994)
Byzantine Armies 1118–1461 AD (Osprey 1995)
The North-East Frontier 1837–1901 (Osprey 1999)
The Sikh Army 1799–1849 (Osprey 2005)

Armies of the Sixteenth Century
1: England, Scotland, Ireland, the United Provinces, and the Spanish Netherlands 1487–1609 (Foundry 1997)
2: The Aztec and Inca Empires, other native peoples of the Americas, and the Conquistadores 1450–1608 (Foundry 1999)

Armies of the Nineteenth Century: Asia
1: Central Asia and the Himalayan Kingdoms (Foundry 1998)
2: China (Foundry 1998)
3: India's North-East Frontier (Foundry 1999)
4: Burma and Indo-China (Foundry 2003)

PREFACE

This series of books is not the first to attempt a collective overview of the armies and warriors of what a 19th-century soldier or colonial entrepreneur might have called, with disparaging undertones, the 'native states' of Asia. However, the few other English-language books that have ventured down this particular avenue of military history have confined themselves to the peoples affected by Britain's overseas ambitions, excluding all mention of those with which other colonial powers came into contact. In addition they approach their subject exclusively from the British Empire's viewpoint. In both of these regards they differ significantly from the book before you. The object of this series, by contrast, is to provide information on the armies and warbands fielded by all of the major, and many of the minor, independent powers and peoples of 19th-century Asia, whether 'tribes', kingdoms, or empires – not just those against whom the European powers fought, but also the indigenous peoples attacked by, conquered, or utterly destroyed in the course of interminable wars with their own more powerful neighbours. In each case the intention is to piece together a picture of their military organisation, fighting-style, and appearance in as much detail as contemporary accounts, modern research, and – above all – space, will permit.

The need to keep within the bounds of economic viability, along with the very vastness of the geographical region covered, nevertheless renders it necessary for me to apologise in advance for any omissions. There are not, I hope, many of these, and there are certainly none of major military or political significance, so that by and large readers should find that these volumes will enable them to envisage with reasonable clarity virtually any of the somewhat shadowy forces which most standard books on 19th-century history pit against colonial expansion in the East.

Japan, the principal subject of this volume, was an enthusiastic latecomer to the concept of colonialism. With the benefit of hindsight, of course, its military operations during the closing decades of the 19th century can be seen as the first fateful steps along a road that would lead, with horrible inevitability, to head-on collision with the Allies in the brutal Pacific War of 1941–45. In the late 19th century, however, Japan's courage, ardour, and determination were not only admired in both the United States and Britain, but were loudly applauded. The horrific cruelty of which Japanese soldiers were to prove capable in the 1930s and 1940s seems to have manifested itself only once during the period under review (at Port Arthur in November 1894), and was quickly glossed over at the time by most contemporary observers, who were far more interested in showering praise on Japan's flattering emulation of Western culture – which was just as well, since Japanese diplomats were quick to remind their critics of the colonial Powers' own less than pristine records in India, Africa, the American West, and other theatres of Imperialist conflict.

The astonishing speed of Japan's social and military reinvention during the century under review must surely be the most remarkable feature of this book. As late as the 1850s, the Japanese Empire remained technologically and militarily stagnant, an isolationist, mediaeval state that had been marking time for the best part of half a millennium; but within just 40 years – in what must rank as the most rapid and comprehensive cultural transformation in world history – it had managed not only to absorb and successfully imitate several hundred years of Western technological progress, but had become one of the late Victorian world's top ten military powers. Halfway through the opening decade of the 20th century it would even defeat one of the very strongest of the self-styled 'Great Powers' of the day, mighty Imperial Russia. But that, as they say, is another story.

Korea, by contrast, participated only reluctantly in this military revolution, and demonstrated a comprehensive dislike of anything tainted by Western 'progress' until forced to adopt a limited programme of reform under foreign pressure – especially Japanese, but also American, Russian and Chinese – in the closing decades of the century. However, such military reforms as the 'Hermit Kingdom' attempted were to prove too little and too late, and were insufficient to prevent it becoming first a puppet state and then a colony of its maritime neighbour. Its attempts to modernise its armed forces are nevertheless fascinating, not least because so little has been written about them in the West.

The last section of this book comprises a detailed index for the five volumes of the series published thus far. A second index, covering the remainder of the series, will be included in the final volume.

Regarding the spelling of foreign names and words, please note that I have opted to stick mainly with the most popular of those likely to be encountered by anyone who consults the 19th- and early 20th-century publications listed in the bibliographies. Any attempt to indulge in a wholesale revision of the spellings and place-names in use at the time seems counter-productive, and potentially more confusing then helpful. Readers will therefore find 'Formosa' rather than Taiwan, 'Kinchow' rather than Jinzhou (or Chin-chou), and so on. Japanese personal names are likewise presented in their customary 19th-century form, with the surname first.

The bracketed dates which frequently occur after the names of 19th- and early 20th-century authors mentioned in the text sometimes differ from those of publication. In such cases they represent the year in which that particular writer was actually present in the country being described.

Finally, I would like to offer my sincere thanks to Ken and Akiko Crawford, Dr David Bullock, Rafaele d'Amato, Rai England, and the ever-generous Peter Abbott, for contributing reference material and illustrations towards the research for this volume. Gareth Simon's 'Pallas Armata' series of facsimile reprints – sadly no longer available – also proved invaluable, while the section on Japanese uniforms benefited enormously from the published work of the talented Ritta Nakanishi.

Ian Heath
March 2011

CONTENTS

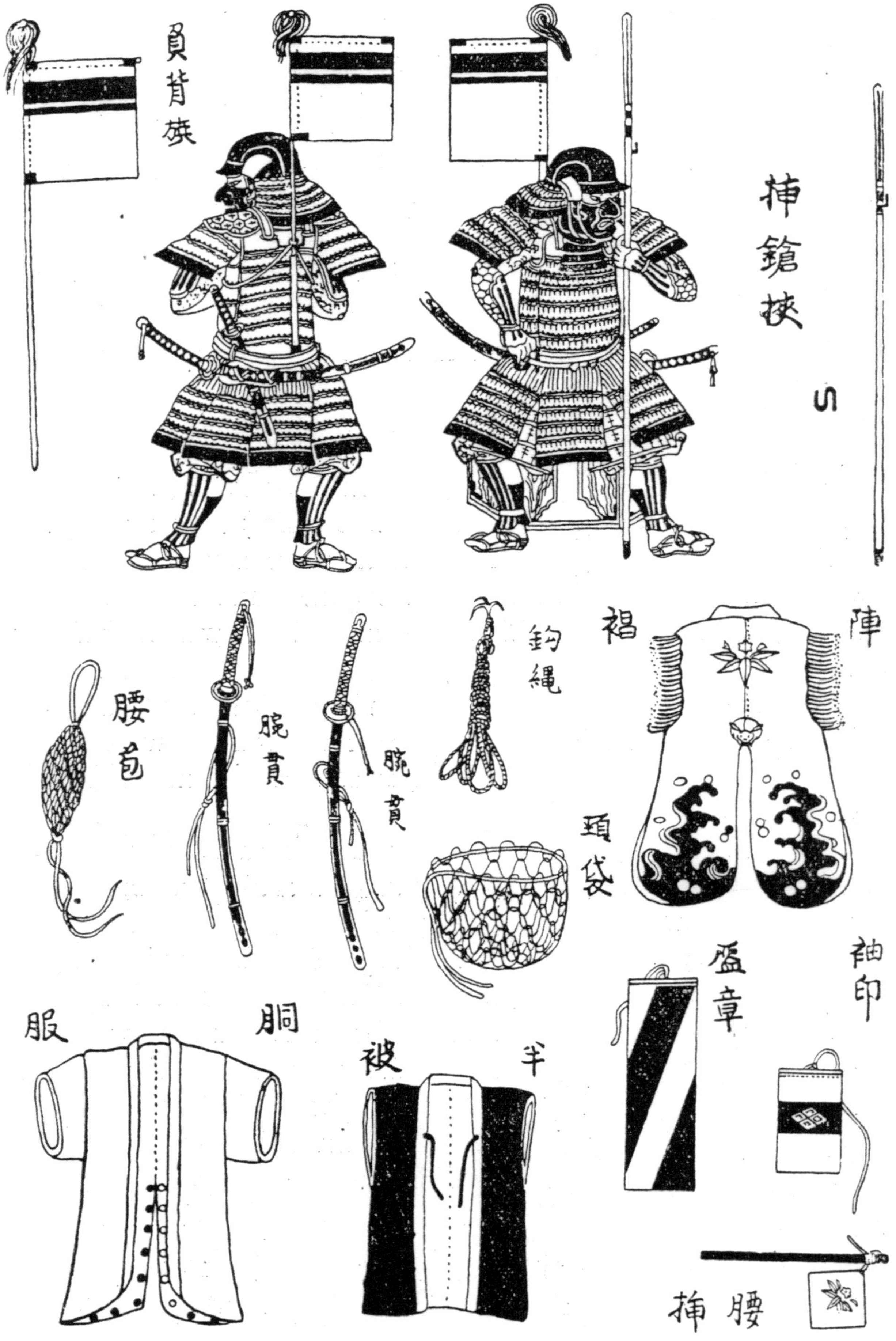
負背旗
挿鎗挟
5
陣
腰包
腕貫
腕貫
鈎縄
頭袋
盔章
袖印
胴服
半被
腰挿

THE EMPIRE OF JAPAN

Known to its people as Nippon ('the Rising Sun') or Dai Nippon ('the Great Rising Sun'), the Empire of Japan had a population of roughly 28 million as the 19th century commenced, which had increased to more than 40 million by 1895. Its geographical extent fluctuated between approximately 3,500 and 4,000 islands,[1] of which only about a quarter were large enough to be of commercial or strategic consequence. The largest, in 1800, were the five islands of Kyushu, Shikoku, Honshu, Yezo (renamed Hokkaido in 1869), and Karafuto (now Sakhalin) – though exploration of the last remained sufficiently incomplete that it was believed to be a peninsula of the Asiatic mainland until as late as 1808, when it was first circumnavigated by Japanese explorers. Other islands of historic significance included Chishima (the Kurile Islands), stretching northwards from Hokkaido towards Kamchatka; the Ryukyu Islands (Liu-ch'iu to the Chinese) between Kyushu and Taiwan, incorporated into the Empire in 1879;[2] and Tsushima and Ko-Saki, a pair of strategically situated islands in the Korea Strait north-west of Kyushu.[3]

Needless to say, Russian ambitions along the Pacific Rim meant that Japan often found its claims to such peripheral island groups challenged as the century progressed. Japanese possession of Tsushima, for instance, which commanded the southern entrance to the Sea of Japan and thereby access to Korea, was threatened in 1861–62, when a Russian warship landed men and tried to establish a naval base before being persuaded to leave by the arrival of a British fleet under Sir James Hope. There were also occasional Russian attempts at settlement of the northern and central Kurile Islands from the 18th century onwards, and Japanese possession of even the two southernmost (Iturup and Kunashir) was only eventually conceded by Russia in 1855.

Having pursued a rigorously enforced policy of isolation since the 17th century, Japan appears to have traditionally looked upon such outlying islands as little more than a buffer zone against foreign influence and interference, and only began to regard them seriously when Russian expansion became steadily more threatening after the mid-18th century. Russian policy in the East, by contrast, had always been to occupy unpopulated territory wherever it was found, which rendered remote Japanese islands – often thinly peopled at best, and sometimes entirely deserted – an invitation too tempting to resist. This strategy had already gained Russia most of the Kuriles before the period under review even began, and left Sakhalin and Yezo, the northernmost of early 19th-century Japan's five principal islands, especially at risk. Though some far-sighted Japanese had long-since recognised and advocated the need to forestall Russian expansion by increasing the number of settlements on both, these islands remained dangerously underpopulated as the century dawned.

Recognising its strategic importance in commanding the northern entrance to the Sea of Japan, Russia announced its own claim to Sakhalin as early as 1804, and used the arrest by the Japanese of several Russian merchants found illegally trading there as an excuse to put small landing parties ashore in autumn 1806, as well as on Japanese-held Iturup in the Kuriles in the spring of 1807. Some fighting ensued, but the question of Sakhalin's ownership remained unresolved. Despite landing several exploratory expeditions during the next half-century it was not until 1853 that Russia established a permanent military post on Sakhalin. Nevertheless, so intense was the diplomatic pressure subsequently exerted that Japan signed away the island's virtually unexplored northern half just two years later, and in 1875 resigned its claims to the southern half too, receiving back in compensation the comparatively worthless northern and central Kuriles, which had been held by Russia for the last hundred years.

However, the second half of the century saw Japan achieve territorial gains that went some way towards compensating for the humiliating loss of Sakhalin. The Bonin Islands (Ogasawara-shoto), originally discovered by the Japanese back in the 16th century, were formally claimed in 1861 and occupied in 1876; the Volcano Islands (Kazan-retto) and Marcus Island (Minami Tori Shima) were added to the Empire in 1891 and 1899 respectively; and Formosa (Taiwan) and the Pescadores (P'eng-hu Liehtao) were ceded by China following its defeat in the Sino-Japanese War of 1894–95, a conflict which also left Japan in virtual control of Korea (see pp.117–118).

Though this ascendancy was seriously threatened by the revival of Russian ambitions after 1896, and in particular by Russia's occupation of Manchuria during the Boxer Rebellion in 1900,[4] it was emphatically reaffirmed by Japan's decisive victory in the ensuing Russo-Japanese War of 1904–5. This not only secured the Empire's position in Korea (which was eventually annexed in 1910) but recovered southern Sakhalin and the Russian-held Liao-tung Peninsula of mainland China. All of these remained in Japanese hands thereafter until the Empire's own catastrophic defeat by the Allies in 1945.

THE MEIJI RESTORATION

Though it retained its Imperial family, which dwelt in secluded semi-captivity in the capital, Kyoto, the Empire had actually been ruled since the 17th century by the Tokugawa, a dynasty of military dictators bearing the title *Sei-i-dai-shogun* ('barbarian-subjugating great general')[5] – usually abbreviated to 'Shogun' in Western sources. This had been founded by Tokugawa Ieyasu (d.1616) following his decisive victory at the Battle of Sekigahara in 1600. Between 1603 and 1868 an unbroken line of 15 Tokugawa shoguns governed Japan from what had become the Empire's administrative centre, Edo.[6] The era

Opposite: various items of traditional samurai dress and equipment, from the 18th-century Tanki Yoriaku. *Top left, a* sashimono *('little banner') and the means of securing it to a warrior's back. Top right, a* yari *(spear). Middle row, left to right: a* kate-bukuro *(provisions bag), two varieties of* udenuki *(sword knots), a* kagi nawa *(hooked rope) for use in climbing walls, a* kubibukoro *bag, used to carry an enemy's severed head, and a* jinbaori *(surcoat). Bottom row, left to right: a* do kimono, *a* happi *(open-fronted jacket), and, in the bottom right-hand corner, three types of identification device – a* kasa-jirushi, *a* sode-jirushi, *and a* koshi-sashi, *for all of which see pp 76–77.*

of Tokugawa rule is consequently usually referred to as the 'Edo period' (though its final phase, the period after 1853, is now generally termed the *Bakumatsu*, meaning 'end of the shogunate').

As many as five Tokugawa shoguns held office during the 19th century, namely Ienari (1786–1837), Ieyoshi (1837–53), Iesada (1853–58), Iemochi (1858–66), and Yoshinobu, better known in the West as Keiki (1866–68). It seems that the final three probably harboured ambitions beyond their already elevated status, since we sometimes find them styled *O-gimi*, or *Tai-kun* (rendered 'Tycoon' by British travellers), a title which, best translated as 'great prince' or 'exalted ruler', properly belonged exclusively to the Emperor. Yet at the same time all but Keiki appear to have been virtual puppets of their own sophisticated bureaucracy, which by the 19th century had usurped much of the political decision-making process.

In order to minimise the effects of foreign influence and religion the shogunate government, or *bakufu*,[7] had adopted a policy of isolation in 1639. Japanese traders had already been forbidden to travel outside the country on pain of death several years earlier (this ban was not lifted until 1866), and the only foreigners to be tolerated within Japan thereafter comprised communities of Dutch and Chinese merchants established on the minute island of Deshima outside Nagasaki harbour. Despite several Russian, British, and French attempts to get this policy reversed during the first half of the 19th century, the situation remained unchanged until the arrival in 1853–54 of an American fleet (still remembered as 'the black ships') under Commodore Matthew Perry. By means of an unsubtle blend of diplomacy and veiled threats, Perry was able to convince the *bakufu* of the West's technological and military might. This led to Shogun Iesada reluctantly signing trade treaties with the United States in 1854 and 1858, which were followed by similar treaties with Britain, Russia, Holland, and France. As a result five ports were grudgingly opened to foreign trade.

Iesada's decision to let foreigners in did not meet with universal approval. Far from it. Though Perry's expedition had convinced the *bakufu* that Japan was, militarily, utterly outclassed, and that the most sensible course of action was to appease the West for as long as it took to improve Japan's own potential to a comparable level, clans traditionally opposed to shogunate policy were appalled by what they considered blatant treason, and loudly expressed the view that if the Shogun couldn't live up to his 'barbarian-subjugating' epithet and keep the foreigners out then it was time for him to go. In addition the Emperor himself, the xenophobic Osahito (1846–67, posthumously named Komei), initially refused to recognise the new treaties, even though he lacked the power to do more than voice his outrage.

Needless to say, this divergence of viewpoints resulted in a power-struggle that was to last for the next decade, with on the one side the anti-isolationist *bakufu* and the Tokugawa and allied clans, and on the other the pro-isolationist Imperial court[8] supported by the south-western clans – particularly Satsuma and Choshu – which henceforth dedicated themselves to removing the Shogun from power and restoring the Emperor. From 1860 on the latter faction mounted numerous murderous attacks on individual foreigners, in the hope of thereby driving a wedge between the Shogun and the West. The new British Legation was attacked twice, and numerous foreign diplomats, seamen, and merchants, as well as anti-isolationist shogunate statesmen, were attacked or killed by samurai gangs or lone assassins calling themselves *shishi* ('determined men', or 'men of high purpose').

The last straw for the British was the murder of merchant C.L. Richardson by Satsuma samurai outside Yokohama in September 1862, for which £100,000 compensation was demanded in spring 1863. Shogun Iemochi agreed to pay the fine (knowing full well that the Satsuma clan wouldn't), but then declared that all foreigners should be expelled from Japan and issued orders to this end, despite being perfectly well aware that the foreigners were far too powerful to be removed quite so easily.

The date of 25 June was set for their expulsion. Significantly, however, when the day arrived only the ambitious and troublesome Choshu clan took action, having entirely failed to realise that it had been set up by the *bakufu* as a scapegoat to divert the foreigners' wrath. Choshu ships and the clan's shore batteries at Shimonoseki, guarding the straits between Honshu and Kyushu, took to firing at passing foreign vessels as they came within range, and American, Dutch, and French vessels were all shot at over the next few weeks, until, on 16 July, an American warship shelled the batteries and sank two Choshu gunboats. Just four days later a French warship also bombarded the batteries before landing detachments to storm and demolish the gun emplacements. Some 700–800 Choshu clansmen were killed in these actions. Isolated attacks against foreign nationals by extremists nevertheless continued elsewhere, and the *bakufu* was eventually pressurised into permitting substantial contingents of British and French troops to land at Yokohama for the protection of the foreign community. These garrisons remained in place until 1875.

Still pursuing its own grievances, Great Britain had meanwhile decided to take unilateral action against the unrepentant Satsuma clan for Richardson's murder, and had despatched seven ships against its capital, Kagoshima. When, on 15 August 1863, the most recent British demand for compensation was formally rejected, three Satsuma vessels moored in the harbour were seized. The Japanese, unsurprisingly, responded by shooting at the British ships, and a vigorous exchange of fire ensued lasting several hours, by the end of which serious damage had been inflicted on the Satsuma shore batteries and Kagoshima itself, though the British flotilla also suffered some loss. The captured Satsuma ships were burnt.

Despite such object lessons – and ignoring *bakufu* orders to desist – the Choshu clan's repaired batteries at Shimonoseki continued to take pot-shots at passing foreign vessels, until the Western powers decided to mount a joint operation to neutralise this particular threat once and for all. Consequently, on 5–6 September 1864, 17 warships (nine British, four Dutch, three French, and one American) and landing parties totalling 1,850 seamen and marines (1,400 British, 250 French, and 200 Dutch) bombarded, stormed, and dismantled the Choshu batteries. Obliged to concede defeat, the Choshu had to pay a total of $3 million compensation to the four Western powers. However, a lesson had now been learnt, and henceforward the Choshu abandoned blind opposition to

A French photograph and an English engraving of the Shimonoseki shore batteries following their capture by British, French, and Dutch naval brigades in September 1864. Eyewitness Ernest Satow described the batteries as 'of earth, having a parapet about 20 feet wide, armed along the edge with a chevaux-de-frise of pointed bamboo stakes. In battery No.7 the guns were mounted en barbette, on carriages with enormous wheels, and worked on pivots. They were of bronze, very long, and threw a 32-pound shot, though marked as 24s... Besides these, there was a short 32-pdr, and on the other side of a traverse, containing a small magazine, was a single 10-inch gun, also of bronze ... In the nine-gun battery were a couple of heavy 11-inch bronze guns ... The next battery ... was divided into two by a traverse containing a magazine, on one side of which were one ten-inch howitzer, two 32-pdrs, and one 24-pdr; on the other side were the same number, with the addition of a single 24-pdr.' (Photograph Wikipedia; engraving *Illustrated Times*, 3 December 1864)

all foreign influence in favour of modernising their own military forces along Western lines.

Ironically, the Choshu clan's pre-eminence within the pro-isolationist camp had by now begun to express itself in a growing rivalry with the powerful Satsuma clan, which, in order to restore its waning prestige, began to advocate an alliance between the Shogun and the Imperial court. Choshu attempts to increase their own influence within the Imperial court at Kyoto had been frustrated by a Satsuma-led coup at the end of September 1863, which had driven out the Choshu and their *tobaku* (anti-*bakufu*) allies. The Choshu clan's heartland in the extreme south of Honshu subsequently became the refuge and rallying point for all Japanese dedicated to the overthrow of the Shogun and the expulsion of foreigners. However, following a failed attempt to re-enter Kyoto by force on 20 August 1864,[9] a fortnight before the Western powers launched their attack on Shimonoseki, the Choshu domain was itself surrounded by *bakufu* troops.

This double crisis of bombardment by the combined Western fleets coupled with the threat of imminent attack by the *bakufu* enabled conservatives within the clan to wrest power from the radicals, and to appease the *bakufu* by ordering the execution of those responsible for the expedition against Kyoto. This led in turn to a civil war amongst the Choshu, from which it was the anti-*bakufu* radicals, under Takasugi Shinsaku and others, who eventually emerged triumphant in March 1865, thanks in large part to the effectiveness of their new *shotai*, or Western-style rifle-armed troops.

The *bakufu* and Choshu now began to rearm and square up for the inevitable final confrontation that would settle the issues of Imperial restoration and intercourse with the West once and for all. The Tokugawa received a French loan and the promise of a French military mission,[10] and appear to have contemplated the utter destruction of the Choshu. The latter, meanwhile, bought 7,300 modern rifles – including 4,300 Miniés left over from the American Civil War – from a British merchant, via their erstwhile enemies the Satsuma, with whom they were formally reconciled in March 1866 when rumours began to circulate that after it had annihilated Choshu the *bakufu* intended to move against Satsuma.

When hostilities (known as the Choshu-Bakufu War, or the Summer War) finally erupted in July 1866 the Choshu *shotai*, with their modern firearms and their superior training and morale, were able to rout the larger but antiquated and divided shogunate forces sent against them, said to have amounted to some 120–150,000 men. Sympathetic towards the Choshu, and wishing to avoid a bloody civil war, many *bakufu* lords failed to give the Shogun their wholehearted support, which resulted in discord and demoralisation. The *bakufu* expedition's attacks from various directions were consequently so badly co-ordinated that the Choshu were able not only to defeat its four individual elements in detail, but to drive them back deep into *bakufu* territory. Shogun Iemochi's sudden death at the end of August 1866 was therefore seized upon by his successor Keiki as an excuse to end hostilities in September, before the situation could deteriorate any further. Emperor Osahito died a few months later, in January 1867, and was succeeded by his 15-year-old son Mutsuhito (1867–1912), who in September 1868 would assume the reign name of Meiji ('Enlightened Rule').

Recognising that Japan's outdated 'feudal' government was disintegrating, Keiki made desperate efforts to introduce a programme of reform and modernisation. However, he was politically outmanoeuvred at court, and, ousted from power in November 1867 following a coup engineered by the Satsuma and Choshu, he was pressured to resign the title and office of Shogun. He seems to have acquiesced to this in the belief that he would be able to exert his influence thereafter via the ruling council of 'feudal' lords and court nobles that was to be set up in his place, but this body never materialised. Instead, on 3 January 1868, a Satsuma-dominated assembly abruptly restored nominal power to the Emperor and ordered that the Tokugawa clan surrender all its lands to the court. All forces friendly to the Shogun were dismissed from Kyoto the same day, and guardianship of the Imperial palace was transferred to the Satsuma, Choshu, and Tosa clans. All of this proved too much for Keiki and his supporters, who assembled some 30,000 men at Osaka – only about half of them soldiers – and marched towards Kyoto to remonstrate. However, they were intercepted by 'Loyalist' (anti-*bakufu*) forces under the Satsuma commander Saigo Takamori on 27 January as they advanced down narrow roads on either side of the Yodo River, and the shogunate army was heavily defeated in four days of fighting generally referred to as the Battle of Toba-Fushimi.

This proved to be but the opening engagement of a conflict known as the Boshin War (*Boshin Seneki*), after the name of the year. Keiki himself withdrew to Edo and, declining French offers of military assistance, swore allegiance to the Emperor before retiring into obscurity (he died in 1913). However, a sizeable number of his kinsmen and followers declined to submit and maintained the struggle for several months more. Edo changed hands twice before finally falling to the Loyalists in April, and the latter were also victorious at the Battle of Ueno on 4 July, where some 2,000 or more Tokugawa adherents calling themselves the *Shogitai* ('Corps of Clear Loyalty') were virtually wiped out in a desperate hand-to-hand combat after occupying a hill-top temple on the outskirts of Edo. The fiercest fighting of the war, however, took

A contingent of traditionally-equipped shogunate troops on the march during the second bakufu *expedition against the Choshu clan, July to September 1866.* (Wikipedia)

This engraving of Tokugawa soldiers at drill, from the Illustrated London News *of 13 August 1864, gives a good idea of the hybrid and colourful appearance of Japanese troops during the early stages of modernisation.*

place at Wakamatsu in October, where the pro-shogunate Aizu clan lost about 3,000 men. Some Tokugawa units under Enomoto Takeaki (commander-in-chief of the shogunate navy) fled to Hokkaido the same month and, capturing Hakodate in a surprise attack, held out until as late as May 1869.[11] Nevertheless, the fall of Wakamatsu had effectively ended the Boshin War. Though skirmishes sputtered on elsewhere on Honshu until January 1869, Emperor Meiji was able to enter Tokyo (formerly Edo) in triumph on 25 November 1868, and was installed as a European-style constitutional monarch.

There was no return to Japan's former policy of isolation – contrary to his supporters' expectations and desires, Meiji proved to be an advocate of Westernisation and strong central government. However, by overthrowing the shogunate the clans had already achieved their key aim, and in time the majority came to accept, albeit grudgingly, that intercourse with the West was the best way of ensuring Japan's long-term security and prosperity. But the abolition of Japanese 'feudalism' and samurai privileges in 1871 led to resentment, humiliation, and rancour amongst die-hard traditionalists, who mounted several futile rebellions against the new order during the ensuing decade. Most notable of these were the revolts of the Hizen clan under Eto Shimpei in 1874 (the Saga Rebellion);[12] elements of the Choshu clan under Maebara Issei and others in 1876 (the Hagi Rebellion);[13] and – most dangerous of all – a large part of the Satsuma clan under Saigo Takamori in 1877 (the Satsuma Rebellion, known in Japan as the *Seinan Senso* or 'South-Western War').

THE SATSUMA REBELLION 1877

The Satsuma samurai Saigo Takamori, who had been a key participant in the Meiji Restoration of 1868, had been appointed commander[14] of the new Imperial army in May 1873, but resigned in protest in October when the government rejected his proposal to invade Korea. Returning in disgust to his home in Kagoshima, he was accompanied by a sizeable number of deserters from the Satsuma contingent of the Imperial Guard and was subsequently joined by 300 more clansmen who had likewise quit the newly established police force. He then established a network of military academies (referred to as *shigakko*, or 'private schools', in order to conceal their real purpose), which subsequently became the rallying point for disaffected samurai from all over south-west Japan. By 1875–76 there were more than 130 of these academies within Satsuma territory, training some 20–30,000 cadets, 7,000 of them in Kagoshima alone.

It has never become entirely clear what Saigo intended to do with the soldiers he was training, though it seems likely he had the security if not the eventual independence of Satsuma territory in mind, and doubtless anticipated an eventual clash with the national government over the clan's semi-autonomous status. Clearly the very existence of the 'schools' and their armed students posed a significant threat to Japan's internal stability, and the government became increasingly uneasy about them, even though Saigo's loyalty seemed to be confirmed by his failure to participate in any of the rebellions which punctuated the period 1873–76, even that of his friend Eto Shimpei. Saigo's eventual seemingly reluctant decision to take up arms against the Meiji regime seems to have been prompted by the alleged confession of a captured government spy, in February 1877, that he was to be assassinated, coupled with the unauthorised actions of up to 2,500 of Saigo's students, who, at the end of January, had defied government attempts to remove munitions from three Satsuma arsenals in Kagoshima and subsequently seized the arms dumps for themselves. Contrary to what he might have expected, however, Saigo's decision to rebel against the Emperor's advisers (he was careful to emphasise his continuing loyalty to the Emperor) did not receive universal support amongst his fellow clansmen, despite his personal popularity and prestige. The Satsuma clan's leader, Shimazu Saburo, was foremost amongst those who remained loyal to the state, while Saigo's own brother, Saigo Tsugumichi, was amongst the Imperialist commanders who took the field against him.

When they marched from Kagoshima towards Tokyo in mid-February, Saigo's forces comprised some 14,000 men, including between 11,500 and 12,000 infantrymen (organised into six regiments), 200 artillerymen, and 1,200 porters. All of them were pupils of the 'schools', it being observed at the time that 'Saigo would not allow any but the pupils of these establishments to accompany the expedition, although considerable numbers of volunteers presented themselves'. Sizeable contingents of traditionally-equipped samurai nevertheless attached themselves to the army as it marched, bringing its effective combat strength to a maximum of 20,000 men. Saigo provided artillery (28 mountain-guns, two field-guns, and 30 small mortars) and an unknown quantity of modern firearms, but most of the students and the volunteers had to provide their own weapons, and were each required to bring 10 *yen*[15] in order to buy provisions, which they had to carry themselves. However, what the army clearly lacked in armament and logistics it more than made up for in morale and superior training, most of the rebel soldiers being ex-samurai veterans of the Boshin War while the Imperialists included many raw recruits drawn from the peasantry and the middle classes. At this stage Saigo seems to have still hoped – rather naively – that he would be able to negotiate a settlement with the government.

After marching north in falling snow for four days, the rebels found their way obstructed at Kawawhiri on 21 February by a battalion of government troops sent out from Kumamoto castle,[16] the commander of which had seemingly been given advanced warning of Saigo's approach by militants in his army determined to provoke hostilities. This vastly outnumbered Imperialist contingent was easily defeated and pursued back to the castle, which, held by a garrison of 3,800 soldiers and 600 armed police, was vigorously attacked from the 22nd until the 24th to no avail, after which the rebels began to dig in for a conventional siege.

A series of skirmishes ensued over the next few days as rebel units collided with Imperialist reinforcements mustering to the north-west, notably at Minaminoseki and Takase. These minor engagements were followed in turn by a full-scale Imperialist offensive led by General Yamagata Aritomo, which commenced on 4 March and lasted for 17 days without either side managing to gain the upper hand, despite the potentially decisive advantage in firearms enjoyed by the Imperialists. The fighting reached its height on 20–21 March, when, in a concerted struggle for possession of the rebel positions at Tabaruzaka, the Imperialists lost 1,766 men killed and 2,399 wounded out of 11,000 engaged, while the rebels lost about 1,200 killed and 2,100 wounded out of some 9,000.

Saigo Takamori, from a contemporary Japanese portrait reproduced in Brinkley's History of the Japanese People *(1914). Saigo is described by Augustus Mounsey as having been 'extraordinarily tall for a Japanese, being a full head above his fellows: he was proportionately broad, had massive limbs, and would have been considered a well-built powerful man in any country.'*

The fighting round Kumamoto was ultimately to prove decisive. By besieging the castle instead of moving rapidly north and invading Honshu, Saigo had given the government the time it needed to mobilise and deploy its forces. At the same time, the endless skirmishing steadily whittled away his own army and exhausted his already inadequate supply of ammunition. It nevertheless took him seven weeks to recognise this, and there were more than 40,000 government troops in the field when he finally raised the siege on 14 April and, breaking through the tightening Imperialist cordon closing around him, withdrew towards the south with his remaining 18,000 men. The Imperialists then deployed in a massive pincer movement designed to prevent his escape, with armies marching south from Kumamoto and north from Kagoshima to trap the rebels between them.

The ensuing series of skirmishes and battles lasted the best part of five months. There was a pitched battle at Miyakonojo in July (where the Imperialists lost 300 men, the rebels many more), and a prolonged engagement in the mountain passes round the castle-town of Nobeoka in mid-August. The fighting here virtually destroyed what remained of the Satsuma army, about half of the surviving 10,000 rebels being captured and the rest dispersed. Saigo was amongst those who escaped, but only a few hundred men were still with him when he emerged from the mountains near Kagoshima at the beginning of September. Repulsed by government troops when he attempted to force his way into the town, he withdrew to the nearby hill of Shiroyama, where his small force – reduced to fighting with swords – was surrounded and annihilated by some 15,000 Imperialists on the 24th. The latter suffered just 30 casualties in the final assault, none of them fatal, whilst the rebels were all either killed or captured. Saigo was among the 300 who died in the fighting. Having been seriously wounded, he appears to have instructed his followers to behead him in order to avoid the humiliation of capture – the nearest he could get to committing ritual suicide.

Several sources record about 40,000 fighting men to have been involved in the rebellion in all (William Griffis gives the suspiciously precise figure of 39,760), but of these only some 20,000 or perhaps 22,000 at best were ever in the field at the same time. Roughly 7,000 of these are believed to have been killed in the fighting, and a further 11,000 wounded. Once the uprising had been crushed, 42,500 people were charged with having taken part, of whom about 39,600 were pardoned or acquitted and 2,850 were punished, mostly by fines or imprisonment for anywhere between 30 days and 10 years. Just 20 of the ringleaders were executed. Imperialist losses in the campaign were about the same as the rebels', being recorded as just under 6,400 dead and more than 10,500 wounded in official sources, representing about 25% of the troops engaged compared to the rebels' 45%. The fact that the actual number of casualties was much the same on both sides, despite the Imperialists' vast superiority in firearms, is said to have been the product of the rebels' desperate bravery and their expertise with the sword in close combat.

The eight-month rebellion was the last and most formidable threat to the stability of the Meiji regime. It was also the first major test of the new national army, which during the course of the campaign had fielded a total of 58 battalions of infantry (56,318 men), two battalions of engineers (1,512 men), half a battalion of military train (310 men), and four battalions of artillery (48 guns), reinforced by naval brigades and some 7,000 armed police. Of this total of 65–70,000 men a maximum of 40,000 were in the field at any one time. Shortcomings which had rapidly become apparent included the army's serious shortage of manpower (it had to mobilise not just its entire front-line strength – slightly less than 34,000 men at this time – but also most of its reservists and cadets, as well as the Hokkaido militia and a significant number of ex-samurai volunteers); the lack of a mobilisation plan; the lack of staff officers; inadequate transport and medical facilities; poor artillery; and the uselessness of its second-line reserves. All of these problems would now be addressed and resolved.

Though it has been argued that the outcome of the rebellion proved once and for all that with the right training conscripted peasants could beat samurai, this is not entirely true: at this stage in its evolution roughly two-thirds of the Imperial army was itself still made up of ex-samurai, and it appears to have been units recruited largely among these which bore the brunt of the fighting. More significant was the fact that the victors constituted a national army that had been mobilised by a Western-style national administration, was organised and trained along Western lines, and was armed entirely with modern firearms. There could be no clearer proof that the age of samurai supremacy was categorically at an end.

THE SINO-JAPANESE WAR 1894–95

Though modernisation of its armed forces was all that prevented Japan from falling prey to exploitation or

Japanese depiction of the bitter fighting at Tabaruzaka during the Satsuma Rebellion. The fire laid down by both sides was so intense (as many as 320,000 rounds were fired in a single day) that researchers walking the battlefield have found bullets that actually collided in midair. (Wikipedia)

conquest by the colonial powers, the country lacked sufficient iron ore and coal to maintain its arms industry for long, let alone institute a programme of commercial industrialisation. The importance of securing the appropriate resources elsewhere in Asia was consequently recognised by leading scholars and statesmen at a very early stage. These advocated expansion on to the Asian mainland and the establishment of a 'Greater Japan' as the only sure way of guaranteeing a sufficient supply of the necessary raw materials.

With the passage of time such suggestions assumed more solid form. Kamchatka, Korea, and Manchuria should all be seized, it was suggested, thereby providing a secure foothold on the mainland that would ensure the decisive defeat of China before Japan turned its attention south and conquered Formosa, the Philippines, and the East Indies – a strategic plan which bears a striking similarity to that which was eventually pursued between 1904 and 1945. However, neither the shogunate *bakufu* nor the early Meiji government proved sympathetic towards aggressive expansion, and during the late 1850s and the 1860s both went so far as to execute several proponents of such ambitious schemes as dangerous agitators. The necessity of foreign conquests was nevertheless tacitly acknowledged in military circles as ultimately unavoidable. All that remained to be decided was where the first blow should fall, and when. In the meantime vast amounts of money were devoted to the enlargement and improvement of Japan's armed forces in readiness for that day: annual military expenditure steadily increased, to 19% of government spending by 1880, 25% by 1886, and as much as 31% by 1890.

Plans for a war with China had already been formulated by the 1880s, and Japan had carried out large-

Map of 'the seat of war' during the Sino-Japanese conflict of 1894–95, from Trumbull White's The War in the East *(1895).*

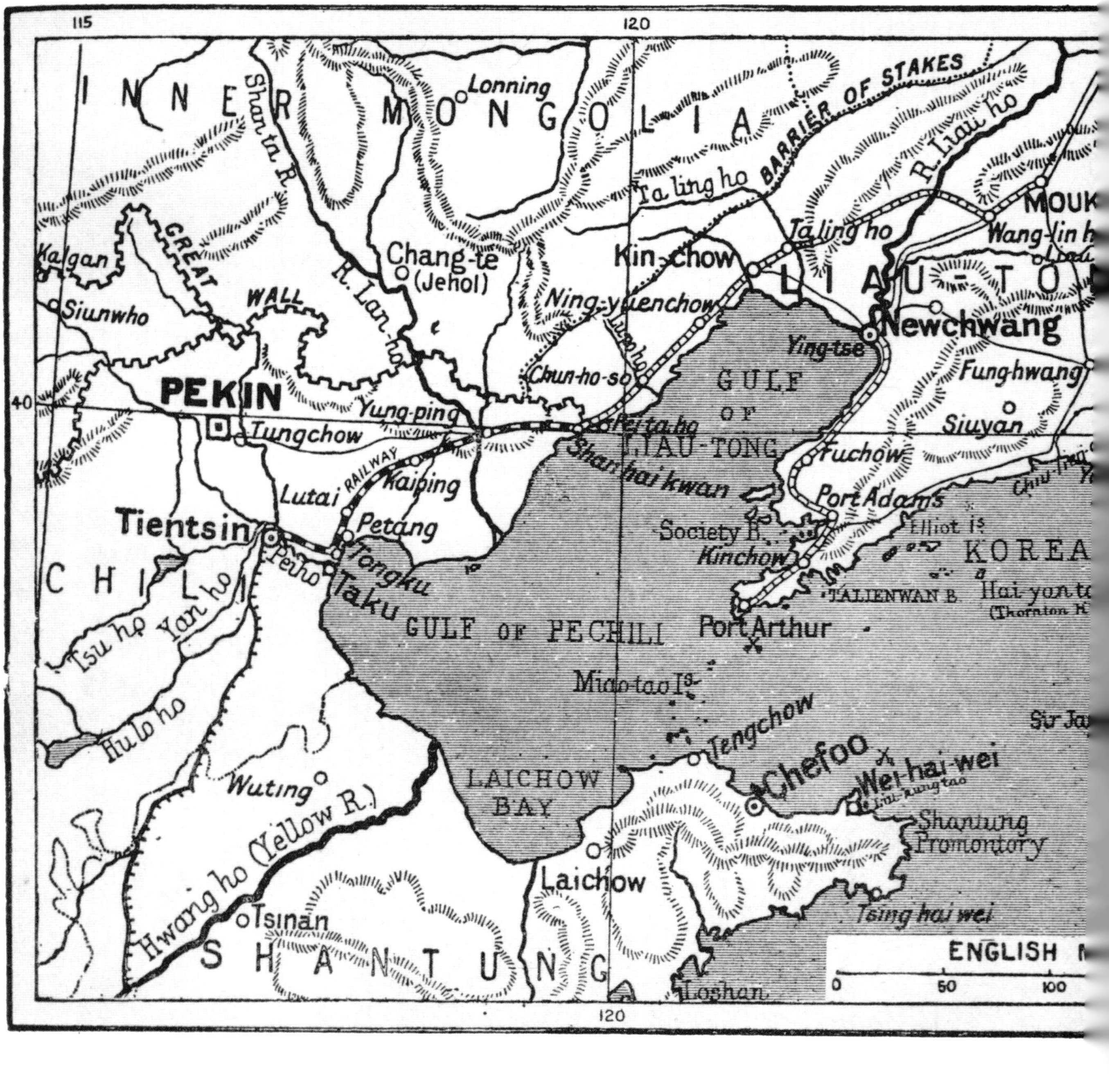

scale manoeuvres in readiness for this eventuality in both 1890 and 1892, involving not only the mobilisation of its reserves but also maritime landing operations. It was the Tonghak crisis (see pp.116–117), resulting in the deployment of both Japanese and Chinese 'peace-keeping' forces in Korea, which provided the necessary opportunity to actually instigate hostilities. These commenced without warning on 25 July 1894, when an Imperial Navy squadron composed of three cruisers intercepted and fired on three Chinese warships (a cruiser and two gunboats) and a troop transport off Pung-do island, forcing one gunboat to beach (where it blew up) and capturing the other. When the transport declined to surrender after lengthy negotiations this too was eventually fired upon and sunk, with the loss of over a thousand lives.[17] Simultaneously with this engagement the 4–5,000 Japanese troops stationed round Seoul under the command of Major-General Oshima Yoshimasa set out to mount a pre-emptive strike against the Chinese army's positions at Asan, the Japanese plan being to eliminate all enemy forces south of the Korean capital before advancing against those stationed round Ping-Yang in the north. The ensuing battle at Songhwan (Söngchon), some 30 miles from Ping-Yang, began at about 3:30 in the morning on 29 July and was over by about 8:00 a.m., when the Chinese defenders – variously given as somewhere between 2,800 and 4,000 men – were finally driven from their redoubts and fled towards Asan, leaving behind 110 dead, 500 wounded, and eight guns. Japanese losses totalled 29 dead and 59 wounded. So swift was the Chinese flight that Oshima found Asan deserted when he arrived there about eight hours later.

War was officially declared two days later, on 1 August, with Japan claiming that hostilities had been initiated 'in the interests of peace'. It was a conflict that ill-informed European pundits believed the Japanese stood no chance of winning.

Following his victory at Songhwan, Oshima turned north towards the city of Ping-Yang itself. Japanese reinforcements consisting of the 5th Division under Lieutenant-General Nozu Michitsura[18] were landed at Gensan, Pusan, and elsewhere in Korea during the first two weeks of August. Organised into three brigades, these joined with Oshima's troops in converging on Ping-Yang from four different directions, forcing their way through outlying Chinese positions at Chunghwa, Singchuen, and Hwangju in a series of engagements on 5 and 6 September.

The Chinese had meanwhile heavily fortified the environs of Ping-Yang, notably by erecting 27 redoubts amply provided with artillery. These were garrisoned by four armies under Wei Jukwai, Ma Yu-kun, Tso Pao-kwei, and Nieh Kuei-lin, plus 1–2,000 fugitives from Songhwan and Asan under their own defeated general, Yeh Chi-chao, who according to some sources was in overall command (others give this post to Tso). In all, the Chinese defenders numbered at least 14–16,000 men and possibly as many as 20,000, plus 32 guns and six Gatlings. Their attackers totalled between 12,000 and 15,600 men, with 44 mountain guns.

The Japanese commenced their assault on the morning of 15 September, possession of the perimeter forts being fiercely contested for much of the day. Several key outworks were nevertheless overwhelmed, and by late afternoon the Chinese found their position sufficiently untenable that they agreed to surrender, requesting only that their formal submission be postponed until the next morning because of heavy rain. Nozu reluctantly agreed, and many Chinese took the opportunity to slip away overnight. The Japanese had lost 180–192 men killed and 506 or 516 wounded in the fighting, but Chinese casualties are less clear. Somewhere between 2,000 and 2,700 seem to have been killed and 600 captured. However, Trumbull White (1895) says that 14,000 prisoners were taken, and that 'less than a fourth of the Chinese army succeeded in escaping'. Tso Pao-kwei was among the dead.

Despite the fact that the war had seven months yet to run, the Battle of Ping-Yang was in effect the most decisive land battle of the conflict: 'Songhwan was the beginning of the end,' wrote Yamada Yoshiaki in 1897, 'Ping-Yang was the real end of the contest. After that, with but few exceptions, every battle was a foregone

Table 1: Japanese order of battle, 1894–95

1st Army (mobilised July 1894) – Marshal Yamagata	
3rd (Nagoya) Division, Lieutenant-General Katsura	
5th Brigade, Major-General Oseko	6th Infantry Regiment 18th Infantry Regiment
6th Brigade, Major-General Oshima Yoshimasa	7th Infantry Regiment 19th Infantry Regiment
3rd Cavalry Battalion	
3rd Artillery Regiment	
3rd Engineer Battalion	
5th (Hiroshima) Division, Lieutenant-General Nozu	
9th Brigade, Major-General Oshima Hisanao	11th Infantry Regiment 21st Infantry Regiment
10th Brigade, Major-General Tachimi	12th Infantry Regiment 22nd Infantry Regiment
5th Cavalry Battalion	
5th Artillery Regiment	
5th Engineer Battalion	
Corps Artillery	
6 × field guns, 12 × 9-cm mortars	
2nd Army – Marshal Oyama	
First portion (mobilised August–September 1894)	
1st (Tokyo) Division, Lieutenant-General Yamaji	
1st Brigade, Major-General Nogi	1st Infantry Regiment 15th Infantry Regiment
2nd Brigade, Major-General Nishi	2nd Infantry Regiment 3rd Infantry Regiment
1st Cavalry Battalion	
1st Artillery Regiment	
1st Engineer Battalion	
6th (Kumamoto) Division (part), Lieutenant-General Kuroke	
12th Brigade, Major-General Hasegawa	14th Infantry Regiment 24th Infantry Regiment
6th Cavalry Battalion, 1 squadron	
6th Artillery Regiment, 2 batteries	
6th Engineer Battalion, 1 company	
Siege Artillery	
4 × 12-cm guns, 12 × 9-cm guns, 8 × 15-cm mortars, 6 × 9-cm mortars	
Second portion (mobilised December 1894)	
2nd (Sendai) Division, Lieutenant-General Sakuma	
3rd Brigade, Major-General Yamaguchi	4th Infantry Regiment 16th Infantry Regiment
4th Brigade, Major-General Fushimi	5th Infantry Regiment 17th Infantry Regiment
2nd Cavalry Battalion	
2nd Artillery Regiment	
2nd Engineer Battalion	
6th (Kumamoto) Division (part)	
11th Brigade, Major-General Odela	13th Infantry Regiment 23rd Infantry Regiment
6th Cavalry Battalion, 1 squadron	
6th Artillery Regiment, 4 batteries	
6th Engineer Battalion, 1 company	
Siege Artillery	
6 × 9-cm mortars	
Third portion (mobilised February 1895)	
Imperial Guard, Lieutenant-General Kitashirakawa	
1st Brigade	1st Guard Infantry Regiment 2nd Guard Infantry Regiment

2nd Brigade	3rd Guard Infantry Regiment
	4th Guard Infantry Regiment
Guard Cavalry Battalion	
Guard Artillery Regiment	
Guard Engineer Battalion	
4th (Osaka) Division, Lieutenant-General Yamazawa	
7th Brigade	8th Infantry Regiment
	9th Infantry Regiment
8th Brigade	10th Infantry Regiment
	20th Infantry Regiment
4th Cavalry Battalion	
4th Artillery Regiment	
4th Engineer Battalion	

conclusion'. The Japanese victory at Ping-Yang was followed just two days later by the war's most decisive naval action, when China's North Sea Fleet was surprised while landing troops at the mouth of the Yalu river and lost five out of its 16 ships, as well as about a thousand men. The Japanese lost none of their 12 ships and suffered just 242 casualties. Though not deemed a convincing victory by some contemporaries (because the two Chinese battleships present had both escaped), the Chinese navy did not venture out of port again, which left Japan in undisputed command of the Yellow Sea.

In the meantime Marshal Yamagata Aritomo had been sent out to assume command of the Japanese forces, bringing with him the 3rd Division under Lieutenant-General Katsura Taro. This was combined with Nozu's 5th Division to become the 35,000-strong 1st Army.

The Chinese were next chased back to the banks of the Yalu, where a defensive line of more than a hundred redoubts had been constructed. By mid-October an estimated 25–30,000 Chinese troops (White says 38,000) were dug in here. Their main body (some 7–8,000 men) was established in 18 encampments round Hushan, which the Japanese attacked soon after dawn on 25 October after throwing a pontoon bridge across the river unopposed during the night. The Chinese were driven out after three and a half hours of fighting, their losses amounting to at least 500 men and a considerable number of guns, while the Japanese suffered about 140 casualties. Nearby Chiu-lien was abandoned overnight along with another 22 guns.

On 24 October, meanwhile, another Japanese force – the 39,000-strong 2nd Army under Marshal Oyama Iwao[19] – had begun landing at Hua-Yuan-k'ou on China's Liao-tung Peninsula. Marching swiftly south at the beginning of November, Oyama attacked Kinchow and the strategic ports of Ta-lien-wan (Dairen) and Port Arthur (Lu-shun).[20] Kinchow fell after offering minimal resistance on 6 November, as did Ta-lien-wan on the 7th. Both Chinese garrisons then fled to Port Arthur, which fell in turn on the 21st despite its considerable German-built defences, comprising a continuous two-and-a-half-mile line of parapets and hill-top forts which almost surrounded the town. These were defended by an estimated 14–20,000 men and an eclectic mix of about 80 guns, ranging from state-of-the-art Krupps to ancient smoothbores. The port itself fell in the late afternoon after 20 perimeter forts had been overrun, and the Chinese abandoned the remaining forts overnight, having lost some 7,000 men killed or wounded. Oyama's forces, which had numbered 12,000, lost just 66 dead and over 350 wounded. Foreign eyewitness accounts report that Japan's mask of Westernisation slipped somewhat following the capture of Port Arthur, when, in American reporter James Creelman's words, the victors 'killed everything they saw'. Some 2–3,000 unarmed civilians and prisoners are said to have been massacred, including women and children.

An almost simultaneous Chinese counter-attack against Kinchow to the Japanese rear, by about 7–8,000 hastily gathered troops under General Sung, was intended to threaten Oyama's base at Ta-lien-wan but was driven off after losing at least 500 men to the 1,500-strong force assigned to its defence. The main Chinese attack had lasted from just after midday until midnight.

Leaving 10,000 men to hold Port Arthur,

The storming of Ping-Yang's Hyonmu Gate, 15 September 1894. The portrait is of Private Second-Class Harada Jukichi of the 18th Regiment, a hero of the attack. Note the use of brass Arabic numerals on the shoulder-straps to identify his unit.

Japanese troops advance against Chinese fortifications at Hushan, defending the line of the Yalu River, October 1894.

Marshal Oyama advanced northwards on 22 November, the Chinese falling back before him to Fu-chou. This was subsequently abandoned and the Japanese were able to enter unopposed on 5 December.

To the north-east, matters in Manchuria had become complicated, with Japanese and Chinese armies marching and counter-marching as Marshal Yamagata sent columns out to reconnoitre and the Chinese attempted to either intercept or avoid them. Fundamentally, the bulk of the 1st Army proceeded in two general directions after it crossed the Yalu, the right wing under General Nozu advancing north-west along the main Mukden road towards Feng-huang, while the left wing under General Katsura advanced south-west, following the Yalu towards the Liao-tung Peninsula. The Chinese, meanwhile, had regrouped into three armies, of which one (about 25,000 men under General Sung) guarded the Mo-tien-ling pass on the road to Mukden; another (30,000 men) was gathered round Kai-ping, south of Ying-k'ou; and the third, of indeterminate but doubtless similar size, under the Manchu General I-ko-teng-a, was situated somewhere towards the north-east.

Feng-huang fell to Nozu on 31 October, its defenders fleeing to Mukden, Hai-ch'eng, and Taku-shan, and he had pushed north almost as far as the Mo-tien-ling pass by mid-November, when the Chinese under General Sung Ch'ing – who continued to hold doggedly to their positions even after the onset of severe weather – unsuccessfully attempted to turn the Japanese right flank in what one contemporary described as the most determined Chinese effort since the fighting at Ping-Yang. This was the Battle of Ts'ao-ho-ku, fought on 25 November, which involved some 2,000 Chinese cavalry, 4,000 infantry, and eight guns, against about a third as many Japanese.

Katsura's column had meanwhile taken Taku-shan on 7 November before advancing against Hsiu-yen from two directions. One column attacked from the south on the 17th, and the garrison of 2,500 infantry and 500 cavalry fled after about an hour's fighting, abandoning all its guns (every gunner having been killed or wounded). The second Japanese column had meanwhile fought its way through the defences north-east of the town and, driving off some 4,000 troops, had captured another three guns.

Early in December, General I-ko-teng-a set out intending to retake Feng-huang, but on the 10th his advance guard of 3,500 men was intercepted and driven off by somewhat over 3,000 Japanese under Major-General Tachimi, defending the right flank of the 1st Army's advance. This was the Battle of Pan-chia-tai. A second element of the Chinese force, consisting of some 7,000 men, nevertheless descended on Feng-huang from an entirely different direction between 12 and 14 December but was beaten in two minor engagements and pursued into the mountains, losing 150 dead and abandoning four guns. The Japanese lost just 75 men. General I subsequently gave up any further attempts against Feng-huang and instead concentrated on attempting to recapture Hai-ch'eng, which had fallen to Katsura's 3rd Division on 13 December. This important town commanded the approaches not only to the major port of Ying-k'ou but also to the Chinese army's principal supply base at T'ien-chuang-t'ai, so its recovery was deemed of considerable strategic importance. A series of massive attacks was mounted to this end between December 1894 and February 1895, but had no effect, despite the fact that the Japanese generally regarded the combat here as no more than a useful diversion which tied down considerable Chinese resources.

The first significant action during this extended struggle round Hai-ch'eng was the Battle of Kungwasai on 19 December, where 5,550 Japanese drawn from the 3rd and 6th Divisions fought 13,000 Chinese for five hours in two feet (0.6 m) of snow. White regarded this as 'probably the most obstinate engagement yet fought by the armies in Manchuria. The Chinese had strongly entrenched themselves ... and they defended their position most vigorously.' Their defences were only overrun at the fourth attempt, the Japanese losing 69 dead and 274 wounded, the Chinese an estimated 300–500 men killed.

The Chinese mounted five further attacks on Hai-ch'eng between 17 January and 27 February 1895, but, despite being mounted in considerable strength (15,000 troops were involved in the attack of 17 January, and about 20,000 in each of the others), these were, in the words of N.W.H. du Boulay (1896), 'of the very feeblest description'. The 'ridiculous ease' with which they were all beaten off is reflected in the casualty figures, the Japanese (whose strength here reached 7,500 men by 16 February and peaked at 9,800 on the 21st) losing just 211 men in the whole five battles, while the Chinese lost about a thousand.

In the meantime, for political reasons too convoluted to be addressed here, Marshal Yamagata had been recalled ('invalided home') at the beginning of December, and was succeeded in command by Lieutenant-General Nozu.

Other than the ongoing Chinese assaults against Hai-ch'eng, severe weather ensured that there was minimal military activity throughout most of January 1895, during which time hundreds of Japanese soldiers were struck down by frostbite. On the 10th, however, a 6,700-strong mixed brigade from the 2nd Army under Major-General Nogi Maresuki[21] (part of Lieutenant-General Yamaji's 1st Division) took Kai-p'ing, attacking in deep snow across a frozen river ('50 to 75 yards of broken ice') in the face of stubborn Chinese resistance that included 12 field-pieces and two well-handled Gatling guns. The fight lasted four hours, 53 Japanese being killed and 296 wounded. Casualties among the 3–4,000 defenders are unknown but are believed to have been considerable: 150 prisoners were certainly taken, while one Chinese officer reported 900 dead and 300 wounded. A Chinese reinforcement of 10–14,000 men en route to Kai-p'ing is said to have 'halted when the fugitives appeared over the hills' and fell back towards Ying-k'ou, joining with forces already entrenched north-west of T'ai-p'ing-shan. These were attacked in turn once the rest of Yamaji's 1st Division came up, and after repulsing the first Japanese attack on 21 January were overwhelmed on the 24th in another battle fought in knee-deep snow and temperatures as low as 0°F (–18°C). The Chinese – said to have numbered 17,500, of whom there appear to have been some 6,000 in the front-line trenches – suffered more than 2,000 casualties, while the Japanese had just 30 men killed and 220 wounded, though a further 1,500 were incapacitated by frostbite.

At the very end of February the 1st Army advanced on Niu-chuang and its port of Ying-k'ou. Niu-chuang was held by just 3,000 Chinese when it was attacked on 4 March by the 14,200 men of the Japanese 3rd and 5th Divisions, but was only taken at the end of a stubborn, day-long street-fight. Du Boulay records that 'the first houses were reached about noon, after firing had been going on for two hours, and from that time onwards the struggle was a severe one. The Chinese made a determined resistance in the houses, and until 5 p.m. no very great success was achieved by the Japanese. After that, however, a more systematic method of attack was adopted, and each house or block of houses was reduced in succession, guns being brought forward in some cases to knock down the walls. In this way the Chinese were gradually subdued, some of them fighting to the last, and others surrendering when they saw that further resistance was hopeless, and at 11 p.m. firing ceased.' The Japanese lost at least 70 killed and 319 wounded (White gives their total losses as 500), while about 1,900–2,000 of the Chinese garrison were killed and 600–700 were captured, along with 21 guns and 216 flags.

It was at Ying-k'ou that elements of Japan's 1st and 2nd Armies finally effected a junction, when part of Marshal Oyama's 1st Division occupied the town itself on 6 March (the forts guarding the mouth of the river only changed hands the following morning). The Chinese made no attempt to hold Ying-k'ou, instead falling back to T'ien-chuang-t'ai, where the last major engagement of the conflict – and, indeed, one of the biggest battles of the entire war – took place on 9 March.

The opposing armies drew up with the frozen Liao River between them. The Chinese, under General Sung, totalled perhaps 20–30,000 men, of whom some 7,000 were in the front line, with 30 guns emplaced along the riverfront. The Japanese under General Nozu, consisting of the 1st, 3rd and 5th Divisions (28,400 men), massed their 84 guns and seven mortars directly opposite the Chinese artillery and launched infantry attacks against

Lieutenant-General Nozu Michitsura (left), appointed to the command of the Japanese 1st Army in December 1894, and Marshal Oyama Iwao, commander of the Japanese 2nd Army.

the Chinese flanks, the 5th Division under General Oku[22] attacking their left and the 2nd Brigade under General Yamaji their right. General Katsura commanded the centre. The attack commenced at 7:30 a.m., and by 9:30 there was fierce fighting at the southern end of T'ien-chuang-t'ai, along the river, and about 4,000 yds (3,650 m) to the north, where the 5th Division, having crossed the Liao, found itself opposed by 3,000 Chinese who eventually scattered at about 10 o'clock. With both its flanks now in disarray the entire Chinese army broke and fled, large numbers being shot down as they crossed the front of the 1st and 5th Divisions. Chinese losses are variously reported as 20 guns and anywhere up to 5,000 men, including about 2,000 dead (1,400 bodies are said to have been counted on the battlefield). By contrast, Nozu lost just 16 men killed and 144 wounded. This brought the fighting in Manchuria to a close and left the way open for an advance on Peking.

The war had meanwhile been carried into North China by the launching of an amphibious assault from Japan against the port of Wei-hai-wei in Shantung province, carried out by the 2nd Division and such elements of the 6th Division as had not yet been despatched to Port Arthur, a total of some 19,000 men. Landings had begun on 20 January 1895, and the eastern forts had all been captured on the 30th after fierce fighting. The garrisons of the western forts abandoned these on 1 February, and the Japanese entered the town the following day. Only the forts on Liu-kung-tao and I-tao islands, garrisoned by some 1,500 men, and the remnants of the Chinese fleet under Admiral Ting Ju-ch'ang (two battleships, five cruisers, a sloop, seven gunboats, and 11 torpedo boats) – holed up here since its defeat at the Battle of the Yalu – put up a determined resistance, continuing to exchange fire vigorously with both the Japanese fleet and the captured eastern and western forts. In an attempt to neutralise the fleet, the Japanese squeezed eight torpedo boats past the boom blocking the harbour entrance on the night of 4/5 February. However, some were intercepted and damaged in exchanges with Chinese guard boats, and only six torpedoes got launched, though these struck and sunk the battleship *Ting-yuen*. Another attack by five torpedo boats the next night was more successful, sinking a cruiser and two smaller vessels. The 11 Chinese torpedo boats were all either sunk or captured when they attempted to escape on 7 February, and bombardment of the remaining ships and defences continued remorselessly until the 12th, when Admiral Ting negotiated the surrender of the fleet and forts and then committed suicide.

With the Japanese thus poised ready to advance against Peking from both Shantung and Manchuria, the Chinese sued for peace, even as Japanese troops overran the Pescadore Islands (23–26 March). Japan was at first inclined to reject the appeal for a ceasefire, but, fearing international condemnation, it subsequently U-turned in embarrassment when a Japanese fanatic shot and wounded Li Hung-chang, the principal Chinese negotiator. An armistice was subsequently agreed on 30 March, followed by the signing of the Treaty of Shimonoseki on 17 April. This awarded Japan 200 million *taels* (about £30 million) in war indemnities and gave her possession of Formosa, the Pescadores, and the Liao-tung Peninsula. However, Russia, France, and Germany (which all had Chinese ambitions of their own)[23] persuaded Japan to return the Liao-tung Peninsula to China in exchange for an increased indemnity, it being patently clear that Russia was prepared to resort to military force in order to have its way. Japanese troops consequently evacuated Liao-tung on 25 December.

This foreign interference, known to posterity as

Painting by Kubota Beisen from Arthur Diósy's The New Far East *(1900), where it is captioned: 'A sergeant of Infantry of the Line in Field Service Order, as in the early part of the War against China (1894)'. However, his rank stripes suggest he is a corporal rather than a sergeant. From 1871 to 1873 the rank of non-commissioned officers and privates was denoted by the yellow/gold edging along the top of their arm-of-service coloured pointed cuffs: one thin line was a private second class, two a private first class, three a corporal, one thick line a sergeant, one thick line crowned by one thin line a senior sergeant, and one thick line crowned by two thin lines a sergeant-major. In 1873 straight uncoloured cuffs were introduced, with horizontal arm-of-service coloured rank stripes above them – one for a private second class, two for a private first class, and three for a corporal; sergeants had a single gold stripe along the cuff line, an inch-wide gap above that, and then one to three arm-of-service coloured stripes above that (one for a sergeant, two for a senior sergeant, and three for a sergeant-major). These rank distinctions continued in use for the rest of the century..*

the 'Triple Intervention', led to outrage and riots in Japan, and the realisation that, despite its many achievements, Japan continued to be regarded in the world at large as a second-rate power answerable to the West. Japan responded to this discovery in the only way it could: by resolving to make itself even stronger in the shortest possible time. Consequently in 1896 military expenditure was increased to a staggering 133.1 million *yen*, representing more than half of all government spending.

The Treaty of Shimonoseki, meanwhile, did not quite end the fighting, since it proved necessary for Japan to mount a bitter four-month campaign against Chinese patriots for possession of Formosa.[24] In all about 135,000 Japanese troops participated in this operation, with some 50,000 in the field at any given time. Casualties totalled nearly 700 killed or wounded and more than 4,600 dead of disease, with another 27,000 invalided home.

ORGANISATION

Tokugawa 'feudalism'

As the 19th century began Japan remained what Western writers inaccurately but conveniently refer to as a 'feudal' state, which had changed very little in the 200 years since Shogun Ieyasu had come to power. The Tokugawa family itself was directly responsible for about a quarter of the entire country as well as all the major cities, while its 23 collateral branches – the greatest of which were the *gosanke* or 'three houses' (the Owari, Mito, and Kii or Kishu clans) – were responsible for about another eighth. The balance was divided up into autonomous territorial districts called *han* (most often translated as 'clans' or 'fiefs', but more accurately rendered as 'domains') over which the Tokugawa exercised an unchallenged hegemony.

There were some 265 *han* during the period under review,[25] each ruled by an hereditary lord known as a *daimyo* (literally 'great name'), whence the *han* is sometimes found described as a 'daimiate' in Western literature. The *daimyo* owed allegiance theoretically to the Emperor, but in reality to the Shogun, and each was in turn owed the allegiance of vassals of his own. His specific military obligations to the shogunate were decided according to the size of his *han*, which was calculated not by its area but by its taxable productive capacity, predominantly in rice, which was measured in *koku* (a unit of volume equivalent, in the 19th century, to 4.96 English bushels or 5.12 American, or roughly 180 litres). Technically the size of each *han* was fixed, and could be neither augmented nor diminished – 'either by marriage, or by purchase, or by might' – without the Shogun's express permission; but it is clear from 18th–19th century records that the revenues of most had either gradually increased over the years or (more probably) had never been accurately calculated in the first place. The problem for the *bakufu* was that it had no way of confirming this without violating a *han*'s autonomy, and therefore had no choice but to leave the traditional tax contributions and military obligations unchanged.

The highest-ranking grades of *daimyo* were the *gosanke* or *orokanomazume kamon* (descended from Shogun Ieyasu's favourite sons), the *tamarinomazume kamon* (descended from his other sons),[26] and the *kokushu*, a term also employed to describe this entire class of senior *daimyo*. The domains of such higher-ranking *daimyo* comprised one or more entire provinces, or lands or revenue of equivalent value. Beneath the senior *daimyo* came the *ryoshu*, who were lords of smaller but still sizeable domains called *ryochi* or *ryobun*; and the *joshu*, whose lordships were known as *shiro* (castles) because they generally comprised a single castle and its adjacent territory. In the mid-19th century there appear to have been 21 *kokushu* (each possessing a domain in excess of 200,000 *koku*), 32 *ryoshu*, and over 200 *joshu*.

Each *daimyo* owed personal military service to the Shogun, accompanied by a contingent of armed men – traditionally a mixture of swordsmen, musketeers, artillerists, archers, spearmen, and standard-bearers, plus 'numberless servants'[27] – proportionate to the assessed income of his lands. Domains of 200 *koku* were required to field five samurai; those of 1,000 *koku* provided 21; 5,000 *koku* 103; 10,000 *koku* 235; and 100,000 *koku* 2,155. The size of these quotas remained relatively unchanged from 1649 until as late as 1861, when they were significantly reduced (for instance, a *daimyo* of 50,000 *koku* who had earlier supplied some 1,000 men was henceforth expected to field just 163).

A more significant subdivision of *daimyo* was that made between those whose ancestors had been Tokugawa vassals prior to Ieyasu's victory at Sekigahara, and those whose ancestors did not become Tokugawa vassals until afterwards.[28] The former group were referred to as *fudai* and the latter as *tozama*. The *fudai* (the name means 'loyal families', but is often rendered as 'inner lords') outnumbered the *tozama* by two to one. They owed their lands and titles entirely to the patronage of the Tokugawa shoguns, whose hereditary vassals they consequently were. Unsurprisingly, they included all of the *gosanke* and *kamon*. Government appointments were made exclusively from the ranks of the *fudai*, though Tokugawa clansmen among them rarely held posts that were anything more than advisory. The Shogun retained ultimate control over *fudai* domains, and could either increase or decrease their revenue at will. He could even order *fudai* to exchange their domains if he saw fit, most often as a means of demotion or promotion. However, this practice became uncommon during the 18th century.

The *tozama* or 'outside lords', of whom there were 98 at the commencement of the 19th century, included the Mori of Choshu, the Shimazu of Satsuma, the Yamanouchi of Tosa, the Mutsu of Sendai, and the majority of the other important families found mostly in the extreme north and the south-west. Though these still had to pay rice tribute and owed nominal service to the Shogun they were otherwise left to manage their own affairs, being considered too powerful to antagonise unnecessarily. (It was said, for instance, that 'a Tokugawa man might not venture into the districts of the great Shimazu family, the lords of Satsuma and its neighbourhood, without more or less peril.') As an indication of their political and military might it need only be pointed out that two-thirds of Japan's wealthiest *han* were held by *tozama*, including the three richest – Kaga, assessed at more than 1.02 million *koku*; Satsuma, assessed at 770,000; and Sendai, assessed at 625,600. Indeed, the already mentioned increases in value since their *han* had been officially assessed back in the 17th century meant that the *tozama* were actually considerably richer than their *bakufu* assessments implied: to cite but two examples, the Higo *han* was assessed at 540,000 *koku* but its actual yield was 721,000, while Choshu, officially assessed at only 369,000 *koku*, actually yielded at least 713,000 and possibly as much as a million. Since it was larger than Choshu it can be supposed that in all likelihood Satsuma similarly yielded somewhere in the vicinity of a million *koku*. Such figures should then be compared to Japan's total official revenue of little more than 20 million *koku* at about mid-century, and the seven million *koku* assessment of the Tokugawa *bakufu*'s own domains.

As we have already seen, it was to be *tozama* lords who would eventually orchestrate the overthrow of the shogunate and bring about the Meiji Restoration, and their wealth proved a decisive factor in this process, enabling them to purchase whatever Western arms they needed. For the best part of the preceding 250 years, however, the Tokugawa government had been able to maintain tight control of the country's *daimyo* by an efficient system of checks and balances, which had involved four key elements: firstly, the prevention of a potentially hostile power bloc arising, by the careful geographical distribution of loyal vassals and pro-Tokugawa *tozama* amongst the *han* held by descendants of *tozama* who had fought against Ieyasu; secondly, by the introduction of the *sankin-kotai* or 'alternate attendance' system, which inflicted ruinous expense on *daimyo* by requiring them to travel with their households to Edo and reside there on alternate years, and to leave their families there as hostages for their good behaviour when they returned to their domains;[29] thirdly, by doing everything it could to prevent the import of foreign technology and weapons which might (and eventually did) upset the delicate balance of power between *bakufu*, *fudai*, and *tozama*; and fourthly, by enforcing Japanese society's adherence to a strict hierarchical mould which denied even the most ambitious any opportunity for dangerous advancement.

Beneath the nobility, the lower rungs of the Tokugawa ladder of social privilege were occupied by the *daimyo*'s personal military retainers, known as *samurai*. Technically this term embraced all Japanese entitled to wear two swords, and therefore included the *daimyo* themselves, but in common parlance it was generally understood to denote only those of non-noble rank, who owed allegiance to their lords in exchange for a 'fief' (see below) or an hereditary fixed stipend (*karoku*), originally paid in rice. In order to qualify for his 'fief' or salary, a samurai was technically required to be aged 15 or more, to have been born a samurai, and to be proficient with horse, bow, spear, and sword. However, John Wigmore (1893) reports that 'these requirements were often not strictly adhered to in practice'.

By the mid-19th century there were about 400,000 families of samurai status, estimated to have represented 1.8–2 million souls out of a total population of approximately 28–30 million. On this basis it is generally accepted that roughly 5.5% of the male population were samurai. Technically all of these owed military service to their *daimyo*, but because the only serious fighting since the 1630s had involved crushing occasional peasant uprisings that duty had become almost redundant, and had largely been replaced by often trivial administrative responsibilities. E.H. Norman (1940) considered that 'the long years of peace after the establishment of the Tokugawa shogunate sapped the martial ardour of the samurai and rendered their existence superfluous, so that they became virtually a parasitic class.' Certainly by the beginning of the 19th century most were little more than armed layabouts, whose most taxing military obligations were to provide their lord with an escort on ceremonial occasions, to accompany him during his biennial residence in the capital, and to perform perfunctory guard duty at his house or castle.

There were considered to be two grades of samurai, known as *seishi* and *kashi*, who Ernest Satow (1921) defines respectively as 'gentlemen' and 'common soldiers'. Following a similar train of thought, Wigmore likened the *seishi* to 'knights, in the strict sense of the term', since 'they alone had the privilege of following the lord to battle on horseback'. *Seishi* were subdivided in turn into two distinct categories. Those who owed allegiance directly to the Tokugawa clan were designated *chokushin* or, more often, *hatamoto* (meaning 'under the banner', describing their traditional post in battle), while those who owed their allegiance to other *daimyo* were known instead as *kerai* or *baishin*. A *daimyo* assessed at 100,000 *koku* probably retained about 1,000 *seishi*, many of whom had samurai retainers of their own. The most powerful *hatamoto* held domains worth 9,000 *koku* and fielded almost as many samurai as the lowest rank of *daimyo*, whose domains were valued at 10,000 *koku*. The Tokugawa family's domains contained some 5,000 *hatamoto*, each customarily maintaining between three and 30 samurai of his own, so that by the *Bakumatsu* era at the very latest they were theoretically capable of mustering more than 60,000 men.

Engraved from a photograph, this is Yoshinobu, better known in the West as Keiki, the last shogun of Japan (1866–68).

The *kashi* or inferior class of samurai traditionally constituted the foot-soldiery. They were known by an assortment of terms dependent on their precise occupation and status within the civil or military establishment, including *doshin*, *kachi*, and *yoriki*, but they are best known as *ashigaru* ('light foot'). *Kashi* belonging to Tokugawa clans were generally known as *gokenin* ('virtuous housemen'), of whom there were theoretically some 17,000. These had a well-earned reputation for conceit and arrogance in their dealings with the retainers of other *daimyo*.

Together, the Tokugawa *hatamoto* and *gokenin* – collectively known as *shomyo* or 'small names' to further distinguish them from the *daimyo* or 'great names' – constituted the linchpin of shogunate government, filling the majority of posts in the civil administration and providing the greater part of what might be termed its regular armed forces (i.e., the virtually permanent bodies of samurai that the *bakufu* maintained for city guard and garrison duties). *Hatamoto* with incomes of less than 10,000 *koku* but more than 3,000 were called *taishin* ('great vassals') when they held active administrative posts, but *yoriai* (literally 'those summoned to assemble', i.e., councillors) – either *kotai-yoriai*, 'alternate councillors', or *hira-yoriai*, 'ordinary councillors' – when their positions were purely honorary. *Hatamoto* assessed at between 300 and 3,000 *koku* were called *omemiye-jo* when they had the right of presentation at the Shogun's court (but *omemiye-ka* when they didn't), and, along with *gokenin* not holding official posts, might also be referred to as *kobushin*. Technically none of the offices held by either *hatamoto* or *gokenin* were hereditary, except where the office was itself the basis of the 'feudal' relationship between vassal and lord, but many became so with the passage of time.

On the left is a saihai, a short lacquered baton used to direct troop movements on the battlefield (see also the caption to Figure 1). It was most often about 15–24 ins long (0.38–0.61 m) with a bushy tassel of hair, leather strips or oiled paper. According to the Tanki Yoriaku *'every captain and all officers of higher rank' carried one. On the right is another officer's symbol of office, the* dansen. *The* Tanki Yoriaku *tells us that this was used 'to ward off arrows and stones and also as a sunshade.' It was generally made either of solid iron or of an iron-covered wooden core, and was usually laminated black and otherwise decorated.*

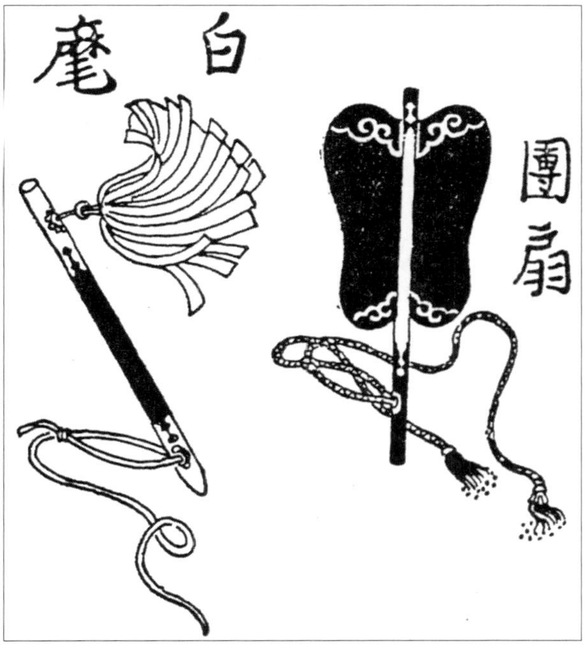

In exchange for their services all samurai received exemption from taxes plus an income which originally took the form of either rice or else a revenue derived from a grant of land that Western writers generally term a 'fief', but which nevertheless differed markedly from its mediaeval European counterpart. Instead of receiving the land itself, a samurai was awarded the right to a set income (*chigyo*) derived from a parcel of land called a *chigyo-sho*, which could vary dramatically in size and might be anything from a single village or a dozen rice-fields up to 50 or more villages. Unlike a feudal European fief, the *chigyo-sho* did not become the samurai's personal property, even though the peasants who farmed it were obliged to provide him with servants in war-time.[30] However, the majority of samurai were not so fortunate as to receive a *chigyo-sho*, instead being granted the right to simply draw an annual allowance of rice from their lord's storehouse. This allowance was known as a *fuchi* or a *hyo-mono*, the latter variety being worth more than the former. Like the *chigyo-sho*, the value of such grants varied enormously, some being sufficient only to keep the samurai himself, while others could feed up to five people and a few were actually worth more than a *chigyo-sho*. On the whole, however, samurai rice stipends were staggeringly low.

Martin Ramming, after closely examining various Japanese records, concluded in 1928 that even middle-ranking samurai had averaged only 100 *koku* at best, which was 'roughly equivalent to the income of a rich peasant', and that 'the average for all samurai' (presumably referring only to those below the rank of *seishi*), was well under 35 *koku*, 'which put them on the same economic plane as a peasant'. Chitoshi Yanaga (1949) calculated their income to be even lower, stating that *bakufu* retainers averaged 28 *koku*, and *daimyo* retainers just 16 *koku*.

In all cases, the need for actual cash meant that much of the rice the samurai received had to be sold in order to buy other necessaries, and it seems to have eventually become acceptable for a samurai's rice allowance to be assessed at the going market rate and paid out in cash rather than kind. However, this was clearly a very late development, since even in 1811–13 Vasilii Golownin, a Russian prisoner, noted that it was only in the northern islands – Sakhalin and the Matsumae *han* (made up of Hokkaido, Kunashir, and Iturup) – that samurai income was paid partly in money as well as partly in rice, while everywhere else, he wrote, 'soldiers receive their pay in rice'.

In addition to pay all samurai also received a place of residence, which was invariably situated within one of their lord's *yashiki* ('castle-towns'). The wealthiest and most influential were required to live in the *han* capital. Those holding official posts also enjoyed much-needed additional income, either in rice or land revenue. Not even the neediest samurai would so much as contemplate engaging in any sort of work, trade, or business in order to improve their financial position, despite the fact that their incomes had generally remained unchanged for centuries regardless of inflation elsewhere in the Japanese economy. Even some *daimyo* felt the pinch sufficiently to cut their retainers' pay; all of which meant that many samurai families became steadily more impoverished with the passage of time. Some samurai were entirely dispossessed of their income, or voluntarily left their master to seek service elsewhere in the hope of improving their fortunes; yet others became desperate enough to resort to crime.[31] Collectively, such incomeless and masterless samurai were known as *ronin* or 'wave-men', in the sense of being 'tossed about hither and thither as a wave of the sea' (Gubbins 1911). According to Chitoshi Yanaga there may have been as many as 100,000 to 200,000 *ronin* by the end of the Edo period.

As those with the greatest appreciation of the desperate need for change in Japan's antiquated and ailing 'feudal' system, it was to be the *ronin* and other impoverished low-ranking samurai who eventually inspired opposition to the country's uncompromising conservatives and the political stagnation they represented. Believing that the Emperor would be a better master than the Shogun, most became ardent supporters of his restoration to power. Many took up the study of Western languages and technology (*Rangaku*, literally 'essentially technical' but usually translated as 'Dutch learning') in open defiance of the *bakufu*'s attitude to foreign influence, hoping that this might give them an edge in the forthcoming struggle. Troops of *ronin* nevertheless served on both sides during the fighting of 1864–68, the best-known such corps probably being the *Seigishi* ('Righteous Samurai') raised by Mori Takachika, lord of Choshu, in 1861, and the Tokugawa *Shinsengumi* ('Newly Selected Corps') and *Shinchogumi* ('New Levies').

The *tozama* of the south-west

Military organisation within the pre-Restoration Satsuma, Choshu, Tosa, and other *tozama* lordships of south-western Japan differed markedly from that found elsewhere, since it depended heavily on a socially inferior class of rustic samurai referred to as *goshi*. The ancestors of some *goshi* had risen to their nominally elevated status from peasant or merchant backgrounds (which was technically illegal, but *tozama* lords blatantly ignored *bakufu* prohibition of the practice), while others were the descendants of samurai evicted from their homes at the beginning of the 17th century when large parts of the original Satsuma and Choshu domains had been confiscated after the Tokugawa came to power.

Unlike other samurai, *goshi* not only received a small allotment of land but in the majority of cases actually farmed it with their own hands, thereby earning themselves the derogatory nickname 'sweet potato samurai'. However, since these allotments were only occasionally worth more than 20 *koku* and often amounted to less than one, many *goshi* lived in a state of virtual destitution, resulting in another of their unique characteristics – their preparedness to participate in trade or industry in order to boost their income. Despite being in effect little more than smallholding cultivators they nevertheless remained genuine samurai, and their existence explains how by the late Edo period as much as 25% of Satsuma's population and 9% of Choshu's were of samurai status, both figures being well above the national average of 5.5%. Because there were so many samurai in such lordships it was obviously impossible for them all to reside in and around the local capital, and they consequently tended to be found all over their respective *han*, much as had been the case throughout Japan in mediaeval times. Their sizeable samurai populations also meant that Satsuma could field some 25,000 rather than the 14,000 called for by its *koku* assessment, and Choshu 11,000 rather than its official 6,000.

The clans' more conventional samurai were divided and subdivided into several distinct classes as elsewhere. The superior grades, equivalent to Tokugawa *hatamoto*, consisted of land-holding nobles (*hitotsu-kadi-mochi* or *isso-machi*) and senior administrators (*yoriai*) with revenues of 3–10,000 *koku*; while beneath these, in descending order, came *koban* and *shimban* (equivalent to *omemiye-jo*), *kosho-gumi* (equivalent to *kerai*), and *yoriki* or *ashigaru* (equivalent to *gokenin*). A sizeable number of these were settled in and around the *han* capitals as usual, but others were based round the sites of former castles which were the seats of administrative districts called *go*, each run by an official known as a *jito*. Samurai of the *kosho-gumi* class – men such as Saigo Takamori, Takasugi Shinsaku, and Okubo Toshimichi – were to be among the leading advocates of the Restoration movement in the 1860s. Their affluent clan leaders, by contrast, were content with preserving the status quo, and only reluctantly joined the revolutionary movement when it became clear that if they did not they would fairly certainly forfeit the loyalty of the men upon whom the administration of their *han* depended.

With its massive revenue and its access to such substantial numbers of samurai 'famed for their intense local patriotism and fierce fighting ability', Satsuma was by far the most formidable of the *tozama* clans. Augustus Mounsey (1879) observed that it constituted a veritable *imperium in imperio*, and that 'each of its inhabitants considered himself a Satsuma man first and then a Japanese'. The province's location in the extreme south-west, astride the most direct line of approach to Japan, also meant that despite the *bakufu*'s isolation policy, not only had Satsuma been able to enjoy covert but highly profitable trading relations with China (via the Ryukyu Islands) throughout the Edo period, but had also, as a result of its early exposure to Western traders, pioneered the import, manufacture, and use of modern Western firearms, building an ordnance factory at the *han* capital of Kagoshima as early as 1854. With as much as 40% of the *han*'s finances being dedicated to military expenditure, another cannon factory and three ammunition plants quickly followed. The bombardment of Kagoshima by the Western powers in 1863 urgently underlined the need for further reform, and not only prompted a rapid increase in the purchase of Western firearms but also led to the clan's *daimyo*, Shimazu Hisamitsu, engaging several Frenchmen – an officer (the Comte de Montblanc) and several retired NCOs – to instruct his samurai in Western drill and tactics.

Even so, Satsuma forces were less well organised (there seems to have been minimal organisation above company level) and far less comprehensively modernised than those of Choshu, for whom see below, probably because they were also significantly more numerous. Swords, spears and polearms therefore continued to feature prominently in most Satsuma field forces – the 5,600 Satsuma clansmen in Kyoto in December 1867, for instance, included at least 2,100

Traditional Japanese horse-harness, from an engraving in the Illustrated London News *of 17 August 1861. Note in particular the stirrups and the straw horseshoes. The latter are described by George Smith that year as 'tied like a bag round the hoof, and laced with straw bands around the fetlock.' As with the similar straw sandals worn by samurai these had a limited lifespan, and a supply of spare horseshoes was always carried, generally in a net suspended underneath each stirrup.*

swordsmen. However, they are said to have 'made up in judicious deployment, zeal, numbers, and leadership ... what they lacked in quality of organisation and weaponry.'[32]

The south-western *tozama* were also the earliest clans to make significant use of the enormous manpower potential of the peasantry, who by tradition were required to perform corvée service (*kayaku*) for the repair and maintenance of roads, dykes, and bridges, but not military service. By the beginning of the 19th century at the latest, however, Japan's social order had begun to show small signs of change, with some of the wealthiest peasants (*gono*) being awarded the right to wear a short sword and to practise military arts. Consequently by the 1840s a handful of radicals were advocating the enlistment of peasants into the military, which led to the creation of the first small *noheitai* or part-time peasant militias in the 1850s. Drilled by samurai but officered by peasant officials, these were intended for use only during emergencies. The enlistment of peasants into clan armies followed during the wars accompanying the demise of the shogunate in the 1860s, an early Meiji source recording that in the immediate pre-Restoration period 'the need frequently arose for each clan to increase the number of its soldiers and, keenly feeling the insufficiency of the samurai, the clans organised troops by summoning the dependants of the regular soldiers, or by recruiting peasants and commoners, Shinto and Buddhist priests, and others. In order to maintain them they gave them stipends and every clan without exception did this.' But the principal reason for the enlistment of peasants appears to have been samurai resistance to the adoption of firearms, which in Japan had become traditionally associated with the very lowest stratum of soldier. The use of commoners in this capacity also meant that modern, Westernised formations could be introduced gradually, without unduly disturbing the traditional samurai military establishment.

The first unit to actually incorporate commoners and samurai side by side appears to have been the relatively short-lived *Mimpei* or 'People's Militia' organised by the Tosa clan of Shikoku in September 1854, to guard its coasts. This was officered by *ronin*, *goshi*, and village headmen (*shoya*), but otherwise consisted predominantly of peasants, townsmen, seamen, and hunters, who were required to be at least 5 ft (1.52 m) tall and aged between 17 and 50. (When the corps was revived as the *Gohei* in 1869 its recruits were required to be 17–30 years old.)

Several other such units appeared in the 1860s, including the Ashikaga clan's *Seishintai* ('Corps of the Whole-hearted') of 1865, eventually numbering more than 200 men. The best-known, however, was that raised for the Choshu clan in June 1863 by Takasugi Shinsaku, an avid student of 'Dutch learning'. Known as the *Kiheitai* (sometimes graphically translated as 'shock troops', but more accurately 'Extraordinary Corps'), this roughly 300-strong formation was equipped largely – but at first not entirely – with modern Western firearms. Like the *Mimpei*, it was recruited from a mixture of samurai, peasants, and townsmen, and was officered by *ronin*, *goshi*, and other samurai (though some of its 'lower officers' were eventually of non-samurai status). Its men received unusually high pay, substituted European-inspired light dress for traditional armour, and were subjected to Western drill[33] and strict discipline. At first the non-samurai element was inconsequential, and even in 1864 only 2.4% are known with certainty to have been of peasant origin (though a further 31% were hunters, townsmen, and priests), but when second and third *Kiheitai* companies were raised this proportion markedly increased, 78 out of 137 men (57%) being peasants in the second company, and 123 out of 277 men (44%) in the third. By comparison, only about 25–33% were samurai, the future marshal Yamagata Aritomo among them.

The *Kiheitai* were, in fact, but one of numerous similar full-time units raised by anti-foreign Choshu extremists at this juncture, all made up about half and half

Typical late bakufu soldiers photographed c.1867, in a typical melange of Western and traditional dress, but all of them still armed with two swords as well as muskets. They have presumably removed their hats for the photograph to be taken. (Wikipedia)

of commoners and samurai. Known as *shotai* (usually translated as 'auxiliary militia'), they included the *Giyutai* (50 men), the *Hachimantai* (100 men), the *Rikishitai* (a small unit made up largely of Sumo wrestlers), the *Shugitai* (50 men), the *Yochotai* (230 men), and – the largest such corps – the *Yugekitai* (500 men), among many others. Some such units were raised by the Choshu *han* government, while others coalesced unofficially under the leadership of charismatic local samurai as a result of alliances between *goshi* and commoners, and were only subsequently 'adopted' by the *han*. All seem to have been initially equipped with a mixture of traditional bladed weapons and firearms, though priority was invariably given to the latter wherever possible. Full Westernisation of their organisation and equipment commenced only during the second half of 1865, when all the *shotai* were brought under *han* control and provided with firearms. There were some 58 Choshu *shotai* by late 1864, and perhaps 156 in mid-1866, but they were repeatedly subjected to disbandment and reorganisation as each crisis of the period 1864–66 waxed and waned, and their numbers fluctuated accordingly. During the latter part of 1866 the *shotai* were comprehensively reorganised, into 36 battalions each theoretically consisting of 400 men divided into ten companies of 40 – a total of 14,400 men in all.

When conservative elements within the Choshu clan came to power following the failure of the radicals' counter-coup in Kyoto and the bombardment of Shimonoseki by the Western navies in September 1864, attempts were made to disband the *shotai* by force in order to placate the *bakufu*. However, the *shotai* retired into the countryside under Takasugi and Yamagata and, joining with other radicals, eventually succeeded in overthrowing the conservatives. The *shotai*'s expertise with Western firearms and tactics proved the decisive factor in this victory, and both were soon thereafter adopted throughout the Choshu clan's forces. One observer noted in 1865 that the Choshu thereafter enjoyed such a mastery of guns and artillery that traditional Japanese 'slash and cut' tactics were useless against them. This was underlined in the fighting against *bakufu* forces the following year, when another contemporary recorded that while the Choshu's 40,000-strong army was 'truly most skilled in the use of Western arms', which gave it 'a formidable power', the *bakufu* 'feudal' vassals against whom it fought used either traditional weapons or else matchlocks and other old-fashioned guns. The latter were consequently outclassed in every engagement, thereby obliging the *bakufu*'s own corps of Western-style infantry to keep coming to their aid. The *shotai* were only eventually disbanded in 1869 following the Meiji Restoration.

Like Satsuma and Choshu, the other south-western clans were also quick to recognise the military advantages of Western technology. Amongst the quickest was Hizen, which, because it included the Dutch trading station off Nagasaki, became the centre of 'Dutch learning' in Japan. Reformers here had begun to cast Western cannon (with Dutch assistance) by as early as 1842, and by 1850 a reverberatory furnace had been installed. Inevitably there were teething problems, but in time such advances enabled Hizen to manufacture guns to virtually the same standard as European factories, and by 1866 it was turning out almost 40 guns a month. (Satsuma did not get a reverberatory furnace until 1856, which produced the 50 or so heavy guns used to defend Kagoshima harbour against the British in 1863.) All Hizen samurai were required to train with firearms after 1857, as were all Satsuma samurai after 1854.

A report of late 1863 assessed the total theoretical military obligation to the shogunate of all the *tozama* at 116 infantry battalions (each of nominally 400 men, making a total of 46,400), 12 squadrons of cavalry (just 1,224 men), and 50 batteries of artillery (3,200 men). These figures include only samurai troops and exclude Choshu's contingent entirely, since it was considered at the time to be beyond the *bakufu* pale. The schedule records the Satsuma clan's obligation as eight infantry battalions, one cavalry squadron, and four batteries of artillery.

THE LATE TOKUGAWA ARMY, 1860–68

Suggestions for *bakufu* military reform had been circulating since the beginning of the century, initially prompted by a growing awareness of the threat posed by Russia. The need for change grew steadily more pressing after about 1830, excited mainly by the shogunate's financial weakness and by Western European advances into Asia. In particular, Great Britain's swift and decisive victory over China in the Opium War of 1839–42 led to a reappraisal of attitudes towards 'barbarian' technology, and dawning realisation of the vast disparity in armaments that separated Japan and the West. Shogun Ieyoshi immediately instigated the purchase of sizeable quantities of foreign guns via the Dutch trading community at Nagasaki, as well as introducing the first basics of machine-based armaments production.

Admiral Perry's arrival in 1853–54 led to the establishment of further factory and foundry facilities at Edo, Nagasaki, and elsewhere. In 1854 the Dutch government presented Japan with her first steam-ship, the *Kanko Maru*, and in 1855 some 20 Dutch instructors were provided to establish a naval and military training college at Nagasaki.[34] Pursuing its traditional policy of isolationism, the *bakufu* initially regarded improvement of its navy and shore defences as more important than army reform, and over the next few years spent huge sums buying warships, building modern coastal fortifications[35] (notably at Hakodate, Kameda, Kamitsushim, Shimoda, and Shinagawa), and financing the study of Western arms and technology. This swiftly generated a massive national debt. Then, as Japan's domestic situation worsened and disaffection spread, shogunate priorities shifted. The need for improved internal security meant that Westernisation and centralisation of the army, not the navy, became the *bakufu*'s primary concern.

The first plan for restructuring the military establishment, presented in the second half of 1862, was drawn up by samurai who had either studied under the Dutch at Nagasaki or had been taught, unofficially, by other foreigners at Yokohama. It called for the creation of a central army corps comprising infantry, cavalry, and artillery units, referred to as the *Sampeitai* (literally 'three bodies of troops') or the *Shinei Jobigun* ('Shogun's standing army'), which was to be at least partially organised and trained along Western lines. This resulted in the formation of an army of 13,625 men recruited half and half amongst higher and lower-ranking samurai, of whom more than 8,300 served as infantry. As many as 6,300 of these were still armoured, and equipped with matchlocks or old-fashioned muskets and swords, but most of the rest substituted light clothing and carried Minié rifles. There were also 1,068 cavalry, provided by the *hatamoto* (900 armed with carbines and swords and the balance with lances), and 2,845 artillerymen. The latter were organised into field artillery (48 × 8-pdr guns and 800 men) and heavy artillery (52 × 16-pdr guns and 2,045 men). The *Sampeitai*'s remaining 1,406 men were officers. Recruits were levied amongst the Shogun's personal vassals at the rate of one samurai per 500 *koku*, three per 1,000 *koku*, and ten per 3,000 *koku*. The men enlisted had to serve for five years, and probably received much the same pay as was recorded in 1866 – seven *ryo* and 1.8 *koku* of rice per annum, plus a uniform, and provisions when in barracks. Theoretical organisation appears to have been into battalions of 600 men, each under a major. Each battalion was made up of five companies under captains, a company consisting of three 40-strong platoons commanded by lieutenants, with half-platoons under second lieutenants. Platoons were probably subdivided into four ten-man squads.

The troop quotas owed to the state by *daimyo* were overhauled at much the same time, and were reduced by at least 50% and in some instances by as much as 85% to purge them of deadwood. It was also agreed that *bakufu* vassals could henceforth pay fines (in money or rice) in lieu of providing men, the revenue generated going towards financing the large-scale introduction of foreign firearms. From January 1863 *bakufu* vassals were required to send selected troops aged 15–45 (some sources say 17–47) to Edo for five years' service as infantrymen, beginning with a course in the use of firearms. Practice with Western firearms by *daimyo* retainers had been encouraged at every opportunity since May 1862, archery practice being simultaneously abandoned, and the adoption of firearms was henceforward enforced with greater and greater rigour.

Outside of the Tokugawa family's own domains, however, firearm training met with only limited success, partially because lords were initially required to buy the muskets and finance the practice out of their own purses, but mostly because of obstinate samurai resistance to the adoption of guns and the accompanying demands that they should drill like common soldiers. Consequently even when the *bakufu* eventually agreed to shoulder the financial burden, samurai firearms training continued to be indifferent in quality, and, since it was not compulsory, was attended with reluctance if at all. John Black recorded in 1865 that 'many of the samurai to whom rifles were offered, refused to use them, or to undergo the new drill, preferring to trust the old bows and arrows, the trusty sword, and the tactics of old Japan.'

A further problem encountered was that, despite or perhaps because of the massive reduction in size of the obligatory military quotas of *bakufu* vassals, sufficient able-bodied men could not be found to fill the ranks of the proposed new units. In fact only about half the required number of recruits could be mustered. This generated a lengthy debate regarding the practicality and desirability of enlisting non-samurai, which ended with a decision in late 1863 to recruit commoners into the infantry. There are indications that they may initially have been employed predominantly in maintenance and transport duties, but as many as 1,500 peasant, or at least non-samurai, soldiers were certainly employed in the field against Mito rebels in 1864, and two rifle-armed

This atmospheric picture of unreconstructed Tokugawa samurai was taken by celebrated photographer Felice Beato, who accompanied Sir Harry Parkes to Japan in 1867. The Tokugawa mon can be seen on the right-hand warrior's jingasa *'war-hat'.*

bakufu battalions raised in 1865 consisted almost entirely of commoners, only the officers being samurai. Thereafter commoners constituted a steadily increasing percentage of all shogunate infantry, not least because they were more receptive to the introduction of Western drill and firearms. Such men were required to be aged between 17 and 45 and, like their samurai counterparts, had to serve for five years. After 1867 they were paid from revenue derived from a tax levied on villages in lieu of militia service. Needless to say, many samurai objected to serving side by side with commoners. Some even regarded serving alongside lower-ranking samurai to be beneath their dignity.

A revised plan for the central army introduced in February 1865 resulted in it being restructured into 12 numbered regular infantry or *hohei* battalions (9,600 men), two cavalry units (264 men), and six batteries of artillery (1,380 men). Foreign eyewitnesses describe some of these units seen at Yokohama that year as 'very creditably instructed'. However, the indications are that reorganisation along these lines was never entirely completed. There were perhaps only 5,400 *hohei* at the end of 1865, and a Japanese officer's claim that the forces which marched against Choshu that year included 10,000 infantry 'altogether equipped and drilled in the European style' is certainly exaggerated. The same officer's statement that these Westernised infantry constituted 'the kernel of the army ... on which the Tycoon more especially reckons for the final success of the struggle' is nevertheless an accurate observation. By early 1867 there were 7,300 such infantry, organised in seven regular battalions and two 'training battalions'. The former consisted of the 1st (1,000 men), 4th (1,000), 5th (800), 6th (600), 7th (800), 8th (800), and 11th (900) infantry battalions, while the two 'training battalions', totalling 1,400 men, were doubtless those undergoing instruction by the French military mission which had arrived in January (for which see below). Note that these battalion strengths are significantly larger than the 500 men (each battalion customarily consisting of ten companies of 50 men) more typical of late Tokugawa practice and recorded for these very same battalions in other sources.

Following Shogun Iemochi's sudden death in 1866, his successor Keiki put together five additional infantry battalions (called *yugekitai* – not to be confused with the Choshu *shotai* of the same name) by combining a number of existing 'feudal' units. The men continued to receive their traditional stipends, but these now took the form of pay directly related to their military service. At the same time *fudai* and *hatamoto* were instructed to convert their samurai contingents to firearms, and, in order to enforce the reluctant compliance of the samurai, the pay of men armed in any other way was henceforth suspended. Formal practice with swords and spears was simultaneously abolished. Other ways of boosting the central army's strength involved a slight increase in the number of men each vassal had to provide for military service;[36] the abolition of various traditional administrative posts and titles and the reassignment of their holders to the army; the disbandment of city watches and elite guard units so that their men could be reassigned to new firearm-equipped battalions; and the progressive

Partially Westernised shogunate soldiers, probably hohei, *sketched at Yokohama in 1866. An engraving from the* Illustrated London News.

consolidation of small military units until they reached battalion strength (most often 400–500 men). In addition an existing unit of Edo magisterial guards was converted into infantry, the senior samurai being put into Western uniforms and formed into a roughly 500-strong battalion of Legation guards (*bette gumi*), while the thousand-odd lower-ranking men were organised in companies of 50 and combined into two infantry battalions known as *hohei gumi*. All of these were armed and trained along Western lines. Some Edo city patrols (*mimawari gumi*) were also gradually converted to firearms, but the patrolmen regarded this as a demotion in status and many consequently deserted.

In order to preserve the distinctions between different samurai ranks while it restructured the army, the *bakufu* initially adopted a policy of creating new units entirely from samurai of the same status – *yoriai* with incomes of 3–8,000 *koku*, for instance, were formed into small units (subsequently amalgamated into battalions) called *kumiai jutai*, other *hatamoto* formed the *okuzume jutai*, middle-ranking samurai became the *yugekitai*, and units made up predominantly of *yoriki* became the *jutai*. All of these were theoretically provided with firearms, but these were often of mixed quality (including everything from 16th-century matchlocks to modern rifles), and many men carried assorted traditional weapons instead. Finally there were the units formed from *doshin* and the very lowest-ranking samurai, who together constituted the largest number of these newly created corps, designated as either *sappei* (artillery guards and gunners) or *hohei* (regular infantry).

This practice of assigning men according to perceived or actual rank inevitably led to recruitment problems by limiting the choice of available men, and it was consequently abandoned in August 1867. Many *sappei* units were then redesignated *hohei*. Even so, there were still as many as 5,000 *sappei* in September, of whom only about 60% were actually of the right age or physical fitness for military service. New battalions of artillery guards raised thereafter seem to have been called *taihotai shojutai*.

Needless to say, traditional troops continued to be fielded alongside such Westernised and partially Westernised contingents, and many continued to dress and arm themselves in full samurai panoply exactly as their ancestors had. This was especially true of the forces raised by the Shogun's vassals, which remained determinedly archaic in both armament and organisation, with units of every imaginable size and composition. Consequently Tokugawa field armies of the period 1866–68 invariably comprised two distinct elements, one made up of enlisted 'feudal' vassals at least partially armed and drilled along Western lines, and the other of unreconstructed *fudai* with their largely sword-, spear- and bow-armed retainers and massive entourages of servants (usually at least equalling the number of fighting men and sometimes outnumbering them several times over). The army mustered at Osaka to march against the Choshu in January 1866, for instance, included nearly 2,000 traditionally armed samurai (mostly swordsmen) arranged in nearly 40 companies of various sizes, alongside some 6,000 firearm-equipped troops organised principally into understrength battalions, including six and a half battalions of *hohei* (2,600 men), six and a half battalions of *sappei* (1,500 men), and an artillery corps of five eight-gun batteries and 320 men.

A typical example of a late Tokugawa 'feudal' contingent is that of the Ii *daimyo* of Hikone, which in 1865 consisted of 1,887 samurai (plus roughly as many porters and servants), of whom 711 were mounted men organised in dozens of small troops averaging about nine men each; 320 were spearmen in squads of 9–15; 447 were musketeers in squads of 25; 65 were men armed with Western rifles formed into five squads; 160 were artillerists equipped with a total of 16 field-pieces; and the balance were swordsmen. The entire contingent was organised into six unevenly-sized battalions of which the smallest comprised 173 men and the largest 493.

The organisation and arms of the most steadfast Tokugawa vassal, Aizu, remained virtually unchanged between 1863 and 1868, with mixed companies about 120–150 strong made up of spearmen, swordsmen, and matchlockmen (the last being finally changed to musketeers and riflemen only in 1868). These companies were thrown together as required to produce as many temporary battalions as a given situation might demand. The general consensus seems to be that the Aizu provided the most courageous and best quality troops of any of the Shogun's vassals, despite the observation made in various sources that they included more spearmen than firearms.

By mid-October 1867 the reorganised Tokugawa central army appears to have comprised some 24,000 men, including the *hohei* regular infantry, troops undergoing French instruction, and 36½ battalions of samurai grudgingly converted to modern firearms within the preceding 12 months, including one battalion of *yugekitai*, seven and a half of *sappei*, two of *taihotai shojutai*, and four and a half of cavalry. In fact the army had now become so large that the *bakufu* economy was unable to sustain it, enabling the authorities to refine it further in November the same year by disbanding as many as 7,000 of its least modernised and most expensive troops (the *kumiai jutai*). This move resulted in considerable unrest, with gangs of redundant samurai roaming the streets of Edo in belligerent mood, and only ended with the re-employment of some 6,000 into the *hohei* as the outbreak of the Boshin War approached.

The shogunate forces assembled in Osaka to march on Kyoto at the beginning of 1868 included 12 battalions of *hohei* (theoretically 6,000 men); two French-drilled battalions of *sappei* (900 men); two battalions of firearm-equipped *okuzume jutai* and *jutai*; three and a half composite battalions (one and a half made up predominantly of *yugekitai* and *mimawari*) provided with a mixture of firearms and traditional weapons; an unknown but small number of regular artillery and cavalry (probably no more than 600–800 men); and assorted clan contingents including artillery (probably about 4,000 men in all, including some 1,600 Aizu). The individual corps into which this army was divided seem to have each included a mixture of all these assorted troop types.

Conrad Totman (1980) succinctly describes such late *bakufu* armies as 'miracles of disorganisation' that 'assembled slowly and unpredictably and fought sporadically'. He observes that those fielded during the 1860s coalesced with excruciating lethargy, and only after suffering initial reverses acquired 'mass and momentum' sufficient to theoretically overwhelm the enemy. The fact that they nevertheless lost in each of their campaigns against smaller but better-trained and armed anti-*bakufu*

A unit of shogunate hohei, *sketched by a Japanese artist in 1864.* (Wikipedia)

forces underscores the ultimate failure of the Tokugawa modernisation programme.

The first French military mission 1867–68

Disillusioned by the performance of its new central army in its conflict with the Choshu in 1864–66, the *bakufu* decided to seek direct foreign assistance in its training instead of relying on self-taught Japanese instructors using dubious translations of foreign military texts. It first considered sending samurai to Holland for instruction, but this idea was dismissed as impractical. Instead, towards the end of 1864, it approached the British, requesting that instructors might be provided from the regiments then stationed at Yokohama. When no positive response was received it turned finally, in January 1865, to French Minister Léon Roches at Yokohama, and in September the French government agreed to provide a training mission. This eventually arrived in January 1867 and established itself at Oya Jinta, Yokohama, before being transferred to Edo at the end of May. In the meantime, in February, the *bakufu* had made training by the French compulsory for all unemployed *hatamoto*.

Commanded by Captain Charles Chanoine, the mission consisted initially of five officers (Chanoine and four lieutenants – two infantry, one cavalry, and one artillery) and ten NCOs and men, joined in November by one or two engineer officers and two more NCOs.[37] It brought with it 2,000 Chassepot 1866 pattern bolt-action rifles, 12 guns (six field and six mountain), and 20 Arab horses, with all the necessary harness and equipment. The French plan was simply 'to teach indigenous instructors and choose them well so that they can instruct others'. To this end they established – according to J.M. Grierson (1886) – three separate schools, which commenced the training of 150 infantry officers, 30 cavalry officers, and 50 artillery officers. But Meron Medzini (1971) says that the 230 pupils comprised 60 infantry officers, 20 artillery officers, and 'a squadron of cavalry officers and the cadre of a battalion of sub-lieutenants and corporals'; while Conrad Totman states that 200–300 cavalry, 'a few' artillery, and 'some' infantry were undergoing training by July, and that by the end of November 'the programme appears to have created a drilled cavalry force of more than 500', but that its infantry and artillery output was 'unclear'. Whatever the strength of its initial draft of cadets, however, it would seem that by the time the Boshin War erupted at the end of January 1868 the French had completed the training of as many as 1,500 infantrymen plus a company of engineers, and that a battalion-strength element of these had already seen action against Satsuma and Choshu Loyalists at the very end of 1867, accompanied by its French instructors (albeit in no more than a supervisory capacity).

The French training programme effectively ended with the outbreak of hostilities, since its pupils were withdrawn to participate in the fighting. The mission retired to Yokohama for the duration of the conflict, and in September 1868 it was advised by the new Loyalist government that its services were no longer required. However, in October about half of its members, including at least three officers – Brunet (artillery), Caseneuve (infantry), and Verny (engineers) – as well as two French naval ensigns (Nicol and Collache), defied France's official policy of non-intervention and joined up with such shogunate forces as remained in the field. Jules Brunet, their ringleader, participated in the fighting round Wakamatsu that month (Algernon Mitford credits him with 'taking command in the Shogun's army when it made its last stand at Wakamatsu in the northern province of Aizu'), and they all subsequently joined a 3,000-strong force under Enomoto Takeaki – about half of which consisted of troops originally trained by the French mission – and took part in the capture of Hakodate in December. Brunet and Caseneuve eventually deserted their wards as Imperial forces surrounded Hakodate in

French military advisor Eugène Collache, who remained with the shognuate forces to the bitter end and was condemned to death following his surrender to the Loyalists in 1869. He was subsequently handed over to the French authorities and expelled from Japan. The picture comes from his article 'Une Aventure au Japon', published in Le Tour du Monde *LXXVII, 1874.*

June 1869, but Collache at least was still with Enomoto when the town fell in July.

Another member of the mission who also remained in Japan, and subsequently offered advice to the new Meiji government, was Lieutenant Albert Charles du Bousquet, who was assigned the post of French military attaché. Though he is sometimes credited with having persuaded the new Japanese government to organise its army along French lines, that was in reality a road along which Japanese military thought was already travelling.

THE MEIJI ARMY

It need hardly be stated that the Meiji Restoration was accompanied by sweeping changes in every sphere of Japanese government, but in military terms the most dramatic departure from shogunate tradition was the complete dismantling of Tokugawa 'feudalism'.

In 1869 the *daimyo* of Satsuma, Choshu, Hizen, and Tosa started the ball rolling by voluntarily resigning their *han* into the Emperor's hands, and most other lords rapidly followed their example. The rank of *daimyo* was abolished and its holders instead became governors (*chihanji*) of what had previously been their domains, receiving in exchange an annual income equal to 10% of the *han*'s former rice tribute assessment. This arrangement was designed to avoid 'the evil of too suddenly terminating the relation between the clans and their lords'. At the same time the *daimyo*, the old court nobility (*kuge*), and the most senior samurai were all made nobles (*kazoku*, literally 'flower race').[38] Samurai of lower rank simultaneously became *shizoku* (gentry) and had their stipends replaced by government pensions which – though they swallowed up nearly half the national revenue – were sufficiently small that most ex-samurai soon found themselves obliged to work for a living if they didn't want to starve. There were at first as many as 18 distinct classes of gentry, but these were reduced to two (*shizoku* and *sotsu*) at the end of 1870, and then to just one in 1872, when half the *sotsu* became *shizoku* and the other half were relegated to the status of *heimin*, or commoners. The *shizoku* enjoyed no special privileges, and in reality there was little difference between *shizoku* and *heimin* beyond the lingering social superiority that, for a generation or so, adhered to the former as ex-samurai. Meanwhile, in August 1871, the clan system in turn had been abolished in its entirety. The old *han* were converted into *ken* (prefectures) and reduced in number, first to 75, later to 68, and finally, in August 1876, to 35. Their castles and fortifications passed into the hands of the new Bureau of Military Affairs, and entire responsibility for the collection of tax was assumed by the central government. In 1876 all remaining samurai pensions were paid off in lump sums.

The old clan armies survived the earliest stages of the 'de-feudalisation' process, and in the interim some continued to pursue their own modernisation programmes and variously adopted Dutch, French, British or German military systems. Perhaps the most interesting of these was that of the Kii clan, which had already converted entirely to the use of Western firearms (including at least 500 Minié rifles) in the late summer of 1866. During 1869–70 it reorganised its troops into eight infantry battalions of 600 men (armed with Dreyse rifles), a pioneer corps, a 150-strong cavalry regiment, and two batteries of mountain guns 'which can be taken to pieces and carried on horses'. All of these units comprised a mixture of samurai and commoners serving side by side, trained by a Prussian NCO (Sergeant-Major Karl Köppen) sent out as instructor with the consignment of Dreyse rifles supplied in 1869.

However, this and all such private enterprises ended with a government decree in October 1870 that ordered all *han* armies to henceforward adopt the French military system. When the *han* were themselves abolished the following year and their armies were disbanded, the best of their troops – usually those which had already undergone at least some form of foreign training – were amalgamated to form the new national army. The samurai belonging to fiefs worth below 10,000 *koku* were disbanded outright, while detachments of the standing forces that had belonged to the larger fiefs were evenly redistributed throughout the newly created prefectures on the basis of one platoon-sized unit to each. The reduction of the clan armies was also utilised as a convenient opportunity to purge from their ranks most if not all of the commoners who had been enlisted during the civil wars. This at least was a victory for the traditionalists, albeit a short-lived one.

Foreign instructors 1872–94

One of the leading architects of early Meiji military reform was a Choshu clansman, Omura Masujiro, widely recognised today as father of the modern Japanese Army. He was the first Minister put in charge of the new Bureau of Military Affairs, and was directly or indirectly responsible for most of the reforms of 1868–71 aimed at eradicating 'feudalism' and commencing the introduction of universal conscription. He also established a military academy at Kyoto in 1868 (moved to Osaka in 1869 and finally to Tokyo in 1871 where eventually, in May 1883, it became the Army Staff College). However, he met with stiff opposition from conservatives even within his own clan, and was assassinated by disaffected Choshu samurai in October 1869. His reform programme was nevertheless carried through by his successor in office, Yamagata Aritomo, following the latter's return from training in Europe in the summer of 1870. Yamagata became Japan's first Army Minister – basically commander-in-chief under the Emperor – when the Bureau of Military Affairs was split into Army and Navy departments in April 1872.

Though some of his fellow reformers variously favoured British, Dutch, and Prussian methods, Omura decided – doubtless as a result of lingering influence left over from Chanoine's *bakufu* mission of 1867–68, and the fact that many Japanese officers were consequently already familiar with the French system – that his academy should teach its drill in French. This in turn influenced the Meiji government's eventual decision in October 1870 to adopt the French military system for its army (but the British system for its navy),[39] despite Yamagata's personal preference for Prussian methods – a view subsequently vindicated by events in the Franco-Prussian War. It was, however, by then too late for the Japanese government to change its mind without losing face (as they saw it). Another military mission was therefore requested from France, which arrived in May 1872 and stayed for eight years. This initially consisted of six officers, six NCOs, and four specialists, but was later increased to a total of 23 men (Emory Upton says 27), under the command of Lieutenant-Colonel Charles-Antoine Marquerie until May 1874, and thereafter under Lieutenant-Colonel Charles Munier.

The French mission established an NCO training school at Toyama in 1873, and a military academy (the *shikan-gakko*) for officer cadets in January 1875 that subsequently inspired the creation of about a dozen similar military schools. Nevertheless, French influence was already on the wane by 1874, as Japanese officers sent for instruction in Europe began to return home advocating German rather than French methods. This led to a pro-German officer, General Torio Koyata, being appointed Vice-Minister of the Army in January 1876. The final decision to abandon the French system in favour of the German seems to have been prompted by the army's various organisational inadequacies that became apparent during the Satsuma Rebellion of 1877. The French mission was consequently reduced by stages from then on and was eventually withdrawn in 1880.

One of the shogunate infantrymen under French instruction in 1867, from a watercolour by Jules Brunet of the French military mission. His uniform is dark blue (but, unusually, without the typical white lines on the sleeves), and his hat was presumably once black but has faded to dark grey. Socks are black. A bright blue shirt is just visible at his wrists. (Wikipedia)

It is often stated that German influence prevailed thereafter, especially after the appointment of Major Klemens Wilhelm Jakob Meckel to the post of senior military advisor at the Army Staff College in March 1885. However, the switch from French to German methods was not a particularly clear cut process, since a third French military mission consisting of four officers under Lieutenant Henri Berthaut was hired in June 1884, and following its arrival in October taught at both the military academy and the Toyama School of Tactics until January 1889.

Indeed, though the pro-German lobby prevailed in Japanese military circles from 1885 until 1894, French influence was never entirely displaced. French tactical methods were used during manoeuvres in 1886, for instance, and in 1887 Henry Knollys could still describe the Japanese Army as 'French to the very core; French in dress, interior economy, and to a great extent in language'. Meckel himself actually left Japan in March 1888 and was replaced by another German officer of considerably less influence, Major von Wildenbrück, who remained until April 1890. Japanese students meanwhile continued to be trained by Meckel in Berlin.

F.J. Norman's view in 1905 was that the foreign influence exerted upon the Japanese military establishment was actually far more complex and cosmopolitan. He considered that in reality the French instructors 'achieved nothing like the success that has been so generally claimed for them, for there can be no disputing the fact that the Japanese army gained greater advantages from the swarms of officers sent to study in Europe than from any instructions it may ever have received from imported instructors. And to say that the Japanese army tactics or organisation are copies of the German is to advance a claim that is absurd; for if they have not adopted more from the French, they certainly have adapted so much from other and various Continental armies that the German share in it is but a fraction of the whole.'

The very last foreign instructor in the Japanese army during the 19th century was nevertheless a German, Major Baron von Grutschreiber, who was hired in 1890. His contract expired in July 1894, and he returned home shortly before the outbreak of the Sino-Japanese War.

The contracts of all such foreign instructors averaged about three years, and they received substantial salaries – up to 400 *yen* per month in the 1880s, at a time when a Japanese full colonel received no more than 200 *yen*.

Conscription and army organisation

The newly-created Meiji army evolved slowly at first as initial steps were taken towards introducing conscription in place of 'feudal' service. As early as April 1868 the *daimyo* were called upon to provide ten men per 10,000 *koku* for service in the capital and a further 50 to serve within each respective *daimyo*'s own province. The conscripts were 'to be picked men from among the people 17 or 18 to 35 years of age. The service extends over three years. For the present, the men are to be equipped with muskets, bedding and other requisites by the fief holders. The Imperial Court will be responsible for the furnishing of uniforms, salaries and board. As to the troops maintained in the provinces, they should always be held ready for Imperial requisition.' By a subsequent decree of February 1870 the 60 men raised from each 10,000 *koku* were designated an infantry platoon, and two such platoons (plus officers and NCOs) constituted a company. Where artillery was raised it comprised batteries of four guns organised in two squads of two guns each. All conscripts were now to be 18–38 years old, and at this stage still had to be of samurai status.

The first universal conscription regulations were issued in November 1870, albeit on an experimental basis only, and in just five provinces (Izumi, Kawachu, Settsur, Tamashiro, and Yamato), all in the vicinity of Kyoto. These regulations called for the selection of five conscripts per 10,000 *koku*, who were to be over 5 ft (1.52 m) tall, aged between 20 and 30, and chosen from both 'the able-bodied men of the military class and the common people'. They were required to serve for four years, during which time they would be paid and provided for entirely at government expense. Once trained, they were organised into garrison districts (*chindai*) intended to protect the coast, the first two, consisting of the Tozan garrison (headquarters Ishinomaki) and the Saikai garrison (headquarters Kokura), being established in June 1871. These were replaced in October by four new *chindai*, based round Chinsei (headquarters Kumamoto), Osaka, Tohoku (headquarters Sendai), and Tokyo, which were used to absorb many of the samurai cut loose from their old 'feudal' obligations by the abolition of the clan system that August. In general terms, however, this first experiment in conscription was not the success reformers had hoped for. The authorities had thought that conscription would be regarded as an honour, but they found that many peasants objected to their new liability to perform military service almost as much as the samurai objected to having to serve alongside them. This widespread opposition delayed the general introduction of conscription for another two years.

Universal military service was finally introduced throughout Japan in January 1873, requiring all male Japanese aged between 20 and 40 to serve in the army (or navy) for three years. Following completion of their term of service in the active army (*jobigun*), they became members of a first reserve (*yobigun*) for a further two years, during which time they were assembled once a year for training. They were then placed in a second reserve, the *kobigun* (often referred to by Westerners as the 'territorial army'), for a final two years. Only NCOs spent their entire seven years' term in the active army, and were therefore exempted from service in the reserves. The first reserve was to be called up on the outbreak of hostilities in order to bring the peacetime establishment up to war strength, but the second reserve was only to be called to arms during emergencies. Service years began towards the end of April, the conscripts being chosen (by drawing lots) amongst those who had reached the age of 20 by the beginning of January the same year. They were then assigned to the various arms of service according to their stature, the artillery taking the tallest and strongest men, followed by the cavalry, then the infantry, engineers, and military train. Individuals who drew what were known as 'supplementary service' lots were not conscripted into the active army but remained at the government's disposal for a year and could be called up at any point during that time in order to fill vacancies in the active army's ranks as they occurred. Such men were still required to perform their obligatory four years' service in the reserves. All conscripts were provided with board and lodging, regular pay, and uniforms.

At this early stage all the officers were inevitably ex-samurai, as were the great majority of NCOs – not least because they were selected by the officers. A shortage of appropriately trained officers continued to be a problem for many years, and was only partially alleviated by the promotion of experienced NCOs and civilian officials who could demonstrate 'a certain amount of knowledge of military matters'. Few peasant conscripts had sufficient education to proceed beyond the rank of lance-corporal, so form the 1880s most new NCOs were consequently supplied by the

Toyama school. Even at the beginning of the 1890s officers still included many ex-samurai (who by now held all the senior posts), as well as NCOs promoted from the ranks and former civilian functionaries. With the passage of time, however, these were gradually replaced by men trained at the various military schools, and by 1892 it could be reported that 'all the officers recently promoted have either passed through the Special Military School or the schools for non-commissioned officers.'

Though the conscription system is variously claimed to have been based on Prussian or French usage, its associated exemption policy was definitely copied from that found in France. Even before universal conscription was enacted, the Meiji government had recognised that it lacked the resources to enlist or train all those who would qualify for service each year, and as a result grounds for exemption were initially very generous. As well as the obvious exceptions – criminals, the maimed, the sick, the insane – others who qualified for exemption included heads of families, acting heads of families, eldest sons, only sons, only grandsons, one of two brothers called up simultaneously, those with a brother already serving, the brother of a man killed or wounded whilst serving, priests, teachers, students, doctors, regional and city councillors, government officials without deputies, everyone under 4 ft 11½ ins (1.51 m), and, until 1883, anyone who could afford to buy exemption for the relatively substantial sum of 270 *yen*.

Cumulatively, these grants of outright exemption could account for up to 40% of a year's potential intake (in 1887, for instance, there were 303,948 exemptions out of 777,972 available conscripts). A further 13% of potential conscripts either chose self-mutilation to render themselves unfit for military service, or else failed to so much as present themselves at the drawing of lots (conscription remained sufficiently unpopular amongst the agrarian population which bore its brunt that it was often referred to as the *ketsu-eki*, or 'blood tax'[40]). In the years 1879–81 as few as 7.5%–8.3% of the men liable for conscription were actually taken into the active army, and the situation had changed very little by the end of the century, when the number of conscripts taken up is recorded to have increased from just 5% in 1895 to 10.6% in 1898; the number of men conscripted into the reserves increased from 12.8% to 24.8% during the same period.

Taking all these factors together, it is unsurprising to find that only about 10,000–10,500 men were conscripted each year during the period 1873–77, and roughly 15,000 per annum in 1877–86. As the government's need for, and ability to finance, more troops increased, so the number of people who qualified for exemption was reduced, notably during the 1880s. Regardless of how it was modified, official exemption policy nevertheless continued to favour the rich and the educated, and throughout the period 1873–1900 the burden of military service was borne predominantly by the younger sons of *heimin* families, especially amongst the agrarian population.

All such men as were exempted from conscription and were aged between 17 and 40 were

Camp scene sketched by G. Bigot during the march on Ping-Yang in August–September 1894, published in The Graphic *on 1 December 1894.*

theoretically enrolled into a newly-established militia, the *kokumingun* – often referred to as the 'national army' – which was only to be called up when the active army and the reserves were insufficient to meet an emergency. Once other able-bodied men had completed their time in the reserves they were likewise required to serve in the militia up to the age of 40. However, to what extent the militia, or come to that the second reserve, existed in any form other than on paper is debatable, since as late as the 1890s foreign military attachés frequently described both formations in such terms as 'unorganised', 'never organised', and 'incomplete'.

Simultaneous with the introduction of universal conscription in 1873 was the reorganisation of the entire country (except Hokkaido) into six military districts or 'garrisons' at the beginning of 1874, consisting of Tokyo, Sendai, Nagoya, Osaka, Hiroshima, and Kumamoto. Each garrison was subdivided into two districts, and those in turn into subordinate garrisons and small outposts. The entire strength of the six garrisons totalled 14 infantry regiments, three cavalry squadrons, 18 artillery batteries, ten companies of engineers, six companies of military train, and nine companies of fortress artillery. If at full strength these would have added up to 31,680 men in peacetime and 46,350 in war, made up as shown in Table 2.

Table 2: Active army strength by arm of service 1873

	Peacetime	*Wartime*
Infantry	26,880	40,320
Cavalry	360	450
Artillery	2,160	2,700
Engineers	1,200	1,500
Military train	360	480
Fortress artillery	720	900
Total	31,680	46,350

However, in 1873 these existed mostly on paper, and there were actually just 12,723 men under arms, almost all of them new conscripts assigned to the garrisons in the respective districts from which they had been drafted. Writing in 1875, visiting American officer Emory Upton records that the 14 regiments of infantry comprised 42 battalions, and that the 18 batteries were organised into nine artillery battalions. Upton also lists only two rather than three squadrons of cavalry, and nine rather than ten companies of engineers. His overall totals therefore come out very slightly lower, giving a peacetime strength of 31,440 and a wartime strength of 46,050. Figures quoted.

Table 3: Active army strength by corps 1877

	Peacetime	*Wartime*
Tokyo garrison	7,140	10,370
Sendai garrison	4,460	6,540
Nagoya garrison	4,260	6,540
Osaka garrison	6,700	9,820
Hiroshima garrison	4,340	6,230
Kumamoto garrison	4,780	6,940
Total	31,680	46,440

by Augustus Mounsey in his book about the 1877 Satsuma Rebellion likewise differ very slightly, and are subdivided by garrison rather than arm of service, as listed in Table 3

Upton also provides us with the first detailed Western account of unit organisation. Infantry regiments consisted of three battalions, each of four companies. The regiment's field and staff officers consisted of a colonel (regimental commander), four majors (three battalion commanders and the regimental surgeon), four captains (the regimental adjutant and three battalion surgeons), four first lieutenants (three battalion adjutants and the regimental paymaster), and three second lieutenants (battalion paymasters). Peacetime company strength comprised a captain, two first lieutenants, two second lieutenants, a sergeant-major, a quartermaster sergeant, eight sergeants, 16 corporals, a commissary corporal, and 160 men (increased to 240 in wartime). An infantry battalion therefore totalled 768 men in peacetime and 1,088 in war; a regiment 2,320 men in peacetime and 3,280 in war.

By the 1870s the accepted Japanese nomenclature for army units comprised, in ascending order: *shotai*, an infantry platoon (but an infantry company during the 1860s), a troop of cavalry, or an artillery section; *chutai*, an infantry company, a cavalry squadron, or an artillery battery; *daitai*, a battalion; *rentai*, a regiment; *shidan*, a division; *ryodan*, a brigade; and *gundan*, an army. A more generic term was *tai*, which could denote a military body of almost any size.

There were various changes to the conscription system as time went by. The first major revision occurred in October 1879, which adjusted the conscripts' terms of service to three years in the active army, three years in the first reserve, and four years in the second reserve, thereby increasing their overall obligation from seven years to ten. Supplementary service reverted to one year after having been reduced to just 90 days since 1875.

E.H. Norman records the active army of 1879 to have comprised 12 regiments of infantry, one and a third battalions of cavalry, ten battalions of field artillery, three and a half battalions of engineers, and a military train corps of one company and two platoons. Its overall strength nevertheless seems to have remained essentially unchanged. In September 1880, however, French military attaché Lieutenant Alexandre Bougoüin recorded the strength of the peacetime active army as 35,000 men, and the reserves as 53,000 men.

Conscription reached what was basically its final form with the enactment of another recruitment law in December 1883, which required conscripts to serve three years in the active army, four years in the first reserve, five years in the second reserve, and then eight years in the militia until they reached the age of 40, having already served for three years in the same body between the ages of 17 and 20. All able-bodied males aged between 17 and 40 who were neither regulars nor reservists also had to serve in the militia, from which there was no exemption. All exempted men also had to serve in the second reserve. Reservists were now summoned for 60 days' training at most (more often 30 days in reality), plus an additional one day for annual inspection when in the first reserve. The number of men owing supplementary service was required to be equal to 40% of active army strength; men performing such service had their first reserve obligation extended to six years. The first reserve was to be used to augment units from peacetime to wartime strength and to form corps depots, while the second reserve's wartime role was to provide garrisons and to maintain the army's lines of communication in the field. The militia was to be called out and organised into units only when more men were still needed even after the second reserve had been deployed.

A comprehensive breakdown of conscripts' periods of service in the various elements of the army during the period after 1883 is provided by Captain Villaret, an officer of one of the French military missions, whose analysis clarifies an otherwise somewhat complicated situation:

Men drawing lowest numbers in the ballot:
Militia service from age 17 to age 20 (three years)
Active army service from age 20 to age 23 (three years)
First reserve service from age 23 to age 27 (four years)
Second reserve service from age 27 to age 32 (five years)
Militia service from age 32 to age 40 (eight years)

Men drawing 'supplementary service' numbers:
Militia service from age 17 to age 20 (three years)
Supplementary service from age 20 to age 21 (one year)
First reserve service from age 21 to age 27 (six years)
Second reserve service from age 27 to age 32 (five years)
Militia service from age 32 to age 40 (eight years)

Men drawing highest numbers or exempted from active army service for secondary reasons:
Militia service from age 17 to age 20 (three years)
First reserve service from age 20 to age 27 (seven years)
Second reserve service from age 27 to age 32 (five years)
Militia service from age 32 to age 40 (eight years)

Men exempted from active army service for special reasons:
Militia service from age 17 to age 20 (three years)
Second reserve service from age 20 to age 32 (12 years)
Militia service from age 32 to age 40 (eight years)

Every conscript's total term of service was therefore 23 years. However, students aged 17–26 who had graduated from government schools, as well as any who had passed a military examination, only had to serve one year in the active army, albeit at their own expense. Such 'one-year volunteers', as they were termed, also served for only two years in the first reserve and five years in the second, often as officers. Graduates of ordinary schools who had studied either law or political economy served just six months in the active army (at government expense) but seven years in the first reserve and three years in the second.

Reasons for exemption had in the meantime been pared down considerably. Henry Knollys nevertheless observed as late as 1887 that exemptions remained 'so numerous as to cause scandal', and that recruits continued to be drawn 'almost exclusively from the lower orders'. There was consequently much discontent and low morale within the army as a whole, as the inequality of conscription and exemption demonstrated a widening social gap between the privileged rich or educated class and the poor. In January 1889 a further conscription act finally abolished the majority of the remaining grounds for exemption, and morale thereafter gradually improved.

The army was also expanded during 1883, theoretically to 28 infantry regiments (inclusive of the Imperial Guard), and seven battalions each of cavalry, field artillery, engineers, and military train. Yamagata Ariyoshi states that the reconstructed army was 'increased to 200,000 men', and that a plan to increase its strength to 400,000 was only frustrated by expenditure elsewhere, on coastal fortifications, arsenals (in Tokyo and Osaka), powder factories, and military education. In reality, however, the army was much smaller. Grierson's comprehensive description of the Japanese military establishment, written in 1886, records the theoretical existence of just 44,000 active army soldiers and 79,000 reservists, or 123,000 men in all, while Henry Norman (1892) records that, excluding the Imperial Guard (and, seemingly, the fortress artillery), army strength at the very end of 1885 was as set out in Table 4.

Table 4: Army strength by arm of service 1885

	Active army	*Reserves*	*Total*
Infantry	38,089	64,293	102,382
Cavalry	671	788	1,459
Artillery	3,817	4,064	7,881
Engineers	1,708	1,814	3,522
Military train	548	54,458	55,006
Gendarmerie	1,435	1	1,436
Total	46,268	125,418	171,686

Grierson records that in the mid-1880s each garrison consisted of two (Hiroshima, Kumamoto, Nagoya, and Sendai) or three (Tokyo and Osaka) infantry regiments, one or two artillery battalions, a company or a battalion (two companies) of engineers, and a half-company of military train. Only the Tokyo and Sendai divisions had cavalry (just a squadron each). Each infantry regiment (commanded by either a full colonel or a lieutenant-colonel) had three battalions, each of four companies that were divided into four platoons (Du Boulay erroneously says three) of four squads. Company strength when on a war footing was variously reported by Western observers as 200, 220, 230, or 272 men but was actually supposed to be 265 (80 more than in peacetime). It was commanded by a captain, and consisted of two lieutenants, three second lieutenants, a sergeant-major, a quartermaster sergeant, eight sergeants, 16 corporals, eight buglers, and 225 privates. Each platoon comprised a lieutenant or second lieutenant, two sergeants, two buglers, four corporals, and 56 privates, each squad a corporal and 14 privates.

These figures indicate that wartime battalion strength was 1,060 men plus field officers (Grierson says 1,073 men in all, which is probably correct), but most sources give considerably lower figures: Knollys (1887) says 'about 740 men all told', while G.J. Younghusband (1894), White (1895), and Du Boulay (1896) say 800, reducing to just 400 in peacetime. Another commentator, writing in 1897, records battalion strength as 660–680 men, while the battalions which operated in North China in 1900 are said to have comprised 868 men. Such figures doubtless indicate that most battalions were generally understrength.

Similar discrepancies occur in the recorded strength of regiments. For instance, although they were writing in the same year (1892), Pierre Lehautcourt records regimental peacetime strength as 70 officers, 14 horses, eight non-combatant officers (two administrative officers and six doctors), 160 NCOs, and 1,440 privates, or 1,721 men in all; while Henry Norman says 69 officers, 12 horses, nine non-combatant officers, 349 NCOs, and 1,920 privates (increased to 2,880 in wartime), a total of 2,347 men – a difference of as many as 626 men. Regimental depots were only constituted on mobilisation.

Table 5: Army strength by corps December 1887

	Strength	
Tokyo garrison	9,210	
Sendai garrison	8,920	
Nagoya garrison	8,267	
Osaka garrison	8,655	
Hiroshima garrison	7,223	
Kumamoto garrison	7,476	
Hokkaido Militia	1,461	
Imperial Guard	5,591	
		56,803
General Staff	2,014	
Military schools	2,910	
Gendarmerie	1,376	
		6,300
First reserve	101,273	
Second reserve	44,939	
		146,212
Total		209,315

Only in 1887 did army strength achieve the 200,000 figure claimed by Yamagata Ariyoshi, Table 5 providing details of the situation at the end of December that year as recorded by Henry Norman – a grand total, he says (though his figures don't tally with the individual totals he gives), of 450 staff officers, 3,360 officers, 10,391 NCOs, and 193,804 rank and file. The General Staff corps he lists had been established in December 1878 in consequence of lessons learned during the Satsuma Rebellion, and was organised along Prussian lines, with Yamagata Aritomo as chief of staff. It constituted the first step towards establishing the independence of the army's command function in relation to its financial administration by the Bureau of Military Affairs. This process was completed in 1882, when it was established that the armed forces were directly responsible to the Emperor, as their nominal supreme commander, rather than to the civil government. (In reality the chief of staff was a power unto himself, and was answerable to no one.) There proved to be some difficulty at first in finding sufficient men capable of performing staff functions, Shigenobu Okuma (1909) recalling that one of the army's greatest difficulties 'was a lack of staff officers; to meet this urgent need ... the Military School in Tokyo turned out graduates after a shorter course of training, while efficient volunteers from different clans were kept on the staff. Under such circumstances there could be no settled rule for promotion, and many NCOs were promoted to be captains within the course of a year, but some of them had subsequently to be degraded for incompetency.'

Figures recorded for 1887 by Knollys are noticeably lower than those given by Norman. He gives the strengths of the individual garrisons as: Tokyo 8,500; Sendai 3,400; Nagoya 4,900; Osaka 8,000; Hiroshima 4,900; and Kumamoto 5,800; a total of 35,500 in all. He also provides what he calls 'a fairly accurate estimate of the actual strength of the different arms', comprising 34,000 infantry (16 regiments, or 46 battalions), 450 cavalry (three squadrons), 2,500 artillery (20 batteries, each of six guns), 1,500 engineers (ten companies), and 550 military train – a total of 39,000 men (3,500 greater than the strength he ascribes to the garrisons, but presumably including the Imperial Guard). He then observes: 'I am quite aware that my numbers fall considerably below the quota in various official publications. But after personal enquiry on the spot, coupled with checking by different sets of figures, I have come to the conclusion that my estimates more closely correspond to actuality than do the theoretical paper establishments. It may be objected that the "war footing" establishment would increase the numbers by about 30,000 men. But I prefer to reckon these among the Reserves. To [the active army] must be added the Reserve, the theoretical strength of which is 45,000 men. I cannot estimate the actual numbers at more than 35,000. In all probability the Government would be able to lay their hands on the majority of these men if required, and therefore the military strength ... on an emergency may be fairly estimated at about 70,000 ... [but] this number is far in excess of that which could be drawn up in "battle array".'

At this point in its development the Army was still regarded by the Meiji government as a largely defensive institution geared towards domestic security – whence its establishment as a network of French-style sedentary garrisons. It was incapable of mobilising effectively in an emergency, since it lacked the necessary supply arrangements, the requisite number of officers, sufficient arms to equip its reservists, and so on. Knollys reported in 1884, for instance, that 'they have left comparatively untouched the questions and even the institutions connected with commissariat, transport, military stores and provisions for the sick and wounded.' However, the year 1888 witnessed a major shift in Japan's military outlook, and the army was henceforward seen as a potentially offensive rather than a principally defensive force. Under the guidance of Klemens Meckel, its six garrisons were restructured into German-style, self-sufficient, fully mobile, all-arms divisions (*shidan*), known as the 1st Tokyo, 2nd Sendai, 3rd Nagoya, 4th Osaka, 5th Hiroshima, and 6th Kumamoto, as set out in Table 6.

Each division was commanded by a general of division from the end of 1890, and consisted of two infantry brigades (each of two regiments and therefore six battalions), a cavalry regiment (three squadrons), a regiment of field and mountain artillery (four batteries of the former and two of the latter), a battalion of engineers (three companies), a battalion of military train (two companies), plus, when mobilised, remount and telegraph depots, seven ammunition trains, two companies of stretcher-bearers, a field hospital, and assorted administrative staffs. However, a Russian observer noted in 1896 that the composition of the divisions was not entirely uniform, since although they all had two infantry brigades, the strength of the artillery, cavalry, engineer, and military train elements varied slightly. Du Boulay similarly noted that though all six divisions were fundamentally alike, some included 'coast defence' troops (i.e., fortress artillery units).

Table 6: Composition of Line divisions 1892

Division	*Brigades*	*Headquarters*	*Regiments*
1st Tokyo	1st	Tokyo	1st & 15th
	2nd	Sakura	2nd & 3rd
2nd Sendai	3rd	Sendai	4th & 16th
	4th	Aomori	5th & 17th
3rd Nagoya	5th	Nagoya	6th & 18th
	6th	Kawazawa	7th & 19th
4th Osaka	7th	Osaka	8th & 9th
	8th	Himeji	10th & 20th
5th Hiroshima	9th	Hiroshima	11th & 21st
	10th	Matsuyama	12th & 22nd
6th Kumamoto	11th	Kumamoto	13th & 23rd
	12th	Kokura	14th & 24th

Du Boulay says that each division had a peacetime strength of about 9,000 men, which increased to some 17,000 in wartime, but Okuma gives wartime divisional strength as 18,492 men, plus 5,633 horses, 24 field guns, and 12 mountain guns. Arthur Hardy gives breakdowns of overall army strength in 1890 by corps, as per Table 7 (which is directly comparable to Table 5), and by arm of service, as per Table 8, and – like Knollys in 1887 – comes up with two somewhat different totals. These indicate that the active army probably consisted of some 55–60,000 men, and the reserves of about 165–185,000.

The paper strength of the peacetime active army reached 63,000 in 1893. When the Sino-Japanese War broke out in 1894 it amounted to some 67,000 men, which increased to 90,000 on mobilisation and eventually more than 161,000 as the conflict progressed. Garrison duties within Japan were immediately assumed by the reserves, the fortress artillery, and the Hokkaido and Tsushima militias (for which see p.48 and note 43), which were 'charged with the duty of defending the fortresses and other imperial places as well as the lines of communication, and, if necessary, were to be drafted into the field forces.' The active army and these assorted corps combined are said to have totalled 220,580 men, 47,221 horses, and 294 field and mountain guns.

Nevertheless, the events of the war and the ensuing 'Triple Intervention' incident demonstrated to the Meiji government that its active army was still far too small. An expansion programme was therefore set in motion which anticipated more than doubling the peacetime army to 164,500 men, and increasing its wartime potential to 545,000, to be achieved by converting the Hokkaido Militia into a full division (this occurred in 1896) and creating five additional divisions. It took until 1903 for this process to be completed. In the meantime, active army manpower reached a peacetime strength of 101,600 in 1896 and 121,000 in 1897, and stood at just over 143,000 throughout 1898–99. Mobilised wartime strength was theoretically 8,200 officers and 314,000 men by 1898. At the end of 1897 the active army is recorded to have comprised 24 Line and four Guard infantry regiments, six Line and one Guard cavalry regiments, six Line and one Guard field artillery regiments, four fortress artillery regiments, seven engineer battalions, and seven battalions of military train.

Table 7: Army strength by corps 1890

	Strength	
1st Tokyo	8,485	
2nd Sendai	7,697	
3rd Nagoya	7,753	
4th Osaka	8,065	
5th Hiroshima	8,022	
6th Kumamoto	8,123	
Hokkaido Militia	1,514	
Imperial Guard	5,435	
		55,094
General Staff	413	
Military schools	613	
Gendarmerie	1,388	
		2,414
First reserve	113,229	
Second reserve	53,137	
		166,366
Total		223,874

Final minor adjustments to Japan's 19th-century conscription regulations were made in March 1895. Military service was now to comprise three years in the active army, followed by four years and four months in the first reserve, and five years in the second reserve, thereby extending service in the active army and reserves from 12 years to 12 years and four months. What used to be termed 'supplementary service' was reclassified as 'conscript reserve' (*hoju*) service, and was now for a term of either seven years and four months or one year and four months (Y. Takata calls these 'first supplementary service' and 'second supplementary service'). The former comprised conscripts 'who remain in excess after the calling out of the recruits necessary to complete the regular units'; these were liable to fill vacancies in the active army during their first year, could be called out in wartime or national emergencies to bring units of the active army up to strength, and were trained for up to 150 days in their first year and 60 days a year thereafter. They passed directly into the militia on completing their term as 'conscript reserves'. The second category consisted of individuals who had been exempted from both regular service and the longer variety of 'conscript reserve' service, and were to be called out only in wartime or emergencies.

There were two Japanese forces in the field as the century closed. The first comprised three composite brigades serving in Formosa, consisting in total of six infantry regiments, three cavalry squadrons, three artillery companies, two fortress artillery battalions, three engineer companies, and a railway guard unit, all 'withdrawn by rotation from the units of the Japanese Army'. The other consisted of Japan's contribution – the largest provided by any of the participating nations – to the Allied expeditionary force operating against the Boxers in North

China. Sent out in July 1900, this contingent comprised a mixed brigade under General Fukushima Yasumasa and the 5th Division under Lieutenant-General Yamaguchi Motuomi. It consisted of four infantry regiments each of three battalions, plus one independent battalion (each battalion being reported as 868 men); the 5th Cavalry Regiment (360 men); the 5th Artillery Regiment (six batteries, 150 men to each) and three independent batteries; a fortress artillery battery (four 12-cm guns); an engineer battalion; a railway battalion 'with bridge equipment'; and a telegraph company – a total of 13 infantry battalions, one cavalry regiment, ten batteries (58 guns), and supporting arms, variously reported as 16,000, 20,000 or 22,000 men in all. The Japanese element of the Allied field force with which Sir Alfred Gaselee marched on Peking included nine infantry battalions, four (sic) squadrons of cavalry, and six batteries, or 9–10,000 men and 24 guns. Some 6,400 Japanese troops were still stationed in North China in April 1901.

Table 8: Army strength by arm of service 1890

	Active army	*Reserves*	*Total*
Infantry	48,145	102,099	150,244
Cavalry	1,085	1,311	2,396
Artillery	5,702	8,115	13,817
Engineers	2,522	3,288	5,810
Transport	3,453	67,964	71,417
Total	60,907	182,777	243,684

The Imperial Guard

In order to provide for national defence until such time as the conscript army was firmly established, troops provided principally by the Satsuma, Choshu, and Tosa clan armies had been formed, in February 1871, into a central army corps, initially called simply the *Shimpei* or *Shimpeitai* ('New Soldiers').[41] This was a shrewd move which placed all of Japan's elite military forces under direct Imperial control. The Satsuma contingent comprised four infantry battalions and two artillery batteries; the Choshu three infantry battalions; and the Tosa two infantry battalions, two artillery batteries, and two cavalry squadrons. This corps subsequently became the Imperial Guard, which with the passage of time became known successively as the *Goshimpei*, the *Konoe* or *Konoehei* (Imperial Guard), and finally the *Konoe Shidan* (Imperial Guard Division).

By about the end of 1873 the government felt strong enough to disband this last vestige of the old clan armies, transferring some of its members to Line battalions and dismissing the more reactionary elements. The Guard was then reconstituted using specially selected conscripts, described by Takata (1921) as 'excellent in body and character', who were drawn from every corner of the Empire. These recruits had to have served for at least six months in a Line unit, and subsequently served in the Guard for a further three full years, but then only had to serve 3½ years in the reserves so that the duration of their overall military service remained seven years. The Guard had no second reserve, and when, later in the century, the required term of service was extended to 10 years, 12 years, and eventually 12 years and four months, ex-guardsmen performed their second reserve service within their local territorial division.

The Guard's peacetime strength at the time of its reconstitution is shown in Table 9. As can be seen, the sources differ slightly regarding its manpower but agree on its constituent elements. Mounsey records its strength in 1877 as 3,961 men. Note, incidentally, that Guard regiments had only two battalions rather than the three found in Line units. This remained the case for the rest of the century.

Grierson, writing in 1886, records the composition of the Guard as fundamentally unchanged since 1873. He tells us that Guard infantry companies differed from Line companies in having an extra eight privates, giving them a strength of 192 men in peacetime and 273 in wartime. Including battalion staff, Guard infantry battalions therefore comprised 779 men in peacetime or 1,105 in wartime. The composition of the cavalry squadron remained unchanged in peace or war, consisting of eight officers (a captain, two lieutenants, two second lieutenants, surgeon, veterinary surgeon, and quartermaster), 30 NCOs, and 151 privates including four trumpeters, or 189 men in all (but only 161 horses). The artillery consisted of one field gun battery and one mountain gun battery, with wartime strengths of 164 and 184 men respectively (or 154 men each in peacetime). The field battery was equipped with Krupp steel breech-loaders, and the mountain battery with French Lahitte *pièces de 4 de montagne*. The engineer company consisted of eight officers and 188 NCOs and privates in peace or war, while the train company comprised ten officers, 158 other ranks, and 161 horses. After adding command cadres, these figures give a total strength of 4,031 men in peacetime and 5,377 on a war footing, the latter figure being very similar to that of 5,591 recorded for December 1887 by Henry Norman.

Lehautcourt, writing in 1892, gives peacetime regimental strength as 1,655 men, made up of 50 officers, four doctors, 125 NCOs, and 1,440 privates, plus 11 horses. This indicates only a slight increase in numerical strength in the intervening five years, but a marked change in composition (Grierson's monograph states that a

Table 9: The Imperial Guard c.1873–75

		Black (n.d.)	*Upton (1875)*
Infantry	2 regiments (4 battalions)	3,200	2,688
Cavalry	1 squadron	150	150
Artillery	1 battalion (2 batteries)	300	260
Engineers	1 company	150	150
Military train	1 company	80	80
Total		3,880	3,328

regiment totalled 1,567 men consisting of 50 officers, three doctors, 226 NCOs, and 1,288 privates, plus 7 horses). The Guard artillery now constituted a regiment commanded by a colonel or lieutenant-colonel, made up of two battalions, each of two batteries of field guns. It was made up of 23 officers, two doctors, two veterinary surgeons, 64 NCOs, and 188 privates, but had a total strength of 493 men (indicating a substantial number of supernumeraries), plus 294 horses. By May 1898 the Guard artillery had been increased to three battalions, and at some point around the turn of the century it was converted back to mountain guns.

In 1888 the Guard was reorganised into the *Konoe Shidan* or Imperial Guard Division, consisting of two infantry brigades (each of two infantry regiments, therefore a total of eight battalions), a battalion of cavalry (three squadrons), an artillery brigade (four batteries), one battalion of engineers (two companies), and one of military train (two companies). Du Boulay gives its peacetime numerical strength in 1894 as about 8,000 men, which increased to 13,000 on a war footing.

The Imperial Guard was one of three divisions which served in Formosa in 1895, the others being the 2nd Sendai and elements of the 4th Osaka.

The Cavalry

Despite the fact that mounted warfare had once been a samurai tradition, by the 19th century Japan possessed surprisingly few horses suitable for cavalry service. Okuma put this down to the fact that the Tokugawa had prohibited commoners from riding, which 'not only made horses mere beasts of burden, but caused a decline in stock breeding'. A crisis eventually arose when, at the outbreak of the Sino-Japanese conflict, it was realised that as many as 40,000 horses were needed to put the army on a war footing and they could not be found. Of those that were available, many turned out to be below the required standard – of the 11,000 raised in one divisional district, for instance, as many as 6,000 were deemed unfit or unsuitable. Thereafter attempts were made to improve the Japanese breed by buying in foreign horses (see the caption to Figures 62–69).

When the Restoration government established its first cavalry units it was hard pushed to raise even two squadrons (one for the Imperial Guard, the other for the Tokyo garrison), and Western observers repeatedly refer to the weakness of Japan's cavalry arm for the rest of the century. Upton noted the existence of just two 'battalions' (actually squadrons) in 1875, each of 120 men in peacetime and 150 in war. Grierson recorded three squadrons in 1886, two of which were Line units – one based in Tokyo and the other in Sendai – and one Guard; the wartime strength of each of the former was 11 officers and 189 men (but only 174 horses), reduced to eight officers and 136 men in peacetime. Each squadron comprised two troops, each of two sections, while the two Line squadrons together constituted a battalion, with a command staff of 25 officers and men with 12 horses.

The terminology used by foreign observers to describe Japanese cavalry units is generally less than helpful, not least in the casual way the words 'squadron' and 'battalion', and 'battalion' and 'regiment', are arbitrarily interchanged. However, it would seem that there were two Line battalions (i.e., four squadrons) by the end of the 1880s, both apparently quartered in Tokyo. Hardy records their total active army strength in about 1889 as 1,085 men, with a further 1,311 in the reserves. Excluding non-combatants, the composition of a battalion at this date appears to have been as set out in Table 10.

Table 10: Cavalry battalion strength c.1889

	Peacetime	*Wartime*
Officers	17	18
NCOs	36	36
Privates	306	426
Horses	(377)	(459)
Total	359	480

A further four Line battalions were raised between 1888 and 1890, so that each of the army's six divisions could have one, and it was decided to increase battalion strength from two squadrons to three at the same time. However, it seems that most or all battalions were still wanting their third squadron when the Sino-Japanese War ended in 1895. Each battalion was commanded by a lieutenant-colonel, and in peacetime each of the three squadrons had five officers (a captain, two lieutenants, and two subalterns), 16 NCOs, and 129 privates, or 150 men in all. Peacetime battalion strength, including the command cadre, was 19 officers, two doctors, two veterinary surgeons, 48 NCOs, 387 privates, and 'a certain number of clerks and artificers', making 512 men (and 462 horses) in all. Henry Norman gives slightly different figures the same year, recording each squadron to have consisted of 159 men and 135 horses in peacetime, and 189 men and 140 horses (therefore 140 cavalrymen) when on a war footing. The fact that several sources, dating to both the 1880s and 1890s, record wartime squadron strength as just 100 probably indicates that in reality most units were considerably understrength. Each squadron was subdivided into four troops.

On paper at least, when the army commenced its expansion programme after the Sino-Japanese War the cavalry arm was increased dramatically, in theory to 17 battalions (henceforward more often referred to as regiments), of which one belonged to the Imperial Guard. However, as with the infantry, it seems likely that this process was not completed until the beginning of the 20th century. Certainly there seem to have still been just seven regiments (six Line and one Guard) in 1897. As each army division gradually received additional cavalry regiments these were paired to form brigades.

The desired increase to 17 regiments (16 Line and one Guard) appears to have been achieved by about 1903, when a Russian source records the existence of 55 squadrons, comprising 400 officers, 9,300 men, and 9,000 horses, plus 17 depot squadrons totalling a further 2,350 men. This information also indicates in passing that regimental strength had now increased from three squadrons to four. The same source makes the observation that the cavalry still represented only about one thirtieth of Japan's armed forces, and that 'this proportion is an excessively small one compared with European powers, where [it] varies from one seventh, in Russia, to one twelfth and one fifteenth.'

The Artillery

The first artillery units raised from scratch by the Meiji Government, in 1870, comprised an unknown number of four-gun batteries, each consisting of two squads of two guns each (which was probably their peacetime strength – see below). Then, when the conscript army was introduced in 1873, 2,160 artillerymen were raised and 18 six-gun batteries were established. By 1875 these had been organised into nine two-battery battalions, with each battery consisting of 120 men in peacetime and 160 (for mountain batteries) or 130 (for field batteries) in wartime. In addition there were nine companies of heavy fortress artillery, each of 80 men (peacetime) or 100 (wartime).

Grierson records that prior to the mid-1880s all batteries were customarily taught to function as both mountain batteries and field batteries 'so as to be available as mountain artillery if required', and adds that field batteries which served during the Satsuma Rebellion had all been converted in this way. He records overall artillery strength in about 1886 as a Guard battalion (consisting of one field battery and one mountain battery) and nine Line battalions, three of field artillery and six of mountain artillery, each commanded by a major. Each battalion comprised two six-gun batteries (each divided into three two-gun sections), with 164 men per field battery or 184 per mountain battery. The latter consisted of five officers (two captains – the senior of whom was the battery commander – two lieutenants, and a second lieutenant), a sergeant-major, 21 NCOs, three trumpeters, six artificers, and 148 privates; field batteries had 20 less privates. When on a war footing, field artillery battalions had a command staff of five officers (including a surgeon, a veterinary surgeon, and a quartermaster) and 17 NCOs and men, plus 48 horses, while a mountain artillery battalion's command staff comprised five officers, 45 other ranks, and 78 horses. Line field batteries were equipped with old French muzzle-loading *pièces de 4* and *pièces de 12*, while Line mountain batteries had *pièces de 4 de montagne*. Additional guns in storage in government arsenals included two batteries of Krupps, three of Broadwell mountain guns, further French *pièces de 4* and *pièces de 12*, and 'a large number of guns and mitrailleuses of various patterns.'

Knollys considered the field artillery units that he saw in 1887 as being very good. In the drill which he observed two batteries (therefore probably a battalion) were commanded by a lieutenant-colonel, with 'one

A mountain battery in action during manoeuvres at Handa in 1898. Though the hooded overcoats suggest cold weather, the gunners nevertheless wear white summer covers on their caps. Writing in 1895, Isabella Bird observed that the horses used by Japanese mountain batteries were 'serviceable animals, 14 hands high, ... equipped with pack saddles of the latest Indian pattern.' A gun required four horses to carry it, and one to transport the ammunition boxes, which held seven rounds each.

captain and two subalterns to each battery of four 9-pdr Krupp guns. To every gun was assigned one mounted sergeant, five gunners, and six horses; and, in addition, there was the usual proportion of staff-sergeants, trumpeters &c.' He also confirms that four guns was peacetime battery strength, and that on mobilisation this was increased to six. Each battery nominally had about 140 men and 80 horses, but they appear to have been 'conspicuously far below the nominal strength'.

With the reorganisation of the army into divisions in 1888 the artillery was restructured into regiments (referred to in some sources as 'brigades' or 'divisions'), one being assigned to each army division. Line artillery regiments comprised three battalions (two field and one mountain – the Japanese had no heavy field artillery), each of two batteries. The Guard regiment differed in having just two field battalions. All batteries had six guns, still organised into three two-gun sections. This gives a total of four Guard field batteries, 24 Line field batteries, and 12 mountain batteries, making 40 batteries in all, or 240 guns. Regiments were commanded by colonels, battalions by majors, batteries by captains, sections by lieutenants or second lieutenants, and each individual gun by a sergeant. Each battery had five officers, ten NCOs, and somewhere between 96 and 112 gunners (sources differ), plus 58–63 horses in a field battery and 29–37 in a mountain battery. In wartime field and mountain batteries received an extra 38 and 30 gunners respectively, field batteries getting a substantial number of additional horses too. There were also sizeable quantities of artificers, drivers, and the like.

In 1892 Line artillery regiments are reported to have consisted of two field artillery battalions and one mountain artillery battalion, each of two batteries. Each regiment was commanded by a colonel or lieutenant-colonel, and contained 37 officers, three doctors, two veterinary surgeons, 83 NCOs, and 576 privates, but had a total strength of 725 men and 311 horses. Henry Norman gives the peacetime strength of an individual battery as 148 men (68 active army and 80 reserve) with 86 horses and four guns, to which ten gunners and two guns were added on mobilisation; and peacetime battalion strength as 12 officers, 51 NCOs, 240 gunners, 180 horses, and eight guns, plus an extra 20 gunners, four guns, and 78 horses when on a war-footing. (He also gives each battalion nine non-combatant officers, but then adds his figures up to 306 men in peacetime and 326 in wartime.)

Army expansion following the Sino-Japanese War saw the artillery increased to 12 divisional regiments. In addition corps artillery had been established for the first time during the war, and led before the end of the century to the creation of two independent artillery brigades, each of three two-battalion regiments. Based in Tokyo, these were intended to form corps artillery in any future conflict. The whole 19 regiments (one Guard, 12 Line, and the six regiments of corps artillery) added up to 38 battalions or 114 batteries, totalling 684 guns, 800 officers, 12,500 men, and 8,800 horses, plus 19 depot batteries totalling an additional 114 guns and 2,650 men. Five regiments (one source says seven) were equipped with mountain guns, and most of the rest with field guns, the one exception being the 7th Hokkaido, which was equipped half and half with mountain and field guns.

Besides field artillery there was also a corps of 'fortress artillery' or 'garrison artillery', responsible primarily for manning the guns defending Japan's fortified harbours and naval establishments (including those on Tsushima and, at the end of the century, Formosa). There were nine companies of fortress artillery by as early as 1875, but the corps seems not to have been organised at any higher level until the second half of the 1880s. By 1890 there were two battalions, which had been enlarged into two regiments by the following year, three regiments by 1894, and four by the end of 1897. Each regiment had varying numbers of battalions and companies 'according to the requirements of the fortress in which the regiment is quartered', but most sources indicate that during the first half of the 1890s they customarily had three battalions, even though there were actually as many as 19 battalions in 1896. Most battalions had three or four companies. Lehautcourt describes a fortress artillery regiment as being commanded by a colonel or lieutenant-colonel and having an effective strength of 74 officers, three doctors, 164 NCOs, 1,404 privates, and ten horses. Other sources give a battalion 660–680 men, and a peacetime company five officers, ten NCOs, 110 privates (increased to 160 in wartime), and three horses. By about 1902 the entire fortress artillery establishment comprised six regiments and three independent battalions (a total of 20 battalions in all), made up of 530 officers, 10,300 men, and 70 horses.

The Engineers

These already existed in some form at the close of the Edo period, Henry Tilley recording 'a corps of artillery and engineers' in 1861. The first French military mission is known to have trained at least one company of engineers in 1867, and small units are recorded accompanying *bakufu* forces in the field during the Boshin War. It is therefore likely that they were present in the Meiji national army from the outset, even though they were only established as an official arm of service in 1872. Upton gives engineer company strength as 120 men in peacetime and 150 in wartime, probably exclusive of officers and NCOs. Grierson lists wartime company strength as five officers (a captain, two lieutenants, and two second lieutenants), a sergeant-major, 22 NCOs, four buglers, and 146 privates, but gives a separate total of 183 for the NCOs and privates; probably the number of privates in the first set of figures should therefore be 156 rather than 146, making company strength 188 officers and men. (This seems to be confirmed by the fact that he records the Imperial Guard's engineer company to have had 188 NCOs and privates in both peace and war.)

The Guard's company and any independent engineer companies (of which there were three in 1878, for instance, and four in 1884) had three additional officers, consisting of a surgeon, a veterinary surgeon, and a quartermaster. The independent companies also had six additional privates, probably indicating that two men were assigned to each of the additional officers.

Engineer battalions may have initially had just two companies but they certainly had three by 1890, and may have done from the outset. The discrepancy is probably explained by Du Boulay's observation that on mobilisation two served as field companies while the third formed bridging and telegraph sections as and when required (each division had two bridges, one 96 m/105 yds long and the other 36 m/39 yds). He describes the

A detachment of Military Train. The nearest horse carries two of the huge bowls used to cook the rice that constituted the staple diet of Japanese troops in the field. (See also the illustration on p.37.)

battalion as 'three companies of the same strength as in the infantry', while Hardy (1890) states that peacetime companies comprised 125 men plus one non-combatant, and wartime companies 221 men and 58 non-combatants. Grierson records the command staff of an engineer battalion as three officers (major, lieutenant, and second lieutenant) and three NCOs, with two riding horses. Lehautcourt (1892) gives the total strength of a peacetime battalion as 392 men (18 officers, 44 NCOs, and 330 privates), and its 'total effective force' – presumably meaning the wartime strength of its two field companies – as 408 men and 19 horses. The Imperial Guard's engineer battalion had just two companies at this date, and comprised 14 officers, two surgeons, 33 NCOs, 220 privates, 11 non-combatants, and 14 horses.

There appear to have been ten companies of engineers by as early as 1875, and theoretically six Line battalions (one per garrison) by 1883, though Takata states that in May 1884 actual strength stood at just three battalions plus four independent companies, even after including the Imperial Guard. Certainly there were still only 1,708 engineers in all in 1885. The six Line battalions were probably completed by 1888, and the peacetime engineer establishment is recorded to have stood at 2,522 men in 1890. Expansion plans following the Sino-Japanese War envisaged the creation of a further six battalions, but doubtless these remained incomplete as the century ended. The anticipated strength of the army's entire 13 engineer battalions (12 Line and one Guard) was 270 officers, 7,000 men, and 215 horses, plus 13 depot companies with a further 1,600 men. A single railway battalion also existed by 1896, and by about 1902 seems to have stood at 20 officers, 550 men, and 15 horses.

A separate Telegraph Corps had been created in about 1884, but was abolished in 1887 and its duties reassumed by the engineers (who seem to have been operating an army telegraph service by 1881 at the latest). Grierson recorded its strength in 1886 as seven sections, two of 32 men to service the army headquarters (apparently he means the Imperial Guard and the Tokyo garrison) and five of 27 men for attachment to each of the other five garrisons. In peacetime the Telegraph Corps was placed directly under the Headquarters Staff. Telegraph sections attached to each division during the Sino-Japanese War had sufficient cable to lay a line of some 30 km (18 miles). As regards other methods of communication, a reporter for the *Times* noted in 1895 that 'the Japanese use no means except couriers, as far as I have seen – no bugles, semaphores, flags, heliographs, or other modern methods. This results in effectively preventing the enemy from knowing their plans.'

The Military Train

Like the Engineers, the Military Train was only formally established in 1872 but had doubtless existed in some form from 1869 onwards. In 1873 it comprised a theoretical 360 men in peacetime and 480 in wartime, organised into six companies. In reality there were probably considerably fewer – just one company and two platoons seem to have existed in 1879. However, by 1883 there were nominally seven companies (one per garrison and one for the Imperial Guard), which in theory, but not in reality, had been expanded to seven two-company battalions by 1886.

It needs to be remembered, of course, that the Military Train's functions were not much required in peacetime, only in war, which explains why in 1885 the numerical strength of the active army's Line commissariat units still stood at just 548 men (5½ companies, each wartime company having seven officers and 107 men when at full strength), while its reserves, intended for call-up in wartime, stood as high as 54,458. The purpose of the regular companies, therefore, was simply to provide cadres for as many coolie corps as might be needed. (This is what Knollys meant when he wrote in 1887 that there was no regular commissariat corps, its functions being undertaken instead by what he calls 'civilian contractors'.) During the Satsuma Rebellion, for instance, tens of thousands of coolies were engaged daily to keep the army supplied. Grierson tells us that 'every year 15,000 men are told off out of the annual contingent for [coolie] duty', and that these were immediately enrolled into the first reserve and eventually the second, which meant that the reserve of coolies stood at 15,000 multiplied by the current length of reserve service in years. He adds that 'one twentieth of the men are called up in their first year of service for a three-months' course of training.'

When the garrisons were converted to divisions in 1888 each had a military train battalion as before. Battalion strength in 1890 is recorded as 14 officers, two doctors, two veterinary surgeons, 42 NCOs, 540 privates, 12 non-combatants, and 298 horses. The Guard battalion at the same date was considerably smaller, having just 24 NCOs rather than 42, and 240 privates rather than 540, but apparently 188 non-combatants and 240 horses. The expansion programme initiated at the end of the century envisaged a corps of 13 battalions (26 companies), totalling 220 officers, 7,740 men, and 40,000 horses, plus 13 depot companies (3,050 men).

Some units were recruited entirely from Japan's untouchables – the despised *eta* leather workers or *burakumin* – after attempts to introduce them into other arms, even in the capacity of boot or saddle makers, met with strong opposition from ex-samurai and commoners alike. Edgerton (1977) records that they ranked so low in the estimation of their contemporaries that the names of those killed in action weren't even listed among 'the honoured war dead'.[42]

On mobilisation military train battalions ceased to exist as such, instead being broken down into numerous

Europeans had considerable admiration for the accomplishments of Japanese engineers. An eyewitness of manoeuvres in November 1901, for instance, observed that 'no fault could be found with the Japanese pioneers, and the European officers were astonished at the ease and dexterity with which they threw up fortifications and constructed bridges.' Following the capture of Ping-Yang it took the engineers less than ten hours to construct nearly 40 miles of field telegraph lines so that news of the victory could be wired to Pongsan and thence to Seoul. This contemporary picture shows such a military telegraph under construction.

detachments variously responsible for regimental transport, divisional supply columns, and divisional ammunition columns, a large number of artillery and infantry reservists also being assigned to the last. The battalion provided all the ponies and carts, and oversaw the many thousands of coolies assigned to the division. The regimental transport was made up of pack ponies, each carrying a load of about 250 lbs (115 kg). Divisional transport, which carried a minimum of four days' rations and ideally eight, was likewise normally carried out using ponies, but during the Sino-Japanese War and the Boxer Rebellion most other transport – the divisional ammunition and supply columns, and the line of communication transport – employed light, two-wheeled Japanese hand-carts, each capable of carrying 300–400 lbs (135–180 kg). These were drawn by either a single pony or three coolies apiece, the latter usually selected among men with experience of pulling rickshaws. Eyewitness H.V. Cox describes such carts as 'too light and flimsy for anything but good roads.' Captured Chinese wagons were also used in both campaigns. Du Boulay describes those seen in 1894–95 as 'drawn generally by five, six or seven animals of different sorts; mules, ponies, donkeys and oxen; all harnessed together. These wagons carry heavy loads and go great distances.' Each division had three supply columns and five ammunition columns.

The workings of the army's logistics arrangements in the field are succinctly outlined in a newspaper report written in 1905. Though describing operations during the Russo-Japanese conflict, this summary is equally valid for the Sino-Japanese War: 'As a rule, the Japanese private carries with him the day's rations and two days' emergency rations. When these fail he has to fall back upon the regimental transport, which is supposed to carry never less than one day's supplies. The Japanese regimental transport consists of a column of pack-horses and light carts, except in the hills, where the military coolie corps takes its place. This transport is found by the train battalion of the division; but it remains permanently attached to the regiment it serves, and is under the orders of the regiment commander ... This transport is so divided up that, if a battalion or company is detached, a section or sub-section of the regimental transport accompanies the detachment. In case of absolute necessity the regimental transport can be pooled and allotted to other pressing needs, but this is rarely done ... It carries baggage, cooking utensils, tools, medical stores, ammunition, and litters, as well as food. In rear of the regimental transport there follows the divisional supply column with four or more days' rations.'

The Medical Service

There was an army medical department as early as the 1870s, which in 1878 included 127 surgeons and doctors and 145 assistants. By the Sino-Japanese War this had become a very substantial organisation indeed. Each infantry regiment was accompanied by six surgeons, 15 attendants, and 48 bearers with six panniers and 12 stretchers, and each cavalry, artillery, engineer or military train battalion by between six and ten surgeons and attendants. In addition every infantry company included four men trained in first aid, who assisted the wounded until stretcher bearers could retrieve them and then returned to the firing line. Each division also had its own medical corps. This consisted of a central unit of surgeons, medical officers, pharmacists, administrative staff and so on (11 officers, 93 men, and 49 horses), a field hospital (eight officers, 108 men, and 44 horses), and two stretcher-bearer companies, each of one officer and 155 men (or 120 in the Guards Division) with 48 stretchers. Field dressing stations were set up wherever needed, and were divided into three distinct categories, being either receiving and forwarding stations (which carried out the triage process), operating sections, or dressing stations.

Du Boulay says that the stretcher-bearer companies were 'composed chiefly of infantry soldiers [who] do not treat the wounded, but carry them to the central staff for treatment. The central staff is composed of medical officers and medical attendants, and they form the dressing stations as required.' Other sources tell us that the bearers were in fact reservists, led by combatant officers.

Western observers were immensely impressed by the bravery and efficiency of the army's medical staff in both the Sino-Japanese War and the Boxer Rebellion, a British naval officer recording during the latter expedition that 'the hospitals, both base and field, were wonderfully good, prompt and skilful attention being received by all the wounded, who were certainly better off in this respect than those of any other nation'. Cox, too, wrote that their hospital equipment was as good, if not better, than that of any of the other Allied armies operating in China in 1900, being 'thoroughly up to date', with 'field sterilizers, and distillers, X-rays, and acetylene searchlights, etc. Their surgical instruments were of the very best, and much envied by our own medical men.'

In addition to the army medical corps there was also the *Hakuaisha*, a benevolent society founded in 1877 to care for the sick and wounded. This was reorganised in June 1886 after being formally enrolled as an international Red Cross society.

The Hokkaido Militia

In order to defend what had become (after the loss of Sakhalin) Japan's northernmost island against the risk of Russian encroachment, an agrarian militia (the *tonden nohei*, or 'military colonists') was authorised for Hokkaido in June 1874 and took shape during 1875–76.[43] Organised into regiments, battalions, and companies along exactly the same lines as in the active army, it consisted exclusively of ex-samurai and their issue until as late as 1891.[44] After receiving the appropriate training in modern warfare, these served as provincial police in peacetime and as militia soldiers in wartime from the age of 18 until they were 35. In exchange they received free transport to Hokkaido, a few acres of land, a house, seed, tools, household goods, arms, and three years' provisions. The land grants were in close proximity to one another, so that the militiamen's houses formed self-contained villages or 'colonies', to facilitate the mustering process. The earliest were established in coastal districts, notably in the Ishikari region, but later colonies were formed in the interior. In 1878 celebrated traveller Isabella Bird saw the principal colony, at Satsuporo (the capital of Hokkaido), which she overestimated as comprising nearly 1,000 soldiers and their families – probably roughly twice the total strength of the Militia as it existed at that time.

In 1882 the Militia comprised an infantry battalion and two 'sections'. By 1886 it had increased to two battalions, each with a theoretical peacetime strength of 24 officers, 84 NCOs, and 500 privates, and by the end of 1887 there were three battalions and one company, with a total strength of 1,461 men.

Revised Militia regulations were issued in August 1890. These required its soldiers to live in 'military houses which shall be provided for them, and shall take part in military drill, in cultivation, and in farming.' Men from other islands wishing to join the Hokkaido Militia were to be 'volunteers from cities and prefectures, and shall change their registered residence to Hokkaido, and live there with their families.' Militiamen were to serve for 20 years, from the age of 20 until they reached 40, serving whenever called upon for their first three years, followed by four years in the first reserve and 13 in the second. Where a militiaman reached the age of 40 before having served for his full term of 20 years, or else died or was incapacitated, a suitable substitute had to be provided to complete the service period (though such service might be remitted if there was no suitable male heir). In addition militiamen were required to perform ten years' 'supplementary service' after completing their time with the second reserve, and could still be mobilised on the outbreak of war or during other emergencies.

By 1891 there were four infantry battalions, a squadron of cavalry, an artillery battery, and a company of engineers, comprising about 4,000 men in all. Organisation and strength remained fundamentally unchanged thereafter until the end of the century. In 1892 Lehautcourt recorded that Hokkaido Militia battalions comprised a command staff of 17 men (including four medical officers) plus from two to six infantry companies, each of 221 men if they belonged to the active army element, or 203 if they were recruited from reservists. The cavalry squadron had a permanent command cadre of five officers, one doctor, one veterinary surgeon, and 19 NCOs, in addition to which there were 143 active army militiamen and 136 horses, plus 160 reservists with as many horses. The single artillery battery of six guns had 113 active army militiamen and 29 horses, and 120 reservists with 33 horses, plus a permanent command cadre of four officers, a doctor, a veterinary surgeon, and 15 NCOs. Finally, the engineer company had 109 active army militiamen and four horses, 120 reservists, and a command cadre of four officers and a doctor.

Shogunate infantry sketched at Yokohama early in 1865, from an engraving in the Illustrated London News. *Note the white stripes on their hats and down the sleeves of their dark blue uniforms, which show up dazzlingly bright in contemporary Japanese paintings and thereby demonstrate how useful they must have been in distinguishing friend from foe, at a time when the uniforms worn by shogunate and Loyalist forces were dangerously similar. See also the caption to Figures 13–20.*

During or immediately after the Sino-Japanese War the Militia was amalgamated with an independent infantry battalion, an independent field artillery battalion, and an independent engineer company, to form a full regular army division, known as the 7th Hokkaido. Its engineer company was enlarged to a battalion in 1897; four further infantry regiments were added in 1899; and a cavalry regiment, a field artillery regiment, another engineer battalion, and a military train battalion were added in 1900. The inevitable end product of this influx of regular army units was the abolition of the Hokkaido Militia itself in September 1903, by which time nearly 40,000 soldier-colonists had settled on the island.

A very small number of Hokkaido Japanese were also conscripted into the active army during the century. These served in the fortress artillery unit based in Hakodate.

WARFARE

Traditional tactics differing little if at all from those employed during the classical age of samurai warfare theoretically still prevailed at the beginning of the 19th century. These involved contingents of mounted samurai armed with spears and bows, supported by lower-ranking samurai fighting on foot, organised into units of spearmen, halberdiers, archers, and matchlockmen. In broad terms, the role of the cavalry was to provide scouts and to attempt to take the enemy in flank, while some infantry archers provided skirmishers and the other missile-men formed the army's front line, the matchlockmen frequently employing 'dropping fire' over the heads of their own men. Firearms and bows were regarded as having advantages when the enemy was on lower ground, but swords, spears, and polearms were considered superior when attacking uphill. Archers and matchlockmen alike were protected when and where necessary by spearmen. Weaknesses in the enemy's line were exploited by the spearmen as they occurred, after which the battle usually degenerated into a multitude of duels between individual samurai until one side or the other eventually broke and fled. The victor would then commit his reserves to ensure that the ensuing pursuit was close, bloody, and decisive. Needless to say, numerous exotic battle arrays are recorded in surviving military manuals, but in essence most important conflicts seem to have boiled down to the basic sequence of events outlined above.

However, with the exception of inconsequential peasant revolts peace had prevailed throughout the country for nearly 200 years by the beginning of the 19th century, and by the time warfare returned to Japan's political agenda in the 1860s traditional tactics had been compromised by the indelible stamp of outside influences – in particular the introduction of more and better Western firearms on an increasingly grand scale. These inevitably encouraged the widespread adoption of barricades and substantial field defences during the civil wars of 1864–77, which in turn led to a dependence on defensive rather than offensive tactics. As the firearms became more numerous and effective so field defences became ever more substantial. Starting out as simple trenches and embankments during the 1860s, they culminated in such sophisticated breastworks as those thrown up by the Imperial army during the fighting round Kagoshima in 1877, described by eyewitness John Hubbard as comprising 'first ... a strong bamboo fence, so crossed as to form a diamond shape. This is seven feet high. Behind it are boards on the ground studded with nails; then a ditch four feet deep and twelve feet wide; next a frame-work of strips of bamboo tied in squares and raised two feet from the ground and twenty feet wide. The squares are just right for a man to step in and flounder about without making any progress. The next trap is another deep ditch twenty feet wide filled with small branches of trees, and then comes the main breastwork ... made of earth and straw bags filled with earth, a wonderful construction about eight feet wide at the base and two feet wide at the top, with an inside embankment'. Writing of the same conflict, Mounsey records that Imperials and Satsuma rebels alike further strengthened their positions by 'planting pointed bamboos and sharp nails in the ground, and covering them with loose earth'.

Understandably there was a reluctance to assail robust earthworks and barricades head-on in the face of heavy musket and rifle fire. The enemy was therefore attacked in flank and/or rear wherever possible, or else lured out from behind his defensive works by means of a feigned retreat, and then ambushed. This strategy was effectively employed by the Choshu clan several times in 1866–68, for instance, though where the *bakufu* forces – who relied almost exclusively on defensive tactics – declined to follow the decoy party, the Choshu nevertheless demonstrated a willingness to return and attack their barricades regardless of losses, relieving each other by half-battalions. They were only usually defeated if they exhausted their ammunition before achieving a result. Roadside ambushes of marching columns were also popular, the most famous engagement of this kind being the Battle of Toba-Fushimi in 1868.

Such exchanges of fire as occurred in the open field tended to be at close range and usually consisted of one short sharp volley, followed almost immediately by a charge and a hand-to-hand melee – which was where traditional samurai fighting skills could still make themselves felt. As an example of the effectiveness of samurai swordsmanship at close quarters it is only necessary to cite the attack by two dissident samurai on the British Minister's escort of 12 mounted dragoons in Kyoto in 1869, in which ten of the latter were 'more or less seriously wounded' (it took a couple of samurai accompanying the Minister's entourage to finally bring down their attackers). But on the battlefield swordsmen were generally overrun by riflemen so long as the latter's ammunition did not fail them – as it did at Toba-Fushimi in 1868, when a body of Satsuma riflemen unable to reload quickly enough were driven back by sword- and spear-armed Aizu clansmen.

That the samurai tradition of hand-to-hand combat persisted for the rest of the century and into the next is apparent not only from the fact that all Imperial soldiers carrying swords still indulged in single combats with the enemy at every opportunity, but also from the Japanese love of bayonet attacks, evident even in the Russo-Japanese War. The traditional samurai practice of decapitating their dead enemies also survived, being recorded in Formosa in 1874 and North China in 1894–95; the customary execution of prisoners, however, seems to have largely ended with the Boshin War.

Post-modernisation

In the closing decades of the century samurai tradition[45] was to prove invaluable in creating the new citizen army's esprit de corps, even amongst non-samurai conscripts not generally considered by their social superiors to possess 'military spirit'. Foreign observers noted with approval that the Japanese taught their soldiers 'to realise that they were in an honourable profession' and 'to set an example to the nation ... by their self-sacrifice'. Individual initiative was encouraged, as was hard physical training, including long-distance runs and forced marches of 60–70 miles in 24 hours 'to increase endurance' (a Russian report seemingly written in 1901 describes the Japanese as having 'a wonderful capacity for marching'). Lehautcourt found Japan's peasant conscripts to be 'enduring, patient, sober, courageous, naturally gay, reckless, and submissive', and C.C. Dix (a participant in the international expedition against the Boxers) adds that they showed 'no fear of anything'. The Russian report observes that 'they take readily to a soldiers' life and adapt themselves easily to discipline'. Several observers even considered that they made better infantry than certain Europeans they could name. Though desertion and even mutiny were not unknown,[46] and the much-vaunted discipline of the Japanese Army was not always what it might have been, the available evidence certainly appears to indicate that Japanese élan was superior to that of some Western armies – not least because the average Japanese soldier put national pride before self-preservation. In his examination of the tactics utilised during the Russo-Japanese War, A. Kearsey considered that Japanese success in the field 'was due to their sense of duty, their spirit of discipline, their abnegation of self and the co-operation of their commanders'. Indeed, unlike some European armies co-operation between officers was high and rivalry between them correspondingly low.

With the transformation of the national army from a defensive organisation into an offensive force in the second half of the 1880s, under the auspices of its chief instructor Major Klemens Meckel, drill and tactical thinking 'modelled on the German system of 1880, with some modifications' was adopted. This was generally adhered to thereafter until the early stages of the Russo-Japanese conflict. The principal characteristic of these nominally German tactics[47] was a dependence on close-

Photograph taken in 1894 showing Japanese troops in action during the Sino-Japanese War. The distance from the stock-cap to the end of the barrel indicates that their rifles are Type 13 Muratas rather than the Type 18s one woud have expected to see at this late date (see pages 71–72). (Wikipedia)

order advances directly into the enemy's fire, heedless of casualties, Meckel's belief being that three- and four-deep formations, with intervals of just one yard between men, maximised the impact of an attacking force.

Though in 1904 they were to prove horrifyingly costly in the face of Russian machine guns, field guns, rifles, and barbed wire, such attacks were almost invariably decisive when employed against the Chinese, whose morale, training, and musketry at that time left much to be desired. A reporter for the *Japan Mail*, for instance, observed of the attack on Kinchow in 1894 that the Japanese 'steady, rapid, unhesitating approach had more effect than anything else in making the Chinese defence weak. To wait for close quarters in those circumstances requires better soldiers than the Chinese.' Another eyewitness similarly observed of the attack on Port Arthur in November that year that the ineffectiveness of the Chinese fire in stopping the Japanese advance 'must have had a somewhat demoralising effect on them'. Frederick Brown, describing the fighting at Tientsin in July 1900, observed that 'the Chinese might shoot them down by the dozen, but those left did not even waver', and William Maxwell (1906) records it being drummed into Japanese soldiers that 'any wavering and lack of dash would lead to increased casualties and diminish the prospects of success.' 'Nothing short of annihilation will stop them once they are let loose,' wrote Cox after the expedition against the Boxers, 'and when they have altered their tactics they will be difficult to annihilate.'

Details of a typical direct assault are provided by Maxime Sauvage's account of the 1894 attack on Port Arthur. He tells us that 'while Matsumitsu's column had before it absolutely unbroken ground, Hasegawa's Brigade could take advantage of a rolling landscape, clusters of trees, and some houses. The latter's task was thus less difficult. It advanced in perfect order, utilising the least cover provided by the terrain.' Du Boulay records that Hasegawa's men were drawn up in two lines, the first of five companies on the right and two on the left, all in extended order – meaning that 'each company had two sections extended and two in support closed up' – with a second line consisting of two companies on the right and two on the left all in line, in close order. But, says Sauvage, Matsumitsu's column 'had to overcome far greater difficulties. No cover could hide its movement, and a scathing fire struck the slopes that it must climb in order to seize the eastern defences. It did not, however, hesitate a single moment. Marching as if on parade, it advanced in methodical order without being disturbed by the gaps which Chinese fire caused in its ranks.' Eastlake and Yamada (1897) tell us that Chinese officers present here attributed the Japanese victory to the fact that 'when advancing to the charge, [they] were not to be repulsed even by the fiercest fire. They seemed to the Chinese to be utterly reckless, storming on as they did under the iron hail of the forts.'

As Sauvage's account intimates, the Japanese were not averse to taking advantage, when they could, of such cover as might be available. Far from it. In describing Japanese operations in Korea and China in

Japanese infantry attacking Chinese positions during the Sino-Japanese War, an illustration from The Graphic.

1894–95 and 1900, various sources specifically state that their infantry were trained 'to make good use of cover' and 'learnt to make the best use of ground, to obtain cover from view and fire by moving rapidly between positions and by rising and getting down quickly after each rush'. Consequently companies operated almost independently when a battalion went into action. 'Sections of companies found positions separately, where the country and the cover favoured them,' observed an American commentator, 'without attempting to preserve long straight lines, while the units displayed great initiative and dash. The rolling ground permitted them to advance by rushes effectively. After firing a few rounds they would dash ahead to another hillock, and, dropping into the grass, empty their magazines again'. John Leader (1903), who had observed the Japanese Army in action in both Korea and China, confirms that they customarily advanced 'by alternate companies and half companies'. In combination with good cover, this sometimes enabled head-on assaults to be mounted with surprisingly light casualties. Nevertheless, some eyewitnesses of their operations in China in 1900 remained unconvinced that the Japanese were particularly well trained in 'taking proper advantage of ground'.

The Russian report of c.1901 already mentioned tells us that the usual Japanese attack formation comprised skirmishers, a firing line, and supports: 'Each company sends out skirmishers to the number of two sections [the American report quoted above says that the Japanese were 'exceptionally good skirmishers'], and as they are not in extended order they are practically in close order of one line with a short space between the sections. In the firing line the men usually lay down and take advantage of any cover. NCOs and commanders of sections kneel on one knee three paces behind the firing line. The supports take their place from 40 to 50 paces behind the firing line, and when the skirmishers are stationary for some time the supports kneel ... Before the firing line extends for an advance the officers go forward to reconnoitre the ground and conditions.' Other sources confirm that the Japanese 'carefully reconnoitred the ground over which they were going to attack ... and they always endeavoured to gain accurate information as to the extent and weak parts of an enemy's position, where the flanks were, and what obstacles there were to the advance.'

'When a company of infantry is ordered to take a position it advances in close order,' continues our anonymous Russian informant, 'and on reaching the position sends out skirmishers, but has no flank guards. Infantry fire is independent or by volleys. Volley fire is adopted at long range, independent fire within a thousand paces. [An American report of 1904 says that though they occasionally used volleys 'most of the time they fire at will, giving the enemy less information of their position, and gaining the advantages of individual marksmanship.'] ... In sighting and loading their rifles the men are quick and accurate. To reinforce the firing line the supports are added ... If additional reinforcements are needed the supports extend and move forward between the companies which are already in extended order. When still further help is required a part of the supports form a second extended firing line behind the first line. In this case the first line lies down, while the second stands or kneels'.

When advancing, the firing line moved at 'the ordinary pace' until it drew near the enemy, 'when the advance is at the double. Rushes are made 40 or 50 paces from the enemy. Sometimes each body rushes forward independently. All the supports double after the firing line, and the advance is usually confused. The men crowd together and move forward obliquely, exposing their flank.' The final assault – sometimes delivered in relative silence (orders were transmitted by means of hand-signals), and sometimes accompanied by a loud *Wa–a–a!* described as sounding like 'a wail of grief' – was preceded by what W.D. Bird (1909) describes as 'rapid but somewhat wild rifle fire'. (A *Times* correspondent covering the Sino-Japanese War considered Japanese infantrymen to be 'very poor shots', claiming that he had witnessed three- to four-hour skirmishes with 'volleys fired at 500 to 1,000 yards' in which not a single man had been killed on either side.) In addition attacks were supported by artillery fire described as 'storms of shrapnel, delivered at rather long range.' If the assault failed, says Kearsey, 'the survivors remained under cover in the vicinity of the ground gained, and a new attacking line was built up; then the final assault, covered by fire, was repeated'.

The Russian report adds that the Japanese seldom fired when advancing, and other sources comment on their reliance on the bayonet in the final assault – their 'decided penchant for close quarters and cold steel', as Dix put it. F.J. Norman noted that Japanese soldiers might not be able to go through sword or bayonet drill with the same precision as British guardsmen but that 'far and away a greater proportion of them' knew how to use these weapons 'better and more effectively'. 'The Japanese love the arme blanche,' agrees Maxwell, 'and never hesitate to use it. With the bayonet they have proved themselves again and again ... whether singly or en masse.' At Liao-yang in 1904, he records, 'a whole division charged and carried a position at the point of the bayonet and never fired a shot ... The Japanese recognised no "lethal zone swept by a horizontal sheet of lead" within 400 yards of an entrenched enemy. They found this the zone of comparative safety from rifle fire, and went in with the bayonet.'

In fact direct frontal attacks continued to be utilised throughout the Russo-Japanese War, though after July 1904 they were no longer mounted in such close order as before, the earlier almost shoulder-to-shoulder Japanese formations (justifiably criticised in more than one source as 'cumbersome') being abandoned in favour of three and eventually five pace intervals between the men. It also became accepted policy thereafter to halt when within about 1,000 yards of the enemy's position and, bringing up the supports to reinforce the firing line as before, attempt to first obtain superiority of fire before 'advancing by rushes' to the final assaulting position. Nevertheless, the losses sustained continued to be severe, and such successes as were achieved had more to do with either the weakness of the enemy, the presence of dead ground in front of his position, or local Japanese superiority in artillery, than with any inherent invincibility in this method of attack. If a purely frontal assault was attempted against a well-entrenched position held by resolute troops success was by no means guaranteed, and losses were frequently prohibitive, especially amongst the command cadre – Japanese officers invariably leading from the front.

Most Western observers considered the Japanese Army's uncompromising head-on approach unimaginative. They criticised its generals and regimental commanders for not making better use of their common sense and for being 'rather prodigal of their men's lives', and observed that it was the ordinary soldiers who 'often, by their doggedness, repaired mistakes of tactics and leadership.' But Japanese generals were, in fact, fully cognisant of the risks inherent in mounting direct assaults, and consequently made use wherever possible of wide flanking or enveloping manoeuvres in support of their frontal attacks. H. Brunker (1911), for instance, observes that though the Japanese 'almost invariably attacked the enemy along their whole front ... an attempt was also made to envelop one or both flanks. The frontal attack, even against well defended positions, was seldom of a mere holding nature, but was as a rule the main attack and as such was pressed with the greatest vigour, the flank attack being intended to assist the frontal attack in capturing the position, and in making victory more decisive by intercepting the enemy whilst retiring. It is also a noticeable feature of the Japanese operations that even a secondary attack was pressed with vigour, as it was realised that it is necessary to approach close to the enemy's position and to assail him in earnest if he is to be prevented from transferring troops to other portions of the field'. The night attack at Pei-tsang in June 1900 (the Japanese were already taking full advantage of darkness in their attacks at least as early as 1894) provides a good

Satsuma artillery in action at the Battle of Toba-Fushimi, from a contemporary print. (Wikipedia)

Japanese field artillery passing through Tungchow en route to Peking, August 1900, a double-page illustration from The Sphere of 27 October that year. The soldiers all wear white summer uniforms. Western-style artillery harness had been in use in the Japanese Army since the 1860s. H.V. Cox, an eyewitness of the expedition against the Boxers, recorded that their guns were drawn by teams of six ponies: 'They use black breast harness, oiled, and black buckles ... Guns are kept clean, but the remainder of the equipment and carriages are allowed to more or less shift for themselves.' All the metalwork of the harness was lacquered black. Field gun limbers carried 40 rounds and the wagon bodies another 50 rounds.

example of such a flanking manoeuvre, where 'the Japanese advanced to within 200 yards of the Chinese trenches before they were discovered, when a heavy fire was poured into them. They charged without faltering; a brilliantly timed flank attack proved successful, and the Chinese were put to flight in less than ten minutes from when the first shot was fired.'

In defence, Japanese infantry formed a long firing line in extended order, strengthened when there was time by trenches deep enough to facilitate firing from a kneeling position. When the enemy approached to within 800–300 paces, the firing line would leave its trenches, fix bayonets, and advance 40 or 50 paces, the supports simultaneously coming up and forming a second line which fired over their heads from a standing position. Our anonymous Russian observer considered that the weak point of a Japanese defensive position was its flanks, on which, he claims, there was 'great confusion' if they were threatened by a turning movement.

On the march Japanese infantry moved in column of fours, the cavalry in column of threes, and the artillery in single column. The average speed of a detachment of all arms was roughly 4½–5 mph (7–8 kph). Each column usually had a small body of cavalry (about half a squadron) forming the point; these were followed in sequence by a sizeable detachment of infantry, the artillery, the balance of the infantry, the engineers, and finally a small rearguard. 'One or more divisions advanced along several roads,' says the Russian report, 'and the advance guard is sent from one column – generally the central ... In war the Japanese send in front an independent body of horsemen, usually the whole of the cavalry attached to the column. The advance guard consists of about one-quarter of the infantry, from one-seventh to one-third of the artillery, a company of sappers, and a troop of cavalry. The point is composed of specially selected cavalry, and sends out patrols to the front. They have neither flank guards, nor fixed patrols.' The advance guard was generally placed some way ahead of the main body and was expected to engage the enemy unsupported until the main body could come up. In a retreat, the bulk of the infantry withdrew first, then the artillery, and finally the remainder of the infantry.

The Cavalry

Cavalry training was somewhat neglected during Westernisation of the Japanese Army, on the grounds that there were few of them, suitable horses were not available, and the country's topography was not suited to this arm of service anyway. Western and Russian sources are consequently unanimous in their criticism of Japanese cavalry. E.G. Barrow, for instance, wrote in 1893 that they were 'indifferent', and that 'their horses possess none of the charging qualities of speed or weight' (see the caption to Figure 4 regarding the size of Japanese horses). Dix describes them as 'the weakest branch of the service ... because of the small size of the horses', which were 'not altogether suitable for several reasons, among others that, being entire horses [i.e., not gelded], they are exceptionally savage, and in camp cause great trouble as well as many casualties.' He too considered that 'on account of their lack of weight, they are unsuitable for shock tactics', but adds that this 'did not prevent them from rendering scouting services beyond all praise' during the advance on Peking in 1900, when they proved to be 'well trained, and with no defects except those already mentioned.' Some contemporaries, however, held the general view that the Japanese were not actually very good horsemen.

During the period under review cavalry functions were mainly restricted to scouting, plus outpost and escort duties, and foreigners who witnessed Japanese manoeuvres in November 1901 felt that even in their execution of these roles they were slow and unconvincing. In a clearly bigoted passage which strongly suggests it was written by a cavalryman, the Russian report of about that date tells us that they took 'little part in actual fighting, and rarely keep watch on the flanks. They are always anxious to seek shelter behind the fighting line, and do not take advantage of any opening to attack the enemy. Even when they see an excellent opportunity they do not ride rapidly forward, being more anxious not to fall off their horses than to quicken their pace.'

Though theoretically trained principally for shock action – despite the unsuitability of their mounts – they were also taught to skirmish on foot. Indeed, in the Russo-Japanese War, in which they were seriously outnumbered by their Russian counterparts and were consequently obliged to act mostly on the defensive, they spent much of their time fighting dismounted. Brunker describes them as 'an arm of the service of which the essential mode of action is rifle fire', and adds that they constituted a battlefield rapid reaction force which could be transferred swiftly to wherever it was needed most.

An example of a cavalry action incorporating all of these elements is provided by an incident during the attack on Port Arthur in 1894, where a 200-strong Japanese reconnaissance force encountered some 2,300 Chinese infantry and cavalry in the open field. The Japanese cavalry spread out in open order and attacked, engaging the Chinese in hand-to-hand combat, but despite being joined by a company of supporting infantry they were eventually forced to fall back: 'By sheer force of numbers the Chinese succeeded at one time in surrounding the Japanese on three sides ... At first Captain Asakawa with his company of troopers led the van; but on seeing that the fight had become general, he rode [with them] over to the right, in order to render assistance in this direction. Noting this the Chinese made a furious attack on that side: so rapidly and fiercely engaging the Japanese that those who had not yet mounted were rendered incapable of doing so; and the cavalrymen had to fight on foot like all the rest. The Brigade commander now ordered Captain Asakawa to disperse the rapidly increasing enemy, and, with only 40 or 50 troopers, the latter charged into the ranks of the Chinese.'

Cavalry also contributed to the screening forces which Japanese commanders customarily placed ahead and on the flanks of their armies in order to conceal their movements from enemy scouts. There were usually numerous such detachments, each comprising 20–40 horsemen supported by infantry – normally on a ratio of four or five foot-soldiers per three or four horsemen – and, sometimes, foot artillery (the Japanese having no horse artillery).

As with the infantry, most cavalry attacks involved very little shouting. We are told (by Henry Knollys, writing in 1887) that commands were given predominantly by means of sword signals, and that trumpets were seldom used.

The Artillery

Japanese batteries could move at a maximum speed of about 5–6 mph (8–9.5 kph). When in action they were nearly always entrenched, with an interval of theoretically 22 paces between guns. The artillery was expected to open a battle, but in the 19th century generally did so at relatively long range (5–6,000 yds, or 4.5–5.5 km), and rarely moved forward in support of the infantry as it attacked, the Japanese apparently having an aversion to moving their guns in daylight.

Though the Japanese rarely concentrated their artillery in great numbers, each battalion fought as a complete two- or three-battery unit wherever ground admitted. Isolated action by individual batteries was disapproved of other than in hilly or broken country, where the lack of adequate space prevented deployment in battalion strength. We are told that 'great stress was laid on the importance of concealing guns from view and fire, and earthworks were ordered to be made wherever possible.'

In firing, Japanese artillerymen are said to have handled their guns with confidence, and their fire is described as slow, methodical, and relatively accurate (Barrow reports their accuracy as 'good, or at least fair'). Du Boulay says of the fire of guns involved in the attack on Port Arthur in 1894 that 'their shooting was most regularly carried out, from right to left of the whole line of guns, with an interval of ten seconds between each round.' Wherever possible they attempted to enfilade an enemy position from two sides.

The Engineers

The Japanese employed their engineers in more advanced positions than was customary in the West. In attacks on fortified emplacements, towns, and villages they were required to remove and destroy obstacles, demolish walls, and blow up gates, even accompanying scouting parties at night in order to remove obstacles that threatened to impede a planned attack. The rest of the time they generally accompanied the artillery, in order to improve roads and to construct the earthwork emplacements that protected their guns.

A classic example of the individual courage of Japanese engineers in action is provided by the Allied attack on Tientsin in 1900, where responsibility for capturing the city's south gate was allotted to the Japanese. Eyewitness Frederick Brown tells us that 'their commanders directed that the outer gate should be blown up. Two tins of gun-cotton were placed in position, and a fuse was attached and ignited; but the heavy fire of the Chinese either cut the fuse or blew out the light. Three times it was lighted, and as often went out. At last a Japanese engineer took a box of matches, ran forward, and touched the powder. Immediately there was an explosion, which blew man and gate to atoms.' His self-sacrifice enabled the Japanese infantry to storm the gateway, and its capture guaranteed the Allies' victory in what was to prove a decisive engagement.

DRESS AND APPEARANCE

Nineteenth-century Western travellers noted the existence of two distinct Japanese types, which they labelled as the 'aristocratic' type, possessing a light yellow or almost white complexion and slight build; and the 'plebeian', of darker complexion 'often to a copper colour' and more robust stature. These distinctions resulted from the marked division of Japan's population into pampered samurai and townsmen on the one hand and peasant agriculturalists on the other. Edward Belcher, for instance, wrote in 1845 that the 'lower orders' were 'of a much browner complexion than the better classes, many of whom are almost white'; and Henry Tilley (1861) observed that though Japanese men were generally 'muscular and agile', with 'warm white' skin which became yellower as they got older, the 'labouring classes' had decidedly brown complexions as a result of going 'generally naked when working'.

As a result of their simple diet, 19th-century Japanese men were considerably smaller than their 21st-century counterparts, averaging only 5 ft 1 in–5 ft 2 ins (1.55–1.57 m). According to Upton (1875) conscripts for the Japanese Army were required to be 5 ft 1 in–5 ft 3 ins (1.55–1.6 m), while Grierson (1886) states that 'the minimum height for artillerymen is 5 ft 4 in [1.63 m]; for cavalry, engineers, and train soldiers 5 ft 3 in [1.6 m]'; but it appears that both these authors have probably erred on the high side. The height of soldiers conscripted in the Tokyo district in 1891, for instance, was only just over 5 ft (actually 1.54 m), while a British report of November 1898 states categorically that conscripts for active army service had to be 5 *shaku*[48] (4.97 ft/1.52 m) tall, while men of 4.8–5 *shaku* 'qualified for the national army'. Barrow in 1893 and Griffis in 1903 both give the average height of Japanese soldiers as 5 ft (1.52 m), and Arthur Diósy in 1906 states that 'the average height of the Japanese infantryman' was 5 ft 0½ in (1.54 m).

The Japanese are naturally more hirsute than the Chinese, and following Westernisation heavy beards and 'very creditable moustaches' became fashionable, especially amongst the military (but only the officers – other ranks were clean-shaven). Their hair is mostly black, though a surprisingly large number actually have very dark brown hair. The traditional hairstyle that we today regard as characteristic of the samurai, but which was in fact worn by most Japanese men, involved shaving the front and top of the head but leaving the hair at the sides and back long. This long hair was gathered up into a little queue, the *magé*, which, with its end neatly clipped and glued together by means of a bandoline preparation, was bent forward to lie over the shaven scalp, and then bound at the base. However, other ways of wearing the hair were also occasionally seen, notably the 'Kobusho style',[49] in which the hair along the top of each temple was also left unshaven and was combed back to form part of the queue; and the far less common 'Osei style', which involved 'an unshaven head with all the hair worn, but made into a top-knot cue'.

With Westernisation, all of these styles gradually disappeared in favour of conventional European haircuts, a process which began in the second half of the 1860s with the sending of students overseas and the adoption of Western military dress by the army. Certainly some Japanese students had adopted foreign haircuts by 1867, as had many soldiers by 1870 at the very latest (when a description of Kii troops, for instance, tells us that 'their hair is cut in military style'). In the autumn of 1872 the government tried to discourage adherence to the old fashion and promoted – but did not enforce – the adoption of Western haircuts; and when, in March 1873, the Emperor himself had his hair cut in the foreign manner a great many of his subjects obediently followed suit. Even so, about 20% of the male population were still wearing their hair in the old style ten years later. According to Chitoshi Yanaga (1949) long hair and topknot finally disappeared in 1889, but Arthur Diósy (1898) states categorically that though the *magé* had become rare by the time he wrote, he had seen older men still wearing their hair in this fashion, 'especially in country districts'.

Some men belonging to the lower orders had their bodies and arms heavily tattooed in blue and scarlet, while at the other end of the social scale court nobles blackened their teeth and shaved their eyebrows until these customs were banned in 1870.

Clothing

For the evolution of Japanese Army uniforms during the century see the figures and captions on pp.79–99. In the following paragraphs we are concerned instead with what nominally constituted 'civilian' dress, worn under their armour by samurai and as fighting dress in its own right by some of their retainers right up to 1877.

Amongst the samurai class male attire started with an undergarment called a *fundoshi* (see the opening illustration on p.64), which was preferably of bleached muslin or linen, or sometimes silk crepe. Over this was worn a plain white silk or cotton shirt (*juban*), to which a short under-jacket of the same material, the *dogi*, was added in winter. In very cold weather two wadded coats, padded with cotton, *panya*, or *tsubana* (the last two described as 'something like cotton, but much lighter in weight'), might be substituted for the *dogi*, the inner one being called a *shitagi* and the outer one an *uwagi*. The name *shitagi* was also used as a generic term to describe an under-jacket worn between shirt and corselet by armoured men. Under-jackets were similar in cut to *kimono*, but were narrower, reached only to the knees, and had closer-fitting sleeves and a thick tape or cord round the waist. They were put on with the left side folding over the right, and the waist cord tied at the back.

Over the shirt and under-jacket was worn a loose, wide-sleeved outer robe called a *kimono* (sometimes rendered 'kirimon' by 19th-century writers), which can best be described as resembling an ankle-length dressing-gown. Isabella Bird (1880) tells us that it was 'made of several straight widths of cotton or silk, fifteen inches wide', with sleeves that were 'a width of the same stuff from three to ten feet long, doubled, joined, and attached to a portion of the armhole'. It was worn with the front folded across the chest from left to right and was secured in place by a waistband called an *obi*. The *kimono* of samurai were of light cotton in summer and heavy silk in winter.

The *Tanki Yoriaku*, an 18th-century guide to the wearing of armour, tells us that the *kimono* was sometimes worn under armour in place of a *shitagi*, but points out that since it was really too long it first needed to be put on with the collar pulled above the head: '[then] tie your *obi*

The Tokugawa family mon, *which could be either gold or silver on blue.*

and pull the collar down to the neck; the lower end will then just cover the knees. As regards the sleeves, you can hold them up with buttons, or you can tuck them under the *watakami* [short suspenders attached to the body of the armour across the shoulders]; in the latter case they will take the place of shoulder-pads. A third way is to hold them up by means of *tasuki* [sleeve-cords – see Figure 24].'

The *obi* or waistband was made of white linen, cotton, or thick silk. According to the *Tanki Yoriaku* it was 16 ins (406 mm) wide, folded down to 4 ins (102 mm), and usually either about 6 ft (1.83 m) long and wound round the body twice, or 9 ft (2.74 m) long and wound round the body three times; Diósy, however, says it was 12 ft (3.66 m) long and folded to a width of 2¾ ins (70 mm), while Bird says it was folded to 'the width of the hand'. It was wrapped 'smoothly and evenly' round the waist and tied at the front or very occasionally at the back. Receptacles for a small pipe, tobacco, medicines, and other necessaries were attached to or tucked into the *obi*. The front of the *kimono*, where it bloused over the *obi*, also doubled as a large pocket.

Samurai generally wore a coat and *hakama* 'trousers' over the *kimono*. The coat could be one of two types – either a waist-length *kataginu*, invariably worn in conjunction with *hakama* (the two together constituting a formal costume known as a *kamishino*), or a knee-length *haori*. The *kataginu* was sleeveless, but had distinctive flared shoulders. In earlier times it had invariably been of the same material and colour as the *hakama*, but contemporary prints indicate that by the mid-19th century it was just as often of a completely different colour. Either way, it was always decorated with the wearer's heraldic badge or *mon* between the shoulder-blades and on each breast. These badges were always white when used on clothing – they are variously described by visitors as stencilled, embroidered in white silk, or else left white during the dying process – and were contained within a circle described by J.J. Rein (1884) as 2–3 cm in diameter, and by Diósy (1898) as 'about the size of a shilling', though the latter admits that their exact size was subject to the vagaries of fashion.

The *haori* was worn on less formal and everyday occasions. It was loose-fitting, wide-sleeved, and was secured by a pair of laces tied (or by the middle of the century often buttoned) across the chest. Like the *kataginu* it bore the wearer's *mon*, usually between the shoulders, on each sleeve, and sometimes on each breast. *Mon* were also worn in these positions on many *kimono*, and at the small of the back on *hakama*. The number and position of *mon* on the *haori* was something which, like the size of the *mon*, fluctuated with the passage of time. A *haori* was occasionally worn under armour in place of the under-jacket or *shitagi*.

A sleeveless but otherwise very similar knee-length garment worn over armour was called a *jinbaori* (literally 'war-overcoat'). Made of rich material, this had deep arm-holes often reaching almost to the waist, and a slit at the back so that the wearer's swords could protrude behind. Theoretically it was not worn in action, instead being intended to give the wearer 'a more important appearance' when in camp or when meeting with other samurai. Numerous late Japanese prints nevertheless show samurai fighting in *jinbaori*, though these may not be an entirely trustworthy source.

Though *hakama* is usually translated as 'trousers', this ankle-length garment actually took the form of a divided skirt, described by Bayard Taylor (1853) as 'a petticoat with a seam up the middle'. Until mid-century only samurai were permitted to wear them ('no commoner dare appear in the streets ... in the *hakama*,' observed John Black, visiting in the 1860s), but following the abolition of the 'feudal' system they began to be adopted by other classes too, and according to Isabella Bird were in widespread use by 1880. A shorter, slightly less voluminous variety, generally reaching just 4–5 ins (100–125 mm) below the knees, were called *kobakama*. Whereas *hakama* were for ceremonial wear and were worn over *kimono*, *kobakama* were intended for everyday and combat use and were worn in conjunction with *shitagi*. The *Tanki Yoriaku* recommends *kobakama* for cavalrymen and states that they were worn over the *shitagi*, but for infantry it suggests another type of trousers called *matabiki*, which were instead worn under the *shitagi* (in fact many infantrymen wore *kobakama*). *Matabiki* were long and close-fitting, and were tied with laces below the knees and round the ankles. *Kobakama* were likewise generally tied by laces beneath the knee when worn in conjunction with armour, but seem to have otherwise been more often worn loose by the 1860s. Both *hakama* and *kobakama* had a crotch which hung well down towards the knees, and were open at the sides from the hip to about mid-thigh (see Figures 5 and 12). They were held in place by two pairs of laces, one attached to the front and one to the back, which were tied round the waist. *Hakama* and *haori* were invariably silk, while *kobakama*, though ideally of silk damask lined with cotton, seem to have sometimes been of linen or cotton.

Kobakama and *matabiki* alike were often worn in conjunction with gaiters called *kiahan*, which were preferably of linen but were otherwise cotton. Soldiers described by Edward Belcher in 1845 as having 'tight pantaloons and gaiters' were doubtless wearing *matabiki* and *kiahan*, like, for instance, Figures 7 and 11.

Footwear comprised socks (*tabi*) and sandals or

clogs. The socks reached only to the ankle and had a separate compartment for the big toe, to facilitate the wearing of a traditional type of sandal with a strap that passed between the first two toes. The *Tanki Yoriaku* says that there were two principal varieties of *tabi*: the *kawa-tabi*, made of tanned skin; and the far more common *momen-tabi*, made of quilted cotton cloth. The sources are unanimous that cotton socks were invariably white, dark blue, or black, in that order of popularity. *Kawa-tabi*, however, were often printed with 'fancy patterns'. In the summer a samurai might not wear *tabi* when at home, but he always wore them when he went out.

The sandals were worn principally in dry weather. They were called *zori* or *waraji* (the latter were intended for hard work and hard walking and were bound tightly to the feet, while *zori* were only suited to light work), and were manufactured from a variety of inexpensive materials, including hemp, palm fibres, and cotton thread; but the majority by far were made of plaited rice-straw. None were particularly robust, and they wore out so quickly that journeys were measured by the number of pairs that would be needed. High wooden clogs (*geta*) were substituted in wet weather, but were not worn for travelling. They were of a distinctive design, with a ground clearance of a couple of inches (50 mm) achieved by means of two transverse pieces of wood, one under the toes and the other under the heel.

Samurai costume was completed by the wearing of two swords (see the section on arms below), which were most commonly thrust through the *obi* at the left hip. Samurai alone had the dearly prized right to carry two swords, but some wealthy commoners either purchased, or else earned 'by some meritorious action', permission to carry one.

No jewellery was worn, and except for a large 'basket-like' hat of willow, bamboo cane, or rattan worn when travelling, most men went bareheaded when in civilian attire, protecting their heads from the sun when necessary by means of a fan or a large paper parasol. However, Tilley tells us that 'in the north, where the winters are often severe, they muffle up their heads in a cloth, so that only the nose and eyes are visible.'

As regards the colours of outer clothing amongst samurai, the closing decades of the Edo period are described by Helen Minnich (1963) as having been distinguished by 'a seesawing between extravagant debauchery and strict sumptuary laws'. In the 19th century this resulted in a short period of lavish costume (called the Bunka-Bunsei era, 1804–29) being followed at the beginning of the 1830s by severe austerity in the form of the so-called 'Tempo Reformation', which saw the manufacture, sale, and wearing of silk prohibited, and government seizure and destruction of garments considered offensively decorative. Such draconian measures inevitably met with considerable public opposition, and the regulations were swiftly repealed. Even so, the costume of Japanese men never thereafter regained its former exuberance, and most 19th-century Western travellers describe the samurai as wearing only 'sombre' or 'quiet' colours, of dark shades in winter but lighter ones in summer. *Kimono* were most often some dull shade of blue, grey, brown, or black – Belcher, for instance, wrote of those he saw in 1845 that, though blue was 'the chief and favourite colour', others were 'light black' or a buff colour. However, he adds that some were 'chequered black and white, some striped [in 'very narrow vertical stripes divided by black lines' according to Diósy], others flowered, many quite plain, some marked with characters on the back, others with various circles and mysterious hieroglyphic devices.'

The *haori* was invariably black in winter, but often of some lighter colour in summer. Its silk lining was what Diósy calls 'some well-chosen colour, such as russet-brown or old gold, with a beautifully woven pattern.' *Hakama* were usually 'sober-coloured', Diósy describing them as 'probably of some bluish-grey tint with narrow vertical stripes', but some were more colourful – in 1860, for instance, Barrington de Fonblanque saw samurai officials wearing 'wide petticoat trowsers' that were 'richly brocaded in gold and colours'. Tilley says that the colour of *hakama* and 'under garments' (by which he appears to mean under-jackets) depended on the status of the wearer.

Needless to say, the costume of commoners was less comprehensive than that of samurai and was made of cheaper materials. In summer labourers and peasants at work in the fields wore just a loincloth (*shita-obi*), or at most a smock-like hemp or cotton *kimono* called a *shirushi-banten* reaching only as far as the calves, plus an *obi* and a pair of *waraji* sandals. In addition a blue cotton kerchief (*hachimaki*) was often wrapped once or twice round the forehead and tied at the back of the head, to stop sweat from running into the eyes. Occasionally 'tolerably close fitting trousers' (*momohiki*) and gaiters were also worn, 'by way of protection against leeches in the rice-fields, or mosquitoes in the forest', but otherwise these, and a shirt or under-jacket, were only donned at the onset of winter. The middle classes wore trousers and under-jacket all year round, plus socks.

Until at least the 1870s peasant *kimono*, shirts, under-jackets, and trousers alike seem to have been almost invariably what Rein calls 'a dirty blue', obtained by means of a locally-produced indigo dye, but prints often depict them white, and in 1895 Trumbull White describes their trousers as 'made of checked cloth'. The *shirushi-banten* was usually marked on the back with either a *mon* or a Chinese character to identify the wearer's employer.[50]

Basil Chamberlain (1890) tells us that 'travellers of the middle and lower classes' could be distinguished by wearing their *kimono* 'lifted up and shoved into the sash behind', as well as by 'silk drawers' called *patchi*, mittens or hand-protectors called *tekko*, and a cape called a *kappa* ('a corruption of the Spanish *capa*').

Westernisation

Western-style military dress had been adopted by elements of the *bakufu* army even before the collapse of the Tokugawa shogunate in 1868, and this proved to be the narrow end of a wedge that was hammered swiftly home during the early stages of the Meiji Restoration. The very first dress regulations of the new Meiji army opted for entirely Western-style uniforms, and in 1872 'foreign' civilian costume was adopted as court dress and was ordered to be worn by most government departments and on all official occasions. George Sansom (1950) observes that this abolition of flowing robes reflected the change from a 'leisurely, processional life' to the 'busy, practical' one that came with modernisation. However, it generally

Satsuma soldiers photographed c.1868. Note that despite their admittedly hybrid Western dress, only one (at the extreme left) has as yet adopted a Western-style haircut.

affected only the upper, ex-samurai classes of society, and such others as came into regular direct or indirect contact with Westerners – i.e., merchants, bankers, students, and the like – and outside of government and court circles changes did not occur overnight even here. Instead, for the next few years a strange melange of foreign and Japanese costume generally prevailed, including *kimono* worn with trousers and boots; frock-coats or morning coats worn with *kobakama*; Western suits worn with *obi* and swords; and so on.

A further break with the past came when the wearing of swords was banned in March 1876 (it had been optional since the autumn of 1871), and this gave added impetus to the adoption of Western dress, so that by the beginning of the 1880s traditional Japanese costume was generally found only amongst the urban working class, the rural peasantry, and a few remaining unreconstructed or 'unenlightened' (as contemporary Japanese referred to them) ex-samurai who clung doggedly to the old ways. The only reason that traditional dress had not been extinguished entirely by the end of the century, and therefore survives to the present day, seems to have been the indignation felt at the West's refusal in 1887 to renegotiate the extraterritorial privileges wrung from Japan under duress back in the 1850s; this, Diósy reports, 'caused a sudden return to many of the old habits and customs.' Starting in 1896 these privileges were gradually relinquished by the Western Powers, but they left behind a sour aftertaste that was to prove but the first step along an increasingly bitter road of resentment and misunderstanding that, over the next few decades, would utterly alienate Japan.

ARMS

Pre-modernisation

Any discussion of Japanese weapons has to begin with their swords. As we have already seen, samurai alone had the right to bear two of these, which constituted what was collectively referred to as a *daisho*, meaning a pair of swords with matching mounts. Both swords were single-edged. The longer of them (the *dai-to*) was the fighting sword, by now usually of a type called a *katana* but in the 18th century still sometimes a *tachi* (a slung sword) or some other variety. These various types of long sword differed fundamentally only in their mounts, having virtually identical blades which were most often somewhere between 26–30 ins (0.66–0.76 m) in length, but might occasionally – in the case of *tachi* – be 33 ins (0.84 m) or more.

Since the 16th century the most popular variety

had been the *uchigatana* or *katana koshirae*. This constituted what is today considered the archetypal Japanese sword. It had a slightly curved blade and a hilt long enough to be grasped in both hands, which was the manner in which Japanese long swords were customarily wielded. The grip was wrapped in coloured silk or thread, with the owner's *mon* or some other device 'beautifully wrought or inlaid in gold and steel under the silken meshes'. The iron guard (*tsuba*) was also usually exquisitely decorated.

The *daisho*'s shorter sword (*sho-to*) was called a *wakizashi*. Used as a supplementary weapon or, more famously, to commit ritual suicide, this averaged some 16–20 ins (0.41–0.51 m). A shorter dagger, either a *tanto* or an *aikuchi*, might be substituted, most of these averaging only 11–15 ins (0.28–0.38 m). Some, however, were actually slightly longer than the *wakizashi*, from which they could nevertheless be differentiated by the style of their mounts. The *Tanki Yoriaku* says that 'the limits of length for the *tanto* are 1 *shaku* 3 *sun* to 1 *shaku* 5 *sun*', which is equivalent to 15.5–17.9 ins (0.39–0.45 m). Because it invariably accompanied its owner into a house (unlike the *katana*, which etiquette required be left at the door), the short sword was often far more ornately decorated than its longer counterpart.

Another type of dagger that might be carried by a samurai was called a *yoroi toshi*. This most often had a blade of some 7½ *sun* (about 9 ins/0.23 m), but could be up to 10 *sun* (12 ins/0.31 m). It was designed to cut through armour, and, the *Tanki Yoriaku* tells us, 'was much used in olden time, and it is wise to carry it even at present.' Because it was carried at the right hip it was nicknamed *metezashi* or 'right-side wear', to distinguish it from the *daisho* carried at the left hip.

Other varieties of sword included the *chisa katana*, basically a short *katana* with a blade of about 18–24 ins (0.46–0.61 m) and a proportionately smaller hilt that could only be held in one hand. By the 19th century such weapons were made largely for such non-samurai elements of society – mostly merchants and rich peasants – as were permitted to carry a single sword. At the other end of the spectrum, the very longest type of sword likely to be carried by a samurai was the *nodachi* (literally 'field sword'), described as 'a very long and heavy sword ... [used] by very strong men.' Being as much as 25% longer than a conventional *katana*, it was not carried at the hip but was instead slung diagonally across the back 'with a narrow belt girdled from the left shoulder to the right side of the waist, so that the hilt will be over the left shoulder and the edge of the blade will be to the left.'

Swords manufactured during the last stages of the Edo period (from the 1780s on) and in the early Meiji period were referred to as *shinshinto* ('very new swords'), and were recognisable by their wider blade, its relatively long *kissaki* or point, and its highly polished, almost mirror-like finish. These were nevertheless relatively heavy, unsophisticated weapons compared to those produced in earlier times. They were joined, in the immediate pre-Restoration period, by swords somewhat inaccurately described as *han-dachi* ('half-*tachi*'), which, being mass-produced for issue to the soldiers of clan armies opposed to the *bakufu*, were nicknamed *kinno-to* ('Loyalist swords'). But a large proportion of the swords still found in use in the 19th century were actually ancient family heirlooms of singular quality, which, 'heavy, and sharp as razors,' as Henry Tilley puts it, could 'sever all they come in contact with, and the first blow is pretty sure to disable, if not to kill outright.'

Scabbards, called *saya*, were almost always made of wood, or at the very least lined with it even where the outer surface was of metal. They were usually lacquered and highly polished – most often black but sometimes red or some other colour – and were often decorated with inlaid gold or silver patterns and figures, which might include the owner's *mon*. However, in describing substantial gatherings of troops seen in the 1850s and 1860s Western visitors often mention seeing sword scabbards covered in plain shagreen, which were presumably either owned by *ashigaru* and similar lower-ranking samurai, or else were those commonly substituted for the more ornate variety when on campaign. Wealthy samurai at least quite often had several different scabbards for different occasions, including a relatively plain one with simple mounts for everyday wear, another sometimes covered with iron for use in battle, and one or more ornate examples for ceremonial occasions.

Daisho scabbards were worn thrust through the *obi* at the left hip. In order to prevent them from slipping through, each scabbard had a small protrusion (the *kurikata*) on one side, through which a flat, coloured silk cord (the *sageo*) might be passed as an additional means of securing it to the belt. The *wakizashi* scabbard (and very occasionally the *katana* scabbard) might also have a slot near the top designed to house either a small knife (called a *go-gatana*) or a skewer (*kogai*, the precise function of which appears to have been forgotten). Foreigners noted that a pair of chopsticks was also frequently accommodated here, which suggests that the *kogai* may have been intended as an eating utensil.

Other than swords, other traditional samurai weapons still in general use consisted predominantly of spears, polearms, bows, and matchlocks. Edward Barrington de Fonblanque also mentions seeing crossbows being carried by a *daimyo*'s escort in February 1860. Spears (*yari*), which in Japan were designed to cut as well as thrust, still featured prominently amongst the armament of *bakufu* forces as late as 1866–68, but proved far more tiring to use than firearms, and consequently – despite the recorded effectiveness of spearmen in hand-to-hand combat during the Boshin War – they contributed adversely to the ability of shogunate forces to maintain a fight. Spears for close-quarter fighting were about 7 ft long (2.13 m) with 6–12-inch (0.15–0.30 m) blades, but others were some 10–12 ft long (3.05–3.66 m) with blades of 18 ins (0.46 m) or more. Some blades had a substantial crossbar just above the socket, which could be used to parry sword-blows or to catch hold of an enemy's armour or clothes and yank him to the ground.

The most popular polearm was the *naginata*, which had a long curved blade shaped much like a sword, and a lacquered shaft. Though, by the 19th century, it was reputedly limited largely to ceremonial use, it is nevertheless shown being used in combat in contemporary pictures of the rebellions that punctuated the period 1874–77. Lighter varieties of the *naginata* were sometimes called 'women's spears' because women were taught to use them for exercise and self-defence (see, for example, Figure 53). Another variant was the *nagamaki*, which was similar but had a less curved blade that resembled a sword

Emotive photograph of a samurai, apparently produced for the Western tourist trade in the second half of the century but clearly taken before the traditional 'samurai' hairstyle had been largely abandoned in the 1870s.

even more closely. Spears and *naginata* alike were always carried with their blades sheathed when not in use, these sheaths being lacquered, most often black or red, and sometimes ornately decorated.

19th-century Japanese war bows (*yumi*) were either plain wood self bows (*maru-ki*) or, more usually, of 'built' construction, being made either entirely out of bamboo laminates glued together, or else from a combination of bamboo strips glued to a mulberry, sumac, or cherry wood core, bound at intervals with rattan, lacquered, and then elaborately decorated if intended for ceremonial use but left plain black if meant to be used in battle. They were invariably exceptionally long. Examples seen in temples by Western visitors measured anywhere between 7ft 3 ins and 8 ft 9 ins (2.21–2.67 m), but these were historical weapons not necessarily intended for practical use; in the 19th century 7 ft to 7 ft 2 ins (2.13–2.18 m) seems to have been more usual, with a few reaching 7½ ft (2.29 m). They were nearly uniform in section from one end to the other, and the grip, of rattan and leather, was set so far below the centre point that the lower arm was only half the length of the upper, thus enabling the bow to be used from horseback or from a kneeling position. There were also some considerably smaller composite bows, measuring only about 3 ft (0.91 m). These were apparently intended for self-defence when travelling in a litter.

War bows were drawn back well behind the ear, so that their arrows had to be correspondingly long, most measuring some 40 ins (1.01 m) overall. These were made of bamboo, usually with a small head and a flight consisting of three or very occasionally four (for arrows with heavier heads) crane, eagle, hawk, or pheasant's tail feathers. Most arrows were relatively heavy, and some of those with more substantial heads weighed up to half a pound (227 gm). They were kept in various types of quiver. That in most widespread use was the *ebira*, a sort of open rack arrangement, which held the arrows apart in order to protect their feathers from damage. Others, the *yadzutsu* and *utsubo*, took the form of a closed container, which completely protected the arrows from rain but were impractical for battlefield use. *Ebira* varied considerably in size and design, but fundamentally comprised a shallow open box (more often than not decorated with its owner's *mon*) divided into compartments by a series of bars to accommodate the arrow heads, with an open frame rising from the back to which the shafts were loosely secured by means of a cord. Normally one quiver (of a type which the *Tanki Yoriaku* calls a *shiko*) was carried at the right hip, while another, the *ebira*, was carried over the left shoulder.

Japanese bows could shoot their heavy arrows to a maximum effective range of about 130 yds (120 m), using a very flat trajectory, and in skilled hands could fire one aimed arrow approximately every six seconds. They remained in use on the battlefield well into the 1860s. At least one of the five British soldiers killed in the attack on Shimonoseki in 1864 was slain by an arrow, and bows and arrows were amongst the weapons captured there.

Japanese firearms were collectively referred to as *tanegashima* or *teppo*. Their matchlocks were robust weapons with round or octagonal barrels that averaged some 3 ft (0.91 m) in length. They had a bore of about 0.5–0.8 ins (125–200 mm), and a maximum range of as much as 300 yds (275 m) but an effective accurate range of only 50 yds (45 m). The barrel was invariably fitted with both a foresight and a backsight. It was fired by means of a trigger-operated, spring-loaded serpentine arrangement that released a smouldering match into a pan of priming powder on the right-hand side of the barrel. As in China, the stock's slightly curved grip was held against the cheek rather than braced against the shoulder, and the recoil was absorbed by letting the musket push the hand and grip back and down towards the crook of the arm. A wooden ramrod was housed in the stock for reloading, a procedure which modern tests indicate may have taken as long as two minutes but probably took less than a minute when carried out by an experienced musketeer. A few weapons had their reddish oak stocks decorated with brass inlay, and most had their barrels either lacquered or, on better quality pieces, engraved and decorated ('overlaid') in gold, silver, brass, or copper.

Until the 19th century, the last major Japanese battle in which firearms had played a significant part had been at Hara Castle as far back as 1638, during the Shimabara Rebellion. Since then there had been no wars, Japan had virtually cut itself off from the outside world, and the further development of firearms had been proscribed. Consequently most Japanese living in 1800 had never even seen a firearm,[51] and in all likelihood there were less than 200,000 in the entire country – about the same number as when Tokugawa Ieyasu had seized power back in 1603. This figure only began to increase after Japanese ports were opened to foreign trade in the mid-1850s.

At the beginning of the century Japanese

firearms still consisted almost exclusively of matchlocks (*hinawaju*), since the production of wheellocks and, later, flintlocks had been actively discouraged by the government, which was not eager to see a proliferation of more advanced firearms that might upset the delicate balance of power which maintained the fragile peace between the clans and kept the Tokugawa shoguns in power. A handful of enlightened individuals nevertheless experimented with imported Dutch muskets during the first few decades of the century and gradually wore down official resistance to their introduction, so that when Perry's 'black ships' arrived in 1853 S. Wells Williams was able to report seeing 'many files' of infantrymen armed with 'muskets with bayonets' amongst the troops assembled at Kurihama. Writing at the time, however, Takashima Shuhan – who had once been imprisoned for advocating the adoption of modern firearms – felt compelled to observe that though every single Western soldier possessed a gun, there were as few as 30 firearms to every 1,000 Japanese soldiers.

Perry's arrival swept away any remaining doubts the *bakufu* may have harboured regarding the wisdom of modernising its armed forces, by forcing it to grudgingly recognise just how far behind its military technology had fallen. A concerted effort to acquire substantial quantities of Western firearms ensued, though most of the earliest shipments foisted upon the Japanese (largely by unscrupulous Dutch and American traders) proved to be obsolete and worn-out muskets of minimal technical merit, most of which had seen at least 20 years' hard service. In 1855, for instance, a single American brig sold the Japanese government 10,000 antiquated flintlocks for as much as $5 apiece.[52] However, it didn't take astute reformers long to realise that much better weapons were available, and by 1862 the *bakufu*, followed within two years by such richer clans as Satsuma, Choshu, and Hizen, had started buying in sizeable quantities of Minié rifles (which they called *Minieru*).

The *bakufu* used these imports to arm its regular infantry (the *hohei*). However, the clan contingents which constituted the larger part of its armed forces stubbornly struggled on with their ancient matchlocks – many of which were 200–300 years old – even as late as 1865, when, eyewitness John Black tells us, 'many of the samurai to whom rifles were offered, refused to use them, or to undergo the new drill'. By contrast, every last Choshu *shotai* was armed entirely with rifles by this date, many of them Miniés, and when they fought the *bakufu* in 1866 their riflemen seriously outranged the latter's antiquated firearms, inflicting such dreadful casualties that the shogunate troops eventually refused to approach the Choshu positions. Though the *bakufu* had 40,000 Chassepot bolt-action breech-loaders on order from France by May 1867, only 3,000 of these at best, and possibly no more than 775, had been supplied by the end of the year, thereby enabling the Loyalist clans to retain their arms advantage throughout the ensuing Boshin War.

The fact that matchlocks made as far back as the 16th or 17th century were still in working order in the mid-19th nevertheless demonstrates how remarkably well they were constructed. Incredibly, in the 1850s and 1860s many were actually modernised into percussion firearms for service in the late Tokugawa and early Meiji regular armies, either by simply strengthening the spring and screwing a nipple into the pan cover, or by substituting an imported Western percussion lock. Even later, during the Sino-Japanese War of 1894–95, several thousand were upgraded a second time by conversion into bolt-action rifles. Perrin (1979) records that several such 'twice-retooled *tanegashima*' survive to the present day with barrels bearing 17th-century dates and makers' marks.

Armour

At the beginning of the century every Japanese fighting man theoretically still wore armour, though its quantity and quality were governed by either his own affluence or that of the *daimyo* who equipped him. However, since the 17th century there had been little opportunity to test it in the field, and gradually practicality had been sacrificed in favour of fashion, as armour became more a statement of wealth and an object of decoration than a means of personal protection. During the 18th century there was a revival of interest in the closely-laced lamellar armour that had been popular as far back as the Heian and Kamakura periods (794–1333), and superbly ornate facsimile *o-yoroi* and *do-maru* armours, as they were called, copied from celebrated examples preserved in Japanese temples, were manufactured to meet the demand. Some actually incorporated surviving pieces dating back to the 13th–16th centuries, often modified or redecorated to suit contemporary tastes. Consequently late Tokugawa armour didn't only *look* archaic, even by Japanese standards; some of it actually was.

However, failure to understand certain features of these early armours, and the frequent substitution of hardened leather and soft iron for the steel used in the originals, meant that the majority of such copies were – like the embossed armours (*uichidashi-do*) that had become enormously popular at much the same time – at best impractical and at worst dangerously inefficient, even though the technical expertise involved in their production remained of the very highest order. This revivalist trend continued into the period under review, barely acknowledging in passing a fleeting return, at the beginning of the century, to more utilitarian armour based on styles worn during the Momoyama period (1573–1603), when one-piece plate corselets called *tosei-do* ('modern armour') had first been introduced as a defence against firearms.

Though Japanese armour looked bizarre to visitors it was extraordinarily light compared to that once worn in the West. A complete laced armour weighed by Matthew Garbutt (1913), very similar to that shown in the sequence of drawings reproduced on the following pages, was just 20 lbs (9.1 kg), plus 7 lbs (3.2 kg) for the helmet (though Garbutt conceded that he had also seen helmets which alone probably weighed as much as 15 lbs/6.8 kg). It was therefore possible for an armoured samurai to run, sit, and jump without any difficulty whatsoever.

A significant quantity of armour was still being worn as late as the Boshin War of 1868–69, but following the Meiji Restoration and the dismantling of the 'feudal' system its manufacture declined rapidly, and within a few years only presentation suits were being made. A small amount of armour was still being manufactured as late as 1940, but for the majority of armourers – except for the few lucky enough to get work restoring or repairing

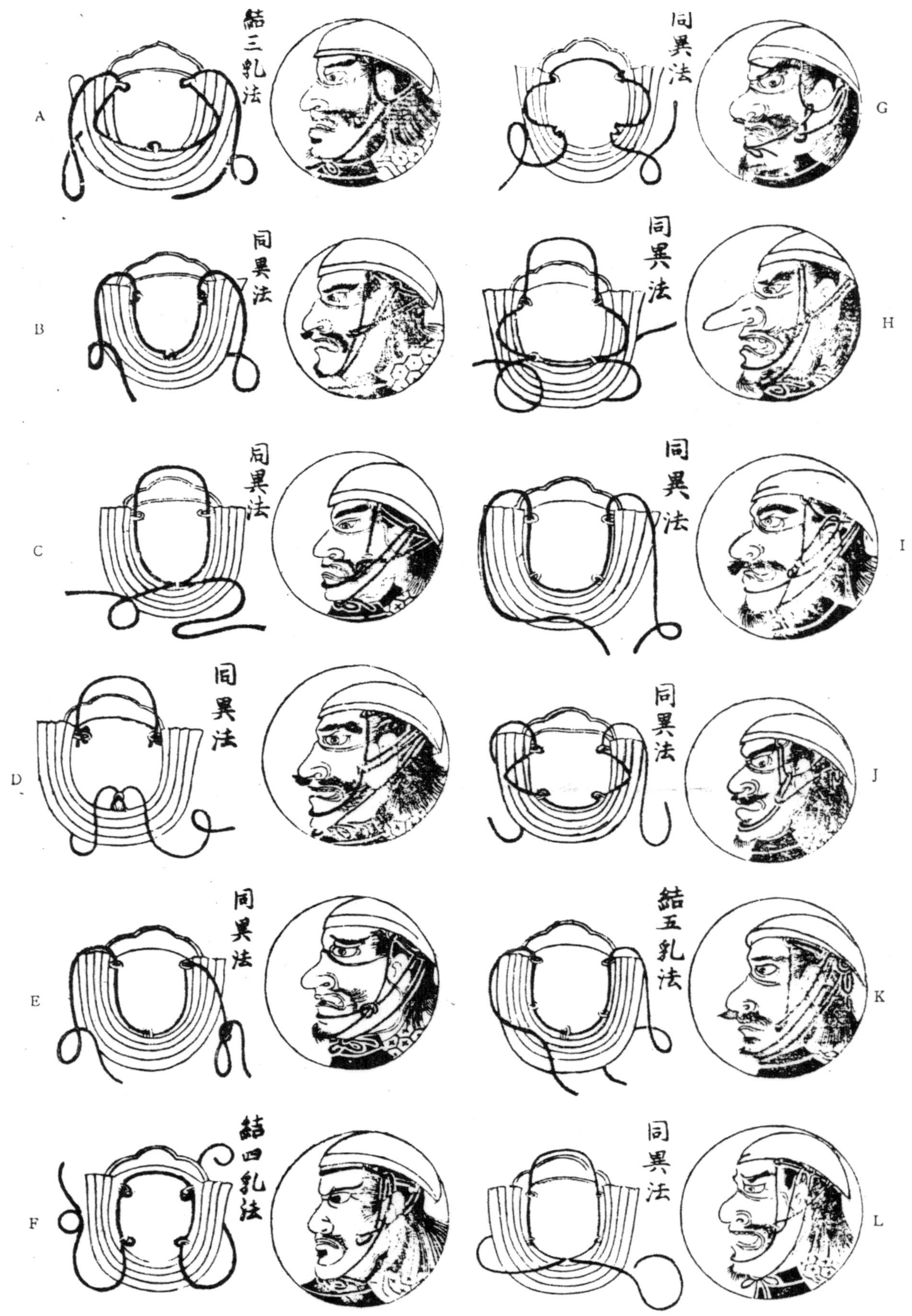

The many different methods of tying on a Japanese helmet, from the Tanki Yoriaku. *The helmets are viewed from underneath on the left, in order to show how the laces were fed through their retaining rings.*

結褌帯
裉襯衣
紮衣帯
服股衣
穿脚絆
履韈子
就草鞋
着臑當

museum pieces – the end of the Tokugawa shogunate meant the end of the road. The very last occasions on which armour is known to have been worn on a Japanese battlefield were during the Hagi Rebellion of 1876 and the Satsuma Rebellion of 1877, when reactionary elements of the Choshu and Satsuma clans donned their 'beetle-headed iron helmets and old armour made of steel and paper laced with silk' one final time.

The best way to understand Japanese armour of the late Edo period is to follow the sequence in which a samurai put it on, as depicted in the 18th-century *Tanki Yoriaku* (translated by Garbutt in 1913). Each of the pictures in this manual shows an item of dress or equipment, and how it was worn. Needless to say, what follows is not an exhaustive description of every kind of body-defence that might have been found in 18th and 19th-century Japan, but it does provide a basic outline of the assorted elements that went to make up a typical late Edo period armour.

Page 64

Top left: This nappy-like piece of underwear is the *fundoshi*, already mentioned on p.56. The *Tanki Yoriaku* says that 'the best material for this is white linen or white cotton. Silk crepe may be used according to one's taste, but plain silk is not suitable. In winter it may be lined with similar material, but in other seasons it is always single. Both ends [i.e., the front and back] are hemmed to put cords through; one of the cords forms a loop to suspend the front end from the neck, and the other secures the back by being tied in front. The length of the *fundoshi* is about five *shaku* [59.7 ins/1.52 m].' Note, incidentally, that the samurai depicted in these drawings has his hair loose, since it was not possible – or at least, was not comfortable – to have it tied up into the elaborate *magé* or queue when wearing a helmet.

Top right: These two items are the *shitagi* and the *obi*. The *shitagi*, it will be remembered, was a garment worn by an armoured man beneath his corselet and usually over an undershirt (not worn here). We are told that there were several different styles, but the anonymous author of the *Tanki Yoriaku* recommends the best type to be 'just about the same as an ordinary *kimono* with very narrow sleeves, a little shorter in length and narrower in width, with a few buttons on the breast, and a thick tape or cord round the waist. It should be put on as though it were a *kimono*, the left hand being first put into its sleeve and then the right, the breast being then buttoned and the waist cord finally tied at the back.' An ordinary *kimono* or a *haori* could be worn in place of the *shitagi*. Whatever form the *shitagi* took, however, it was advantageous to wear an *obi* or waistband with it 'because the *obi* will support the lower end of the *do* [corselet] and thus reduce the weight upon the shoulders.' The *obi* was ideally white linen or white cotton rather than silk. Its length depended upon the size of the wearer, 'whether he is fat or thin', but as we have already seen it was most often either 6 ft (1.83 m) wound twice around the body or 9 ft (2.74 m) wound thrice.

From other sources we know that an additional set of garments, the *yoroi hitatare* or 'armour robe', might be worn over the *shitagi*. This consisted of a short, baggy-sleeved *kimono* and matching *hakama* trousers, usually made of rich brocade but often of hemp. Like much late Edo period armour, the *hitatare* was a revival from mediaeval times, and was intended to be worn with facsimile armour copied from the same epoch.

Middle left: Here we see the samurai donning his *kobakama* or short trousers, sometimes called *kesho-bakama*. 'There are a few different styles,' says the *Tanki Yoriaku*, 'generally a little narrower than ordinary *hakama*, and of such a length as will reach about four or five inches [102–127 mm] below the knees.' Two pairs of cords, one at the back and one at the front, were both tied in front, leaving a deep vent at each hip.

Middle right: Socks (*tabi*) and gaiters (*kiahan*). As well as the principal varieties of *tabi* already mentioned – the *kawa-tabi* or tanned skin socks and *momen-tabi* or cotton cloth socks – there were also *momi-tabi* ('red silk socks'), described as very soft but 'used only by effeminate persons.' Quilted cotton *tabi* were those generally used. *Kawa-tabi* were not considered ideal for mounted men, while *tabi* without soles were recommended for fighting on foot. Linen was considered to be the best material for gaiters, but cotton cloth could also be used, 'lined or unlined according to season, but unlined ones are always preferable.' Gaiters were held in place by means of laces at the top and bottom, tied on the inside of the leg.

Bottom left: There were various ways of arranging the cords used to tie on the *waraji* or sandals, but the *Tanki Yoriaku* comments on the importance of using an 'extra tie across the instep, as it is a great help in marching on steep, snowy, or muddy roads, and in crossing swamps or rivers ... An extra pair of sandals must be carried at your waist; this is quite as important a thing as carrying provisions.' An earlier type of samurai footwear consisted of bearskin shoes called *tsurumaki*. Though these had long since been generally abandoned in favour of sandals they were revived in the late Edo period and can be found accompanying armours produced as late as the mid-19th century – they are worn, for instance, by Figures 1 and 2. Soft boots called *kusari-no-tabi*, of which the uppers were covered with either metal plates or mail, might also be found.

Bottom right: Next the *suneate* or greaves were put on. The picture shows a very popular type consisting of narrow vertical plates joined together by hinges or mail and usually, but not always, lined with cloth. In order to prevent chafing when on horseback a leather guard was always fixed to the inner side at the point which came into contact with the stirrup. Solid plate *suneate* had been abandoned in mediaeval times as 'interfering with free movement'. At the top of the *suneate* there was always a rounded extension known as a *tateage* to protect the knee. Sometimes made up of three separate parts for greater flexibility, this was most often made of padded brigandine armour (*kikko*), which comprised small hexagonal iron, steel, or hardened leather plates sandwiched between layers of quilted cloth that were stitched together following the outline of the plates.

Page 67

Top left: The *suneate* were followed by thigh protectors called *haidate* ('girt shields'), which most often took the form of a split leather or heavy brocade apron in which the lower part was covered with either mail or small overlapping metal or leather lamellae (*sane*), or sometimes a combination of all three. See the description of his *do* or corselet below for details of Japanese lamellar armour. The upper part of the *haidate* didn't need to be armoured because it was covered by the skirt of the corselet. The cord at the top edge was used to secure the apron in place by being passed right round the waist and tied in front. Some had additional cords at the bottom enabling the flaps to be tied close to the legs.

Top right: *Yugake* were gauntlets (actually archer's gloves) made of tanned leather, sometimes with a small, usually heart-shaped hole in the centre of the palm for ventilation, to prevent the hand from getting too sweaty. The second and third fingers were usually made of softer leather than the rest of the glove and were of a different colour. Some archer's gloves were lined with mail on the back of both the hand and the cuff.

Middle left: Armoured sleeves (*kote*) consisted of a fabric foundation, most often of padded silk brocade, covered with mail, brigandine, or small metal plates. They came in a wide variety of forms, the type depicted here, with the two sleeves joined together, being known as *aigote*. Most *kote* ended in plate half-gauntlets (*tekko*) which covered just the thumb and the back of the hand. Though rare, separate gauntlets of mail and/or articulated plates were also sometimes worn. Once the sleeves had been pulled onto the arms, the *aigote*'s laces were fastened across the chest. Some armoured sleeves called *kigote* incorporated in addition a padded collar (*erisuwari*), shoulder-pads (*kata-ate*), and armpit protectors (*wakibiki*). The *Tanki Yoriaku* says that there were several different kinds of *kote* which didn't differ greatly from one another, but that the type called *yumigote* or *igote* was specifically intended for archers, even though it was also possible to shoot while wearing an ordinary *kote*.

Middle right: This is the *wakibiki* mentioned in the preceding paragraph. As with most other elements of a Japanese armour, the *wakibiki* came in a variety of types, including *kusari-wakibiki* (which were made of mail), *botan-gake* (which were fastened with buttons), *kohaze-gake* (fastened with hooks), and *himo-tsuki* (fastened with laces).

Bottom left: This is the *do* or corselet, which was the central and most important part of any Japanese armour. It consisted of a back plate, a breastplate, epaulettes (*kohire*), shoulder-straps (*watagami*), and usually a skirt piece made of several individual flaps called a *kusazuri*, though some corselets had a separate detachable skirt called a *gessan*. If the corselet opened at the side it was termed a *do-maru*, and if at the back a *haramaki-do*.

The specific variety depicted here is one of the mediaeval types revived during the 18th century. It was constructed from small overlapping metal or leather lamellae, or more often a mixture of the two with the metal lamellae being used for those areas in need of the greatest amount of protection (generally the front and the left side). The lamellae were punched with a series of small holes, and were bound tightly together in horizontal rows by means of a leather thong passed through the lower group of holes. These horizontal rows were next bound to each other vertically, overlapping upwards (creating what several experts have succinctly described as 'a sort of Venetian blind appearance'), by means of a prodigious amount of elaborate and colourful silk braid lacing passed through the upper group of holes. The closeness of this lacing appears to have varied according to the owner's wealth and status – basically as his rank got higher, so the lacing became closer. Lamellar construction of this type was used for many parts of a Japanese armour, even where the *do* itself was made of plate, including the *kusazuri* or corselet skirt (often referred to in Western sources as 'tassets'), the thigh-pieces, the *sode* or shoulder-defences, and the helmet neckguard.

Armour which used a large quantity of lacing was repeatedly condemned in 18th–19th-century sources, not least because the laces trapped the points of lances and arrows and prevented them from glancing off. (Embossed armour was condemned for the same reason.) Sakakibara Kozan, who wrote a book on armour published posthumously in 1800, adds that abundantly laced armour became very heavy when soaked with water, and dried very slowly, 'so that in summer the weight is oppressive and in winter the whole may freeze'. The volume of lacing also made it virtually impossible to keep such armour clean.

On the back of the *do* there was a socket at waist level, and between the shoulder-blades a hinged bridge-piece ending in a ring. These were used to hold the staff of a small rectangular banner called a *sashimono*, which was generally made of silk and measured 3 *shaku* deep by 1 *shaku* wide (roughly 3 ft by 1 ft or 0.91 by 0.31 m). The *sashimono* could carry an infinite number of devices, but most often bore a family or clan *mon*. The *Tanki Yoriaku* says that it was replaced 'in night attacks, ambushes, sea fights, and on stormy days' by a *sode-jirushi* (shoulder badge) and/or a *kasa-jirushi* (helmet badge), for which see the caption to Figures 1–4.

Bottom right: Another linen or cotton waistband, properly called an *uwa-obi*, was bound round the outside of the corselet and tied in front. As with the inner *obi*, this was wound twice or thrice around the body, its length therefore being dictated by the girth of the wearer.

Page 68

Top left: Here the samurai is putting on his *sode* or shoulder plates, most of which were of relatively modest dimensions intended to protect the gap between the top of the armoured sleeves and the *watagami* or shoulder straps, to which they were fastened by means of hooks. Though the picture shows them under the *kohire* or epaulettes, Sakakibara Kozan says that this is incorrect, and that they were supposed to be worn over the epaulettes. Larger shoulder plates called *o-sode* or *chu-sode* were worn only by high-ranking officers.

Top right: Next the samurai put on his characteristic two swords. There were many different ways of carrying these, most of which involved pushing them between the folds of the *uwa-obi* in various ways, and further securing them either to the waistband or to each other by means of the *sageo* (silk cords) attached to their scabbards. The long sword might also be tied to a looped leather pad called a *koshiate*, suspended at the left hip from a cord tied at the right side.

Middle left: The throat was protected by means of a U-shaped plate either tied with laces or secured with a clasp at the back of the neck, from which a series of laced horizontal plates was suspended. There were various different types, but the *Tanki Yoriaku* says that

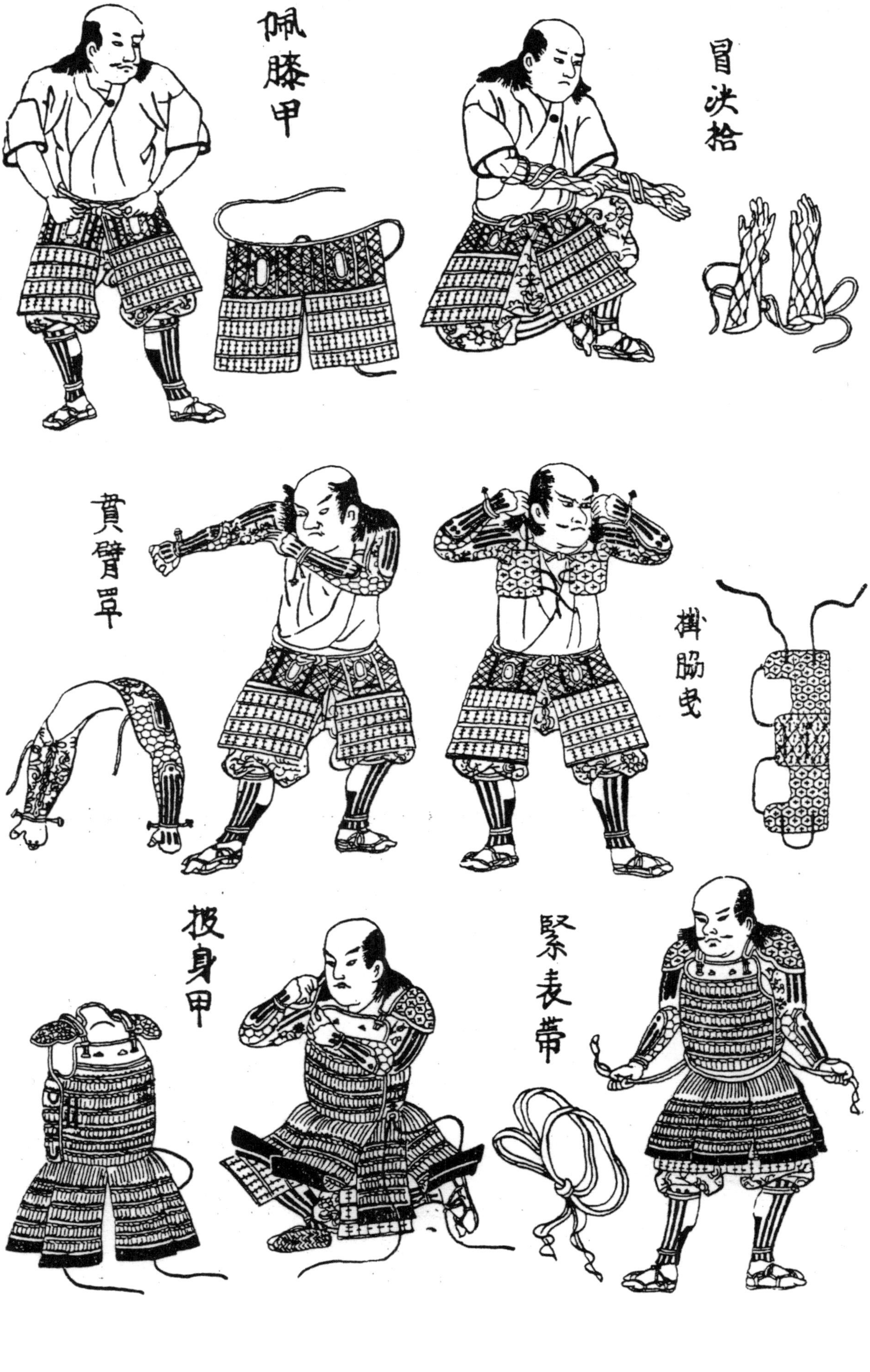
佩膝甲
冒決拾
貫臂罩
掛脇曳
披身甲
緊表帯

繋肩罩
帯两刀
旋喉輪
纏顱巻
裝頬當
戴頭盔

'they are all called *nodowa* ... The *tentsuki* style is the most popular. The *meguriwa*, *eriwa*, and *manju* are the latest designs.' The presence of a *nodowa* here is actually a good example of the failure of Edo period armourers to understand the earlier styles of armour that they were copying. The *nodowa* had originally been worn in conjunction with a separate facemask, but since later masks generally included a throat guard of their own (called a *yodarekake* or 'baby's bib') it was now in effect redundant. In this series of drawings, however, *nodowa* and facemask with 'bib' are worn together.

Middle right: This is the *hachimaki* or headscarf, which was 'put around the head so as to make a padding to receive the helmet. The best material is cotton cloth of either light blue or *kaki* [reddish yellow] colour; its length is about five *shaku* [59.7 ins/1.52 m]. To put the *hachimaki* on, undo your hair and comb it backwards and ... wind [the headcloth] round the head and tuck the ends between the folds.' A skull-cap called a *momi zukin* or *asano zukin* could be worn in place of the headscarf.

Bottom left: The steel or, very occasionally, leather facemask came in several different forms, of which the most commonly encountered were:

– the *somen* ('all-covering mask'), which protected the whole face;

– the *mempo* ('face cheek', also frequently found spelt *menpo*, *menbo*, and *membo*), a half-mask which covered everything below the eyes (this is the variety shown in the picture);

– the *hoate* ('cheek protection'), which covered just the chin and the cheeks;

– *hoate* variants with smaller cheek-guards, known as *hanbo* or *hambo* ('half cheek') and *sarubo* ('monkey cheek');

– and the *tsubamebo* or *tsubamegata* ('swallow cheek' or 'swallow pattern'), which only protected the jawline and the chin.

The *Tanki Yoriaku* says that 'the first and last are not good, because the one is over complete and the other too much abridged.' A sixth, rarely seen variety, the *happuri*, protected only the forehead and the cheeks, George Stone (1934) observing that 'it is the rarest form because it is the least useful'. The most popular variety was the *mempo*, sometimes made of a single plate but more often having a separate, removable nosepiece, enabling it to be converted into a *hoate*. The *somen* was likewise occasionally made of one plate but was more often of three, with detachable brow and nosepieces so that it could be converted into either a *mempo* or a *hoate* as required.

Somen and *mempo* usually came with a ferocious expression, glued-on moustaches or whiskers, and sometimes gilded or silvered teeth. Some varieties of mask were even named according to the type of face they represented ('old man's face', 'woman's face', 'mountain demon's face', 'ghost's face', 'Korean's face', and so on). Josiah Conder (1881) tells us that 'older men were advised to wear masks depicting younger-looking countenances, and younger men those with older-looking countenances.' All masks were lacquered red on the inside and shaped to fit tightly to the contours of the face. They were worn over a *fukusa* (a kind of handkerchief), which provided padding between the mask and the chin and was fastened by laces on the top of the head 'slightly towards the back'. Under the chin the mask usually had a small pipe or hole to let perspiration run out.

Bottom right: Finally we have the helmet or *kabuto* (the drawing shows it from underneath). This was most often constructed from a large number of narrow curved plates, riveted together, with raised edges at the joins. There was a small metal peak (*mabizashi*) at the front and a deep, flared neckguard (*shikoro*), made of steel or hardened leather lamellae, at the back. Because of the popularity of anachronistic armour one or more of the *shikoro*'s uppermost rows of lamellae were often turned back and outwards at the sides of the head to form rudimentary earguards called *fukigaeshi* – a style that had become unpopular during the 16th century but had never entirely disappeared. These turn-backs, often referred to as 'winglets', are absent in the particular example depicted here.

More often than not a curved plate called a *kuwagata*, of iron or gilded copper, was attached to the front of the helmet just above the peak. Though this resembled a pair of horns more than anything else (Russell Robinson describes them as 'flat antlers') it actually represented the leaves of a sagittaria, a species of water plant. The *kuwagata* came in assorted shapes and sizes, but in the majority of cases the two protrusions flared towards the ends and were relatively small. Some helmets

Various types of hoate *face-masks, as depicted in the* Tanki Yoriaku. *Top to bottom they are the* membo, hoate, sarubo, tsubamegata, nodowa, meguriwa, *and* eriwa.

substituted *taka-zuno*, in which the 'horns' had tapering, rounded ends. Between the curves of the *kuwagata* or *taka-zuno* or elsewhere on the crown there might also be some sort of ornament or crest. At the back of the helmet bowl there was a brass ring (the *kasa-jirushi no fan*) through which a thick tasselled silk cord was tied in a large bow (*agemaki*) to stop it jangling. This ring was used for attaching a streamer-like identification badge or *kasa-jirushi*, 'worn in battle for the purpose of distinguishing sides'.

Needless to say, there were innumerable different types of helmet, most of them distinguished by the shape of the crown and all of them designed to impart 'a fierce and monstrous appearance'. The *Tanki Yoriaku* says that the most popular kinds were those called *kashira zukuri*, *sakugata*, *shiigata*, *momogata*, *kimen*, *sohatsu*, *tokwan*, and *tatamijiku*, 'besides which there are thousands of other shapes'. Its author adds that there were also several varieties of *shikoro*, two different kinds of *mabizashi*, and two kinds of *fukigaeshi*.

The bowl of the helmet had a quilted silk lining known as an *ukebari*, and the inside of the *shikoro* was generally lacquered bright red, said by Conder to be 'for the purpose of reflecting a fierce colour on to the face of the wearer. From this it seems that the mask-shaped visor attached to the helmet was not always worn' – which, indeed, it wasn't (see below). The underside of the peak was likewise frequently lacquered red or else lined with red leather, but might also be gilt. Inside the rim of the helmet were three to five rings, through which was passed the immensely long white silk or white cotton cord which secured it in place on the head. This could be tied in a considerable number of complicated ways, most of which involved it being passed beneath or round the front of the chin two or three times – whence the desirability of some sort of face mask in order to prevent the tightly-drawn laces from digging into the wearer's bare flesh. Indeed, with the helmet and face mask both tied firmly in place it is hard to see how the samurai could have opened his mouth (several authorities categorically state that he couldn't) – which may be the origin of the later tradition of attacking in near silence, commented on by foreign observers during the Sino-Japanese War.

Sometimes a much lighter metal or leather half-helmet or skullcap called a *hanburi* ('half-head') was worn in place of the *kabuto*. Some of these, described as being of 'a shallow cup shape', covered no more than the crown. Others covered the forehead and temples and were constructed from a series of hinged plates, with holes left for the ears and the wearer's queue. Some even had a *mempo* attached, or a mail hood. Many were covered with leather, with a length left on each side for tying under the chin. In fact Stone says that *hanburi* varied more in shape and construction than any other type of Japanese head defence. According to Conder such helmets were generally used 'for night sorties or by foraging parties, etc', circumstances in which a conventional *kabuto* would have been more of a hindrance than a help.

Putting Japanese armour on a piece at a time was, understandably, a time-consuming process, and it was therefore recommended that on campaign one should make certain preparations beforehand; thus the *kote* and the fittings for the *sashimono* and 'other small adjuncts' should be secured to the corselet in advance, and the horns, crest, and *kasa-jirushi* should be attached to the helmet. In addition 'all hooks and fastenings must be prepared'. It was then possible to don the larger part of an armour very quickly, either by hanging it up 'at the level at which it will be when you stand erect in it' and then kneeling down and rising up into it from beneath, inserting the arms into the sleeves as one did so; or else by putting it on top of a box and easing sideways into it through its opening at the side or back. Besides, not everything was necessarily worn in the field. The author of the *Tanki Yoriaku* says that a samurai should not wear *haidate* or face mask when fighting very hard, and that 'all unimportant items of equipment are then better omitted'. Indeed, contemporary pictures of samurai in battle during the period 1866–77 indicate that by that late date the majority of samurai wore, at most, arm-guards, a corselet with or without skirt, and occasionally a helmet or shinguards.

Inevitably, *ashigaru* and other low-ranking samurai wore much simpler armour than that outlined above, typically consisting of a helmet, a simple corselet, and, sometimes, arm defences. The helmet was most often a roughly circular type called a *jingasa* ('war hat'). This came in many different sizes and styles, some being conical, others almost flat, and the rest of every shape in between. Nearly all had a large brim, which frequently arched slightly upwards at the front to improve vision. Most were made of iron or steel, but some were copper or leather, and all were lacquered. There were also wooden ones which Stone describes as 'intended mainly for parade and ceremonial occasions and ... often well decorated' – Satow, for instance, records *bette gumi* officers wearing such 'mound-shaped lacquered wooden hats'. Metal ones could be either plain or embossed. There were generally two pieces of padding in the crown, and a padded loop hanging down below the ears on either side through which a white cord or a length of folded white cloth was passed and tied under and in front of the chin.

Alternative types of *ashigaru* helmet were the *kusari-kabuto* or mail helmet, also found referred to as a *tatami-kabuto* ('folding helmet'); the copper hat (*akagane-gasa*); and the leather hat (*kawagasa*), which was basically a hardened leather *jingasa*. The *kusari-kabuto* was made of small iron plates linked by double mail and sewn to a foundation of padded cloth or leather, the skull-piece and the neck-curtain both being manufactured the same way. Conder describes its shape as being very similar to the 'padded fire-bonnet' worn by Japanese firemen (see Figure 9). The *kawagasa* was most often lacquered black and usually had a gold-coloured *mon* badge on the front; the best of them were considered superior to mail helmets.

Ashigaru body-armour was similar in general design to the corselets worn by the higher-ranking samurai, but was much simpler and often made of leather rather than iron and steel. Conder says it was called *nuko* or *ban-gusoku*: 'The corselets worn by the lower ranks were the *sewari-gusoku*, the *uchi-awase-gusoku*, the *tatami-gusoku* and the *hara-ate* or *hara-ate-gawa* ... The *sewari-gusoku* was a leather corselet made in large pieces of *neri-kawa* lacquered black ... fitted and laced together to form one piece, opening at the back, for which ... reason it was sometimes called *yoroi-haramaki* ... [The opening] was closed either by clasps or by laced silk cords. There were several different shapes, of which the pigeon-breasted one was considered the best. The trunk was generally short and had five *kusadzuri* [tassets] attached, which were also short ... Upon the black body the crest of the lord was marked in gold or red. The *uchi-awase-gusoku* [differed] only ... in that front and back are separated, being joined at both sides after putting on ... Of the *tatami-gusoku* there were two kinds, one of iron and the other of leather.' The *hara-ate* or *hara-ate-gawa* was a leather corselet that protected only the front of the body from the neck to the knees.

Post-modernisation

Unsurprisingly, the widespread introduction of modern Western firearms quickly rendered traditional Japanese equipment obsolete, and soldiers of the newly-established Meiji army wore no armour and were armed exclusively with foreign rifles. However, their firearms were initially of very cosmopolitan origins, having, by necessity, been obtained chiefly by confiscating those of the disbanded clan armies. Others were imports obtained from America (surplus stock left over from the Civil War) and from British merchants based in Hong Kong. The majority by far appear to have been Enfields (*Geberu*), Snider breech-loaders (*Sunaidoru*), and Spencer repeaters, but they also included small quantities of Miniés, Chassepots, Zündnadels, Albinis (Albini-Braendlins), and doubtless others besides, most of which are said to have been scrapped soon thereafter (though Black records seeing a unit armed with Chassepots in Tokyo as late as February 1872). The Spencers were issued to the cavalry, engineers, and military train, while the Sniders and Enfields went to the infantry. Before long the Snider breech-loader was recognised as the Japanese Army's first official-issue rifle and remained so thereafter until the introduction of the home-produced Murata in the 1880s. The army's last remaining muzzle-loading Enfield muskets were converted into breech-loaders in 1877.

According to contemporaries, the new Murata rifle (which took its name from its designer, Major Murata Tsuneyoshi) 'borrowed heavily', at the very least, from either the 1871 Beaumont (inspired in turn by the Chassepot), the 1871 Mauser, or the 1874 Gras, and as far as some were concerned was 'an exact copy'; the fact that they rarely agree on which weapon it was an exact copy of suggests that experts who looked upon it as an amalgam of the best features of several different foreign rifles were actually nearer the mark. The first model, the Type 13 (denoting its issue in the 13th year of Emperor Meiji's reign), began mass production in 1880. Sighted to 1,600 yds (1,460 m), this single-shot breech-loader used old-fashioned paper case cartridges. It weighed about 9 lbs (4 kg) excluding bayonet, had a calibre of 11 mm/.429 in (compared to the Snider's 14.9 mm/.581 in), and was 1.29 m (4.23 ft) long, with a sword-bayonet (*juken*) of 0.71 m (27.6 ins).

The Type 18 introduced in 1885 was also a single-shot weapon, but used metal cartridges. At 1.275 m (4.18 ft) it was slightly shorter than the Type 13 and had a shorter bayonet of 0.58 m (22.6 ins). It was followed in 1889 by the bolt-action Type 22, the first Japanese magazine rifle, which was sighted to 2,000 m (2,190 yds) and had a maximum range of 4,000 m (4,375 yds). Calibre was reduced to 8 mm/.312 in, length to 1.22 m (4 ft), and eight rounds were held in a tubular magazine beneath the barrel, making it a ten-shot repeater (one additional round being carried in the feed chamber and another in the breech). The bayonet was also reduced yet further, to just 0.37 m (14.4 ins). Overall weight excluding bayonet was now 4.17 kg (9.2 lbs).

Finally, in 1897, there came the 6.5 mm/.256 calibre Type 30 Arisaka (popularly referred to as the Meiji), a Mauser-type rifle incorporating a certain amount of Mannlicher influence. It measured 1.275 m (4.18 ft), weighed 8.6 lbs (3.91 kg), and had a five-round clip magazine and a 21-inch (0.53 m) dagger-bayonet. Like the Type 18 it was sighted to 2,000 m, and was reported as capable of sustaining unaimed fire at a maximum rate of 25 rounds per minute. The earlier Muratas had produced minimal smoke and made little noise, but the Arisaka was the first Japanese rifle to use smokeless powder.

The Type 30 Arisaka rifle of 1897. Length including bayonet was 5.44 ft (1.66 m), and weight 9.6 lbs (4.36 kg). It was developed from an experimental model, the Type 29, that had been briefly produced between mid-1896 and April 1897.

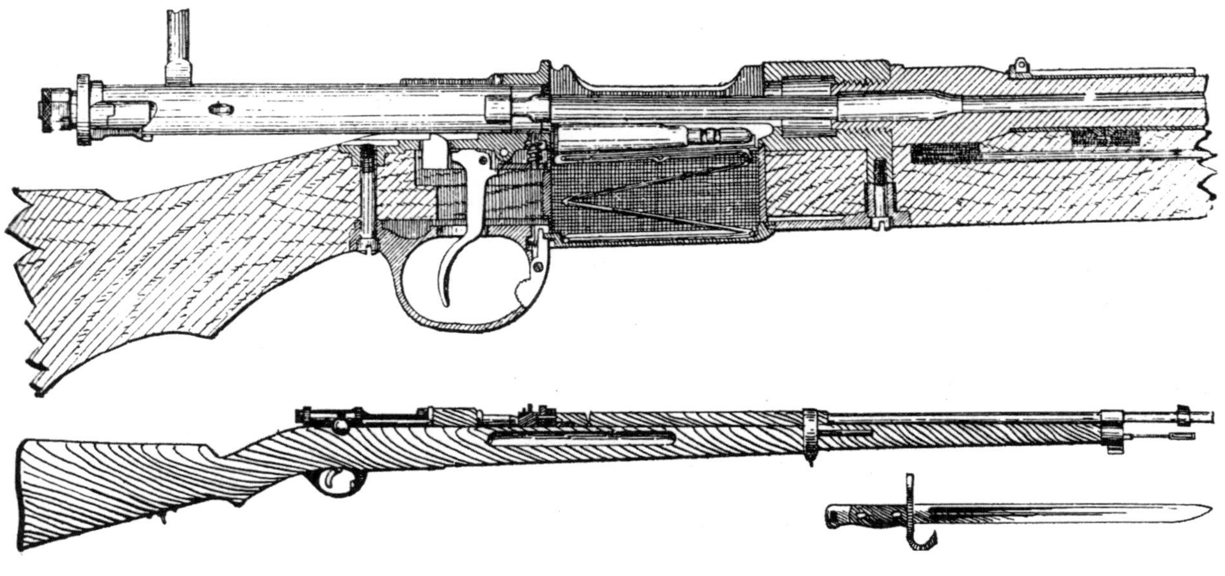

So much for the production sequence. The speed, or rather the lack of it, with which these weapons entered service was quite another matter. As late as 1886, for instance, only the Imperial Guard had as yet been equipped with even Type 13 Muratas (and then only since as recently as 1884), while the rest of the infantry were still armed with Sniders. Despite the fact that Grierson records the expectation that 'by the end of 1887 enough will have been made to re-arm the whole army', Knollys noted the following year that sufficient quantities of the Murata had yet to be produced. In 1892 the army seems to have still been equipped with a mixture of the Type 13 and the 1885 Type 18, and despite the fact that in 1893 Barrow was told that the government was then 'rapidly providing the army with a magazine rifle' (the 1889 Type 22), and that allegedly 60,000 of these had been produced, Japanese infantry are nevertheless recorded to have fought with the Type 18 throughout the Sino-Japanese War (when numerous eyewitnesses observed that whereas the Japanese were only equipped with single-shot breech-loaders, the Chinese had magazine rifles). Some are said to have still been in service as late as the Russo-Japanese War.

In fact only the Imperial Guards and the 4th Division had been partially equipped with the Type 22 by 1894. Neither took part in the fighting in Korea or China though both served in Formosa in 1895, where according to most authorities the new rifle saw action for the first time.[53] The whole active army may have been re-equipped with the Type 22 by 1897. It was certainly the rifle which eyewitnesses record in the hands of Japanese troops participating in the expedition against the Boxers in 1900, even though by this time the 1897 Arisaka is said to have already entered general service – which is unlikely. Significantly several observers reported during 1900 that Japan was just about to rearm her infantry, doubtless with the Arisaka, and this rearmament appears to have been finally completed in 1901–2. The Type 30 Arisaka remained in service thereafter until the introduction of an improved model, the Type 38, in 1905. The army's Type 18 and Type 22 rifles had meanwhile been passed over to depot troops and other second line units. According to a Russian report the armament of such units also included imported Peabody and Remington rifles.

In 1894–95 infantrymen armed with the Type 18 carried 100 rounds into action, in addition to which there were 30 rounds per rifle with the battalion transport and a further 50 rounds per rifle with the divisional ammunition column. These figures seem to have remained largely unchanged for the Type 22, though men recorded serving in China in 1900 carried 90 rounds in their pouches plus 30 in their knapsacks. With the introduction of the Type 30 Arisaka the number of rounds carried on the person increased to 150, of which 120 were carried in the pouches and another 30 in two three-clip cardboard boxes in the knapsack. The reserve ammunition with the battalion transport and the divisional ammunition column also increased, theoretically to 100 rounds in each case, though in practice (during the Russo-Japanese War) the battalion transport seems to have carried only 60. During the latter conflict the number of rounds carried by each soldier actually averaged 200, was sometimes officially increased to 350 or 380, and in the closing stages of the war was occasionally as high as 500. Each five-round clip weighed roughly 4 ozs (actually 1,808 grains, or 0.258 lb/117.1 gm), so that 200 rounds would have weighed in at about 10 lbs (4.5 kg) and 500 rounds at a hefty 25 lbs (11.3 kg).

The cavalry were armed with lances and sabres on ceremonial occasions, plus a carbine when serving in the field. Contemporary prints show lances being used in action in 1876–77, held two-handed at waist-level to the right of the horse's neck, with the left arm stretched out almost straight and the right hand almost resting on the right hip. However, Line units had abandoned the lance by 1894, though it remained in service with the Imperial Guard.

The cavalry's first official-issue carbine was the seven-shot, lever-action Spencer, which was only eventually replaced by a Type 22 Murata carbine in 1889. The Murata was 0.96 m (3.15 ft) long and had a five-round tubular magazine rather than the eight-round magazine of its longer infantry counterpart. Calibre was 8 mm/.312 in, and it was sighted to 1,500 m (1,640 yds). Like its Spencer predecessor, it was invariably carried on the back by means of a sling across the left shoulder, carbine buckets not being used. It was replaced towards the end of the century by a 6.5 mm/.254 calibre Type 30 Arisaka carbine with five-round clip magazine. However, this proved to be a somewhat temperamental weapon. Misfires and jams were commonplace, and it was found to be susceptible to dirt and cold weather. Nevertheless, John Leader, who saw Japanese cavalry in action in 1900, reports that when it was working the Type 30 'could do good practice ... up to 800 metres.'

Many cavalry sabres were European imports, initially from France and later from Germany, but there were also Japanese-manufactured copies, consisting of the Type 7 of 1874, the Type 25 of 1892, and the Type 32 of 1899. These differed from one another principally in the shape of the guard: the Type 7, for instance, had a pierced guard and a long hilt with a prominent bulge in the centre, while Types 25 and 32 had a solid brass guard and a shorter hilt. Those in use in 1894, presumably Type 25, are described as being only slightly curved, with a 33-inch (0.84 m) blade and a horn grip for officers but a wooden grip for other ranks, a black leather wrist-strap (but gold for company officers and red and gold braid for field officers), and a plain steel scabbard, suspended from the belt by a single sling as in Germany. No sabretache was worn. However, in the field many officers and NCOs replaced their official-issue sabres with traditional *katana*, albeit with a modern-style hilt substituted for 'the two-handed haft of Old Japan'.

Artillerymen were armed for self-defence with what foreign observers usually referred to as a sword-bayonet but was actually a simple hanger or short sword, which doubtless saw more service as a tool than as a weapon. This seems to have been used during the period 1885–98 not just by gunners but also by engineers. It had a straight blade measuring about 20½ ins (0.52 m) and a five-inch (0.13 m) hilt that is brass in one surviving example and wood in another. The scabbard, worn in a leather frog like an infantry bayonet, was of wood covered in black leather with brass fittings. Each battery was also provided with 18 cavalry carbines by the 1890s, and by the end of the century all artillery NCOs carried a Smith & Wesson revolver. The NCOs also customarily carried a sword, as did drivers until 1886 (when it was replaced by a hanger).

Officers of all arms carried a revolver and a

Japanese guns captured by the British in the 1860s, as depicted in the Illustrated Naval & Military Magazine *vol. V (1890). Note that the original caption says 'Japanese ordnance taken at Yokohama 1865', presumably an error for 'Kagoshima 1864' since there were no military undertakings against Yokohama.*

sword. Small numbers of revolvers had begun to find their way into Japan as early as the 1850s, and in the 1860s and 1870s Colt Navy, Lefaucheux, and Smith & Wesson revolvers were all imported in sizeable quantities. The Smith & Wesson Type 1 was adopted as the regulation firearm for officers in 1877, and it was not until 1893 that a home-produced handgun, the Type 26 Nen Kenju, arrived on the scene ready to replace it. This 9 mm/.351 calibre six-shot revolver, which combined technical features from several American and European weapons (most notably the Smith & Wesson), actually entered service in 1894, when it was issued to officers and cavalry troopers. However, it was found to be an inferior weapon and was held in low esteem by its users.

The first regulation combat sword for officers probably appeared c.1871. This was followed by a Western-style sword (probably inspired by a French, or possibly an American, original) at some point between 1873 and 1875, which was replaced in turn by a modified version in 1886. Those intended for field use had a slightly curved, traditional *katana*-style blade – as already mentioned, many officers actually substituted old blades by celebrated makers at their own expense – and a long grip (suited to two-handed use) that could be of black or white samé (rayskin), shagreen, or leather, or sometimes black horn, with spaced brass wire binding. The guards, however, were of Western rather than Japanese type. Parade scabbards were of black leather with gilded brass fittings, but on campaign a plain steel scabbard was normally substituted. During the 1870s warrant officers and NCOs also still carried swords, but their steel scabbards were probably blackened to help differentiate them from officers at a glance. Infantry officers', cavalry officers', and artillery officers' swords were all fundamentally very similar, but subtle variations of the guard distinguished different ranks and arms of service.

Artillery

Despite the general abandonment of firearms in the 17th century, a small amount of interest had continued to be shown in artillery for the purpose of coastal defence. However, for many years the Japanese laboured under the delusion that the largest guns it was possible to manufacture safely were 8-pdrs, and despite the fact that acquaintance with Dutch traders had eventually disabused them of this notion most Japanese field and coastal guns alike were still at best 8-pdrs even when Perry arrived in the 1850s; many were even smaller (3, 4, 5 and 6-pdrs are all mentioned by visitors in 1853–54). Nor did the Japanese have much experience in handling them – a Swedish visitor reported in 1776 that Japanese shore batteries tested their pieces no more than once every seven years!

Many guns were also of considerable age. Few new pieces had been cast since the 17th century, and Vasilii Golownin likened the artillery he saw in 1811–13 to that found in mediaeval Europe: 'The Japanese artillery is still extremely imperfect,' he wrote. 'Those cast in Japan are of copper; and, in proportion to the calibre, uncommonly thick. The breech is unscrewed in order to load; the Japanese therefore load their cannon very slowly, and do not fire until all the artillerymen have retired to some distance; one of them then discharges it with a long linstock ... The Japanese have no cannon of large calibre;

they have however some Dutch 18- and 24-pdrs ... They use besides, little falconets, which however are extremely heavy on account of their thickness; their carriages are very bad, and so heavy that they cannot be moved but with the greatest difficulty.'

A more unusual variety of primitive gun was encountered in service as late as 1877, when the arms of Satsuma rebels defeated at Nobeoka were found by eyewitness John Hubbard to have included two wooden cannon, of which 'one was eight feet six inches long, with a nine-inch bore, made of two hollow pieces of wood and hooped its entire length with bamboo hoops. It ... did not appear to have been used, but was mounted in a pile of sandbags ready for use. A smaller one, about six feet long, was lying near and dismantled; this had been fired and was badly burst.' Four guns of the same type are also recorded to have been discovered in one of the batteries taken by the British at Shimonoseki in 1864. These 'were about four feet long, and were constructed of single logs with a bore about eight inches in diameter, having a chamber behind capable of holding about a pound and a half of powder. Bamboo hoops surrounded the gun from breech to muzzle, then came a layer of boards, and then more bamboo hoops; the wood itself was only about three and a half inches thick. The shot consisted of a small bag of pebbles fastened to a wooden disk, and was intended to act like grape at close quarters ... These curious weapons were simply laid on the earthen parapet, and were not calculated to be used more than once.'

Reliance on primitive or antiquated guns vanished with astonishing rapidity after 1853. Some clans had bought in Western furnaces even before Perry's arrival, and by mid-century many Japanese artisans had already learnt how to cast modern artillery. The shogunate government also began to import sizeable quantities of finished guns, initially from the Dutch but before long from American, British, and other foreign merchants. Very soon Japanese foundries were producing every size and variety of gun to standards that improved almost daily, from tiny 3-pdr mountain guns to massive 150-pdr coastal batteries, all copied from prototypes or plans provided by Western governments and entrepreneurs. In the civil wars that marked the end of the Tokugawa shogunate both sides were equipped with mortars, howitzers, smoothbores, and rifled cannon, firing everything from roundshot to chain-shot and shrapnel to shell. Indeed, the sheer variety of guns and calibres resulted in immense logistical difficulties when it came to providing ammunition, and, recognising this, the *bakufu* – under the guidance of its French military advisers – in 1868 began a rationalisation process designed to limit the army's field guns to a nucleus of 4-pdr, 8-pdr, and 12-pdr pieces. During this period gun carriages appear to have been either plain brown or lacquered.

When the new Meiji army was created standardisation continued to be pursued, so that, according to Okuma, at the time of the Satsuma Rebellion

Japanese bronze field-gun designed on the Krupp system and manufactured in Japan under licence. Photographed by Hugues Kraft in Tokyo in 1882. (Wikipedia)

'the only cannon the Imperial troops possessed were bronze, muzzle-loading, 4-pdr mountain pieces, the Imperial Guards alone having twelve 7.5 cm Krupp half-steel guns.' However, James Buck (1973) describes the army's 100-plus guns at this date as including 20 Krupp field guns (doubtless Okuma's 7.5 cm 'half-steel guns'), 45 mountain guns and nine field guns (which he describes as being 5.28-pdrs rather than 4-pdrs), one Armstrong, and 14 mortars; and in 1887 Knollys says that the guns he saw held in an arsenal included 'smooth-bore field pieces of the French pattern, 12-pdr Armstrongs from Elswich dated 1868, and smooth-bore mortars of any date you please.' Gun carriages of the early Meiji period were either left plain brown or else painted green in keeping with French practice. They appear to have remained green thereafter, doubtless the same 'bronze green' as was recorded during the Russo-Japanese War. The iron fittings and bronze barrel were left their natural colour.

Production of Japan's first home-manufactured breech-loading gun (if one excludes copies of the British Armstrong produced by the Hizen clan in the 1860s), began in 1882. This bronze 75 mm (2.95-inch) calibre piece of Italian origin was manufactured under licence at Osaka,[54] and by the late 1880s had replaced the last of the army's old French guns. Described as being 'made on the Krupp system, slightly modified', it came in both field and mountain versions, the mountain gun having a shorter barrel and being mounted on a smaller, lighter carriage than the field gun but having the same calibre and firing the same projectile, which weighed 6 kg (9.31 lbs). The field gun was drawn by just four horses, while the mountain gun could be either drawn by the horses or dismantled and carried on their backs (one carried the barrel, one the wheels, and two the carriage parts; a fifth horse carried ammunition boxes). Japanese artillery horses were provided by the country's small native ponies, which stood only about 13–14 hands. This meant that the loads they could haul had to be comparatively light, and that the mobility of the artillery as a whole was necessarily somewhat slower than might have been hoped for.

Field batteries were accompanied by 142 rounds per gun and mountain batteries by 144 rounds, with the same amount again being available from the ammunition column in each case. A field gun detachment comprised five gunners and a sergeant, of whom two gunners sat on the axle-tree boxes and three on the limber box when the battery was moving at a trot, but otherwise all but the driver generally walked. Mountain gun detachments were larger, consisting of six gunners, five drivers, and a sergeant. Gunners and drivers were all interchangeable. Sergeants and officers rode in all cases.

Though the 1882-model bronze guns remained in use throughout the conflict with China in 1894–95, this campaign showed them to be 'too heavy for a hilly country and only fairly accurate'. Consequently once that conflict was over a replacement was developed by the same Colonel Arisaka Hariakira responsible for the design of the infantry rifle of that name. This all-steel 75 mm 'Q.F.' (quick-firing)[55] gun, the Type 31, was officially introduced in 1898, but re-equipment was a slow process. In May 1900, for instance, G.F. Browne records that the Japanese remained 'indifferently equipped with the antiquated bronze gun which was used in the war with China'; a Russian report records batteries on Formosa being still equipped with them in 1902; and some even saw action during the Russo-Japanese War. Small wonder, therefore, that in 1899–1900 it was felt expedient to import as many as 600 guns from Europe, mostly Krupps. However, it was Arisaka guns that accompanied the Japanese contingent that served in North China in 1900, where they were drawn by teams of six horses. The Arisaka mountain gun was basically the same as the field model but with a lighter carriage, a shorter barrel, and a considerably reduced range of only 4,300 m (4,700 yds) compared to the field gun's maximum of 6,200 m (6,800 yds). Curey (1905) says Arisaka guns were painted 'cinnamon colour', i.e. reddish-brown, but other sources say bronze green.

In addition to 40 rounds per gun limber, 40 per wagon limber, and 50 per wagon body, each Arisaka regiment had an ammunition column comprising 27 wagons each holding 90 rounds, plus three further columns of the same description with the divisional ammunition column. This made an overall total of 400 rounds per gun, of which 355 were shrapnel and 45 common shell. The shrapnel shells weighed 6 kg (13.23 lbs) and the high explosive shells 6.1 kg (13.45 lbs). B. Vincent (1904) notes that case shot was not used, 'shrapnel with time fuzes set at zero being considered sufficient at close quarters.'

As regards heavy artillery, this was updated only slowly, and a large number of obsolete bronze guns survived right up to the beginning of the 20th century. By 1897, however, there were also a great many modern guns and mortars, though few saw any action during the 19th century. The only time that a siege train was fielded was during the Sino-Japanese War, when the 2nd Army was accompanied by four 120 mm guns, twelve 90 mm guns, eight 150 mm mortars, and twelve 90 mm mortars. Du Boulay records each of the mortars being carried slung from bamboo poles between two coolies during the attack on Wei-hai-wei in January–February 1895.

Machine guns

The Japanese army had two Gatlings and a Mitrailleuse by the time of the Satsuma Rebellion in 1877, and at least one of these may have been used against Saigo Takamori's sword-wielding adherents at the Battle of Shiroyama. Otherwise, the army's earliest use of machine guns in action was not until 1895, when an experimental unit armed with 11.25 mm/.443 in Osaka-manufactured Maxim guns saw service in Formosa. These were rendered highly manoeuvrable by being mounted on light carriages pulled by their crews, but proved mechanically unreliable, their cartridges frequently jamming. Several machine guns also accompanied the Japanese contingent which landed at Amoy during the Boxer Rebellion. However, the army's first two machine gun batteries were not officially formed until 1902. Each consisted of three officers, 52 men, and six guns (Maxim guns in one battery, Gatling guns in the other). These were attached to the 1st and 2nd Divisions, the plan being to assign a section (two guns) to each of these divisions' infantry brigades in wartime.

Machine guns were still in short supply during the early stages of the Russo-Japanese War in 1904, when each infantry division theoretically had ten Hotchkiss guns and each cavalry brigade six.

FIGURES

1–4. SAMURAI 1800–77 Figure 1, wearing a *do-maru*, is from a studio photograph of the 1860s; Figure 2, wearing a plate *tosei-gusoku* or 'modern armour', comes from an undated 19th-century Japanese print; Figure 3 is from a late-century photograph; and Figure 4 comes from a Japanese arms and armour book dating to 1855. As has already been noted, traditional samurai armour largely disappeared with the Meiji Restoration in 1868, but the least essential parts had already begun to be discarded during the last few years of the Edo period. Nevertheless, these four warriors still wear the full panoply typical of the first half of the century, before the introduction of modern firearms disabused its wearers of any hope that it could do more than proclaim their social status. Note that Figure 3's armour appears to be made of mismatched pieces, probably a not uncommon state of affairs – samurai armour was, after all, very expensive, and since it was made in many parts individual elements could be replaced on a modular basis. He has yet to put on his throat guard, faceguard and helmet.

Despite the fact that rifle bullets had been found to pass clean through even the strongest helmet,[56] full armour was still being worn by unreconstructed traditionalists as late as the Boshin War. Algernon Mitford, for instance, records seeing Tokugawa samurai marching out to fight in January 1868 'clad in the old armour of the country carrying spears, bows and arrows, falchions, curiously shaped, with sword and dirk, who looked as if they had stepped out of some old picture of the Gempei wars in the Middle Ages. Their jimbaoris, not unlike heralds' tabards, were as many-coloured as Joseph's coat. Hideous masks of lacquer and iron, fringed with portentous whiskers and moustachios, crested helmets with wigs from which long streamers of horsehair floated to their waists, might strike terror into any enemy. They looked like the hobgoblins of a nightmare.' And just three weeks later he records being met at Fushimi by similarly-equipped anti-*bakufu* Tosa clansmen, 'wild-looking fellows, clad in armour with their faces hideously masked and long elf-locks of black or white horsehair hanging down from their helmets over their shoulders.'

Black and white drawings have no hope of doing justice to the beauty of Japanese armour, which was as elaborate and colourful as any the world has ever seen. In particular the heavily laced lamellar varieties revived in the Edo period lent themselves to vibrant decoration. The armour elements were lacquered in a wide range of colours – often applied in alternate rows, panels, or linear patterns – that included black, red, green, yellow, blue, gold, silver, tortoise-shell, and 'rusted iron colour'; and the fabric parts were trimmed with dyed leather or coloured silk braid. There were also *mon* badges on the breastplate and helmet, and a silk *sashimono* ('little banner') was often attached vertically to the back of the corselet, with its edges stiffened by strips of leather to ensure that the heraldry it bore was visible at all times.

Other identifying badges might be attached to the shoulder and helmet. The former was called a *sode-jirushi* ('sleeve badge'), and consisted of a rectangular piece of silk or cotton cloth about 6–7 *sun* long (7.2–8.4 ins/0.18–0.21 m). Its top edge was tied by laces to two rings fixed to the right *sode* or shoulder-guard, while the other end was left 'to flutter in the wind'. Conder records that 'it generally bore some crest or the name of Hachiman, the god of war, in some fixed colour. The device upon the badge was fixed by the general, being ... used [to distinguish] friends and foes, and only put on on the eve of some action.' *Sode-jirushi* sometimes differed between the individual contingents of an army, whence the *Tanki Yoriaku*'s observation that 'they are used as regimental badges'.

The *kasa-jirushi* ('hat badge') was similar but somewhat larger, being generally 10–13 *sun* long (11.9–15.5 ins/0.30–0.39 m). It was either tied to a ring on the back of the helmet or was attached to a small rod about 20 ins (0.51 m) long fixed to the front. Conder records *kasa-jirushi* to have been most often white, with their device in black.

A third variety of recognition device encountered somewhat less often was the *koshi-sashi*, described in the *Tanki Yoriaku* as 'the badge of a cavalryman. It is made of leather or thick paper, and is about 3 *sun* [3.6 ins/90 mm] square. It is attached by a short cord at one corner to a short stick, and carried stuck into the *uwa-obi* at the back of the waist.' Less sophisticated field recognition devices were also used on occasion. For example, a contemporary history of the late Edo period, the *Genj Yume Monogatari*, notes that Choshu samurai fighting in Kyoto in 1864 (reported to have all been 'clad in complete armour') simply wore a piece of white cotton cloth tied round the leg.

Other details to note are the largely unarmoured right arm of Figure 2 to facilitate the use of his bow; the *eboshi* or *samurai-eboshi* (a distinctive soft cap, usually black) worn by Figure 3; and the fur covering (*shiri-saya*) on the bottom half of the first two figures' scabbards. Such coverings were originally worn by samurai when out hunting, but by the 19th century they seem to have been used as a status symbol by some senior samurai. They were mainly of bear fur, or less often tiger, leopard, or deerskin. Figure 3 also carries a commander's *saihai* or *zai*, a baton used to signal troop movements on the battlefield, which was secured round the wrist by a braid loop. When not in use it was stuffed through the *uwa-obi* at the back of the waist.

Traditional Japanese horse-harness can be seen in Figure 4 and the illustration on p.27. This used leather only for the saddle itself, while the headstall, reins, straps, crupper and so on were made of silk cord, usually with plenty of fringes and large tassels. Japanese saddles were considered 'high, uncomfortable things' by foreigners. They were constructed from four pieces of wood laced together and decorated according to the rank of the owner, sometimes being inlaid with metal and invariably being lacquered. The stirrups (*abumi*) were of a distinctive, curved, slipper-like shape with no sides. They were usually made of iron, weighed 8–10 lbs (3.6–4.5 kg) each, and were lacquered to match the saddle. Iron horseshoes were unknown in the first half of the century, when Japanese horses wore straw sandals instead (these can be seen in the picture on p.27). However, the Japanese were very quick to start copying Western horseshoes once they discovered them.

The horses – or, more accurately, ponies – were invariably stallions, whose small stature of about 13–14 hands[57] belied their 'vicious propensities amounting to ferocity'. There were no geldings, and mares were kept only for breeding, not for riding. Though Westerners greatly admired the strength and endurance of Japanese horses, they were unimpressed by their looks. Vincent describes the average pony as 'a straight shouldered, leggy, cow-hocked, coarse looking brute'. However, the Japanese artist of the picture on which this figure is based has depicted this horse rather too large and magnificent – the picture on page 27 is a far truer representation of a typical Japanese horse of the period.

Traditional horse-harness survived into the early Meiji period. Visiting Tokyo in 1871, for instance, William Griffis records seeing a mounted samurai (still with 'a lacquered helmet on his head', so clearly a diehard conservative): 'His feet rest in wide iron stirrups, curved up like a skate-runner, and have room to spare. His saddle has enormous flaps of gilt leather. He grasps the reins, one in each hand, at about six inches from the bit, holding his horse's head so that the lower lip is higher than the space between his ears ... The horse's mane is tied up in a row of stiff pompoms; his tail is incased in a long bag of silk. Enormous tassels hang from the horse's shoulders.' However, by this time such harness had already been abandoned by the new national army.

A small amount of leather and fabric horse armour was produced in the late Edo period, but there is apparently no evidence of it ever being used in battle.

Even in full armour samurai carried some provisions with them, which were contained in a provision bag (*kate-bukuro*). Made of twisted paper strings woven like fine basketwork, this measured about 1 *shaku* by 8 *sun* (11.9 ins/0.30 m by 9.6 ins/0.24 m). It was carried at the waist on the right side. A second bag might also be carried, containing about a pound of rice, as was a water-bottle capable of holding about 1–2 *go* (a *go* was equivalent to 5.1 fluid ounces, or 143 ml). Sometimes pickled plums were wrapped in small pieces of cotton cloth and hung from the corselet shoulder-straps.

5–6. SAMURAI 1868–77 These figures differ from the preceding group in being far less comprehensively equipped. Figure 5 is a Tokugawa adherent from a picture of the desperate fighting at Ueno in July 1868. He wears a simple corselet and armoured sleeves, and has an apparently white *hachimaki* tied round his head. Headscarves worn on their own like this sometimes incorporated an iron plate to protect the forehead. Figure 6 is a *Shimpuren* from a print depicting the Hagi Rebellion of 1876, which shows the rebels wearing sundry combinations of civilian and military dress; this particular man wears a breastplate and a *gessan*.

7–10. LOWER RANKING SAMURAI 1800–77 Warriors wearing considerably less armour, or even no armour at all, are to be found illustrated and described in innumerable contemporary sources. These represent *kashi*, the inferior class of samurai variously referred to as *ashigaru*, *gokenin*, *doshin*, *kachi*, and *yoriki*. Of the four depicted here, Figure 7 is from an armour book dating to 1801, Figure 8 is from the same source as Figure 2, Figure 9 is a reconstruction based on a late-19th century Western engraving and a surviving late Edo mail corselet, and Figure 10 is from the same source as Figure 4 and dates to 1855.

Figure 7 is, somewhat unusually, entirely unarmoured, but Figures 8 and 10 wear typical munition armours – though that of the latter is largely concealed beneath his *mino*, which was a straw overcoat often worn in wet weather (notice also the ingenious arrangement designed to keep the firing mechanism of his musket dry – though it must have impeded accurate aiming). Japanese munition armours generally comprised a simple lacquered

Fig 5 Fig 6 Fig 7 Fig 8 Fig 9

leather or thin metal *do*, a *gessan* (detachable tassets), a light helmet – most often a lacquered *jingasa* – and sometimes light armour for the arms and, much less often, the legs; the arm-pieces of Figures 8 and 10, for instance, consist of no more than small plates sewn to a thick fabric foundation, the plates being linked with mail in the latter example. Note that the *jingasa* was almost always black and usually had a cloth neckguard attached at the sides and back, most often white but occasionally coloured.

Figure 9 wears mail instead of a munition armour, consisting of corselet (*kusari-katabira*), sleeves (*kusari-kote*), and cap (*kusari-zukin*), each sewn to its own fabric foundation. Japanese mail, or *kusari* (literally 'chain'), was invariably either mounted on fabric or leather or else sandwiched between two layers of cloth. It also differed from European mail in being constructed from circular links joined to one another by straight-sided 'oval' links turned edge on to the surface of the mail. In most cases each circular link was joined to its four nearest neighbours by four of these straight-sided links, creating a pattern of squares, but sometimes it was joined to six of its neighbours instead, resulting in an hexagonal pattern. Other items of mail armour also sometimes encountered include leggings (*kusari-kiahan*) and close-fitting breeches called *kusari-bakama*, in which the fronts of the thighs were covered in mail. Note that the skirt of this man's corselet is only partially of mail, leaving the cloth foundation exposed in a checkerboard pattern. In other examples a similar checkerboard pattern was created by the incorporation of small metal plates, which could be round, square, elliptical, hexagonal, or octagonal. A mail corselet might be worn under other armour as well as on its own.

Figure 9's hood is reinforced at the front by horizontal plates, being a variety of the type of head defence known as a *hanburi*. More often the *hanburi* comprised small coin-sized plates stitched inside a brigandine (*kikko*) hood.

The men depicted are armed with a *naginata* and matchlocks, but others might carry a spear or bow. The majority also carried the usual two samurai swords, though such soldiers are very occasionally seen carrying only one – Figure 7, for instance, who substitutes a long holster (to hold his matchlock) in place of the second sword; note that he has removed the 'lid' which would cover the butt and is carrying it in his right hand. Armoured *ashigaru* equipped with matchlocks, who would have doubtless resembled Figures 8 and 10, are frequently mentioned during the civil wars which punctuated the collapse of the Tokugawa shogunate in the 1860s. The *Tanki Yoriaku* recommends that armoured men going out to fight with matchlocks should fasten the *kuchigusuri-ire* (priming flask) and *seseri* (bamboo or wooden cleaning rod) to a hook attached to the right shoulder-strap of their corselets. Ammunition and powder were carried in bags at the waist.

11. TAKASHIMA SHUHAN'S COMPANY 1840s The earliest significant advocate of the modernisation of Japanese tactics and weapons was Takashima Shuhan, an official in the Nagasaki city magistrate's office. He had learned a good deal about Western military methods from the Dutch community in Nagasaki during the 1830s, and, using his own money to buy Dutch artillery pieces and muskets, by c.1840 had trained some 300 disciples to use them (including, significantly, samurai sent from both Satsuma and Choshu), organising these into two infantry companies and an artillery battery. In June 1841 he was invited to Edo with 125 of his cadets in order to give a demonstration before *bakufu* officials, who were sufficiently impressed to purchase his guns and to commission him to open a training school. However, reactionaries amongst them who feared innovation of any sort regarded his use of Dutch words of command as treasonable and in 1842 arranged to have him arrested on trumped up charges and held in prison until 1846. He was only eventually pardoned in the wake of Commodore Perry's visit, when the *bakufu* suddenly woke up to its desperate need for his understanding of Western military organisation and technology, and in 1856 he was appointed an instructor to the army.

This figure wears the special close-fitting

uniform Takashima designed for his soldiers, in accordance with his belief that mobility was paramount and armour obsolete. It comprises a *tonkyogasa* (a type of battle hat invented by Takashima), a jacket, and *momohiki* trousers, here worn with gaiters. Detail 11a is a rear view of the hat, which was secured on the head by means of the same sort of long lace, knotted in front of the chin, as had previously secured a samurai's helmet (see page 63); such lace arrangements persisted well into the 1860s. His uniform is dark blue, with the white edge of his shirt just visible at the collar. The *obi* is white, and belts, scabbards, and socks are black (socks worn with uniforms seem to have been invariably black in the Edo period). The hat is also black, with yellow edge and piping and a gilt badge. He is armed with a Dutch musket.

12. KOBUSHO CADET 1856 This is the uniform worn by infantry trained in the Kobusho military academy established by the *bakufu* in 1856, which became the Rikugunsho in 1867. It was dark blue in winter and white in summer. The hooded cap is of a type that could be tied just below the nose, or else worn loose as in Figure 15, which also shows a variant of the cap shape. The headscarf is white, but all else is blue except for the cap, belts, and the hem of his baggy trousers, which are black. Others substituted *momohiki* for the culotte-like *kobakama* trousers. Detail 12a depicts the hairstyle popularised by Kobusho students. The Kobusho academy continued to teach swordsmanship and other traditional martial skills alongside more modern (but often already outdated) Western military techniques.

13–20. SHOGUNATE REGULAR INFANTRYMEN 1863–68 This group of figures shows the various evolutionary stages undergone by *bakufu* Westernised infantry during the closing stages of the shogunate's existence. Such uniforms appear to have been worn by *hohei*, *sappei*, and *bette gumi*.

Figure 13 wears an 1863 pattern uniform, which can be found in sources dating to the period 1863–66. It was made of white cotton or imported woollen cloth in summer, and blue woollen cloth in winter. Dark blue was henceforward the usual colour for nearly all Japanese winter uniforms, but this seems to have occasionally been of such a deep hue that some eyewitnesses described it as black; very possibly some uniforms actually *were* black. His trousers are a closer-fitting variety of *hakama* known as 'narrow *hakama*', which (though it can't be seen here) retained the characteristic deep vent at each side. These had the wearer's battalion or company number on the back in the same position that *hakama* had *mon*. Only a short sword – probably a *chisa katana* – seems to have been worn with this uniform. His distinctive hat, with its brim folded down at each side, was called a *nirayamagasa* after the office of its inventor, the governor of the Nirayama district. He has a rolled cloth 'bag' called a *danbukuro* tied diagonally round his body. This was used to hold his provisions and personal effects.

Figures 14–16 are all *bette gumi* or Legation Guards seen at Yokohama, from pictures dating to 1864–66. Note that Figure 14's bayonet scabbard is attached to his crossbelt, where it would not impede or be impeded by his two swords. Figures 15–16 come from an engraving in the *Illustrated London News*. The original actually depicts all of them wearing Western shoes, but this is unlikely, albeit not impossible, at such an early date. Note that Figure 16 wears a conventional Western-style knapsack in place of the traditional *danbukuro*. It was probably troops dressed and equipped like these figures which John Black saw marching out of Edo to fight the Choshu clan in June 1865, who included 'a regiment of about 600 men, four deep, armed with Enfield rifles and bayonets. Their dress was a curious hybrid between Japanese and foreign. They were in heavy marching order, with knapsacks, and each had drinking utensils, &c. These men marched with the greatest regularity, and evinced good drilling.' (By contrast the costume and equipment of the regiment behind them was 'purely Japanese – and the variety of colours in their tunics presented a very gay appearance.')

Figure 17 is a *hohei* infantryman dating to 1866. He wears a blue uniform and black belts, with a white *obi*

Fig 10 *Fig 11* *Fig 12* *Fig 13*

and a white vertical stripe on each jacket sleeve. These vertical stripes – of which there was most often one on each sleeve but might be as many as three – were unique to *bakufu* regular troops, and were not found on the otherwise often extremely similar uniforms worn by the troops of either pro-Tokugawa or Loyalist *daimyo*. For the next couple of years the caps worn by *bakufu* troops usually had an arm of service badge on the front. That of the main figure is the infantry badge, which was in yellow, usually with one or more vertical bars within the circle, apparently to denote battalion number; detail 17a is the artillery badge, in white; and 17b is the cavalry badge, also in white. Infantrymen repeated the badge on their ammunition pouches.

The pattern of white diamonds on his *momohiki* trousers was seemingly also an infantry arm of service distinguishing device; artillerymen substituted a line of 17a devices, likewise in white, while other infantrymen used a row of overlapping blue-outlined white discs. However, such trouser devices were not in use for long and they rarely feature in contemporary sources. Their precise meaning is now a mystery.

The cap was often worn with its brim turned up (as in Figures 15 and 16), and its neck-curtain was usually split at the back (as in Figure 72d). A black-lacquered *jingasa* like those of Figures 19 and 20 was sometimes worn in its place.

Figure 18 is from another engraving of *bette gumi* at Yokohama in 1866, published in the *Illustrated London News*. Such pictures are amongst the first to show Japanese troops wearing Western, rather than *Westernised*, uniforms, complete with buttons, though foreign shirts and jackets (albeit worn in conjunction with traditional *kobakama*) had seemingly been introduced in an experimental infantry unit created by Choshu reformer Uemon Yamada as early as 1859. Another picture depicting regular troops of much the same date as Figure 18 shows an otherwise identically dressed infantryman apparently wearing a bowler hat. Though a *jingasa* like that of Figure 24 may be intended, numerous contemporary pictures and written accounts indicate that Japanese soldiers often wore assorted items of Western civilian attire, notably hats, jackets, waistcoats, and bow ties, and bowlers are certainly depicted in some pictures. Shogunate troops seen at Himeji in 1865 actually included a few men in full European civilian dress. See also Figures 39 and 40.

Figure 19, from an engraving of 'part of the Tycoon's body-guard' at Osaka (reproduced in the *Illustrated London News* of 10 August 1867), and Figure 20, a shogunate infantryman from a print of the Battle of Toba-Fushimi in 1868, are dressed in the Western uniforms (based on designs by Captain Jules Brunat) that were introduced in the corps instructed by the first French military mission. These were presumably the uniforms known to have been issued to shogunate *hohei* some time between November 1866 and January 1867 (which is when the mission actually arrived). However, very similar uniforms to that of Figure 20, with buttoned shell jackets, seem to have already been in use (but worn in conjunction with a soft kepi rather than a *jingasa*) by 1866. The uniforms depicted are dark blue with white sleeve stripes and trouser stripes; white waist belt and crossbelts; black ammunition pouch, scabbards, and boots; a black *jingasa* with a yellow arm of service badge; and a brown leather knapsack with brown straps. The blanket on the knapsack is red. Traditional Japanese sandals are still worn in preference to Western boots.

Note the shortness of Figure 19's trousers, and the voluminous proportions of his jacket, which tally with the observations of the commander of the French mission, Chanoine, that the uniforms didn't fit very well: 'The trousers did not fit, the boots were large and heavy which the old habit of dragging the sandal unfitted them to wear; the coats were made of black [perhaps very dark blue?] cloth profusely covered with silver lace, and had a slit up the back to allow the long sword to stick out behind'.

A photograph of shogunate troops being trained by the French at Ota Jinya, Yokohama, shows that artillerymen wore the same uniform as the infantry. More

Fig 14

Fig 15

Fig 16

Fig 17

17a 大 騎 *17b*

Fig 18

Fig 19

Fig 20

Fig 21

interestingly, exactly the same uniform is shown being worn by Loyalist troops in a print by Taiso Yoshitoshi that depicts them escorting the Emperor to Edo Castle in November 1869. This would seem to indicate that old shogunate uniforms were issued to Meiji troops as a stopgap measure before brand new uniforms became available for the national army in 1870.

It appears to have been a regiment dressed like Figures 19 and 20 that Ernest Satow saw at Tokushima in 1867, whose uniform he describes as being 'in imitation of European style', comprising 'black' jackets and trousers, the latter with a red stripe down the seam, plus 'hats of papier-mâché, either conical or of dish-cover shape, with two horizontal red bands'. He adds: 'happy the soldier who could muster a pair of boots, the rest had only straw sandals.' These were not French-trained troops, however, since Satow records that 'they used the English infantry drill, with the quaint addition of a shout to indicate the discharge of their firearms.'

Note that in all of these pictures just one sword is usually carried, only officers and NCOs apparently being permitted to carry the traditional two swords of a samurai.

21–25. TRADITIONALLY ATTIRED TROOPS 1850s–1860s These generic types from various sources give a good idea of the appearance of unreconstructed elements of the clan armies that participated on both sides during the civil wars of 1864–69. There was generally no uniformity whatsoever to their basically civilian attire – whence the pressing need for recognition badges (see Figure 30) – except where some had the collars of their jackets in a particular colour or pattern that denoted their unit. However, uniforms of a purely Japanese type were not unknown during the Edo period, when the followers of many *daimyo* were rigged out in matching costumes reflecting their lord's personal tastes, much like the liveries worn by the retainers of mediaeval European noblemen. Examples seen by Russian prisoner Vasilii Golownin during his captivity in 1811–13 included light blue *haori* with a white cross on the back, black *haori* with a white square on the back, and *bakufu* troops in black silk *haori* with white *mon* on breast and back. Such soldiers would have resembled Figure 22, who dates to c.1850, their uniforms comprising at most a *haori* and *kobakama* (or some other variety of trousers) 'all of the same cut', worn over the soldiers' own clothes. The *haori* was doubtless often discarded in action, as in Figure 23.

Taylor records that the infantry seen at Uraga during Perry's visit in July 1853 mostly wore blue *haori* 'with white stripes on the sleeves, meeting at the shoulder, so as to form a triangular pattern, and a crest, or coat-of-arms [i.e., *mon*], upon the back. Others had gowns of red and white stripes, with a black lozenge on the back. Some wore upon their heads a cap made of bamboo splints, resembling a broad, shallow basin inverted, but the greater number had their heads bare.' Elsewhere he describes the shogunate troops wearing uniforms 'of a dark grey colour, having full trousers, gathered below the knees, a broad sash around the waist, and a white cloth, similar to a turban, bound about the head. They were armed with the old Tower muskets ... with flint locks and bayonets. Those on the right wore a different uniform, exhibiting a mixture of dull brown and yellow in its colours, and carried matchlocks of an antique fashion.' He also mentions seeing units wearing dark brown, blue, and purple jackets 'bound with a girdle at the waist'.

The print of c.1867 by Gountei Teishu from which Figure 21 comes shows two such uniformed units undergoing musketry drill. The uniform of the soldier depicted comprises a black-lacquered *jingasa* with a white 'chinstrap', a white coat with a blue pattern and a blue central portion which may possibly be a light corselet, a yellow *obi*, blue trousers and gaiters, white socks, and a dark grey ammunition pouch and shoulder-strap.

Figures 21–23 are armed with foreign muskets or rifles, but many of the men fielded by *daimyo* were still traditionally armed with spears or polearms. Figure 24, from a Japanese print, wears vambraces and *jingasa* but is otherwise unarmoured, while Figure 25, from the *Illustrated London News* of 13 January 1855, has no armour at all; some spearmen, however, still wore full armour. The baggy sleeves of Figure 24's *haori* have been

hitched up out of the way by means of a narrow sash called a *tasuki* which was passed round both arms from the front, crossed diagonally between the shoulder-blades, and was tied in front of the shoulder.

The minimum equipment and provisions expected to be carried by a typical clan soldier (in this instance a Tatebayashi clan rifleman) are recorded in a document of 1868 as two swords, a bag containing 40 rounds of ammunition and miscellaneous odds and ends, a rifle, an ammunition pouch holding another 20 rounds, at least two pairs of sandals, and sufficient food – consisting of rice, pickled plums, and soy paste – for two meals.

Though the troops of pro-shogunate clans were more traditionally attired than many of their anti-*bakufu* counterparts, most had at least some of their troops dressed much like Figures 13, 14, and 26–29, complete with a wide assortment of headgear. The resultant hybrid appearance of the contending armies in the closing days of the shogunate is succinctly summarised by eye-witnesses Algernon Mitford and Ernest Satow.

In describing Loyalist troops seen in June 1868, Mitford observed that 'of the dresses of these men, it would require a quick artist's eye for each samurai. They represented all the colours of the rainbow. Their hats alone were as diverse as the nations of the earth. Some wore black cone-shaped wooden basins, some a Chinese winter felt hat, others glazed plaited cotton the shape of which might compare with an umbrella whose ribs were broken; some had a taste for the Western fashions, some had French caps, others the British naval style. Amongst them were also to be seen the Australian digger's felt slouch, and some had a fancy for the lion's mane, or the skin of a grizzly bear. There were ponderous iron helmets, and light bamboo and straw. It may be imagined, with such a variety of headdress, how varied their nether costume was ... Now came the daimyo, with their men all armed with foreign rifles and native swords ... Almost all the daimyos' samurai were dressed alike, in black camlet suits with brass buttons, and their distinguishing badges. These latter consist of stripes, crosses, diamond-shaped patches, triangles, etc; or in the case of some, calico marked with a "mon" device, fastened to the shoulder by a piece of paper string.'

Ernest Satow reports that shogunate troops seen at Osaka in January the same year comprised 'men in all sorts of military costumes'. The Shogun's own troops consisted of 'a long train of drilled troops ... followed by a herd of men in fantastic costumes, some wearing helmets with long wigs of black or white hair reaching half-way down their backs, others in ordinary helmets, basin-shaped war-hats (*jingasa*), flat hats, armed some with long spears, short spears, Spencer rifles, Swiss rifles, muskets, or the plain two swords.'

26–29. LOYALIST TROOPS 1865–68 These four generic figures are characteristic of the *shotai* and similar modernised troops fielded by the Choshu clan after about 1863 and by the Satsuma, Tosa, and other anti-*bakufu* clans from about 1865 until the fall of the shogunate. Their uniforms are a characteristic mixture of foreign and Westernised Japanese styles. They appear to have been invariably dark blue or 'black' (which, as already conjectured, may simply denote a very dark blue), with white crossbelts, and black hats, socks, ammunition pouches, and scabbards. The only splash of any other colour on the particular figures depicted here was the decorative red lace *agemaki* bow at the back of the conical *hatsumurigasa* hat worn by Figure 27, a Satsuma infantryman (detail 27a). Figure 26 is another Satsuma infantryman, based on an undated photograph; the large white 'patch' over the elbow of his right sleeve is a recognition device (see Figure 30), bearing the black cross within a circle device of the Shimazu, lords of the Satsuma *han*. Choshu clansmen fighting the Tokugawa during the Summer War of 1866 appear to have been dressed very similarly.

With the assistance of British and American merchants (who, from 1864 on, smuggled considerable numbers of modern firearms to the affluent Choshu and Satsuma clans in particular), the Loyalists gained an early lead in the arms race that they never thereafter lost.

Consequently when the final showdown came in 1866–68 many Loyalists were equipped with breech-loading rifles, while the *bakufu* army mostly had muzzle-loaders. Satsuma had purchased as many as 7,300 breech-loaders (mostly Sniders) in 1865 alone, and by 1868 had over 16,000 Model 1865 Spencers – doubtless the 'American breech-loaders' Shozan Yashi recorded in their hands during the Boshin War – and the Hizen clan about 2,000 more, though other clans had only a few such up-to-date weapons between them. However, Samuel Mossman (1873) states that the Satsuma troops contributed to the national army at its creation were armed instead with Enfields.

In addition to a rifle and bayonet, one or two swords were also invariably carried. In theory all soldiers of such modernised Loyalist units were permitted to wear two swords, even if they were *heimin*, or commoners, but in practice most men carried just one.

30. IDENTIFICATION DEVICES 1865–69 Since the troops of the pro-*bakufu* and anti-*bakufu* factions were virtually indistinguishable (even where uniforms were worn, these were universally dark blue or black), identification devices were of vital importance in telling friend from foe. These generally took the form of either a piece of coloured cloth tied round the right arm (the Aizu clan wore a yellow armband in 1868, for instance, and the Satsuma clan a white one), or a relatively large rectangular piece of cloth attached most often to the upper left sleeve or the left breast, but occasionally to the right sleeve (see Figure 26). These were still known as *sode jirushi*, but they appear to have been smaller than those previously worn with armour, which were 7–8 *sun* long (about 8.3–9.5 ins/210–240 mm).

Most bore devices that were often, but far from universally, derived from clan or family heraldry. They came in an almost infinite variety of forms, of which only a few examples can be depicted here, but most seem to have been white with the charges painted or printed predominantly in blue or black. Amongst traditional clan contingents they were also sometimes used to emphasise social divisions, the badges of senior samurai often differing from those of lower-ranking samurai, which might differ in turn from those worn by commoners. The examples depicted here are:

30a. Aizu clan: white, black device (in 1868 sometimes with a red five-pointed star at the top).
30b. Aki family, Asano clan: white with three blue lines.
30c. Awa clan: white with blue checkerboard pattern.
30d. Azushi clan: white with blue device.
30e. Bizen clan: white with black device.
30f. Todo family, Ise clan: white, black device.
30g. *Shinsengumi* corps: white, red lettering and zigzag.
30h. Kato family, Mizuguchi clan: white, crenellated black line and red device.
30i. Kizuki clan: white with blue device.
30j. Nabeshima clan: white and black for lower rank soldiers, yellow and black for upper ranks.

Though identification devices of this type were worn predominantly by troops in Japanese dress, they were also worn by some troops clothed in Western-style uniforms. However, the latter could more often be told apart by cuff markings worn on one or both sleeves, such as the examples depicted in 30k–30t. Some men wore both *sode jirushi* and cuff markings.

30k. Aki family, Asano clan: three white stripes (compare to 30b).
30l. Bizen clan: white diamond (compare to 30e).
30m. Choshu clan: single white stripe.
30n. Echizen clan: row of white spots.
30o. Hojoh family, Sayama clan: white triangle.
30p. Kato family, Mizuguchi clan: white device (compare to 30h).
30q. Kurume clan: white inverted chevron.
30r. Ogaki clan: single yellow stripe.
30s. Sakurai family, Amagasaki clan: two vertical white lines.
30t. Tatebayashi clan: three red stripes.

Fig 26 *Fig 27* *Fig 28* *Fig 29*

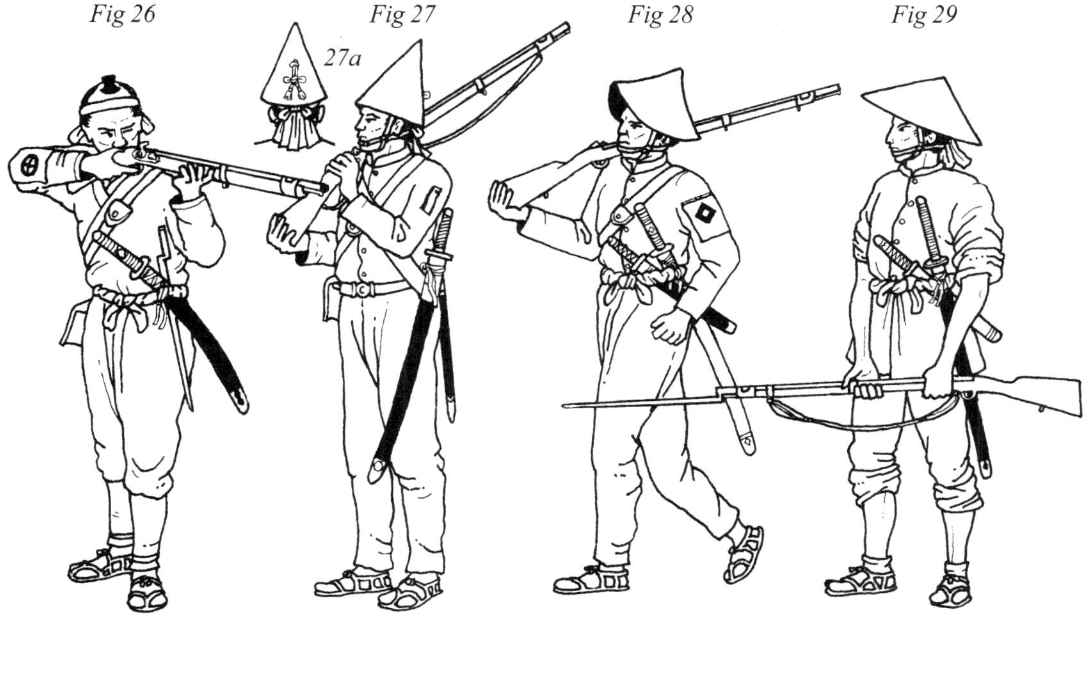

Fig 30

Other recognition devices included a simple unmarked strip of cloth attached to the upper sleeve or the breast, most famous of these being the *kingire* or 'brocade shreds' worn on the left shoulder by Loyalists in 1868 (whence the Loyalists were themselves nicknamed *Kingire*). These were of gold brocade on the front and white cloth on the back. Surviving examples are about 160–180 mm deep and 65–70 mm wide (6½–7 ins by 2½–2¾ ins).

31–42. OFFICERS 1860s The infinitely varied dress of officers during this period of transformation is plainly evident from the dozen figures depicted here. Basically anything went, from full traditional Japanese civilian dress to frock coats and kepis that wouldn't have been out of place at Gettysburg, and business suits of which a London bank manager would have been proud – and, of course, any and every combination of these various extremes.

Figure 31 comes from a series of late 19th-century Japanese prints depicting the evolution of army uniforms in the late Edo and Meiji periods. Though commander of a unit of troops attired like Figures 26–29, he is conservatively attired in *kobakama* and *haori*, and further links himself with the past by carrying one of the *dansen* fans that had been traditionally carried in battle by Japanese senior officers since mediaeval times and are still carried by Sumo referees today.

The Owari clan officer depicted in Figure 32 (from a later photograph of a man in a surviving costume of the Boshin War period) wears much the same outfit as the last, but is interesting for his *guma*, a traditional 'bear' fur (actually yak hair) wig or cap worn by unit commanders in some clan armies. These were dyed in assorted colours; for instance, those of the Choshu and Owari clans were white (*haguma*), Satsuma's were black (*koguma*), and Tosa's were red (*shaguma*). Figure 33, a Choshu officer dating to 1868, confirms that such caps were not only worn in conjunction with Japanese dress. Note that despite his blue foreign-style uniform the latter still wears an *obi* rather than a waistbelt, even though his sword scabbard is nevertheless suspended from a white leather shoulder-belt. Note too the *kingire* on his left sleeve, and the *sode jirushi* in front of Figure 32's shoulder.

Figure 34 is a shogunate officer in 1863 pattern uniform. His outer jacket is of a type called a *sansai-baori*, in which some Western features – a vent at the back (allowing a samurai's swords to protrude behind) and close-fitting sleeves – had been adopted. This was dark blue all year round, but the under-jacket and trousers were white in summer. His hat is black with a yellow arm of service badge on the front.

Figure 35 is another shogunate officer, this time

Fig 31

Fig 32

Fig 33

Fig 34

dating to 1867 but again wearing a blue uniform and *sansai-baori* and black *jingasa*. Soon after his accession Keiki had introduced a system of hat markings to denote officers and NCOs in the regular *bakufu* army. For most officers these involved using gold lines across the crown of the *jingasa* to divide its surface into two to six equal segments, each – except the one at the front – charged with the wearer's clan or family *mon*. The segment at the front often had an arm of service device instead. Basically, the more segments, the higher the wearer's rank. However, some contemporary pictures show officers in hats with no dividing lines at all and just a single *mon* on the front. The four or five segments of this man's hat would seem to denote he is an officer of some seniority, probably the equivalent of a colonel.

Figure 36 is a shogunate cavalry officer of 1867, in a dark blue uniform with brass buttons, brown belts, and a black scabbard and boots. His black-lacquered *nirayamagasa* hat is decorated in blue. Figures 37 and 38 are infantry officers dating to about 1866–67 and 1867–68 respectively. Colours of the former are unknown, but the latter wears a blue uniform with gold piping and rank chevron, and a red trouser stripe, plus a white belt, a black *jingasa* without rank insignia, and black boots. His sword scabbard is plain steel.

Figures 39 and 40, from engravings in 1866–67 editions of the *Illustrated London News*, are probably clan officers. Many Satsuma officers were still to be seen in such fundamentally civilian attire – incongruously worn in conjunction with the usual pair of samurai swords – during the rebellion of 1877 (see, for instance, Figures 49 and 50).

With the single exception of Figure 42's sword, the last two figures, based on contemporary photographs, wear dress that would not have looked out of place in virtually any Western army of the period. Figure 41 is an officer of the Choshu clan's *Kiheitai*, while Figure 42 is an officer of the shogunate troops that held out in

Fig 35

Fig 36

Fig 37

Fig 38

Fig 39

Fig 40

Fig 41

Fig 42

Hakodate under Enomoto Takeaki until 1869. The uniforms of both are probably dark blue, with brass buttons and black or brown belts, scabbards, and boots.

43 & 44. INFANTRYMEN 1870s Figure 43 (from a picture in the 22 February 1873 issue of *The Graphic*) wears the first government-issue uniform of the Meiji period. Introduced in 1870, its French inspiration is readily apparent. That worn here is the dress version, consisting of a dark blue jacket with red collar and cuffs (the latter with a single inverted yellow chevron denoting him to be a second-class private – first-class privates had two such chevrons) and seven brass buttons, pale blue-grey trousers (replaced by dark blue trousers in 1871) with a yellow stripe, white gaiters, brown boots and belt (with brass buckle), and a black bayonet scabbard. The kepi is dark blue with a gold-embroidered chrysanthemum badge on the front and yellow piping round the sides – one band for second-class privates, two for first-class privates, three for corporals, and a single thicker band for sergeants (plus one thin band for a senior sergeant and two for a sergeant-major) – and on the crown, where it formed the outline of a five-pointed star. The blanket wrapped round his knapsack is also dark blue.

Imperial Guard infantry differed in still carrying a traditional long sword, in having yellow piping down the front of the jacket, round the hem, and at the bottom edge of the collar, and in wearing a white *obi* (the ammunition pouch being suspended at the right hip from a brown shoulder-belt). Imperial Guard artillery substituted a yellow *obi* and red trousers with a black stripe, and did not carry a sword. All arms of service substituted white uniforms during the summer.

A contemporary Western account of the introduction of this uniform would seem to indicate that the general effect was initially not all that had been hoped for. 'The Japanese soldier, though small,' wrote James Summers in 1870, 'looked imposing in his own native dress, and larger and stronger than he really was. Now, in a dingy, shoddy, black coat, not made, nor apparently meant, to fit him, with the cartouche-box under the garment instead of neatly belted round the outside, and thus giving him the appearance of being hump-backed ... the undersized Japanese looks even smaller, feebler, and less to be dreaded than he is'. Another eyewitness, Samuel Mossman, wrote in 1873 that the general appearance of the newly uniformed Meiji infantry was 'rendered more ludicrous' by the way they dragged their feet as a result of being accustomed to wearing sandals rather than boots.

Their unprepossessing appearance was further compounded by the fact that uniforms were clearly in very short supply to start with, so that many units had to make do with whatever they could lay their hands on. Soldiers seen in Tokyo by William Griffis in January 1871 were 'dressed in every style of hybrid costume. One, in a broadcloth suit, finishes with bare head and clogs on the feet. Another has a foreign cap, but a Japanese suit. This man has on a pair of cowhide boots, against which his kilt [i.e., his *kobakama*] flaps ungracefully ... This one has a zouave jacket and native kilt. The soldiers look as if they had just sacked New York.' And yet these were 'chiefly the retainers of the daimios of Tosa, Satsuma, Choshiu and Hizen', who constituted the Imperial Guard! Again, writing this time of troops seen at Fukui in May 1871, Griffis records how 'a regiment of soldiers paraded in non-descript dress, a hybrid of native costume and foreign clothes, civil, military, and neither. Straw sandals and high boots, tight trowsers and the *hakama* petticoats, caps, wide-brimmed hats, chapeaux, and bare heads, top-knots with shaven scalps, and hair cut in foreign fashion, alternated confusedly.'

But things gradually improved. Mossman continues: 'After various attempts at improving the uniform and accoutrements of the Imperial army, in order to distinguish the men from the provincial regiments, it was decided to clothe the infantry as follows: – Grey trousers with a yellow stripe, a blue jacket, a red cap or kepi, black braided, wide peak, with the Mikado's crest in gold lace over the peak, and foreign leather boots, instead of native sandals, which the provincial troops continued to wear. This was a curious mixture ... having a motley appearance, but the clothes were of good material and fitted the men pretty fairly. While the privates and inferior officers were thus clad, the superior officers of both

Imperial and provincial regiments went in for abundance of gold-lace over their tunics, caps and trousers. So much was this the case that the demand ... far exceeded the supply; so that one of the army tailors ordered through a foreign mercantile firm 20,000 yards of gold lace [from] Belgium.'

Clearly, however, this is not exactly the same uniform as is worn by Figure 43, and Japanese official records confirm that the 1870 uniform rapidly underwent several modifications before settling, in 1874, on the simplified service dress depicted in Figure 44. This comprised a short dark blue jacket with one or two red stripes round the cuff (to denote second- or first-class privates respectively), dark blue trousers, a brown belt (now with a white metal buckle), and a small dark blue forage cap with or without a black peak, with yellow piping, brass badge, and a yellow band (but red for the Imperial Guard), plus gaiters, boots, and bayonet scabbard as before. On campaign, however, traditional *waraji* sandals were generally worn in place of the boots. James Davidson (1903), for instance, records that during the expedition to Formosa in 1874 'the Japanese soldiers wore close-fitting leg-coverings from the knee to the ankle, and soft thick sandals, both familiar articles of Japanese dress, while extra sandals were carried suspended from the waist.' In summer the jacket, trousers, and cap were of white cotton rather than dark blue cloth, and it was this white summer version that was worn by most of the troops involved in the Formosa expedition.[58] The summer trousers were also often seen worn in conjunction with the winter jacket. Contemporary prints indicate that the blue service dress was worn by the majority of Imperialist troops fielded against Saigo Takamori's rebels in 1877. Henceforth and for the rest of the century, incidentally, all Imperial Guard troops wore a red band on their hats rather than yellow, in order to distinguish them from Line units.

It should be mentioned in passing that the introduction of leather equipment met with a certain amount of resistance, since leather offended the sensibilities of many Japanese (see note 41). Diósy records that Karl Köppen, the German instructor hired by the Kii or Kishu clan in 1869–70, organised the local leather industry to produce equipment for the *daimyo*'s troops 'and shoes were the first thing he wanted; later he commenced to introduce leather belts, cartridge-pouches, and knapsacks. But there was a curious disinclination on the part of the samurai to put on leather shoes, although in the olden days warriors of high rank wore shoes with the uppers made of black bearskin. Yet, as late as 1872, these Samurai were almost in a state of rebellion because they were required to put the skin of animals on their feet; perhaps, also, because the shoes crippled them very much. So the Kishu troops wore European uniform and their native socks and sandals, and marched about exceedingly well because their feet were at ease ... When it came to supplying them with leather belts and cartridge-pouches a stratagem had to be employed. A very good imitation of leather belts and cartridge-pouches was produced out of oiled paper.'

Arm of service colours were also introduced in the 1870s, with yellow for infantry, red for Imperial Guard infantry, light green for cavalry, and black for artillery being in use by 1871. In 1875 the system was revised and expanded, and the following service colours were introduced. These remained in use for the rest of the century.

Infantry	Red.
Cavalry	Light green.
Artillery	Yellow.
Engineers	White (changed to brown, sometimes described as 'dark red', in 1890).
Military Train	Dark blue (sometimes described as 'violet' or 'purple').
Gendarmerie	Red (plus black after 1882; see caption to Figures 83–84).
Medical Corps	Dark green.
Music Corps	Blue.
Veterinary Corps	Purple.
Pay Corps	Grey (variously described as 'silver grey', 'light grey', and 'blue grey').

Fig 43

Fig 44

Fig 45

Fig 46

Fig 47 Fig 48 Fig 49 Fig 50

After 1875 it became customary for kepis to have the chrysanthemum badge on the front, while peaked forage caps substituted a brass five-pointed star. The chrysanthemum badge's rounded petal-ends became serrated and angular in 1886.

45–48. POLICEMEN 1860s–1870s During the first half of the 19th century the samurai who performed city guard or police duties were the nearest thing Japan had to a permanent military establishment, and following the Meiji Restoration the police remained at first as much, if not more, a military body than a civilian one. The new government started by creating a force called the *Shichu Torishimari* in Tokyo in 1868, but this was soon disbanded, and the following year samurai were conscripted from various *han* to form a brigade of *Fuhei* or 'City Guards', controlled by the governor of the Tokyo prefecture. In 1871 these were reorganised and renamed the *Rasotsu* ('Patrolmen').

This corps was initially just 3,000 strong, but by 1877 there were 18,000 such 'well-drilled and efficient policemen' throughout the country, of whom the greater part were drafted in to help suppress the Satsuma Rebellion following the decimation of the national army. These formed a separate corps known as the *Battoh-Tai*. Mounsey (1879) records that at the Battle of Tawarazaka on 20 March 1877 sword-armed Satsuma rebels 'found their match with this weapon in the corps of armed policemen, chiefly samurai, who formed the storming parties [in the Tawara and Kichi-ji passes] under cover of the fire of the regulars'. He adds that such hand-to-hand fighting 'had shown the Tokyo government the advisability of obtaining the services of men accustomed to the old methods of Japanese warfare – of opposing samurai with samurai – and they accordingly proceeded to enrol swordsmen of different clans as police or gensdarmes. By selecting men from the clans which in former days had had feuds with Satsuma [in other words, ex-Tokugawa adherents] ... and by the offer of high pay, they soon induced considerable numbers of this class ... to enrol themselves'. But note the government's careful policy of keeping these men out of the regular army by employing them as armed police. Note too that though equipped with firearms, Japanese policemen of the 1870s invariably relied on their swords in combat.

Isabella Bird records that by 1880 there were 23,334 police, of whom 5,672 were stationed in Tokyo. She says that as many as 30% of them wore spectacles, which probably indicates that by this time the police force was composed at least in part of men passed over as physically unfit for army service.

Figure 45 is included as a guide to the general appearance of pre-Restoration shogunate patrolmen (who were samurai of *doshin* rank). Dating to 1864, he is a *mimawari-gumi* or Edo city patrolman, wearing typical civilian dress including an *eboshi* cap and a *shiri-saya* scabbard cover. On duty such patrolmen were armed with a mixture of spears and specialist arms such as the *jitte* in this man's left hand (a steel rod fitted with a side hook near the hilt to catch an opponent's blade), which was in effect a patrolman's symbol of office, much like a truncheon was in the West; and the *yagara-mogara*, also known as a *sode-garami* ('sleeve entangler'), a polearm with several barbed hooks at its end and about dozen spikes down the first half-metre or so of at least three sides of its shaft, all designed to catch in a wrongdoer's clothing. Some were also carrying firearms by the mid-1860s – the March 1864 *Illustrated London News* engraving on which this figure is based shows three patrolmen of whom at least two have handguns that may be revolvers. Officers at least are recorded to have sometimes worn mail corselets under their coats. At least some pre-Restoration police corps were uniformed, insofar as they wore *haori* of the same colour. The baton in his right hand with its bushy 'tassel' of gilded paper is a *sai-hai*, a symbol of rank amongst samurai.

Figure 46 comes from a print depicting Meiji policemen who have just defeated a peasant uprising at Makabe in February 1876, while Figure 47 is from a print that shows policemen in action against Satsuma rebels in 1877. The former wears the official dark blue police service uniform, with red kepi (with black peak and silver cap band and badge), red trouser stripe and cuff markings, black belt, white metal buckle and buttons, and steel scabbard. The dress of Figure 47, on the other hand, has been modified by service in the field, which has resulted in the addition of pale blue-grey gaiters and white sashes in lieu of crossbelts, and the substitution of a white *obi* for his waist-belt, white civilian trousers for his official blue ones, and black *tabi* and straw sandals for his foreign boots. In addition his cap is apparently black rather than red, and he wields a traditional *katana* rather than a Western-style sword. In the original picture some men have even cut off the constricting sleeves of their European-style jackets, either at the elbow or at the shoulder, for more ease of movement when wielding their swords.

Figure 48 is a *Battoh-Tai* officer in his full dark blue uniform. As with that worn by the army, the blue of police uniforms was sufficiently dark for some observers to describe it as black.

49–53. SATSUMA REBELS 1877 Saigo Takamori's army was not uniformed, but Mounsey observes that the *shigakko* students who constituted its greater part 'wore Japanese costumes sufficiently similar in cut and colour to give the appearance of uniformity'. What he doesn't say, but what other sources do – supported by several surviving photographs and contemporary Japanese prints – is that many, possibly even most of them, also wore items of Western clothing. Figures 51 and 52, for instance, from contemporary prints, both wear foreign shirts, to which Figure 52 has added a waistcoat, while Figure 49, from a photograph, wears a Japanese under-jacket and *obi* combined with frock coat, trousers, boots, shirt and bow tie. Some wore full Western civilian dress – Figure 53, for instance, is from a photograph of Murata Shimpachi, one of the rebel army's battalion commanders – and a handful are known to have worn their Imperial Army uniforms, among them Saigo himself and two of his leading generals, Kirino Toshiaki and Shinowara Kunimoto. Eyewitness John Hubbard records of rebels he saw captured in August 1877 that 'their clothes were of all sorts, sizes and description. Hats seemed to be the main uniform; of the greatest variety and worst looking that one could imagine; there were even black and white felts of all shapes ... My attention was called to two fellows in black frock coats, no pants, but tall black top hats.'

Their armament was equally varied, not least because most men had to provide their own. Nevertheless, they appear to have been fairly well supplied with modern firearms to start with (Mounsey records them to have been in possession of 'a very considerable supply of Snider and Enfield rifles'), but had only about 1.5 million rounds of ammunition, which one modern authority (Buck 1973) estimates to have been equivalent to at most 100 rounds per rifle – an utterly insignificant supply when one reads that in the fighting at Kumamoto the Imperialists were firing off about 320,000 rounds *per day*. Consequently as time passed and ammunition rapidly dwindled the rebels found themselves having to depend more and more on traditional weapons such as swords, spears, polearms, and matchlocks.

In particular all the sources agree that they relied heavily on their 'keen double-headed swords of feudal times'. Mounsey records that they 'placed the greatest reliance' in their swords, 'feeling that that weapon in the hands of samurai, would be more than a match for a rifle in those of a *heimin*' – virtually echoing the report of an American eyewitness that 'it seemed to be their opinion that patrician samurai could rush into close quarters with the *heimin* and easily rout them.' Griffis records how 'defending themselves in some instances by making a shield of the light, thick floor-mats, or *tatami*, the rebel swordsmen, by a sudden charge, drew the fire of the [government] troops harmlessly, and rushing on them with their swords butchered them easily.' Most modern authorities are of the opinion that by the end of the fighting their swords constituted the rebels' primary, and often their only, weapon. However, this view needs to be tempered by Hubbard's statement that when he was shown the rebel arms captured at Nobeoka

Fig 51 *Fig 52* *Fig 53* *Fig 54*

as late as 17–18 August they still included Springfield muskets and Spencer and Remington rifles (though he adds that 'among the most numerous of the firearms were the old-fashioned matchlocks', and that the captured swords were heaped in a pile more than ten feet tall).

The Satsuma forces also had 'a small park' of artillery. Mounsey mentions just 16 guns, but the entire park, organised into two battalions, appears to have totalled 28 mountain guns, two 16-pdr field guns, and 30 mortars of assorted calibres. But these, too, were provided with insufficient ammunition, and by the end of the rebellion such artillery as the rebels still had was of an improvised nature, consisting of a handful of wooden guns of a traditional design (see p.74 for details).

Various sources tell us that some of the rebels' wives and daughters also fought for the Satsuma cause. The lady depicted in Figure 53, her long hair tied back with a headband, and her *kimono* sleeves contained by means of a *tasuki* sash looped round her arms (as shown in Figure 24), comes from a print depicting Satsuma women defending a bridge against Imperialist cavalry. She is armed with *naginata* and short sword. Most women also carried a short knife called a *kaiken*, used for self-defence and, when necessary, to commit suicide. In October 1868, during the Boshin War, women of the Aizu clan had similarly assisted in the final defence of Wakamatsu against the Imperialists.

54. PEASANT REBEL Localised peasant uprisings (*ikki*) were fairly commonplace in Japan, and there were at least 2,800 in the period 1590–1868, most of them in the second half of the 18th century and the 19th. There were a considerable number in the 1830s, 31 between 1844–51, 40 in 1853–59, and as many as 86 in 1860–67. Nor did they end with the collapse of the Tokugawa shogunate. Quite the opposite. Violent opposition to the social changes resulting from the Meiji government's modernisation programme – and in particular to the introduction of new taxes and conscription – led to more than 190 incidents in the ten years between 1868 and 1878, peaking at 42 in a single twelve-month period in 1869–70.

Such uprisings could involve anything up to a couple of hundred thousand rebels, though the largest in the post-Restoration period (the Chichibu Uprising of November 1884) seems to have involved no more than 7–8,000 armed men. E.H. Norman (1940) observes that in the early Meiji period disaffected samurai attempted to exploit such unrest by trying 'consciously to direct the peasant movement against the government', but adds that 'such a peasant-samurai alliance was bound to fail because the interests of these two classes did not run parallel'.

The figure portrayed is based on contemporary prints depicting rebellions of the post-Restoration period. He is clothed entirely in white, except for the use of a coloured sash inexpertly tied *tasuki*-wise round his shoulders to hike his baggy sleeves out of the way. Armament was inevitably varied. Though farm tools doubtless predominated, edged weapons became more widespread following the abolition of the 'feudal' system.

55. INFANTRYMAN 1886 The uniforms introduced in 1886 remained fundamentally unchanged for the best part of two decades. The service version is discussed in the caption to Figures 70–75, but the figure depicted here, from a Quinto Cenni plate, wears the dress version. This consisted of a dark blue single-breasted jacket with five brass buttons and red collar, piping, and facings for Line infantry, yellow for Guards, and white for engineers; dark blue trousers with a stripe of the facing colour; white gloves and spats (i.e., gaiters worn under the trousers); a low, dark blue shako with black peaks front and back, a brass five-pointed star in front (but note that Cenni shows the earlier chrysanthemum badge still being worn), and a white plume with a red base; and black or very dark brown belts, ammunition pouches, and bayonet scabbard. Guard units substituted white belts and pouches, and a red shako in place of the blue one worn by Line units. As Knollys observed the following year, this new uniform and

Fig 55

Fig 56

56a

Fig 57

Fig 58

Officers' kepi rank insignia, 1870 to 1890s

	1875 pattern	1886 pattern
Second lieutenant	2 thin horizontal lines 1 vertical line 2 stars on crown	1 thin horizontal line 1 vertical line 1 star on crown
Lieutenant	3 thin horizontal lines 1 vertical line 2 stars on crown	2 thin horizontal lines 1 vertical line 1 star on crown
Captain	4 thin horizontal lines 1 vertical line 2 stars on crown	3 thin horizontal lines 1 vertical line 1 star on crown
Major	5 thin horizontal lines 2 vertical lines 3 stars on crown	4 thin horizontal lines 2 vertical lines 1 star on crown
Lieutenant-colonel	6 thin horizontal lines 2 vertical lines 3 stars on crown	5 thin horizontal lines 2 vertical lines 1 star on crown
Colonel	1 thick line, 1 thin line 2 vertical lines 3 stars on crown	6 thin horizontal lines 2 vertical lines 1 star on crown
Major-General	1 thick line, 2 thin lines 3 vertical lines 4 stars on crown	1 thick line, 1 thin line 3 vertical lines 1 star on crown
Lieutenant-General	1 thick line, 3 thin lines 3 vertical lines 5 stars on crown	1 thick line, 2 thin lines 3 vertical lines 1 star on crown
General	1 thick line, 4 thin lines 3 vertical lines 6 stars on crown	1 thick line, 3 thin lines 3 vertical lines 1 star on crown

equipment continued to bear 'a strong resemblance' and 'a first cousinship' to those of the French Army.

56 & 57. ENGINEERS 1886–1900 Taken from the same Quinto Cenni plate as Figure 55, the first of these two figures wears a variety of the 1886 pattern service uniform, comprising blue trousers, white-piped blue tunic, blue peaked forage cap, and white gaiters. As with the infantry, the cap band was yellow for Line units and red for Guards. Full service dress as worn in the field was indistinguishable from that of infantrymen except in the substitution of white (but brown after 1890) collar, piping, and facings.

Figure 57 is based on a *Graphic* engraving depicting engineers in the field during the Sino-Japanese War (reproduced on p.47). Note that he wears an old-pattern peakless cap like that of Figure 44 rather than the more normal peaked variety worn by other engineers in the same picture, and traditional gaiters and sandals rather than boots. Detail 57a, from a December 1894 edition of the *Graphic*, depicts the five-pointed, presumably yellow or perhaps white cloth star worn for identification purposes on the backs of the tunics and shirts of civilian labourers who assisted the Engineer Corps during the Sino-Japanese conflict.

58–61. OFFICERS 1870s–1880s These figures are reconstructions from Japanese prints, photographs, official regulations, and surviving items of dress. Figure 58 wears an 1873 pattern uniform, which is in effect much the same as that of Figure 43, but with the addition of gold piping on his jacket and kepi, plus tall boots (which, because of the Japanese custom of removing their boots indoors, were 'very easy-fitting' so that they could be 'kicked off and pulled on without any trouble'). As a company officer the front edge of his gold trouser stripe would be in his arm of service facing colour to a third of its width, while for field officers the arm of service stripe occupied the middle portion instead. General officers had a plain gold stripe. The crown of the kepi was at this stage decorated with the outlines of two five-pointed gold stars for company officers (i.e., second lieutenant, lieutenant, and captain), three stars for field officers (major, lieutenant-colonel, and colonel), four for a major-general, five for a lieutenant-general, and six for a full General, as well as a progressively larger number of thin gold lines round the cap band (plus one thick gold line at the bottom for senior officers) and one to three thin vertical lines at the front, back, and sides. The number of stars on the crown was reduced to one for all officer ranks in 1886. Overall, officers' kepi piping during this period was therefore as listed above.

The jacket collar was in the appropriate arm of service colour, edged in gold (in the Guards) or silver (in Line regiments) to one-third of its width for company officers, and to two-thirds of its width for field officers, but left entirely gold or silver for general officers. 1875 and 1886 pattern trousers had a single arm of service stripe for warrant officers (1886 pattern only), a slightly wider stripe for field and company officers, and a thin stripe between two wide stripes for general officers (whose arm of service colour was henceforward red). Company and field officers' riding breeches had no stripe, while those of general officers had only one. Staff officers were distinguished by an aiguillette.

An 'Attila' – a short-skirted patrol jacket with five braid loops across the chest – was generally worn in the field. This is shown in Figures 59 and 60, who date to

1877 and 1874 respectively. Such jackets were dark blue with black braid loops and black fur edging in winter, and white with white braid loops in summer. The winter version was such a dark colour that many contemporaries described it either as blue-black or simply black. On ordinary jackets and dress Attilas rank was denoted by silver or gold 'Austrian knots' (trefoils) on the sleeves, made up of between one and seven lines of lace (one for a second lieutenant, two for a lieutenant, three for a captain, four for a major, five for a lieutenant-colonel, six for a colonel, and seven plus other distinctions for general officers; generals' knots also comprised three loops on each side rather than just one). Like the jacket buttons, the sleeve knots were silver for Line regiments and gold for the Imperial Guard, but on service Attilas they were black on winter uniforms and white on summer uniforms. Service Attilas had no colour distinctions to denote arm of service, whereas dress versions had coloured collars and cuffs.

A peaked forage cap could be substituted for the kepi. The version introduced in 1886 had a cap band and piping round the crown which were both in the appropriate service colour, plus a silver five-pointed star on the front, and one, two, or three narrow horizontal black stripes circling the arm-of-service band, which denoted the wearer to be a company, field, or general officer respectively. This type of cap is worn by Figure 61, who also wears an 1886 pattern greatcoat. Note that greatcoats had an entirely different series of cuff marks denoting rank. In 1875 these comprised a single horizontal lace band (in arm of service colour) for field officers, with beneath it two five-pointed stars for a major-general, three for a lieutenant-general and five for a general. From 1886 the greatcoats of field officers bore two horizontal cuff bands, company officers bore a single band, and the number of stars borne by the three grades of general officer diminished from two, three and five to one, two and three respectively.

Note too that Figure 59 (from the 27 October 1877 issue of *The Graphic*) wears shoes and gaiters rather than riding boots; this was customary when in marching order or fighting on foot (officers up to and including the rank of captain all fought on foot). There were no regulations covering what or where personal equipment such as binoculars,[59] map-cases, holsters, satchels, water-bottles, etc, should be carried, and officers generally equipped themselves as they saw fit. Being in marching order, this figure has a knapsack and water-bottle.

62–69. CAVALRYMEN 1862–1900 The shogunate's first regular cavalry unit was organised in the latter part of 1862 or early 1863. Figure 62 is a shogunate cavalryman of the mid-1860s in an all-blue uniform and a black *jingasa* with an arm of service badge in white on the front. His *obi* is also white. Figure 63 is another shogunate cavalryman, this time dating to 1867 and wearing a distinctly French-style uniform consisting of a blue tunic, white trousers, white-covered cap with neck-curtain, yellow waist sash, and black or dark brown belt, ammunition pouch, and boots. Note that spurs have now been adopted, and remained in use hereafter. The saddlecloth is white edged in blue, and the horse-harness is of a French pattern. Arms comprised a *katana* or a Western-style sabre, a carbine suspended from a white shoulder-strap, and a lance measuring 2.22 m/7.28 ft overall (shaft 1.4 m, socket 0.35 m, and blade 0.47 m), here slung from the left arm by its strap. The pennon is red over white. A black-scabbarded bayonet for the carbine was attached to the waist-belt behind the left hip.

The Meiji cavalryman depicted in Figure 64 dates to 1871. His uniform consists of a yellow-piped dark blue jacket with red collar and cuffs and brass buttons; red trousers with a yellow stripe, of which the fore-edge is green; a yellow-piped red kepi with a white plume and black peak; a dark brown belt and boots; and a plain steel scabbard. Guard Cavalry jackets were initially (but very briefly) light green – with yellow-edged red shoulder-straps, yellow piping, and brass buttons – but were soon changed to dark blue with yellow piping and no shoulder-straps. The kepi and trousers were as described for Line cavalry, except that the kepi plume was red on the right and white on the left.

Figure 65 comes from a print by Nagayama Umosai depicting cavalry in action during the Satsuma

Fig 59

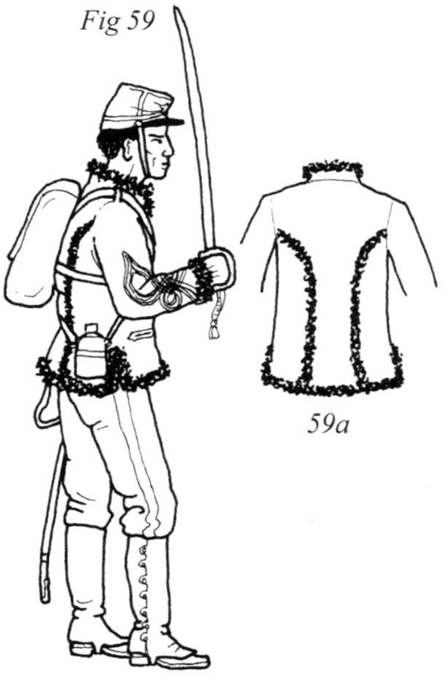

59a

Fig 60

Fig 61

61a

Fig 62 *Fig 63* *Fig 64* *Fig 65*

Rebellion of 1877. He wears a dark blue coat with pale green frogging and piping and a white-edged green collar, a red shako or kepi with a gold band and a white plume (the shako should actually have a black leather cap band and crown, and a brass chrysanthemum badge), red trousers with a green stripe, black boots, and a red-over-white lance pennon as shown in detail 65a. Detail 65b depicts an alternative pennon from a print of Imperial Guard cavalry dating to February 1889; other sources show the field divided by the more usual plain horizontal line. Cenni shows saddlecloths dark blue edged in green, but dark purple edged in red was more usual. A white cotton uniform was substituted for dark blue in summer, with a white cover and neck-flap over the shako.

Figure 66 wears an 1886 pattern uniform, consisting of a double-breasted dark blue jacket with a green collar and piping, brass buttons, and red shoulder straps; red trousers (Grierson erroneously says blue) with a green stripe; a blue forage cap with a yellow band (red for Guards); brown boots and belts; and a steel scabbard. The double-breasted jacket was soon thereafter replaced by a single-breasted variety. Note the typical way that he carries his carbine, slung over the shoulder rather than suspended from the crossbelt. Younghusband observed in 1894 that because of this every cavalry uniform he saw was 'rubbed in holes by the friction of the carbine'. The cross-belts supported a water-bottle on the left and a single ammunition pouch on the right, containing just 16 rounds according to Younghusband, but 30 according to Cox. In wartime an additional 40 rounds were carried in the saddle holsters.

Figures 67 and 68 are variant uniforms (dress and field service) both worn during the Sino-Japanese War. Figure 67, based on Japanese prints and an engraving in the *Graphic* of 8 December 1894, is a Guard Cavalry warrant officer. His jacket is a dark blue dress Attila with yellow-piped light green collar and cuffs, red button loops and piping, and red epaulettes; detail 67a provides a rear view. His dark blue cap has a red band, a black peak, and a brass star. His uniform is otherwise as before. Not shown, because they were not worn on campaign, are the saddlecloth, holster-covers, and the cover over his rolled greatcoat strapped behind the saddle. These were dark purple edged in red, with a red chrysanthemum embroidered on each holster cover and each end of the greatcoat cover. His rather small and shaggy mount is clearly a Korean pony, probably acquired locally to replace a horse lost on service.

Figure 68 comes from an engraving in the *Black & White* of 11 August 1894, and being a newspaper print is not in colour. However, the publication date and the fact that his trouser-stripe looks dark strongly suggest that he is wearing white summer trousers, albeit probably in conjunction with a winter jacket. He also wears a yellow-piped red kepi in place of the last figure's peaked forage cap, complete with chrysanthemum badge. He appears to be a sergeant. The cross-straps support a water-bottle at the left and a haversack at the right.

Finally, Figure 69 comes from a Japanese print of cavalry in action against the Boxers in 1900, published in *The Sphere* on 17 November 1900. He wears a white summer uniform, and his cuff insignia identify him as a second lieutenant. In winter officers generally wore dark blue Attilas on campaign, just like their infantry counterparts. Cox considered the uniforms worn by the cavalry he saw in China in 1900 as 'badly made and ill fitted'.

By the end of 1865 some shogunate cavalry were already using Western-style horse-harness, and following the Meiji Restoration French harness was officially adopted for the army. At some point after 1886 this was changed for German harness. Either way it was left the natural colour of the leather. The saddle was constructed from two side-boards supported by front and back arches beneath a padded leather covering, and had a low cantle. Younghusband criticised this for placing the rider 'rather high off the horse's back'. The saddle was placed on one or sometimes two blankets. In front of the leg there were two 'holsters' (actually 'capacious soft wallets'), and behind the leg were two large saddlebags. A dark blue greatcoat was rolled up and strapped to the back of the saddle. Usually a plain double bridle was used, a plain breast-strap, no crupper, and light, quite small stirrups, but some observers noted that Japanese cavalry equipment was 'not uniform'. Imitations of Western horseshoes, meanwhile, had begun to appear well before the end of the 1850s, and were used for the Meiji army's cavalry corps from the outset. Cox nevertheless observed that as late as 1900 Japanese horses were still shod 'very badly'.

As we have already seen (in the caption to Figure 4), native Japanese horses or ponies were of a testy disposition and not very large – 'small, ugly, and stubborn,' wrote Lehautcourt in 1892; and 'certainly not much to look at, but ... capable of great endurance', says a report of 1901. As in Edo times, they were also still predominantly stallions, only the especially bad-tempered ones being castrated (at least in the artillery), the rest being left 'entire'. The poor quality of Japanese cavalry compared to that of the Western powers was blamed entirely on their horses, which, as well as being small and aggressive, were said to be badly trained and not particularly healthy (of the 450 horses of the single regiment serving in North China in 1900, only 60 reached Peking).

As regards their size, descriptions dating to the 1890s indicate that, unsurprisingly, the largest were selected whenever possible, since most reports put them at about 14 hands. Attempts were also made – albeit reportedly 'without much success' – to improve the native breed by crossing it with foreign stock. The French government had presented 15 Arab stallions and 11 mares to the Shogun as early as 1861, and by 1868 the *bakufu* had bought in some 265 more foreign stallions, including 96 Algerian and 65 American, the rest being largely Arabs. Others were imported by individual *daimyo*. The Arabs were found to be the best sires. In the 1880s and 1890s such crossbreeding programmes as did not involve Arabs used Hungarian, American, or Australian horses. The limited nature of such success as was achieved is apparent from an allusion in Lehautcourt's description of the Japanese Army in 1892, which seems to intimate that only officers rode such crossbreeds.

Including its rider, a Japanese cavalry pony had to carry on average 232 lbs (105 kg). In the 1860s it was fed on 'chopped straw and water, or hay soaked in water, and boiled peas, administered warm', and this remained its customary diet at the end of the century, when regulation daily feed comprised 10 lbs (4.54 kg) of hay and 14 lbs (6.36 kg) of grain, the latter being 'half a mash of beans, and half barley'. For his own sustenance, each cavalryman carried one day's rations (chiefly rice), and two days' emergency rations. The regimental transport carried another one day's rations, and the supply column – which, for the sake of mobility, used pack-horses rather than wagons – another four days'. However, judging from reports written during the Russo-Japanese War the Cavalry's logistical arrangements were often found wanting, and units frequently had to reprovision themselves from Infantry supply trains.

70–75. INFANTRYMEN 1894–1900 As we have already seen, the uniform worn during the Sino-Japanese War and the Boxer Rebellion – and, with little change, the Russo-Japanese War too – had been introduced in 1886. It marked a switch from the army's earlier preference for French styles by incorporating numerous German elements, the most obvious of which was the

Fig 66 *Fig 67* *Fig 68* *Fig 69*

Fig 70 *Fig 71* *Fig 72* *Fig 73*

new service dress peaked forage cap adopted by all arms, with its yellow band for Line units and red for Imperial Guards. This new uniform is shown in Figures 70 and 71, which are derived principally from contemporary prints of the Sino-Japanese War and surviving items of dress.

For Line infantrymen the winter uniform consisted of a short-skirted jacket and trousers of a thick woollen cloth, dyed a blue that was still dark enough to seem black to many eyewitnesses. There was a yellow stripe on the trousers, while the jacket had a red collar, and red shoulder-straps (for both Line and Guards) with brass Arabic numerals identifying the wearer's regiment, but no piping. The rank stripes round the cuffs were yellow for Line regiments and red for Guards (in other arms of service the shoulder-straps, trouser stripe, cap band, and rank stripes were all in the appropriate service colour); in 1886 these stripes had encircled the cuff, but contemporary pictures indicate that by 1894 they were sometimes applied only to the outer surface. The bayonet scabbard was black, but belts, pouches, and boots were dark brown. All buttons and buckles were brass. The trousers are described as 'made like riding breeches', in that they ended well above the ankle, 'where they are made to fit tight to the limb, being fastened by tapes instead of buttons.' Socks were white and very short, reaching only to the ankle, and were of traditional *tabi* style, which enabled them be worn with sandals when required. The knee-length canvas gaiters were officially white, but several contemporaries describe them as grey, and they are also depicted light grey in a number of Japanese prints. Soldiers seem to have customarily tucked their chopsticks inside them.

Note that Figure 70 wears traditional straw *waraji* rather than official-issue boots. This was not unusual, and had been accepted practice since as early as the Satsuma Rebellion, when Imperialist troops wearing European leather boots in action for the first time had abandoned them in favour of native sandals. It was not that their boots were heavy (at just 3 lbs/1.36 kg they were actually a pound lighter than those worn in the British Army at that time): most Japanese simply found them uncomfortable. Sandals were invariably worn by soldiers when off duty, and the authorities turned a blind eye to them being worn on campaign. In fact the practice was so well established that during the Sino-Japanese War infantrymen were required to include four pairs of sandals in their kit as well as two pairs of boots. Some men nevertheless coped with wearing foreign boots, a *Times* correspondent accompanying the Japanese Army in Korea in 1894 explaining this by observing that 'though men after three years of training under the Conscription Laws get on all right in boots, there are now many in the field who had finished their three years and returned to private life and native foot-gear'. The practice of wearing sandals was eventually discouraged, at least in cold weather, after numerous incidents of frostbite during the winter of 1894–95, most infamously in January 1895 when as many as 1,500 men were struck down in a single 24-hour period after marching in sandals through 2 ft (0.61 m) of snow for a whole day.

In cold weather a hooded greatcoat might be worn, as depicted in Figures 73 and 74 (from illustrations in the *Black & White* of 25 August 1894 and the *Graphic* of 29 October 1894). These had been introduced for all branches of the army in the early 1870s, and seem to have alternated between single- and double-breasted styles at various times thereafter so that in almost any one year both types could be found in use somewhere in the army. In 1894–95 the infantry officers' variety was double-breasted, while those of other ranks were single-breasted. Greatcoats were ordinarily of woollen cloth with bone buttons, but during the war with China a cold-weather version was introduced, made of thicker cloth and having a deep, fur-trimmed collar. 'From the middle of the edge of this collar,' writes a nurse who saw such coats during the Russo-Japanese War, 'a cotton cap or hood can be pulled out so as to cover the head, and over this can be worn the ample detached woollen "cold-proof" hood.'[60] Though officially described as dark blue, Japanese army greatcoats were sufficiently dull in colour that some observers considered them to be grey.

In winter most men also either provided themselves, or were provided with, large, thick gloves or mittens, variously described as being of felt or wool.

These were hung from the neck by means of cords. The nurse mentioned above adds that in the Russo-Japanese War 'a sheepskin waistcoat with the wool outside' was also issued in very severe weather. This fastened at one side. However, during the Sino-Japanese War the army's logistics arrangements were far less well organised, to the point where troops fighting in Manchuria were still wearing their summer uniforms even after the onset of winter. Overcoats and mittens were only eventually issued during November, and seem to have been paid for largely by public subscription.

Figure 71 provides us with a view of the standard knapsack arrangement. The pack itself, which Cox states was 'similar to the French one', was made of brown cowhide with the hair left on, its shape being maintained by means of an internal wooden frame. Most sources state that when full it weighed about 42–47 lbs (19–21 kg; one source, however, says only 35 lbs/16 kg). This compared very favourably to the 60–66 lbs (27–30 kg) of most European armies and the 70 lbs (32 kg) of the Russian Army. Full campaigning kit comprised the knapsack, an undyed canvas haversack, and an aluminium water-bottle and canteen (both blackened on the outside). The greatcoat and a dark blue blanket were rolled up and strapped round the outside of the knapsack, a spare pair of boots was strapped one to each side, and the canteen was strapped to the knapsack flap. In addition each man carried a section of tent rolled up and strapped on top of the blanket/greatcoat roll ('which increases the bulk of the pack very largely', says Diósy). A proportion of men also had an entrenching tool secured to the back of the knapsack; alternatively this might be attached to the belt alongside the bayonet.

Amongst the knapsack's contents were spare ammunition, an aluminium mess tin, a small medicine case, a toothbrush, a tin of insect powder, a filter, two changes of underclothing, two shirts, two handkerchiefs, two pairs of socks, four pairs of straw sandals, and rations for between two and four days (sources differ; one says one day's full rations and two days' emergency rations, which may go some way towards explaining the discrepancy).[61]

In summer a white cotton drill uniform was substituted for the blue cloth one, and the cap was given a white cover which left only the coloured band and the peak visible. This cover could also have a neck-curtain attached; by the end of the century this was made of three separate flaps (one at the back and a smaller one at each side), but during the Sino-Japanese conflict it more usually consisted of two overlapping flaps as seen in detail 72d (rear view). During the Boxer Rebellion several eyewitnesses noted with surprise how clean the Japanese soldiers managed to keep these white uniforms.[62] Even so, this campaign and the earlier Sino-Japanese War had amply demonstrated the obvious disadvantages of white uniforms in modern warfare, and they were replaced by khaki in 1904–5. Figure 72 comes from a print depicting Japanese troops in summer uniforms fighting against the Boxers in 1900.

Elements of winter and summer uniforms could often be seen worn together. Figure 75 comes from a photograph taken at Pusan in 1894 that shows just how much Japanese uniforms could actually vary once troops were in the field. Of the 14 men clearly visible in the original, one wears half-boots, another has knee-boots, and the rest either shoes or straw sandals; three wear blue winter trousers and grey gaiters and the rest of them white summer trousers and no gaiters; the cut of the trousers varies from baggy to close-fitting; two wear no jacket; eight wear rolled greatcoats or blanket-rolls of assorted hues, over either the left or the right shoulder; three have no white cover on their caps, and only half-a-dozen have a neck-curtain.

What *looks* like a rolled blanket or greatcoat wrapped diagonally round his body may not be what it seems. That worn by Figure 72 certainly isn't. Although coat and blanket were, indeed, often worn in this way, such rolls might just as easily be an item of kit called a *gassai-bukuro*, referred to by foreign observers as a 'cloth holdall'. This took the form of an elongated cloth sack made of 'stout blue drill', 8½–9 ins (0.22–0.23 m) wide by 6–6½ ft (1.83–1.98 m) long when laid flat. This was open at both ends but sewn across the centre, forming two separate compartments. It was carried empty in the knapsack until a fight was anticipated. The cumbersome knapsack was then discarded, the soldier's rations, a change of clothes, and his spare ammunition being transferred to the holdall, which was wrapped diagonally round the body banderole-fashion and secured by having its ends tied together. *Gassai-bukuro* were also issued to troops not provided with knapsacks, such as the Military Train.

Note the battalion pennon attached to the bayonet of Figure 71, another surviving example of French influence. See the caption to Figure 90 for details of battalion colours. Details 72a–c depict a variety of sun-helmet which had begun to enter service by 1895, when it is to be seen worn by a single background figure in a 16 March engraving in the *Graphic* (72b) and by five (out of 14) soldiers in a photograph taken at Keelung on Formosa at some point soon after its capture in June that year (72a). It doesn't seem to have been in very widespread use, however, and isn't mentioned in any of the foreign descriptions of Japanese troops published between 1894 and 1900. Technically it was intended for use with the summer uniform (though this doesn't explain how it can have been seen and sketched in North China by the *Graphic*'s artist in about January), and was itself white, but in the Keelung photograph it is a distinctly darker shade than the men's white uniforms, which probably indicates that it was provided with a grey or tan cover for winter use.

An unofficial item of dress that seems to have been worn for the first time during the Sino-Japanese conflict was the *senninbari* or 'thousand-person-stitches' (usually rendered in the West as 'thousand-stitch belt'), a sort of good luck charm that was believed – at least by those who made them – to protect the wearer from harm on the battlefield. It comprised a length of white cloth sewn with (theoretically) 1,000 red stitches or knots, prepared for the soldier by female members of his family, who persuaded as many women as necessary to each add a stitch. It was worn round the lower abdomen beneath the uniform.

76–78. ARTILLERYMEN 1860–1900 Figures 76 and 77 are both shogunate artillerists dating to c.1867. Figure 76 wears a dark blue coat and black *jingasa* over civilian dress, while Figure 77 wears the uniform introduced under the auspices of the French military mission (for

Fig 74

74a

Fig 75

Fig 76

Fig 77

details see the caption to Figures 19 and 20). His shoulder-harness is a bricole, a hook on a length of rope which was attached to the hub of a gun's wheel to haul the piece back into position after firing; here it has been doubled up several times and looped through itself to make it more manageable. At this date a Japanese 4-pdr crew comprised six men, and a 6-pdr, 8-pdr or 12-pdr eight men, plus a driver and 'ammunition handler' in each case. A 12-pdr Armstrong needed a smaller crew, just six or seven men.

During the Meiji period artillerymen's uniforms were virtually identical to those of the infantry in all but facing colour (yellow rather than red) and the fact that they sometimes wore tall boots, in which circumstances written sources describe them as wearing uniforms similar to the cavalry but without the braid. They carried a knapsack, albeit a somewhat smaller variety than that described in the preceding caption. This was said to have held 'only two reserve rations and a few absolutely necessary articles of equipment', but still had spare shoes, aluminium canteen, and rolled greatcoat strapped to it. Figure 78 is a fortress artillery sergeant dating to 1890.

79–81. MUSICIANS Their traditional enjoyment of drum music meant that the Japanese readily embraced the infantry side-drum when they Westernised their army. Indeed, the earliest foreign military instructors introduced into Japan (Dutchmen in Nagasaki in the 1850s) noted that drum-playing was their pupils' favourite lesson and was invariably well attended. However, though Japanese infantry appear to have often been accompanied by substantial numbers of drummers (and fifers) in the 1860s and 1870s, these proved to be a passing fad, and in the 1890s it was observed that they didn't use drums in the Japanese Army at all, only bugles. Figures 79 and 80 are shogunate drummers based respectively on a somewhat later Japanese print representing *bakufu* troops of 1864, and an engraving in the 10 August 1867 edition of the *Illustrated London News* depicting 'the Tycoon's body-guard'. Figure 81 comes from a sketch in Trumbull White's *The War in the East* (1895). Infantry bugles had red tassels.

Full military bands were introduced relatively late in the Westernisation process. Writing in 1896, Du Boulay believed that 'bands have only recently been started', but there was certainly at least one, as well as a school for military music, by 1886. However, in 1894 the army still had just two bands – one with the Guards Division and the other with the 4th Division at Osaka – and this number had only increased to three by the end of the century. The 1886 pattern uniform for bandsmen consisted of a dark blue jacket with red cuffs and yellow-piped red shoulder-straps, a red kepi with yellow piping and white plume, red trousers with a blue stripe, white belt and gaiters, and brown boots. Cuff rank markings comprised a single blue line for a private, and a wider band with up to three narrow lines above it for NCOs. Officers consisted of Deputy Band Masters (in effect a warrant officer rank) and Band Masters, the former denoted by an inverted yellow chevron above the cuff, and the latter by a single 'Austrian knot' in gold. The Band Master's kepi also had gold piping in place of yellow.

82. MEDICAL ORDERLY 1894–95 This figure from a contemporary print wears the usual 1886 pattern dark blue uniform and white gaiters, and is identifiable as a member of the medical corps by his white armband with its red cross and the green facings of his uniform (cap band, collar, shoulder-straps, cuff rank stripes, and trouser stripes). The shoulder-straps also had a white metal badge depicting Aesculapius' serpent-entwined staff. Officers carried a sword for self-defence, while other ranks carried a hanger. Infantrymen trained in first aid (of whom there were four per company) wore the usual infantry uniform plus a plain red armband on the upper left arm.

Detail 82a is the badge worn on cap and cuffs by medical staff between 1872–86, before affiliation with the international Red Cross had taken place. Comprising a red bar on a white shield, it was also used as an identification device on medical corps pennons, baggage, knapsacks, and so on.

The Medical Corps had some female nurses

from 1887 (according to Trumbull White) or 1894 (according to Eastlake and Yamada), but these did not serve outside Japan. They were dressed exactly like their European counterparts.

83 & 84. GENDARMERIE 1886–1900 The Tokyo Gendarmerie was formed in March 1881, and similar corps were gradually established in each territorial division. The men were selected from 'time-expired NCOs and privates of exemplary conduct'. There were three such corps (two at Tokyo and one at Osaka) by 1886, four by 1889, six by 1890, and seven (i.e., one for the Guards and one for each Line division) by 1894. Each corps seems to have comprised a battalion of three companies. There are considerable discrepancies in the strength of the Gendarmerie as reported in sources of the period, but among the more reliable figures are (in chronological order) 1,435 men in 1885, 1,655 in 1886, 1,376 in 1887, and 1,388 in 1890. About 50 of these appear to have been officers, and perhaps 250 or so were NCOs. All the officers were mounted, but less than 10% of other ranks. On mobilisation the Gendarmerie supplied the army with its military police, armed with rifle, sword, and revolver.

Their uniform was basically the same as for the infantry, with red cuffs, shoulder-straps, and collar, but the kepi was green with red piping. Headwear changed to a green forage cap with a black peak and red piping round the edge of the crown in 1882, and to a red forage cap with a black band and peak and yellow vertical piping in 1886. In dress uniform trousers were red with a black stripe, but in the service uniform they were dark blue with a red stripe. Also in service dress, other ranks' cuff markings took the form of red reversed chevrons rather than the usual horizontal bands. One thin chevron denoted a private, one thick beneath one thin a corporal, one thick beneath two thin a sergeant, and one thick beneath three thin a sergeant-major. On the greatcoat there was just one thick red chevron for privates, crowned by a thin yellow one for NCOs. Note that the Gendarmerie were unusual in having, in effect, two facing colours, fundamentally using infantry red but with the addition of black for dress uniform trouser stripes after 1882 and for cap bands after 1886.

Figure 83 is a sergeant-major dating to 1890, wearing an 1888 pattern uniform, consisting of dark blue jacket with brass buttons and red collar, shoulder-straps, and cuff markings; a yellow-piped red kepi with black band (officers seem to have generally worn kepis rather than forage caps); red trousers with a black stripe; white gloves; black belts and boots; and a steel scabbard. Figure 84 depicts a private of 1894 in an 1886 pattern service uniform. Tunic and trousers are dark blue, with red collar, shoulder-straps, cuff markings and trouser stripe, and the yellow-piped red forage cap has a black band. The jacket is closed using hooks and eyes rather than buttons.

85–89. OFFICERS 1890–1900 Officers attended Military School for a year, having first served six months in the ranks. Promotion thereafter had to be approved by all the officers of the regiment. It took on average 12 years to reach the rank of captain, 20 to become a major, 26 to become a lieutenant-colonel, and 32 to become a full colonel. Lieutenants were not allowed to be older than 45, captains 48, majors 51, colonels and lieutenant-colonels 54, major-generals 65, and lieutenant-generals 70. At the beginning of the decade it was highly uncommon if not unknown for an officer to be promoted from the ranks, but a deficit in trained cadets throughout this period meant that by its end it had become relatively commonplace for sergeants to be promoted to the rank of second lieutenant for exceptional bravery in the field. By the very end of the century as many as 400 NCOs were being made officers every year. In the mid-1880s subalterns were paid 22–26 *yen* a month, lieutenants 28–38, captains 48–58, majors 87–96, lieutenant-colonels 137–146, colonels 187–196, generals 250–350, and marshals 400. (Privates received just 1.25–2 *yen*, and NCOs between about 3 and $9\frac{1}{4}$, dependent on rank and arm of service.) A decade later subalterns earned about 29–32 *yen* a month, captains 54–62, and colonels about 200.

The majority of officers continued to come from samurai families – especially those of the anti-*bakufu* clans that had engineered the Meiji Restoration – and

Fig 78

Fig 79

Fig 80

Fig 81

Fig 82

82a

Fig 83

Fig 84

Fig 85

their numbers only began to show real signs of decline after about 1890. Writing in that year, Hardy observed that 'the four great clans of Satsuma, Choshu, Tosa and Hizen' furnished the great majority of officer candidates, and that 'three-fifths of the commanding officers of all ranks in the army and navy' were provided by Choshu and Satsuma respectively. At the end of the century the Choshu clan still dominated the army, and the Satsuma clan the navy.

The figures depicted here all date to the Sino-Japanese War, and wear variations of the 1886 pattern uniform already described in the caption to Figures 58–61. Figures 85 and 86 are from the 27 October 1894 and 25 August 1894 editions of the *Black & White*; while Figure 87 is a company officer, and Figures 88 and 89 are Generals, from contemporary Japanese prints. Though they are all shown with Western-style swords, Younghusband wrote in 1894 that 'an infantry officer ... assured me that in time of war each officer would cast away his regulation sword and take to the two-handed sword of his ancestors.'

In 1893 officers' sleeve insignia on summer uniforms changed from 'Austrian knots' to one to three horizontal bands of white braid round the lower cuff above one to three five-pointed stars, as follows:

Second lieutenant	1 band over 1 star
Lieutenant	2 bands over 1 star
Captain	3 bands over 1 star
Major	1 band over 2 stars
Lieutenant-colonel	2 bands over 2 stars
Colonel	3 bands over 2 stars
Major-General	1 band over 3 stars
Lieutenant-General	2 bands over 3 stars
General	3 bands over 3 stars

90. FLAGS Those carried in battle in the pre-Restoration period customarily bore family badges, inscriptions, and

Fig 86

Fig 87

Fig 88

Fig 89

Fig 90

so on – the Choshu forces attacking Kyoto in 1864, for example, were led by two white flags with the names of gods painted on them. The three flags in 90a–c, from a print depicting the shogunate army marching against the Choshu clan during the Summer War, are typical of this period. Figures 90a and b are each about 8 ft deep and 20 ins wide (2.44–0.51 m), while 90c is probably about 5–6 ft (1.52–1.83 m) square. They are respectively blue and white, black and white, and blue and white.

During the first half of the century the Tokugawa themselves frequently used flags with a gold, white, or red *hinomaru* 'sun' disc on a white or blue field. Then, in July 1854, following the opening of Japanese ports to foreign trade, the *bakufu* ordered that all Japanese ships should henceforth fly a white flag with a red disc for international recognition purposes (90d), and the use of this flag was subsequently extended to the government's armed forces. This was the flag under which *bakufu* armies fought during the Boshin War of 1868–69, while the Imperialists fought under a red flag charged with a 16-petalled gold chrysanthemum as depicted in 90e. Confusingly, the latter is also sometimes found referred to as a 'sun' by Western writers – describing the fighting in 1868, for instance, Satow mentions 'the Mikado's standards, the sun in gold on a red field and the moon in silver' (the latter presumably indicating that some flags bore a white disc on a red field). In January 1870 the red disc on a plain white field became Japan's national flag, while military flags added 16 red rays as seen in 90f. The chrysanthemum flag, meanwhile, became the Emperor's personal standard.

Though Okuma says that regimental colours were first issued in 1874, some other sources put the date at 1870 (the year in which the rayed sun was first adopted as a military flag). Either way, the general form of regimental colours remained unchanged thereafter. A typical example of an infantry regimental flag is depicted in 90f. This is white with a red sun and theoretically 16 red rays (though numerous 19th-century Japanese pictures can be found that show anywhere between 8 and 18 rays, so the exact number may have taken a while to settle down). At the bottom is a small white canton on which the name of the regiment was written in black Chinese characters by the Emperor himself. Though they are often depicted larger in contemporary Japanese prints as a result of artistic licence, the flag's dimensions were set at 3 *shaku* 3 *sun* long by 2 *shaku* 6¼ *sun* deep, or about 39.3 ins by 31.3 ins (1.0 m by 0.8 m, therefore in the proportion of five by four), with a purple fringe for active army (*jobigun*) units and a red fringe for second reserve (*kobigun*) units. Cavalry standards were smaller, at 2 *shaku* square (23.8 ins/0.6 m), but were otherwise fundamentally the same design.

Figures 90g–i are the flags of an infantry

regiment's three individual battalions. These were white with coloured zigzags known as 'mountain markings', and no fringe. In active army units the first battalion's flag had a single red zigzag line (90g); the second battalion's a red-white-black zigzag (90h); and the third battalion's a red-black-red zigzag (90i). Second reserve flags substituted a black zigzag for the first battalion; a black-white-red zigzag for the second; and a black-red-black zigzag for the third; while the two battalions of 'national army' (*kokumingun*) units substituted a single purple zigzag for the first and a purple-white-purple zigzag for the second. Active army independent battalions had a single red zigzag with the unit's details inscribed in black Chinese characters at the bottom edge of the field. Flagstaffs were topped with a brass disc shaped like the Imperial chrysanthemum seen in Figure 90e.

While contemporary Western engravings and Japanese prints alike frequently show flags in use, there are indications that in reality they were rarely carried on the battlefield following modernisation of the army; indeed, one of the *Graphic*'s correspondents specifically stated in 1895 that flags were customarily 'absent from a Japanese force'. On the other hand, in 1905 Diósy reported that they 'always take their colours into action', though what he may have meant was that they always took them on campaign, which, of course, isn't the same thing at all.

91. MARINE The Marine Corps was established in 1873 and abolished in 1878, and during its brief existence it was trained by an officer provided by the British Government, one Lieutenant Hawes of the Royal Marine Artillery. Marine contingents participated in the expedition to Formosa in 1874, landings on the Korean coast in 1875 and 1876, and the suppression of the Satsuma Rebellion in 1877.

The figure depicted is a petty officer in blue service dress and white gaiters. His cap has a black chin-strap, and on the crown five lace loops and a button which was yellow for infantry and red for artillery. The circular brass cap badge had a corded edge and bore crossed rifles (infantry) or crossed gun barrels (artillery), petty officers' badges adding a cherry blossom above these. The tunic has yellow collar, shoulder-straps, and piping, and brass buttons, while the trousers had a red stripe which was thin for infantry and thick for artillery. The 'mountain markings' rank insignia on his sleeves are red. These consisted of two lines for a lance corporal, three for a corporal, and four for a petty officer second class. Full petty officers added crossed flags above the stripes (the Japanese flag – white with a red disc – towards the front, and a white flag with two red 'mountain markings', presumably the Marine Corps' own flag, towards the rear); small arms POs had a cherry blossom above the stripes and crossed rifles on the forearm; artillery POs had a cherry blossom above the stripes and crossed gun barrels on the forearm; and instructors had just a cherry blossom above the stripes. Chief petty officers had five stripes, while privates had no sleeve markings whatsoever; nor did the latter have the lace loops on top of their caps. Belts and boots were black for all ranks.

Officers wore a peaked blue cap and either a blue jacket or a blue Attila with black frogging and a black Austrian knot on the sleeves, those of company officers having a black collar with the upper part coloured gold, while field officers had completely gold collars. Trousers were blue and boots black. Company officers had a single gold line round the cap band while field officers had two. The cap badge bore the usual crossed rifles or gun barrels and cherry blossom, but smaller than those of other ranks, with an arrangement of leaves on each side and no corded edge. Rank insignia on jacket (but not Attila) cuffs comprised thick and thin inverted gold chevrons: one thick for an ensign, one thick surmounted by one thin for a subaltern, two thick for a lieutenant, three thick for a lieutenant-commander, three thick surmounted by one thin for a commander, and four thick for a captain. In summer all ranks substituted a white uniform.

92–95. NAVAL BRIGADE 1868–1900 After 1878 the role played by marines in other navies was filled in the Japanese by naval small arms companies that Western observers invariably continued to label as 'marines'.

Fig 91

Fig 92

Fig 93

Fig 94

Fig 95

Fig 96

Fig 97

Fig 98

Naval Brigades served with distinction during both the Sino-Japanese War and the Boxer Rebellion, most notably at the Battle of Ping-Yang in 1894 and in the attack on the Taku Forts in 1900.

Figure 92 is a seaman of the late Edo period equipped for fighting on land. His uniform is entirely blue, except for a white *obi* and the collar of a white shirt showing at the neck. Belt and pouch are black. Western-style naval uniforms also began to be introduced in the late Edo period.

Figure 93, armed with a Martini-Henry rifle, is a Meiji seaman from pictures in the *Graphic* of 19 October 1878. His 1873 pattern uniform is a copy of that worn by the British Royal Navy, setting a trend which was followed in subsequent dress regulations of 1883, 1887, and 1896, in which the main changes were largely restricted to the inordinately complicated system of rank insignia and specialist badges worn on the sleeves. Consequently, despite the intervening regulations of 1896, contemporary Japanese and Western illustrations depict seamen dressed exactly like Figure 94 participating in both the Sino-Japanese War and the expedition against the Boxers. The originals, doubtless drawn in many cases by men who were never anywhere near the scene of action, variously depict the naval brigade involved in the latter operation as wearing blue winter uniforms, white summer uniforms, or blue winter blouses and caps combined with white summer trousers – sometimes with and sometimes without the white or grey gaiters. Very probably all such varieties of dress were worn at one stage or another. Belts, boots, and ammunition pouches were black. The band round the cap was also black, with the ship's name in gold characters and a small gold anchor on each of the ends hanging at the back of the neck.

Officers' service dress also underwent little substantial change after 1873, and certain 1883 pattern uniforms could still be found in widespread use at least as late as 1900. Figure 95 is from a Japanese print of Lieutenant Shiraishi, one of the officers who led the Japanese naval brigade that stormed the Taku Forts in June 1900. He wears a dark blue double-breasted jacket with gold buttons and rank insignia, a black-peaked dark blue cap with a gold band and badge (a chrysanthemum over a circle containing an anchor, sitting in a nest of cherry leaves), a white shirt with a black bow tie, white trousers, and black belt and boots. Though the original shows him wearing a profusion of medals it is unlikely these would have been worn in action; it also shows him armed with only a sabre (the scabbard is black with brass fittings), but doubtless he also carried a handgun of some sort. In the 1870s naval officers had favoured Adams revolvers, but by this late date it is likely they would have been issued with a Japanese-made Type 26.

96–98. COOLIES A tradition left over from samurai days was the army's reliance on huge numbers of porters for its commissariat arrangements. Writing during the Formosa expedition of 1874, for instance, Edward House records that 'the old idea still prevails to a considerable extent that the soldier belongs to a superior class, and is not properly liable to menial offices or the particularly fatiguing labours of the field ... [Consequently] a body of a hundred soldiers [might be] accompanied by nearly an equal number of coolies to do the work of building shelter, cooking, and a good part of the digging of trenches.' Eyewitness B.W. Bax says that the expedition's 2,500 fighting men were accompanied by as many as 1,000 coolies, and Mounsey tells us that during the Satsuma Rebellion three years later the Imperialist army had some 50,000 coolies in its employ on any one day.

Though, by the end of the 1880s, pack animals were being used whenever possible, Japan's insufficiency in horses (there were only a million and a half in the entire country in 1881) meant that it was still largely dependent on 'transport on the backs of men' during the Sino-Japanese War. Conservatives contended anyway that coolies were 'far more satisfactory in every way for transport than horses, as they cost less, carry more, and are far more to be relied upon.' Consequently in 1894–95 about 800 porters were attached to each regiment serving in the field. These carried their loads either by means of a carrying frame similar to the Korean type (for which see Figure 132), or else slung from a bamboo pole carried between two men.

After attempts to utilise Korean coolies during the war with China had ended in failure (see the caption to Figure 132), tens of thousands of Japanese coolies were shipped in, and by the end of the conflict some 154,000 had served in either Korea or North China. These were recruited mostly among the more robust elements of Japanese society, especially farmhands and rickshaw-pullers, but some were ex-policemen in search of excitement, and late in the war a few hundred assimilated Hokkaido Ainu were also recruited. Officially all army porters were supposed to be aged 21–50. They were organised into companies of 50 and 100, and paid 40 *sen* per day, or 75 *sen* for 50-man overseers and a *yen* for 100-man overseers (increased by 10, 20 and 25 *sen* respectively, plus a daily allowance of provisions – rice and dried fish three times a day – once they arrived in Korea or China). Such vast numbers were fielded during the conflict that the normal pool of military reservists from whom they were customarily drawn was drained very nearly dry. This situation was worsened by a colossal casualty rate amongst the army's beasts of burden (one division lost in excess of 75% of its animals in a single march), so that there were never enough coolies available to take up the slack.

Despite their importance, traditional social bigotry meant that coolies were regarded with utter contempt by most of their army compatriots. They were often treated with appalling disregard for their health or safety, and suffered severe losses from disease, cold, injuries, and enemy action. Isabella Bird describes Japanese coolies seen tramping back from Manchuria in 1895 as being 'in rags and tatters, some clothed in raw hides of sheep, their feet, hands, and lips frost-bitten, and with blackened stumps of fingers and toes protruding from filthy bandages.'

Yet on occasion they got involved in the fighting. The following anecdote is provided by Eastlake and Yamada: 'Although unarmed,' they write, 'the Japanese coolies attached to the various Army Divisions had, on several occasions ... to fight for their lives, and in no single instance did they fail to rout the foe. The following is one of the most striking examples of their naked valour. It was just two days after the fall of Port Arthur that a body of about 800 Chinese soldiers made an attack on the Commissariat Quarters. The camp was 30 *li* [about 9 miles/14.5 km] from the Port, and there were only 50 Japanese troopers guarding it ... Their ammunition was almost expended ... when the commanding officer approached at the head of 700 transport coolies. These men were employed simply in the capacity of porters and camp-servants, so had no arms. A few only carried staves [doubtless the bamboo poles used to carry their loads]. Nevertheless the headman of the coolies begged the commander to permit them to engage in a hand-to-hand encounter with the Chinese ... "[to] keep them busy until reinforcements come up." To this the officer rather unwillingly consented. In a moment the coolies were off at a full run, yelling and hurrahing. They fell on the astonished enemy with their naked hands, wrenched the swords or guns away from many, and fought like so many demons. The Chinese broke ... and fled, the cavalry leaving their horses and the foot-soldiers their guns in the hands of the victorious coolies. Of the enemy thirty were killed and many others taken prisoner. On the part of the coolies, the total casualties were only five killed and wounded.'

The coolies depicted here are all from illustrations in March 1895 issues of the *Graphic*, and give some idea of the variety and mixture of Japanese and Western dress to be found amongst them. The colour original from which Figure 98 comes shows him wearing a white shirt and trousers, a brown sleeveless jacket (possibly a long waistcoat) and crumpled deerstalker with a white Havelock, and dark grey gaiters and *tabi*. The bag tied round his chest is blue and the sword scabbard black. Theoretically coolies were issued with 'a sort of uniform' said to have comprised 'a thick wadded coat of light blue cotton' and close-fitting trousers, and this may be the outfit worn by Figure 96. They were also provided with a change of underwear and 'a food-bag, etc, like the soldiers' – probably an allusion to the cloth *gassai-bukuro* described in the caption to Figures 70–75 and apparently worn by Figure 98. However, in reality they either wore what they liked or made do with what they could get. Some are shown stripped to the waist. Most wore sandals or else went barefoot, very few having Western boots. It seems likely that the 'mountain markings' shoulder badges of Figures 96 and 97 were a means of identifying the battalion to which a coolie was attached (compare to the flags depicted in Figure 90g–i).

In the earlier part of the war Japanese coolies were allowed to carry a knife for self-defence (Figure 98 has interpreted this regulation with sufficient generosity to permit himself a traditional *chisa katana*), but after numerous atrocities, murders, and other incidents they were eventually, in January 1895, forbidden to carry weapons of any description. However, most eyewitnesses aver that the worst excesses attributed to them – the massacres and looting which followed the fall of Port Arthur in November 1894 – were actually the work of the army, not the coolie corps.

NOTES

1 This figure stands at about 3,400 today, following territorial losses resulting from the Second World War.
2 Though his people were linguistically and culturally Japanese rather than Chinese, the king of the Ryukyu Islands had acknowledged Chinese as well as Japanese suzerainty (as a vassal of the *daimyo* of Satsuma) since the 17th century, whilst simultaneously considering himself independent of both. This 'ambiguous state of affairs' had persisted until the 1870s. Following the murder by Bunun tribesmen of the crew of a Ryukyu junk wrecked on Formosa's east coast in 1871, it was the Japanese who mounted a 3,500-strong punitive expedition – a mixture of regulars, marines, and volunteers, commanded by Saigo Tsugumichi – in May–December 1874, after China had denied all responsibility for the Bununs' actions (see the section on Formosa in volume 2 of this series, *China*, pp.99–100). China's eventual agreement to pay compensation, by covering the expedition's substantial expenses, was regarded as a tacit admission of Japanese ownership of the Ryukyu group, and despite Chinese protests – which persisted ineffectually until 1879 – Japan retained possession ever after.
3 These would be the site of a decisive Japanese naval victory over the Russians in May 1905.
4 See volume 2 of this series, *China*, pp.74–75. Though the Russian presence in Manchuria was to prove one of the catalysts of the Russo-Japanese War in 1904, the outbreak of the Boxer Rebellion which had brought about its occupation in the first place was, ironically, perhaps the only reason why war had not broken out between Japan and Russia in 1900. As early as May that year the air was reported to be 'full of rumours of a war between Russia and Japan', and pundits predicted that if such a war erupted it would generate a sequence of international crises.

G.F. Browne, for instance, believed (rightly) that Japan would prove victorious, and that 'China would probably throw herself into Japan's arms, and with the resources of that Empire at her disposal, it is difficult to see the limit of Japanese ambition, possibly, but not certainly, at the conquest of the Philippines, Sumatra, and Borneo. Then again, if Russia is crushed in the Far East, it will tend to make her concentrate her energies on Persia and Afghanistan.'

5 The office of *Sei-i-dai-shogun* had been introduced as far back as the 8th century. The 'barbarians' to whom the title referred were the Ainu, who were then still a major threat to the security of northern Honshu.

6 Edo – usually spelt 'Yedo' in 19th-century Western literature – was renamed Tokyo ('the Eastern Capital') in September 1868 following the fall of the shogunate. The Emperor took up residence there soon afterwards and it effectively, though not officially, became Japan's new metropolis, replacing Kyoto. The latter briefly became known as Saikyo ('the Western Capital'), but soon reverted to its traditional name.

7 *Bakufu* meant 'camp office', or more literally 'curtain government', and derived from the Shogun's original function as military commander-in-chief, a Japanese commander's field headquarters being customarily surrounded by screens or curtains. George Preble noted that even in 1854 canvas screens marked with a lord's personal device were still in widespread use 'to surround his camp or station ... I saw a great many of these ornamental screens, and always found them enclosing a military station or surrounding the residence of an official.'

8 The court nobility or *kuge*, who dwelt in the Imperial palace quarter of Kyoto, had been 'reduced to penury and impotence' during the Edo period, and were more than ready to join those *daimyo* opposed to the Tokugawa when resistance commenced in the mid-19th century. This alliance was known as the 'Union of Court and Military', or *Kotu-Gattai*.

9 The Choshu forces were driven back by the Satsuma and Aizu clan armies amongst others, in a confused and bitterly contested street-fight lasting four hours. Known as the Battle of Hamaguri-gomon, this resulted in several Kyoto suburbs being destroyed by fire. (With so many buildings being constructed from wood and paper, fighting within Japanese towns almost invariably resulted in extensive fires.)

10 Unsurprisingly, in consequence of its attacks on Western ships and citizens, the French, British, and other powers regarded the xenophobic anti-*bakufu* faction as a threat to the expansion of foreign trade with Japan. Hence France's preparedness to champion the pro-Western *bakufu* cause.

11 Held prisoner until 1872, Enomoto became a vice admiral in the new Meiji navy following his release. The star-shaped fort at Hakodate, incidentally, was the very first Japanese fortification to be built in Western style, having been constructed in 1855–64 to the design of a Japanese military engineer who had studied in the Netherlands.

12 Eto Shimpei was one of the councillors who supported Saigo Takamori's call for an invasion of Korea in 1873, and, like him, resigned in disgust when the government declined to act. He withdrew to his home prefecture of Saga and, allying with another group of disaffected samurai under Shima Yoshitake, rebelled at the beginning of February 1874. The 2,500 rebels, armed with a mix of swords and modern rifles, were defeated in just ten days, with a loss of some 400 men (compared to 350 on the government side). Eto and Shima were amongst a dozen leaders captured and beheaded.

13 The rebels, calling themselves the *Shimpuren* ('The Band of the Divine Wind'), failed to co-ordinate their attacks and were destroyed piecemeal. The most successful were the 500–600 who managed to surprise the Imperial garrison at Kumamoto, killing or wounding some 300 men. They were defeated a fortnight later. Most members of the various rebel bands not killed in the fighting committed *hara-kiri*.

14 The Emperor was commander-in-chief.

15 Under the Tokugawa shoguns the principal unit of Japanese currency had been the *ryo*, equivalent in value to 220 gm of silver, but in 1871 this was replaced by the *yen*. Both coins were of basically identical value, but whereas the *ryo* consisted of four *bu*, and a *bu* most often of four *shu*, a *yen* consisted of 100 *sen*, a *sen* of 10 *rin*, and a *rin* of 10 *mo*. A silver *yen* was worth 4s 2d (roughly 21p) in 1874, but steadily declined in value over the next two decades, until in 1897 it was worth little more than 2s 0d (10p). The gold *yen* similarly declined, being equivalent to 1.5 gm of gold in 1871 but only half as much in 1897.

16 Castles (*yashiki*) had been pivotal to Japanese strategy since the last quarter of the 16th century and continued to demonstrate their usefulness during the social upheavals of the 1870s. Most readers will have seen photographs of surviving examples and will be familiar with their skilful combination of strength (provided by several lines of broad moats and imposing earth-backed stone walls) and beauty (the decorative, but insubstantial, towers of tiered wooden buildings erected in the centre). Vasilii Golownin, a Russian captive held between 1811–13, tells us that Japanese castles were 'situated upon the banks of rivers or upon lofty eminences, and ... occupy a large extent of ground. Most of them have three enclosures, each with its fosse, and a wall either of earth or stone, with a gate well fortified. The lord lodges in the centre in a square white tower of three storeys, with a small roof in the form of a crown or garland. In the second enclosure are lodged the principal officers of the household; whilst the other one is occupied by soldiery [and servants etc]. The empty spaces are either cultivated as gardens or sown with rice. [They had] white walls [and] the central tower [was] covered with paint and varnish ... The fortifications, though not very strong, are yet sufficient for a country where cannon are scarcely in use ... The proprietors are obliged to keep their castles in good repair; but if any part falls down, they are not permitted to rebuild them without an express permission from the Emperor [*sic* – actually the Shogun]; a permission seldom given, the policy for the last century not allowing any new ones to be erected.' Englishman Rutherford Alcock, writing in 1863, adds that the walls were 'generally built of mud intersected with layers of tiles, and plastered over; sometimes with parapets and loopholed for musketry.'

17 The crew of the transport (a hired British vessel) had surrendered their ship, but the troops it was carrying refused to acknowledge this and after four hours of negotiations started firing at one of the Japanese warships, which consequently shelled and sank her. Japan's unannounced attack on this flotilla, without a formal declaration of war, established an infamous precedent for the events of both 1904 (when Russian fleets were destroyed without warning at Port Arthur and Chemulpo) and 1941 (when the American fleet was attacked at Pearl Harbor).

18 General Nozu would command the 4th Army in the Russo-Japanese War of 1904–5.

19 Marshal Oyama would serve as commander-in-chief during the Russo-Japanese War.

20 Lu-shun had been christened 'Port Arthur' in the West in commemoration of the British Royal Navy's Lieutenant-Commander Arthur, who had surveyed this part of the Chinese coast in 1858.

21 General Nogi had participated in the capture of Port Arthur, and would do so again in 1905 as commander of the 3rd Army during the Russo-Japanese War.

22 General Oku would command the 2nd Army in the Russo-Japanese War.

23 China leased the Liao-tung Peninsula and Port Arthur to Russia in 1898.

24 See volume 2 of this series, *China*, pp.101–2.

25 The exact number is unclear but seems to have averaged about 265. Western and Japanese writers of the period 1860–80 variously report the existence of 262, 264, 265, 267, 268, or even 300 *han* in the late Edo period, the discrepancies being explained both by occasional fluctuations in their number and the fact that some *han* comprised several scattered fragments.

26 There were nine of these, the *daimyo* of Echizen and Aizu being the most prominent. The *han* held by *gosanke* and *tamarinomazume kamon* lords were known as *shimpan* ('related

A Japanese 'dungaree fort' or sham fortification seen by Dumont d'Urville in the 1820s, as depicted in his Pittoresque Autour du Monde, *published in 1834. See note 35.*

han').

27 Only about 20% of a traditional samurai army consisted of fighting men, the remaining 80% comprising an exotic array of servants and menials ranging from armour bearers to sandal carriers.

28 Contrary to what is usually implied in Western books, not all the *tozama* had fought against Ieyasu at Sekigahara. Some had remained neutral, while others actually fought alongside the Tokugawa. Tosa was one of the latter category, but its *daimyo* nevertheless found himself in the anti-*bakufu* camp in the 1860s because many of his samurai had long memories, and were descended from families which had originally owed their allegiance to the lord displaced by his ancestor back in 1600.

29 The population of Edo was consequently very large (about one million by the second half of the 18th century) and consisted half and half of townsmen and *daimyo* with their retainers. The *sankin-kotai* system remained unchanged until October 1862, when it underwent considerable modification. Henceforward the highest ranking *daimyo* were only required to reside in Edo once every seven years, and those of the 'second rank' once every three years, though the rest still had to attend every year as before. But *daimyo* families no longer had to remain in Edo as potential hostages, and attendance was now only required for 100 days rather than a full year. With the change of government in 1868 the obligation was abolished entirely.

30 However, samurai of *hatamoto* rank were notorious for extorting incomes way beyond their official entitlement, and for treating their *chigyo-sho* like personal estates.

31 In the 1860s some samurai 'disengaged themselves from their masters' simply so that they could attack foreigners without having to be answerable for their actions.

32 Conrad Totman's excellent *Collapse of the Tokugawa Bakufu 1862–1868* (1980).

33 One of the foreign adventurers employed as an instructor by the Choshu in May 1864 was a certain 'disreputable American' whose name is scrambled in Japanese sources to 'Borudein'. Was this Henry Andrea Burgevine, disgraced ex-commander of China's Ever Victorious Army? Certainly he had been deported to Japan towards the end of 1863. For his career in Chinese service see volume 2 of this series, *China*, pp.81–82 and 148–49.

34 Conservatives were violently opposed to such training. Aimé Humbert (1874) records that samurai sent to Nagasaki 'to learn the use of firearms under the tuition of the Dutch officers ... were not very well received when they returned to the capital and were quartered in the barracks for the purpose of instructing the new Japanese infantry. Their former comrades shouted "Treason!" and threw themselves on them with arms in their hands.'

35 Prior to this the defence of Japan's coasts depended as much on bluff as effective deterrents, most famously by the use of dummy forts painted on canvas and unrolled along sections of coastline to frighten foreigners from approaching. In 1846, for instance, George Howe, a seaman shipwrecked on Iturup in the Kuriles, records seeing 'what appeared to be a fort, but on coming nearer we found it was a piece of cloth extended about three-quarters of a mile, and painted so as to represent a fort with guns'. On encountering such sham defences in 1853 Commodore Perry's men christened them 'dungaree forts'.

36 In 1861 these quotas had been dramatically reduced, so that, for example, samurai with an income of 600 *koku* owed just two men, those with 1,000 *koku* owed three, and those with 3,000 *koku* owed ten. In 1866 these obligations were increased to three, six, and 24 men respectively, with an extra man being owed for each additional 125 *koku* above 3,000.

37 Chanoine eventually became France's Minister of War in 1894, but resigned after just three days in consequence of the

Dreyfus scandal. The actual strength of the mission itself is variously reported, but certainly at the outset it officially consisted of Chanoine plus 16 officers and men.
38 A Western-style peerage was introduced in 1884, comprising the ranks of Prince, Marquis, Count, Viscount, and Baron.
39 The formation of the modern Japanese navy had begun in May 1868. British naval instructors were provided to the Tokugawa government in 1867 (these were withdrawn during the Boshin War) and to the Meiji government in 1873–79. Much of the machinery and armament used on Japanese warships throughout the 1880s and 1890s was also imported from Britain.
40 Draft evasion remained commonplace amongst Japan's agricultural class for much of the century, and pamphlets providing guidance on how to avoid conscription were reportedly in widespread circulation right up until the Sino-Japanese War.
41 This term had earlier been used to describe small bodies of Loyalist irregulars raised during the Boshin War. Recruited mainly from *ronin*, some of these were armed with modern rifles, but none appear to have received any foreign-style training.
42 This contempt resulted from the Buddhist belief that it was sinful to handle any part of a dead animal – though even devout believers were prepared to compromise their religion sufficiently to permit the use of animal skins once these had been processed into leather by the *eta*.
43 Similar militia units were also established on Tsushima, the Ryukyu Islands, and Goto-Retto (an island group to the west of Kyushu). According to Lehautcourt, by 1892 the Tsushima Militia comprised 'a staff and two corps, one infantry and one artillery; the staff consists of 37 men and two horses, with a lieutenant-colonel or commandant, one lieutenant-adjutant, one administrative officer, three doctors; the corps of infantry has 102 men, of which there are four officers, and that of the artillery 122 men, of which there are five officers.' By the Russo-Japanese War it had increased to a battalion of infantry, a cavalry squadron, a mountain battery, and a fortress artillery battalion.
44 One of the principal factors behind establishing Hokkaido's defensive corps as a militia had been to relieve samurai families reduced to destitution by the dismantling of the 'feudal' system.
45 Occasional resort to ritual suicide (*hara-kiri*) was one of the samurai traditions which lingered on amongst the Japanese military even at the close of the century. An officer overcome by a bout of dysentery during the attack on Port Arthur in 1894, for instance, returned there a week later and committed *hara-kiri* to expunge his dishonour in having had to drop out of the attack; and as late as 1912 General Nogi was to commit suicide as a mark of respect following the death of the Emperor Meiji.
46 The most famous instance of mutiny, known as the 'Takebashi disturbance', involved the 300 artillerymen of the Imperial Guard in August 1878, who were resentful that their loyalty during the Satsuma Rebellion had not been more generously rewarded. After a prolonged firefight, in which some 30 men were killed, they were eventually overwhelmed by the Guard Infantry.
47 As we have already seen (pp. 35–36), though much was made of the 'German' nature of Japanese tactics some observers considered them to have been influenced just as much by those of other European powers.
48 The *shaku* or Japanese foot consisted of ten *sun*, and was equivalent to approximately 11.94 English inches, or 303 mm.
49 This took its name from the *Kobusho* military school set up in Edo by the shogunate in 1854, the students of which wore their hair in this fashion.
50 Henry Tilley records that 'all retainers, whether officers, doctors, wrestlers, soldiers, or serfs, wear the coat of arms of their lord printed on their dress, be it the silk or crape of the two-sworded followers, or the coarse blue cotton of the inferior caste.'
51 The *Genj Yume Monogatari* records that as late as 1862 the people of Kyoto 'had seen firearms in pictures or on the stage, but no one had ever seen a real matchlock [except] on rare occasions they had perhaps seen the weapon of some hunter from the distant wilds'.
52 Tilley records that 'the bayonets, which were a dollar extra, they would not take ... They took one, indeed, as a model, and soon afterwards manufactured themselves as many as they required.'
53 However, the fact that small numbers of the Type 22 must have been issued to elements of the divisions that fought on the mainland seems evident from the following passage in the *Pioneer* newspaper of 10 July 1895: 'From reports which have been received from China it would appear certain that the bullets of the small-bore Muriatta [sic] rifle, used by the Japanese, behave exactly the same as the Lee-Metford pellet ... The Chinese soldiers wounded in action experienced very little difficulty in getting away, even after two or more bullets had hit them ... [and] owe their lives to the invention of the small-bore rifle. The Japanese were only partially armed with the Muriatta; the majority of the infantry had a rifle carrying a much heavier bullet, and this it was that did real execution in the decisive actions.' Since we know that most Japanese infantry were armed at the time with the 11 mm Type 18 this must be the rifle referred to as 'carrying a much heavier bullet'; in which case the 'small-bore Muriatta' can only have been the 8 mm Type 22.
54 One of the only six foreign officers still in Japanese service in 1892 was an Italian 'superintending the making of ordnance at Yokosuka'.
55 The British General Staff's official report on the Russo-Japanese War states that the Arisaka was 'not a quick-firing gun', but other observers say that it was.
56 However, in 1868 Dr W. Willis found by experiment (using armours taken from Tokugawa arsenals) that most helmets were proof against revolver bullets.
57 Curiously, several sources refer to Japanese ponies being 'of a breed larger and much superior to the Chinese'. Superior they may have been, but hardly larger. Chinese ponies were between 12½ and 14 hands tall, while the *maximum* height quoted for Japanese ponies in any contemporary source seems to be just 14-2 hands. Many describe them as no more than 13 or 13-2 hands.
58 The official changeover dates for summer and winter uniforms were the end of May and the end of September respectively. Operations in Formosa lasted from May to December, so it seems likely that the troops involved had switched to winter dress before they were withdrawn.
59 By 1894 sergeants and perhaps even corporals also customarily carried binoculars. A *Times* correspondent accompanying the Japanese Army on campaign that year certainly wrote that 'all above the rank of private carry field-glasses.' Cox reports that these were of French manufacture.
60 The report of Red Cross nurse Miss McCaul, published in the 'Military Notes' section of the *Journal of the Royal United Service Institution* XLVIII, 1904.
61 Upton wrote in 1875 that Japanese soldiers' rations were 'principally rice and fish, but meat is issued twice a week. Bread is also to form part of the ration, but, for want of skill in making it, the men ... preferred rice.' According to Cox, daily rations in 1900 comprised 1.5 lbs (0.68 kg) of 'bread and vegetables' or rice, and half a pound (0.23 kg) of dried meat, plus tea and an unstated allowance of 'country wine' (saké). Other sources indicate that during the Russo-Japanese War they consisted of a quart (1.14 litres) of rice, a third of a pound (0.15 kg) of beef or fish, a third of a pound of dried or pressed vegetables, pressed *shoju* (extract of beans), and six-tenths of a fluid ounce (17 ml) of saké. 'Emergency' rations seem to have comprised different things at different times. Rice, pickled plums, and dried fish 'as hard as a deal board' (described by one observer as looking 'most uninviting') are all mentioned.
62 In 1892, however, Lehautcourt's opinion was that 'there is nothing prepossessing in the exterior view of the Japanese [soldier], and Europeans are often disagreeably surprised at seeing their uniforms unsewn, torn, and dirty'.

THE AINU

Though the name Ainu means simply 'men', the Japanese – and consequently many early Western visitors – rendered it instead as *Aino*, meaning 'mongrel' or 'half-breed' (in allusion to a Japanese legend that they were descended from a human being and a dog). Modern books sometimes call this people the Emishi or Ezo instead. They were the principal aboriginal people of Japan,[63] having occupied the entire archipelago before being driven slowly north following the arrival from the Asian mainland of the ancestors of today's Japanese. Despite putting up a tenacious resistance throughout the early mediaeval period, they had been pushed back as far as the northern tip of Honshu by the end of the 9th century. The last few pure-blooded Honshu Ainu were forced out during the 17th century, and by the beginning of the period under review Ainu were found only in Hokkaido (called Yezo or Ezo, meaning 'wild' or 'barbarian', until as late as 1869), southern Sakhalin, and the Kurile Islands.[64] Their final futile efforts at armed resistance against the Japanese were crushed on Hokkaido in 1786 and the Kurile island of Iturup in 1789.

By the 19th century their numbers had dwindled to virtual insignificance. The census of 1807 showed just 21,700 on Hokkaido and 2,100 on Sakhalin. By the mid-1870s there were at most 18,000[65] and more probably 15,000 on Hokkaido (16,100 were recorded in 1854), 2,400 on Sakhalin, 800 on the southern Kurile islands of Iturup and Kunashir (where there had been about 2,000 in 1800) and little over 100 on the northern islands of Paramushir and Shumshu, the central portion of the Kuriles from Urup to Onekotan being uninhabited by this time. (These figures should be compared to the growth of the Japanese population on Hokkaido, from about 30,000 in 1800 to 287,000 by 1885.) Following the cession of Sakhalin to Russia in 1875 in exchange for the entire Kurile archipelago, some 850 Sakhalin Ainu (referred to as Tsuishikari Ainu) were removed to Hokkaido, though most drifted back to their old homes on Sakhalin during the next few years (they were evicted to Hokkaido again in 1945). The northern Kurile Ainu were similarly removed to the southern Kurile island of Shikotan in 1884, since – having been Russian subjects since the 1770s[66] – their proximity to the Russian frontier was considered by the Japanese government to render them a potential security risk.

Hokkaido, along with the southern Kuriles, was governed by the Japanese Matsumae clan until 1789, when growing anxiety about Russia's intentions in the region prompted the Japanese government to assume direct control of about half the island, before extending its authority over the other half, as well as Sakhalin and the Kuriles, in 1807; this followed Russian attacks against Japanese settlements on the former and the rout of the small Japanese garrison at Shana on Iturup. Though administration of Hokkaido was restored to the Matsumae in 1821, direct rule of the southern Kuriles (Iturup and Kunashir) was resumed in 1854 and maintained thereafter until their garrisons were withdrawn to Honshu to fight for the Tokugawa faction during the civil war of 1868–69. This conflict also witnessed Hokkaido's only significant entry into the annals of 19th-century military history, when its largest town, the port of Hakodate, was surprised and taken by pro-shogunate forces in October 1868 and held until May 1869.

Though Japanese colonisation was steadily intensified after 1874 Hokkaido continued to be regarded as wild frontier territory, and was administered by the government's colonial office, the *Kaitakushi*. Most of the Japanese were concentrated in settlements along the coast of the island's south-western peninsula, which left the Ainu of the interior largely undisturbed and, to all intents and purposes, independent, until quite late in the century.

ORGANISATION

Ainu society was clan-based, there being about half-a-dozen principal clans on Hokkaido. Each of their villages (which were found mostly along the rivers) was governed by its own chief and two elders or deputy chiefs. Chieftainship was for life, or until age or incapacity necessitated the title being passed on. Though a chief could choose a competent son to succeed him if he had one (leading some contemporaries to mistakenly conclude that the office was hereditary), he was just as likely to select 'the most suitable man in the village'. There do not seem to have ever been any Ainu kings, but the chief of Piratori (now Biratori) seems to have once been considered paramount chief among the Hokkaido Ainu, receiving tribute from all the other chiefs and acting as

Japanese painting of an Ainu armed with bow and sword, dating to 1799. His baldric is red with white-edged light blue clasps, and the borders of his gown are dark blue with white decoration.

their commander-in-chief when fighting the Japanese. Each chief led the men of his own village during military expeditions.

The Ainu were exempted from the conscripted militia service introduced on Hokkaido by the Japanese authorities in 1874.

WARFARE

Despite being described as un-warlike by travellers (Isabella Bird considered them 'gentle, good-natured and submissive'), their passivity seems to have been an illusion. Certainly in the 16th century the Ainu had been considered 'bold in war', so that they were 'much feared by the Japanese', and a tradition of inter-village and inter-clan hostility survived into the 19th century. John Batchelor, who lived amongst the Hokkaido Ainu from the 1870s until the 1920s, states that it had 'not yet entirely died out' even in his time. Most such petty conflicts resulted from disputes between neighbouring villages regarding hunting or fishing rights, which were frequently resolved by armed raids. Sometimes these fights were no more than brawls involving sticks and stones, but on other occasions bows, spears, and clubs were employed to murderous effect.

Batchelor wrote in 1892 that 'when the Ainu were at war with one another it was a case of every able-bodied man and woman turning out to fight ... The women were left to fight their own sex, whilst the men fought the men ... Not infrequently too, the Ainu made night raids [*topat-tumi*] one upon another. On such occasions nearly the whole of the male population was murdered during sleep, whilst the women and children were carried off as slaves ... The women are said to have generally accompanied their husbands when they went on these night raids, and to have rendered very effective service.'

In earlier times the Ainu had employed their primitive dug-out canoes (up to 25 ft/4.5 m long) to take them on raids as far afield as Kamchatka and the northern coast of Honshu, and it seems likely they were still used in raids against neighbouring villages where appropriate. Also in earlier times the Ainu of Hokkaido had built rectangular fortifications comprising earth banks and wooden palisades, sometimes with at least two corner towers for lookouts. Still in use in the 17th century, these had been abandoned before the 19th, when the handful that were pointed out to Western visitors were little more than unrecognisable lumps in the ground.

DRESS AND APPEARANCE

Ainu men were much the same height as Japanese (most visitors record them averaging between 5 ft 2 ins and 5 ft 4 ins, or 1.57–1.63 m), but were more robustly built. Bird described them in 1878 as broad-chested, broad-shouldered, and 'very strongly built, the arms and legs short, thick and muscular, the hands and feet large'. Their complexion is variously described by contemporaries as both lighter and 'scarcely darker' than that of the Japanese, the contradiction being explained by the Ainu of Hokkaido's northern coast being darker than those from the south, and the fact that many were noticeably bronzed by exposure to the sun. Bird likened their colour to that of Spaniards and southern Italians. A.H. Savage Landor (1893) described them as 'light reddish-brown', Romyn Hitchcock (1891) as 'rather brown than yellow', and H.C. St.John (1873) as 'a copper colour with an olive tint'. According to Batchelor the darkest were of a 'coppery brown' hue resembling that of Native Americans.

Ainu could be easily distinguished from Japanese by their hairiness. Though this aspect of their appearance has frequently been exaggerated, they are undeniably more hirsute than the Japanese, with thick black or occasionally (in north-east Hokkaido) dark brown hair, beards, moustaches, and eyebrows, and often a 'heavy growth of stiff hair on the chest and limbs'. They wore their hair parted in the middle, and sometimes kept it in place with a headband tied at the back of the head. It was cut short at the front, as well as in an arc at the back to leave the nape of the neck exposed, but could reach to the shoulders at the sides. When it was not simply cut at the front the first 2½–3½ ins (60–90 mm) of the forehead was shaved instead. The Tsuishikari Ainu of Sakhalin shaved off all their hair forward of a line across the crown from just behind the ears (see figure detail 99b). All Ainu men also wore thick, wavy beards which sometimes began immediately below the eyes and covered the entire lower part of the face, Batchelor writing that he had seen 'fine bushy beards more than a foot long'. Their hair and beards went grey at a comparatively early age.

The climate of Hokkaido produced short, warm summers and long, cold winters, and these extremes were reflected in Ainu dress. In summertime, for instance, men

Two Ainu men of 1880, from John Batchelor's Ainu Life and Lore. Note the tasselled inao (lucky charms) attached to the quiver of the right-hand figure. Their bare feet don't tally with their winter attire, and are probably the artist's attempt to prove to his Victorian audience that the Ainu were 'primitive'.

traditionally went almost naked, frequently wearing no more than a loincloth. When other garments were worn the chief item was a calf-length gown (ankle-length for women) called an *attush*, which was folded across the chest from right to left and held in place by a narrow belt. It was made of a durable, canvas-like bast cloth produced from elm-bark, said to have been rough and brittle when dry but very strong when wet. Occasionally birch-bark fibre was substituted, while in the north, and especially on Sakhalin, nettle fibre predominated. These coats are reported to have been generally very grubby, an impression to which the natural hue of the cloth – variously described as beige, reddish yellow, buff, and dirty brown – doubtless contributed. Some, called *kunnep* ('black things'), were rendered darker by means of a vegetable dye obtained from oak or alder bark, which gave them a reddish black tinge. Those worn on holiday occasions were heavily decorated with zigzag geometric or fret-work patterns of red, blue, and white embroidery, and even those intended for everyday use generally had embroidery on the back, cuffs, collar, and hem. The patterns (which differed in style between men and women) varied between villages, so that it was theoretically possible to determine a man's place of origin from the embroidery of his coat. The belt was made either of the same material or else sealskin or bearskin.

Those Ainu who could afford it had their *attush* made instead from Japanese cotton, blue or blue-black material being preferred. Native bast cloth consequently became gradually less commonplace, and by the 1890s was said to be 'by no means abundant'. In fact Landor tells us that some Ainu living in southern Hokkaido either 'adopted Japanese kimonos altogether' or at the very least made their *attush* in the same style, and we know from written accounts and contemporary pictures that village chiefs at least often wore a Japanese *haori* over the *attush*. The Southern Kurile Ainu had meanwhile adopted Japanese dress in its entirety.

Batchelor says that no shirt was worn beneath the gown, but according to Bird some wore 'a skin or bark-cloth vest'. The only other item of clothing commonly worn when hunting or travelling consisted of tight-fitting gaiters (*hoshi*) made of elm bast cloth, coloured or patterned Japanese cotton, plaited reeds (in summer), or animal skin (in winter). Those made from bast often had embroidered decoration on the upper part, while those woven from reeds or rushes were left with fringes at top and bottom to keep mosquitoes away. Landor describes *hoshi* being worn 'fastened just under the knee by means of the two upper strings, then wrapped tightly round the leg and bound round the ankle with the lower and longer ribbon.'

In winter men generally wore in addition one or sometimes two (Bird says 'one, two, or more') shapeless, sleeveless fur pelisses, sewn together from bear, deer, dog, badger, otter, marten, fox, wolf, seal, or even (in the Kuriles) bird skins. Batchelor says that similar skin trousers had also once been worn – presumably before our period – while Bird adds that skin hoods still were. Alternative winter wear included a longer, sleeved deerskin jacket worn mostly, but not exclusively, by women, and skins sewn over a bast or cotton *attush*. On Sakhalin such coats were usually of sealskin decorated with a pattern of fabric and fur appliqué.

Though they generally went barefoot in summer, vine or walnut bark sandals and deerskin or horsehide moccasins tended to be worn for long journeys or when hunting (or, presumably, raiding). These were replaced in winter by boots made from salmon skin, which we are told were 'good for walking on ice, as they were very rough'. Landor adds that when in the field, an Ainu protected his moccasins or boots 'by slipping over them a pair of thick rope sandals, which protect the sides, the back, the toes, and sole of the foot.' For added warmth, boots and moccasins alike might be stuffed with straw or dried grass. For getting around in frozen conditions the Ainu had snowshoes and, on Sakhalin, skis.

A headscarf was also often worn in wintertime, while some Ainu on Hokkaido's north-east coast wore hats, consisting of a 30-inch (760 mm) disc of plaited rushes folded across the top of the head as shown in Figure 100, kept in place by a string tied under the chin.

The only jewellery worn by Ainu men comprised an occasional bead necklace and silver or sometimes brass earrings, or, lacking these, a piece of red silk or cloth stuffed through the hole bored in each earlobe. The earrings were 1½–2 ins (38–50 mm) in diameter, and generally incorporated a glass bead, usually blue, at the point where the ends came together.

The Kurile Ainu

Though we know from Japanese prints published in 1854 that the Sakhalin Ainu dressed identically to those of Hokkaido, we also know from various contemporary reports that the Kurile Ainu did not. By the late 18th century the Ainu of the Southern and Northern Kuriles were instead well on their way to adopting Japanese and Russian costume respectively. Unsurprisingly, the southerners of Kunashir and Iturup were heavily influenced by their proximity to Honshu, and at the beginning of the 19th century began to adopt Japanese dress and hairstyles and to shave or at least trim their beards, while their northern cousins (called *Kuriltsy* or 'Kurils' by the Russians) were pressured into adopting not just Russian dress and haircuts, but also Orthodox Christianity and the Russian language. *Kuriltsy* dress is reported by J. Milne (1878) and Landor (1893) to have comprised an upper garment which, according to the former, 'although made of skins, was European in form', being shaped like a shirt or short tunic. This was made of sea-birds' skins with the feathers on the inside, decorated on the back with yellow puffin feathers and sometimes trimmed with seal fur. It was secured round the waist by means of a sealskin or sea-lion hide belt, which Landor says was often ornamented with 'molten lead buttons' or Chinese coins. Some men also possessed Russian hats, shirts, and trousers, obtained by trading with the crews of passing ships. Footwear consisted either of the usual moccasins and salmon-skin boots, or else fur-lined, knee-length sealskin boots. Following their removal to Shikotan, the Japanese government presented them a gift of Western-style clothing, consisting of old police caps and overcoats.

ARMS

The Ainu were armed with bows, spears, clubs, swords, and knives. Since they lived by hunting they were skilled archers, though their 4 ft to 4 ft 4 ins (1.22–1.37 m) bows, made of a single stout length of inelastic yew with the bark left on, were not especially powerful, and depended for their effectiveness on the use of an aconite-based poison. The 20–22 inch (0.51–0.56 m) arrows were constructed from three pieces, comprising a barbed head with a cavity on one side to hold the poison; a wooden foreshaft or a sharpened, fusiform piece of bone about four inches long, to which the head was 'very slightly fastened'; and a 14-inch (0.36 m) reed shaft, which might or might not be fletched. The idea was for the detachable head to break off in the slight wound it inflicted, leaving the poison to do its work. It was said that a single wound could kill a full-grown bear in ten minutes, and that if a man was wounded by a poisoned arrow 'the only cure is immediate excision of the part'. Nineteenth-century Ainu claimed that such poisoned arrows were only used for hunting, but remarks made by earlier writers suggest that they had previously been used in war too. By the beginning of the 19th century the arrowheads were chiefly of bamboo or bone, but flint heads had remained in use in some areas as recently as the late 18th century. Iron arrowheads only came into use very slowly, in the course of the 19th century.

Spears were long and thin, with a shaft measuring up to about 9 ft (2.74 m) and, in some cases, a detachable head similar to those of Ainu arrows. Most, however, were of Japanese origin, and had steel blades. Some of these had been captured in battle while others were imported from Korea. Either way, spears do not appear to have been popular weapons, and Bird was told in 1878 that they were by then only used for hunting.

The traditional Ainu defensive weapon was a wooden club about 2–2½ ft (0.61–0.76 m) long and weighing somewhat over a pound (0.45 kg). Some were plain and straight, while on others the upper extremity was carved with a series of ridges or knobs in parallel lines. A few (Landor says 'some of the very old clubs') had a piece of stone set into one side – not as a blade, but simply to add extra weight – while others might have pieces of leather or rope knotted round the end 'to make the blow more severe'. Batchelor recorded a fairly typical example in his collection as having a handle 3 ins (75 mm) in circumference, and a head 7½ ins (190 mm) in circumference: 'The front part of the club has notches cut six inches down its face, whilst on the back of it a hole has been cut seven inches long, one wide, and three-quarters deep, in which to put a stone or some other heavy substance to render the instrument more weighty'. Clubs were secured to the wrist by means of a rope or leather loop passed through a hole at the end of the handle.

Ainu swords were invariably Japanese weapons, sometimes of considerable antiquity. Some visitors stated that 'for centuries now the Japanese have forbidden the Ainu to possess swords', but they may have been misled by the fact that few were carried except on special occasions. In fact the Ainu possessed a great many swords, and Japanese armourers continued to manufacture sword blades specifically for the Ainu market even in the 19th century; however, such weapons generally spent their time on display amongst a family's treasured possessions. The more ancient blades had mostly been captured in battles against the Japanese, and were cherished family heirlooms, but some – probably war-trophies dating back to the 16th century – were imported from Korea. The Ainu carried their swords suspended at the left hip from a broad cloth or bast fibre baldric, worn across the right shoulder. This was most often red.

It seems that the majority of 19th-century Ainu knives had started their lives as either swords or spears, since they were manufactured from the broken pieces of Japanese weapons. Though some were long enough to pass for short swords, the majority were only about 6 ins (150 mm) in length. All were one-edged, with a carved wooden or sometimes 'ivory' – doubtless whalebone – handle and sheath. They were carried tucked through the waist-belt.

The only firearms possessed by the Ainu comprised a handful of matchlocks handed out by Hokkaido's Japanese administrators, from the 1870s at the latest, to such men as hunted on their behalf.

FIGURES

99–101. AINU WARRIORS, 16th–19th CENTURIES

It is clear from the accounts left by earlier visitors that the dress and arms of the Ainu did not change at all between the mid-16th century and the period under review. The selection of figures portrayed here, based on 18th–19th-century Japanese prints and the photographs of 19th-century Western visitors, depicts the various combinations in which traditional Ainu costume might occur, ranging from the winter dress of Figure 100 to the summer dress (or, rather, lack of) of Figure 101.

Figure 99 wears an *attush* and is armed with the traditional Ainu combination of bow and club. Ainu clubs came in an enormous variety of shapes – see also Figure 103 and details 103a and 103b for some of their many other forms. Detail 99a shows the 'quarter moon' shape (as Batchelor describes it) into which the hair of Ainu men was cut at the back, while 99b depicts the variant hairstyle of the Sakhalin Ainu. Figure 100 holds a pair of the skis used on Sakhalin. Made of wood covered with sealskin, these measured about 5½ ft (1.68 m) long and 7½ ins (190 mm) wide, and were fastened to the feet by means of a leather strap. The Hokkaido Ainu substituted primitive snowshoes each made from two strips of wood bent to a U-shape with their overlapping ends bound together.

Note their characteristic conical or quadrangular arrow quivers (*ika*), made of willow wood, bound with bark and often lacquered and decorated. These had a lid and a pair of decoratively carved wooden pieces attached along the sides, to one of which was tied the strap worn over usually (but not always) the right shoulder, from which the quiver was suspended under the same arm. One or more small *inao* or charms (rods with hairy tassels) were customarily attached to the quiver to bring luck. The bow was fired with the arrow to the right of the bowstave, using the primary release technique (i.e., with the arrow and string held between the thumb and forefinger).

The Ainu are reported to have been very good horsemen. They rode without stirrups, generally either bareback or sitting on a bearskin. Their usual riding position was with the knees slightly bent and the legs hanging so that the toes were lower than the heels and turned inwards. However, Isabella Bird recorded in 1878 that an Ainu who accompanied her rode 'with his hairy legs crossed over the horse's neck, a fashion in which the Ainos ride any horses over any ground with the utmost serenity.'

Landor describes their ponies as 'short, sturdy,

punchy brutes, not more than ten or twelve hands high, with a rather large and massive head, and thick, crooked legs'. They were unshod, shaggy haired, and had a long mane. Figure 101's wears a typical Ainu bridle, described by Landor as 'based on the lever principle'. He says that it 'worked exactly in the same way as a nut-cracker, the pony's nose being the nut ... By pulling the rope hard, and thus squeezing the animal's nose, it's head is turned in the direction in which it is pulled'. The wooden arms of the 'nut-cracker' were about 12 ins (0.3 m) long, and were operated by means of a single rein about 5–6 ft (1.52–1.83 m) long held in the right hand. Rather impractically, this had to be flicked from one side of the horse's head round to the other in order to exert the appropriate pressure to make the horse turn in the required direction.

102. ARMOURED WARRIOR This hypothetical reconstruction is based principally on a surviving corselet of sealskin lamellae held in the Sakhalin Regional Museum. That some Ainu armour survived in use into this period is confirmed by H. Russell Robinson's *Oriental Armour*, which states that the 19th-century Hokkaido Ainu 'still had some leather lamellar armours of similar make to the lamellae coats found in burial mounds in western Japan'. Batchelor also mentions corselets of leather lamellae, and observes that some Ainu (period not stated) wore Japanese armours taken from the bodies of men killed in battle by their ancestors. A 17th-century Dutch visitor mentions seeing Ainu wearing 'coats of small planks fastened together', presumably meaning rod armour such as was worn in the Aleutians (some Aleuts were living in the northern Kuriles even in the 19th century). An anthropologist working on Hokkaido in 1938 records that in earlier times the Ainu had protected themselves from enemy arrows by means of corselets of salmon skin lamellae which 'they coated with a thick layer of clay' – presumably the source of early Japanese texts that describe Ainu warriors wearing 'stone armour'.

Though helmets are often mentioned in Ainu folklore written down in the 19th century, and were doubtless worn with armour, they do not seem to be described anywhere, and I have come across no references to any examples having survived. Consequently the one depicted here is entirely conjectural.

103. AINU WOMAN It is not recorded how Ainu women were armed for combat, but it seems likely that a club would have supplemented the all-purpose knife they customarily carried at the waist. Though contemporary sources are in general agreement that their dress comprised a longer version of the *attush*, which is confirmed by pictorial evidence, Albert Bickmore (1868) mentions seeing Ainu women wearing 'a shorter dressing gown coming down to the hips, and beneath this a piece of cloth wrapped round the waist and hanging nearly down to the knee.' Note the distinctive blue tattooing round the mouth, on the forearms, and on the hands.

NOTES

63 Others may have included a race variously referred to in old Japanese chronicles as the *Tsuchi-gomo* ('Earth-Spiders'), *Kobito* ('Dwarfs'), or *Koropok-guru* ('Pit-Dwellers'). These may have been conquered and assimilated by the Ainu prior to the arrival of the Japanese, or may even be the Ainu in an earlier guise; the jury is still out on this complex question. Some of those experts who believe there were two distinct races consider that the now extinct Northern Kurile Ainu were actually a surviving remnant of the 'Pit-Dwellers'.

64 Some of the peoples found in Kamchatka and the Amur region of Manchuria also seem to have been of Ainu origin. Central and northern Sakhalin were occupied by the Orok and Nivkh respectively.

65 A.H. Savage Landor (1893) records Japanese estimates of 15–17,000, though he personally considered that 'at least half this number are half-caste, and in my opinion ... the number of thoroughbred Ainu [on Hokkaido] does not exceed 8,000'.

66 Russian exploration of the Kurile Islands began in 1711, and spasmodic (often unsuccessful) settlement of the central and northern islands occurred during the next hundred years, especially after the 1730s. Ainu resistance to Russia's southward advance through the Kuriles was crushed following their massacre of an expedition on Urup in 1771. Though Russia ambitiously claimed possession of the entire Kurile archipelago in the 1780s, it never penetrated further south than Urup, where it established a short-lived colony in 1795–1805. Because it was still theoretically Russian, Urup was briefly occupied by an Anglo-French fleet in August–September 1855, during the Crimean War.

KOREA

During the period under review, Koreans generally called their country Chao-sen ('Land of the Morning Calm'), which was usually rendered Chosen or Choson by Western authors. However, the rest of the world continued to favour its older and much better-known name of Korea (albeit often spelling it 'Corea'), ultimately derived – via such Japanese and Portuguese mispronunciations as *Ku-rai*, *Kori*, and *Koryo* – from the title borne by its mediaeval kings (*Kao-li*).

Measuring roughly 85,000 square miles (220,000 square km), it was made up of eight provinces or *do*, three (Ham-kiung, Kang-wen, and Kiung-sang) on the eastern side of the country and five (Cholla, Chung-chong, Hwang-hai, Kiung-kei, and Ping-Yang) in the west. These are said to have comprised 60 districts and some 3,800 cantons. There were 330–360 so-called 'cities', of which Trumbull White (1895) points out that only 60 or so (doubtless the district capitals) were actually entitled to the name, 'the remainder distinguishing themselves from the larger hamlets and villages merely by the walled-in residence of the chief government official.' In fact, with a total population of perhaps only 10–15 million[67] large urban centres were relatively uncommon, and, unlike those found in neighbouring China, few boasted any defences. Notable exceptions were Ping-Yang (Pyongyang, now capital of North Korea) and the four extensively fortified cities – Sunto to the north, Kangwha to the west, Suwen to the south, and Kwang-chiu to the south-east – which guarded the approaches to the capital, Han-Yang ('Fortress on the Han River'), more usually known simply as Seoul ('the Capital'). However, forts and redoubts could be found crowning many headlands along Korea's coasts and rivers – especially along the Han River – in order to enforce its xenophobic policy of isolation, which had earned it the nickname of 'the hermit kingdom'. Though such coastal defences were effective in deterring foreign shipping from attempting to trade, they were unable to prevent French missionaries slipping into the country from the 1770s onwards.

The provinces of Ping-Yang and Ham-kiung (now Hamgyong) constituted Korea's frontier with China (and, after 1860, Russia), from which it had been insulated since the 16th century by a densely forested neutral zone beyond the Yalu and Tumen rivers. This strip of theoretically unoccupied territory was some 30 miles (50 km) broad near the mouth of the Yalu but widened further north. Its southern boundary was regarded as the Korean frontier, while its northern edge denoted the frontier of Chinese Manchuria. The Chinese boundary had originally been marked by stakes, palisades, and a stone wall described as 'strong, high, guarded and kept in repair', but these defences had long since been abandoned and were now apparent only as overgrown mounds and ruins. Predictably, this no-man's-land became a haven for bandit gangs from both countries, whose depredations in the 19th century grew to such proportions that eventually, in 1875, the Chinese general Li Hung-chang sent a sizeable expedition (supported by a steam gunboat on the Yalu) to disperse the outlaws, and subsequently encouraged Chinese farmers to settle there. Two years later China swallowed up the neutral zone entirely by advancing its frontier to the Yalu unchallenged.

Korea had been regarded as a vassal state by China since suffering defeat at the hands of the Manchus as far back as 1636–37, and it paid annual tribute to Peking. However, Japan also claimed suzerainty following its own invasions of 1582–98, and maintained a permanent colony of merchants at Fusan that it provocatively referred to as the *Su-ja-ri* or 'Frontier Guard'. Japan continued to receive its own occasional tribute from Korea until 1832, and its claim of suzerainty was not officially renounced until as late as February 1876, when a treaty was finally signed recognising Korea as an independent nation. Even thereafter, however, this historic claim on Chao-sen continued to exert a baleful influence on Japan's attitude towards its Chinese, Korean, and Russian neighbours.

Korea had been ruled by the Yi dynasty since 1392, represented at the end of the 18th century by King Chongjo (1776–1800). He was succeeded by his son Sunjo (1800–34), and he in turn by a grandson, Honjong (1834–49), and a more distant kinsman, Ch'olchong (1849–64). When the latter, like his predecessor, died without male issue palace intrigues resulted in the family matriarch, Queen Cho (widow of King Sunjo), enthroning one of Chongjo's great great grandsons, Kojong (1864–1907). However, since he was only 12 at the time his father Yi Ha-ung was appointed to act as regent during his minority, and received the title of *Ta-wun-gun* ('Prince Parent'), generally rendered 'Taewongun' in Western sources.

The Taewongun held power until 1873. Described by a contemporary as having 'bowels of iron and a heart of stone', he was a traditionalist, a ruthless advocate of Korea's closed-door policy, and 'a rabid hater' of Christians, foreigners, and progress, in whatever order one cared to place them. Unsurprisingly, therefore, it was not long before he instigated a persecution of Catholic missionaries and their converts. There had been earlier anti-Christian purges in 1788, 1801, and 1837–49, and the execution of three French priests in 1839 had prompted the somewhat belated despatch by the French in 1847 of the warships *La Gloire* and *La Victorieuse* to exact retribution (both ships ignominiously ran aground on a mud-bank and broke their backs when the tide turned;

French launches land troops on Kanghwa island under fire during Admiral Roze's expedition of 1866. (Wikipedia)

their crews had to be rescued by a British vessel); but the Taewongun's pogrom surpassed all of these, and the execution in February 1866 of as many as nine French missionaries resulted in another French expedition, this time consisting of seven ships – a frigate, two corvettes, and four gunboats[68] – under the command of Admiral Pierre Gustave Roze, carrying 600 troops drawn from the French garrison then serving in Yokohama.

Arriving off the Korean coast in mid-October 1866, Roze landed his troops on Kangwha (Ganghwa) island at the mouth of the Han and Imjin rivers and on the 18th stormed both Kangwha town – which fell in less than an hour but was 'almost wholly deserted' – and a decoy Korean position at Tongjin, that was found to be manned by hundreds of straw dummies dressed up in uniforms. A week later the French moved against the strongly-fortified monastery of Chong-jok some 12 miles (19 km) away, approachable by only one path guarded by a crenellated rampart. Some 4,200 Koreans under General Yang Hon-su had assembled here, whereas the French attacking force numbered just 160 men. Met by a withering hail of fire from the 500 defenders of the Korean breastwork as they struggled uphill, the French suffered at least 35–50 casualties within minutes (compared to one Korean killed and three wounded); in fact Homer Hulbert (1905) claims that as many as half the invaders were rendered hors de combat.

Following this costly reverse, Roze re-embarked his troops the following day after setting Kangwha town ablaze, and sailed away without having achieved his purpose. Needless to say, Korea viewed its repulse of the French as a significant victory, and its persecution of Christians consequently continued unabated before finally petering out in 1870.

It was also in 1866 that the seeds of confrontation with the United States were sewn when the merchant schooner *General Sherman*,[69] unwisely attempting to enter the port of Ping-Yang, was burnt after firing over the heads of the Korean boats which had surrounded it, and its crew was massacred. This eventually resulted in the despatch in 1871 of an American flotilla of five warships, several small steam launches, and 1,300 men, under Admiral John Rodgers. The warships consisted of the *Colorado*, described as a heavy frigate 'of the most antiquated type'; the corvettes *Benicia* and *Alaska*; an iron paddle-wheel gunboat, the *Monocacy*; and an armed steam tender, the *Palos*.

After an exchange of fire with several forts on Kangwha island at the beginning of June, the Americans landed somewhat over 600 men and seven guns at 3:00 p.m. on the 9th (under covering fire from the *Monocacy* and *Palos*) and attacked the nearest fort, which was hastily abandoned by its garrison. The Americans then bivouacked for the night and attacked a second defensive work, Tokjin (which they nicknamed 'Fort Monocacy'), at 6:30 the following morning, before proceeding against the principal defensive work, Kwang-song ('Fort McKee'). Described as 'a breastwork placed on the summit of a rocky eminence', this contained a sizeable part of the island's 3,000-strong garrison under General O Yo-jun. It was nevertheless taken at the point of the bayonet after 'a frightful slaughter had been wrought among the Korean garrison' by a 30-minute enfilade of rifle and artillery fire delivered from both flanks. The Americans lost just three killed and seven or ten wounded in this action, while somewhere between 350–500 Koreans may have been killed in the battle or the ensuing rout, during which many drowned themselves or cut their own throats. Less than 40 prisoners were taken, only about a dozen of whom were unwounded. Two further forts were also captured before the day was out, bringing the total to five. Lacking the authority to take matters any further, however, Rodgers re-embarked his troops on the 12th and eventually sailed away three weeks later (3 July), his unexpected departure being interpreted by the Korean government as yet another decisive victory over Westerners.

RELATIONS WITH JAPAN 1868–85

The Taewongun's dislike of foreigners was not limited to the Western powers. As a traditionalist, he also harboured a burning animosity towards the Japanese, who were regarded by most Koreans 'with a hatred three centuries old'. Consequently he declined to acknowledge the Meiji Restoration in 1868, thereby angering a sufficiently large number of influential Japanese to prompt the creation of the *Sei Kan-ron* or 'Conquer Korea' movement. The Japanese government became so alarmed by a spate of popular unrest in support of the *Sei Kan-ron* that its leaders were eventually arrested and executed. Nevertheless, even in Japanese official circles there was a growing feeling that possession of Korea – even if only to frustrate Russian ambitions – was essential to Japan's national security, and plans for its conquest were mooted from 1870 on.

There was a deliberate Japanese attempt to provoke hostilities in September 1875, when an Imperial Navy warship, the *Unyo-kan*, was sent to take soundings off Kangwha island and landed 20 men ostensibly to seek fresh water. After these were fired on by the garrison of the local fort (who apparently mistook them for Americans or Frenchmen because of their Western-style uniforms), the *Unyo-kan* bombarded the fort and landed a strong detachment of marines, which routed the garrison and burnt the fort before re-embarking and sailing down the coast to Tongnae, near Pusan, where there were further clashes between the Koreans and Japanese landing parties. As anticipated, these incidents were followed by renewed Japanese calls for war, and provided the excuse for a fleet of five Japanese ships, carrying troops under General Kuroda, to be despatched to Seoul at the beginning of 1876. However, though a contingent of marines was landed there was no more fighting, a settlement in Japan's favour being reached on 27 February 1876 which forced Korea to restore its diplomatic relations with Japan and to open three ports (Chemulpo, Pusan, and Wonsan) to Japanese trade. This was followed by the establishment of a Japanese Legation at Seoul in 1879 and the appointment of a Japanese instructor to the Korean army in 1881.

Though Japanese influence steadily increased it was counterbalanced wherever possible by the machinations of King Kojong's pro-Chinese wife Queen Min – strong-willed, aggressive, and ambitious – who had been responsible for retiring the Taewongun when her husband came of age in 1873 and had since installed some 40 of her Min relations in various influential government posts. A Japanese-inspired progressive movement was nevertheless able to push through several reforms, including the Westernisation of the army and the signing of treaties with half a dozen foreign powers (America, China, France, Germany, Great Britain, and Italy), before the ultra-conservative Taewongun felt the time had come to overthrow the Mins and restore Korea's traditional administration.

His chance came in July 1882, when a reduction of rations in the army – which was already disaffected by the introduction of Japanese training and the fact that its pay was 13 months in arrears – enabled him to incite a mutiny on the 23rd known as the *Imo Kullan* ('Military incident of the Year of Imo', sometimes referred to simply as the Soldiers' Revolt). The mutineers killed a Min minister, their Japanese drill instructor, and half-a-dozen other Japanese residents, and then burnt the Japanese Legation, obliging Minister Hanabusa Yoshitada and his 40-odd guards and staff to fight their way to the safety of a British warship. The next morning the mutineers and other rioters sacked the palace, killed several more Min ministers, and tried to assassinate the queen herself (an unfortunate maid being killed in mistake for her). Order was only restored when King Kojong capitulated to the mutineers' demand to reinstate the Taewongun, who persuaded them to disperse by driving the remaining Mins from court and persuading the king to abandon his programme of military reforms. When Minister Hanabusa returned with a Japanese warship and a contingent of troops three weeks later the Taewongun feigned friendship and agreed to all of Japan's demands for restitution. The

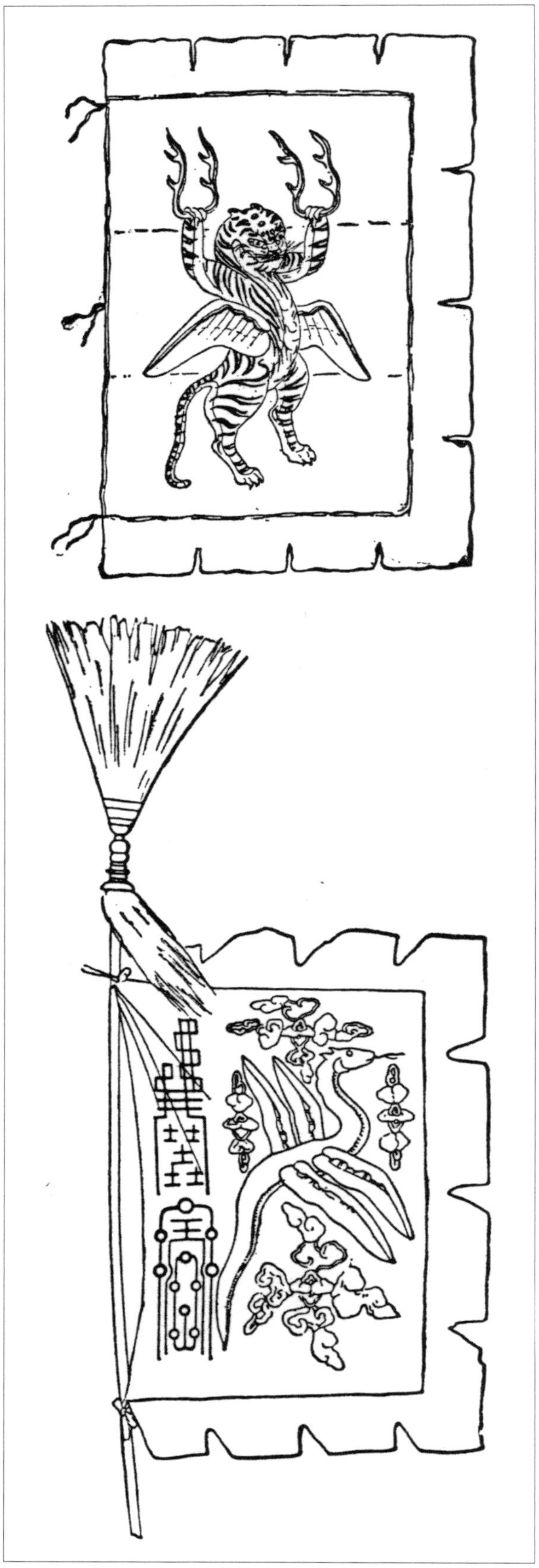

Two of the flags captured by American forces in 1871. The top picture is one of the royal standards – comprising a winged tiger on a yellow field – that at this date seem to have been carried by each battalion.

Yi Ha-ung, who ruled Korea as the Taewongun or Prince Regent 1864–73, and meddled in the country's foeign affairs for considerably longer.

principal mutineers were arrested and punished, sizeable compensation was agreed, and the Japanese were permitted to install a considerably larger Legation guard, consisting of some 200 men.

The devious Taewongun's victory was short-lived, however, and after just 32 days in power he was forcibly deported by a Chinese army under Wu Chang-ching and his subordinate Yüan Shih-k'ai.[70] This had been despatched to Korea by Li Hung-chang at Queen Min's urgent request. Whether the Taewongun's removal was designed to save him from Min vengeance, or was intended as an unsubtle expression of Chinese suzerainty, is impossible to say. Erecting forts to command the Han river against the possibility of Japanese attack, 3,000 Chinese troops (or 4,500 according to some sources) were subsequently stationed in and around Seoul, and Wu transferred political power to Queen Min, sidelining the ineffective king and thereby enabling the Chinese to influence and control the Korean government through the queen.

It wasn't long before the troops of both foreign powers became further entangled in Korea's shaky domestic situation. On 6 December 1884 pro-Japanese reformers led by Kim Ok-kiun received the support of Hanabusa's replacement, Minister Takezoe Shinichiro, and his 180-strong Legation guard in their attempt to overthrow the pro-Chinese conservatives and establish a modern, Japanese-style government. This was referred to as the *Kapsin* Coup (after the name of the year) or sometimes the Post Office Coup, from the fact that many of the Min officials who were killed had been attending a dinner at the Postmaster General's home. Needless to say, the conservative faction immediately received the support of the 1,500 Chinese troops still based in Seoul,[71] 600 of whom, under Yüan Shih-k'ai, joined with 3,000 Korean soldiers and civilians in attacking the revolutionaries, who had seized the Ch'angdok palace and, briefly, the king (soon recovered by the Chinese). Sources are confused and sometimes contradictory regarding the course and timing of subsequent events, but it would appear that after beating off the conservatives' attacks throughout the afternoon of the 6th, during which some 200 Koreans and Chinese were reportedly killed, the Japanese and their own Korean allies slipped back to their Legation under cover of darkness, and at dawn on the 7th formed a hollow square with their families in the centre, fired the Legation buildings, and marched to the safety of Japanese ships anchored at Chemulpo (modern Inch'on).

Though the Japanese, appropriately reinforced, subsequently returned to Seoul and, as in 1882, forced Queen Min and her supporters to pay reparations, in April 1885 Japan and China signed an agreement (known as the Tientsin or Li-Ito Convention) to withdraw most of their troops from Korea, excepting only their respective Legation guards. This treaty also agreed that neither Japanese nor Chinese instructors should henceforth take any part in the training or organisation of the Korean army, and that if either country should ever deem it necessary to reintroduce troops into Korea, the other was to be notified in advance and would be entitled to despatch a contingent of similar strength.

THE TONGHAK REBELLION AND THE SINO-JAPANESE WAR, 1894–95

Though there were localised peasant rebellions against corrupt officialdom on several occasions during the 19th century, notably in Ping-Yang province in 1811, on the island of Quelpart (now Cheju-do) in 1813, and throughout the southern provinces in 1862–63, none posed a more serious threat to Korea's very existence than the Tonghak (or Donghak) rebellion of 1894.

The Tonghaks were a religious movement loyal to the throne but opposed to the privileges and abuses of Korea's hereditary gentry, the *nyang-pan* or 'two orders' (more often rendered as *yangban*). The cult had originated in Kiung-sang province in 1860 and flourished until 1864, when their monotheist beliefs had led to the Tonghaks being identified with and persecuted as Roman Catholics – despite their hatred of Christians and foreigners and their adoption of the name *Tonghak*, meaning 'Eastern Learning', specifically in order to distinguish their ideology from Catholicism or *Suhak* ('Western Learning'). When their founder, Ch'oe Che-u, was himself arrested and executed the movement went underground. Proof that it had nevertheless survived came in 1871, when there was an ultimately unsuccessful Tonghak insurrection at Mun'gyong, involving just 500 adherents. Little was heard of the Tonghaks thereafter until spring 1893, when Ch'oe Che-u's successor, the *Sinsa* (Divine Teacher) Ch'oe Si-hyong, refused to let his followers resort to violence in their struggle against corrupt officials. This resulted in a schism within the movement, the Tonghaks of southern Chung-chong and Cholla seceding under their own leader, Chon Pong-jun (declared a heretic by Ch'oe), who subsequently rebelled against the government on 19 February 1894 in response to the wrongs perpetrated by local magistrates.

Photograph of Korean soldiers guarding Chinese prisoners during the Sino-Japanese War (two Japanese soldiers can just be made out in the background). This is doubtless a propaganda shot, arranged by the Japanese to demonstrate that the only reason they were in Korea was to support the legitimate government. In fact, what little contemporary evidence there is of their activities during the conflict suggests that most Koreans fought against rather than alongside the Japanese. (Wikipedia)

Several small but well-equipped detachments of government troops sent to intercept Chon Pong-jun's advance on Seoul were easily defeated by his ill-armed followers, whose numbers increased from 4,000 to perhaps 10,000 as they marched. In May the Tonghaks won significant victories at the battles of Changsong and Hwangt'ohyon, and on 1 June they captured the walled city of Chonju, provincial capital of Cholla. Here they were besieged by government troops under General Hong Kye-hun, and a stalemate ensued, the Tonghaks being unable to disperse the besiegers, while the latter found themselves unable to expel the rebels.

It was at this juncture that events began to generate a momentum all of their own. Alarmed at the scale of the Tonghak rising, which had meanwhile spread from Cholla to neighbouring Chung-chong and Kiung-sang provinces, and painfully aware of the inadequacy of Korea's own tiny army, a powerful courtier of the Min faction, one Min Ying-chong, now took the ill-considered step of appealing to China for assistance against the rebels. The Chinese obliged by putting ashore 1,500 men (subsequently augmented to 2,000) at Asan, south-west of Seoul, on 8 June. However, according to most authorities they failed to notify the Japanese government as was required by the treaty of 1885. Consequently when Japan learnt of the Chinese landings it immediately despatched 400 marines to Seoul, who arrived on 9 June. These were followed by an additional 4,000 men on the 12th. At the same time, instructions were sent from Tokyo that the Japanese Resident in Seoul was to 'use any pretext available' to justify military intervention. By the end of June the Japanese military presence round Seoul had increased to as many as 8,000 men, under the command of Major-General Oshima Yoshimasa.

Back at Chonju, meanwhile, negotiations between Hong Kye-hun and Chon Pong-jun had resulted on 14 June in the Tonghaks agreeing to return to their homes after being promised that their grievances would be investigated, Chon – a patriot at heart – being genuinely concerned that his actions had resulted in the introduction of so many foreign troops into Korea. The dispersal of the Tonghaks enabled the Korean government and the Chinese to argue convincingly that the crisis was over, and that China and Japan could therefore recall their respective armies. Though the Japanese ostensibly agreed, they subsequently decided that the withdrawal of their sizeable force would constitute a serious loss of face, and remembered that their failure to get sufficient troops into Korea in both 1882 and 1884 had already lost them two opportunities to install a Korean government dedicated to Japanese-style reform. Consequently they prevaricated, and in the interim brought in yet more troops, so that by about mid-July 15,000 were encamped around the capital. Once these were in place the irrevocable decision was made to seize control of Korea's government and to oust the pro-Chinese Min faction.

On 23 July, after a 20-minute fire-fight with pro-Chinese guardsmen loyal to Queen Min, Japanese troops under the command of Minister Hashi Toru seized the Kyongbok palace for the loss of just one man killed and one wounded, and by gaining control of King Kojong ended the Mins' decade-long hold on power. The Sino-Japanese War (1894–95) began two days later with Japan's unprovoked attack on a Chinese flotilla at Pung-do, and the opening stages of the ensuing conflict were fought entirely on Korean soil.

Under Japanese pressure, Kojong formally announced Korea's independence from China on 16 August, declaring 'all treaties hitherto signed between itself and China to be abrogated and all political connection between the two countries to be at an end'. (China acknowledged Korea's independence at the conclusion of hostilities with Japan in April 1895.) Ten days later he signed a formal treaty of alliance with Japan that theoretically guaranteed Korean independence, and agreed to assist in the transport and provisioning of Japanese troops fighting against the Chinese. Korea's own troops, however, officially took no active part in the war, and where there are occasional indications that any might have – unofficially, one assumes – they seem to have fought on the Chinese side rather than the Japanese; foreign newspapers, for instance, reported the presence of as many as 2,000 Korean soldiers amongst the Chinese defenders of Ping-Yang on 19 September, and some contemporary pictures show Korean soldiers fighting the Japanese. White records that the majority of ordinary Koreans remained openly hostile to the Japanese and 'were everywhere welcoming the Chinese as their friends', and that 'except the strongly guarded positions in the provinces of Seoul and Hwang-hai and the country round the treaty ports which were under Japanese influence, the peninsula was in the possession of armed Koreans and Chinese.'

The Tonghaks, meanwhile, remained at large and were stronger than ever, since Japan's seizure of power had finally persuaded the orthodox Tonghaks under Ch'oe Si-hyong to join forces with Chon Pong-jun to repel the invaders. So widespread did support for the rebellion become, in fact, that one Korean official was prompted to observe that 'the term Tonghak can now be applied to the whole population of Korea outside the capital with the exception of the three northern provinces, where the influence of the society has not yet reached.'

After several minor raids against Japanese lines of communication[72] – attacking their supply depots and cutting telegraph lines – Chon marched north towards Seoul in October 1894 at the head of 10–20,000 men, intending to rescue King Kojong from the hated Japanese. However, he was decisively defeated in the vicinity of Kongju on 29 November at the end of a seven-day running battle against 3,000 Korean regular troops under Sin Chung-heui (described by Hulbert as 'the highest Korean general'), supported by 200 Japanese soldiers and advisers.

The survivors fled south-west into Cholla and southern Chung-chong but were defeated again, Chon himself describing how Tonghak numbers were whittled down to 3,000 and how 'after two more battles, only about 500 were left. We had to retreat and went to Kumgu looking for new recruits. Although our number showed a slight increase ... the Japanese troops pursued us, and there were two more battles. We were defeated and dispersed.' Chon was captured by local militiamen at Sunch'ang on 28 December and was executed the following March. Ch'oe Si-hyong suffered a similar fate.

Operations against the Tonghaks continued until the end of January 1895, when their remnants dispersed to become the basis of several of the patriotic guerrilla forces – calling themselves *Uibyong* or 'Righteous Armies'[73] – which maintained the struggle against Japanese occupation thereafter. Until the conclusion of peace between China and Japan on 17 April, some of those in the north were joined by stragglers left behind when the Chinese were driven back across the Yalu. Opposition to the Japanese became even more widespread from the end of 1895, following their installation of a progressive government (the pro-Japanese 'Enlightenment Party') and the introduction of the so-called *Kabo* Reforms, which sought to undermine every aspect of Korea's traditional culture by modernising (i.e., Westernising) its administration.

Queen Min's attempt to end Japanese influence by replacing the Enlightenment Party with a pro-Russian cabinet, and disbanding the army's recently created, pro-Japanese *Kunrentai* corps, led to her murder on 8 October 1895 in an attack on the palace by the *Kunrentai*, assisted by the Japanese Legation Guard and several dozen Japanese thugs (*sashi*).[74] After being a virtual prisoner for the next four months, King Kojong was whisked away to safety in the Russian Legation on 14 February 1896 by

This photograph of 'Righteous Army' soldiers comes from F.A. McKenzie's The Tragedy of Korea *(1908). He says that one wore 'the old uniform of the regular Korean Army', another had a pair of military trousers, and the rest were in ragged Korean dress. 'Around their waists were home-made cotton cartridge belts, half full. One wore a kind of tarboosh on his head, and the others had bits of rag twisted round their hair.' Their firearms included ancient matchlocks, obsolete army rifles, rusty sporting weapons and horse-pistols; some were of Chinese origin.*

a detachment of 127 Russian seamen and marines sent up from Chemulpo, thereby depriving the Japanese and their allies of ultimate control over the government. The Japanese Resident, General Miura Goro, was meanwhile recalled for his participation in the queen's murder.

From the safety of the Russian Legation, where he stayed for the next year, Kojong was able to restore order throughout much of the country by simply rescinding the unpopular *Kabo* Reforms and by signing a new treaty with Japan, by which, under Russian diplomatic pressure, it was required to reduce its military presence to just 800 men. Steadily accumulating power back into his hands as the significance of the pro-Japanese faction was whittled away by assassination, exile, and imprisonment, Kojong was finally able to return to the palace in February 1897, upon which – doubtless in the hope of emphasising Korea's independence from both China and Japan – he adopted the title of emperor and declared that his kingdom should henceforth be known as *Taehan Cheguk*, 'The Great Han Empire'.

Japan had, in the meantime, attempted to limit further Russian influence by proposing that Korea be divided at the 38th parallel into Russian (northern) and Japanese (southern) zones of influence. Needless to say, Russia – which made little effort to conceal its ambition to bring the whole country under its control – rejected this offer and suggested a joint protectorate instead. In treaties signed in June 1896 and April 1898 Japan and Russia agreed to recognise the independence of Korea, to refrain from interfering in its internal affairs, to maintain no more than a thousand troops on its soil (posted in Seoul and the treaty ports, theoretically to protect their legations and mercantile interests), and to have no further involvement in the instruction of its army. In reality all that these cynical arrangements actually achieved was to temporarily postpone the inevitable outbreak of hostilities.[75] By as early as May 1900 – when, regardless of the treaties, there were reported to be some 8,000 Japanese troops stationed throughout the country – the air was already 'full of rumours of a war between Russia and Japan'. Occupation by Japanese forces when that war eventually came in 1904–5 marked the end of Kojong's short-lived Korean 'Empire', which was declared a Japanese protectorate in November 1905. Formal annexation followed in August 1910, following the suppression of a nationwide rebellion against the Japanese that had begun in 1908 in response to Kojong's forced abdication and the disbandment of the army. Korea remained a Japanese colony thereafter until 1945.

ORGANISATION

The Korean government consisted of an inner cabinet of eight ministers, supervising six boards or departments (Appointments, Justice, Revenue, Ceremonies, War, and Public Works), each headed by a president (*pan-so*), a vice-president (*cham-pan*), and a secretary (*cham-wi*), and each with its own small body of 'soldiers' (or, more accurately, gendarmes). The six presidents and their 12 assistants constituted the General Council, while the presidents and the two assistants of the president of the Board of Appointments (also referred to in some books as the Board of the Interior, or Civil Offices) held the cabinet's eight ministerial posts.

Each of Korea's eight provinces was the responsibility of a governor (*kam-sa*) and had its own six administrative departments as well as, traditionally, its own army,[76] of which the *kam-sa* was himself often its commander. The soldiers for these armies appear to have been raised on the basis of one man out of every ten or so *hoo* (units of a varying amount of land), with the remaining *hoo* supporting the soldier's family while he was away. By the 19th century, however, these so-called 'armies' had degenerated into inexperienced militias, employed in the capacity of provincial policemen whose only specifically military service was to parade in Seoul once every eight years. The prefects of the country's 300-plus urban centres provided the men, each prefect having a retinue of at least 50 and sometimes up to as many as 1,500 followers. Since their pay was obtained by 'squeezing' the local population, the exact size of these retinues was dependent on the prefecture's wealth.

Ultimate control of all Korea's armed forces belonged with the civilian-run Board of War, which superintended its archaic, Chinese-style military examinations, governed the lands set aside for the army's maintenance, and collected the taxes these owed. However, Korea's uneasy status as the much abused shuttlecock of its neighbours China, Japan, and Russia meant that the Board of War, like the army itself, was in a perpetual state of flux throughout the second half of the century, and in the 30 years between 1864 and 1894 it saw some 50 presidents come and go.

In earlier times military service had been theoretically owed by all adult males aged 16–60 (Hulbert says 15–40), but over the centuries this requirement had been largely commuted into a tax paid, unusually, in bolts of cloth. Popularly referred to as the *yangyok* or 'commoner's duty', this was initially paid by individuals, at the rate of one bolt of cloth per annum after 1750, but in the 1860s the Taewongun had abolished the old system and introduced the taxation of each village as a single entity. The obligation to provide military service when called upon nevertheless remained in force, and was still utilised to muster the small bodies of men employed as armed police in the provinces. These were raised in the same way as the earlier provincial armies, in which those owing military service – who were, broadly-speaking, the rural peasant class (the nobility, monks, artisans, performers, and slaves all being exempt) – had been subdivided into 'regulars' (*chongjong*) and 'reserves' or 'attendants' (*pongjok* or *poin*). Each 'regular' performed the actual service, which was financed by the taxes of two or more 'reserves', the actual number varying throughout the provinces. Tours of duty seem to have been usually for two months a year, served in rotation.

The only armed force of any significance as the 19th century dawned was the central army based round Seoul and in a handful of scattered strategic posts. Financed by the *yangyok* tax, this permanent establishment of paid, regular soldiers was known as the *Ogunyong*, a term variously translated as the Five Garrisons, Five Camps, or Five Regiments. Originally founded in 1464 and reconstituted under King Sukchong (1674–1720), its five divisions consisted of the Military Training Garrison (*Hullyon Togam*), the Northern Approaches Garrison (*Ch'ongyungch'ong*), the Southern Approaches Garrison (*Suoch'ong*), the Capital Garrison (*Kumwiyong*), and the Royal Guards (*Oyongch'ong*). Each Garrison was an independent, all-arms force theoretically comprising infantry, cavalry (of whom there were actually very few), and artillery, and consisted of five brigades (*pu*), each of four regiments (*t'ong*) made up of battalions (*yo*), companies (*tae*), and platoons (*o*).

So much for the theory. In reality, military neglect resulting from centuries of prolonged peace, combined with traditional Confucian contempt for the military arts (Korean civilians considered their soldiers to be but 'one step above the beggar', and militarism to be 'one of the worst features of a barbarism which they had

Assortment of Korean armour, weapons and paraphernalia, including shoes, pouches, fan and even a pair of folding sunglasses, from a journal published in 1891. The armour comprises black, red and gilded scales mounted on a fur-edged, red fabric foundation. The helmet plume is also red, as is the scabbard, which is decorated with a heavy blue tassel. The bowcase and quiver are lacquered black.

outgrown'), had led to the Five Garrisons becoming little more than a ceremonial force, with civilian officials for officers, and soldiers who paid to enlist so that they might enjoy various immunities and privileges, including exemption from corvée labour and taxation.[77] Percival Lowell wrote in 1885 that the army was purely 'for the purpose of swelling the king's retinue on procession days, and for being detailed in squads to perform the same function at promenades of the magistrates.' Indeed, by mid-century the Garrisons had declined so far from combat status that as much as a quarter of their strength consisted of such non-combatants as servants, couriers, clerks, and flag-carriers. Most units were also kept deliberately understrength by their commanders, who pocketed the money intended to pay and equip the missing soldiers. When official inspections were anticipated, it was customary to either borrow troops from another corps or else press-gang civilians into donning uniforms for a day, in order to create the impression that a unit was at full strength. Even as late as 1897, after the army had theoretically undergone several years of modernisation, Russian instructors are recorded to have been 'much amused at the shifting of Koreans from one barracks to another in order to make it appear that each had its complement'.

The Anglo-French defeat of neighbouring China in 1860 to some extent stirred Korea from its torpor, but few of the army reforms suggested at that time were ever put into effect. Consequently when Korea was itself confronted by Western forces in 1866 and 1871 its military resources were found seriously wanting – so much so in 1866 that the only way of mustering sufficient troops to defend Kangwha was by recruiting volunteers and tiger-hunters.[78] Most of the Five Garrisons' theoretical strength of, at this time, some 30,000 men must therefore have existed only on paper.

Despite the Korean government's self-delusory claims of victory over both Roze and Rodgers, assorted military reforms were put in hand during the period 1866–73. Every town in the country was ordered to levy and drill its own garrison of 120 men, numerous new forts were constructed to guard the coast (each garrisoned by a few hundred men levied among the tiger-hunters), and, starting with the *Hullyon Togam* in 1867, serious efforts were made to rid the Garrisons of the greater part of their non-combatants by forming these into a distinct auxiliary unit. Regular training and Western firearms were also introduced during 1871–73, not only in the Garrisons but also in provincial units. A more curious reform was the Taewongun's decision to raise troops from such previously exempt elements of society as entertainers, sorcerers, fortune-tellers, and butchers, in the belief that soldiers drawn from the country's very lowest classes would be less inclined to disobey or argue with their officers. No attempt was made to improve the quality of the officers themselves, however, and these continued to be provided by scholar-officials drawn from the privileged *yangban* class, who to attain their rank had to do no more than pass a worthless examination which gave priority to 'proficiency in archery and the capacity to write verses'.

More serious attempts at reform and modernisation did not begin until 1881, when the old Board of War was abolished and replaced by the *T'ongnigimu Amun* (Office of State Affairs), and the Five Garrisons were reorganised into just two, called the *Changoyong* (Capital Guards Garrison) and the *Muwiyong* (Palace Guards Garrison). In addition a new elite unit called the *Pyolgigun* (Special Skills Force) was created in May, consisting initially of just 80 men trained by Lieutenant Horimoto Reizo of the Japanese Legation. This was intended to provide the nucleus of a fully modernised army, and had grown to a strength of some 200 (or perhaps even 300) by July 1882. By then, however, its preferential treatment, superior provisions, and higher pay had provoked sufficient resentment amongst the rest of the central army that the latter were easily goaded into mutiny by the devious Taewongun, who was ardently opposed to the modernisation process. Instructor Horimoto was murdered in the ensuing disturbances, and in order to appease the mutineers King Kojong was obliged to restore both the Five Garrisons and the Board of War. The strength of the former, however, had by now dwindled to a mere 3,700 men.

Chinese troops having helped in suppressing the mutiny, it was to them that Kojong turned next for assistance. Their commander, Wu Chang-ching, agreed to form a new *Changoyong* division for the king, placing it under the instruction of his deputy Yüan Shih-k'ai. This consisted of four 'barracks' or battalions (designated the Left, Right, Front, and Rear), each theoretically of 500 men and therefore equivalent to, and doubtless organised along the same lines as, a Chinese *ying*.[79] At the same time, 69 Koreans were sent to the Tientsin arsenal in China for military training, while a further 14 were sent to Toyama in Japan the following year,[80] doubtless as a sop to appease the radical, anti-Chinese elements within the government. Whether the individual 'barracks' ever achieved their proposed strength of 500 men is doubtful, since foreigners recorded seeing units of just 300 men in both April 1883 and November 1884; but this, too, would be in accordance with Chinese practice, where *ying* were frequently considerably understrength. Interestingly, one foreign eyewitness (H.A.C. Bonar) noted of the unit he saw that the words of command were 'muttered in English' by its two Korean officers, which must indicate that their Chinese instructors had themselves originally been trained by the British, presumably either at Tientsin some time between 1862–70 or at Feng-huang-shan in 1864–73.

Some indication of the effectiveness of the Chinese training programme can be found in an American report written in 1885, which observed that the four Capital Guards battalions had been 'well exercised in the use of modern rifles by long continued target practice', and obeyed orders, but remained 'sadly deficient in training as to the manual of arms, company or platoon drill, or fighting tactics'. From another report it is apparent that some were already considered sufficiently well-trained by November 1884 to be sent out 'to impart instruction to their fellows'. The king was nevertheless prevailed upon by the reform lobby to dismiss the *Changoyong*'s Chinese instructors in mid-1884, only for these same instructors to be taken on instead by the Palace Guards Garrison's Min commander, with whom they continued to serve for several months more.

For obvious reasons, Kojong had never been comfortable about relying on either the Chinese or the Japanese for military advice, and as early as October 1883 he and Queen Min had requested instructors from the United States through Lucius Foote, American minister to

Korea; and the covenant signed between China and Japan in April 1885 agreed with them that any military advisers in Korea should henceforth come from a third party. The American government, however, prevaricated, the king meanwhile declining offers of instructors from Russia (with which Korea had signed a commercial treaty in 1884) and Germany. It was not until 1888 that America finally relented and sent a curiously unorthodox military mission led by William McEntyre Dye, who had previously served as a colonel in the Union army and later (1873–78) as a staff officer to the Khedive of Egypt. His assistants were Edmund H. Cummins, a former Confederate cavalry major; Dr. John Grigg Lee, who had no previous military experience; and John Nienstead, who had served as a U.S. Navy pay-clerk. On their arrival between April and May 1888, this oddball assortment were given the task of establishing a military academy for some 40 cadets, and were subsequently also asked to train 160 NCOs for the king's bodyguard.

The cadets presented for training were all *yangban*, unused to hard work or physical exertion, who, even after receiving their modern military training were still expected to pass a traditional Korean military examination before receiving an army post.[81] As well as having to work with such unpromising material, other problems the Americans encountered following their arrival in April 1888 were those of language (none of the Americans spoke a word of Korean) and equipment (Korean purchases of Western firearms were carried out on an entirely ad hoc basis). In addition the Korean government often failed to provide Dye or his associates with pay, assistants, facilities, or even water. The Americans' relationship with their employers was consequently often strained, and Cummins and Lee were dismissed in September 1889 for openly criticising Korean officials in the press. Dye and Nienstead, by contrast, eventually earned sufficient respect to be appointed respectively Vice-President and Councillor of the Board of War. However, Lord Curzon noticed during his visit of 1892–93 that they were allowed to 'exercise no command' and were not permitted to accompany their men in the field.

Though John Ford says that the 'whole army' comprised only 2,500 men in May 1894, while Dye later claimed the existence of 10–12,000 Korean soldiers in his time, every other source indicates that in all probability there were some 4–5,000 regulars based in Seoul throughout the period 1890–94, of whom 500 constituted the 'royal guards'. By 1892 Dye and Nienstead appear to have 'trained' most or all of these, despite vigorous resistance from the traditional military establishment, which, sensitive to the threat that foreign instructors posed to its own privileged status, put hurdles in their path at every opportunity. However, the opinions of visiting Westerners vary regarding the standard of training that the Americans achieved. George Gilmore, for instance, observed in 1892 that Korean soldiers had hardly any idea of military discipline, lacked precision and punctuality, 'had no esprit de corps' and that 'hardly any instruction has been given', while Henry Norman described the drill of two regiments he saw in 1894 as 'a very amusing sight ... a sort of cross between Swedish gymnastics and the soldiers of a Drury Lane pantomime'. In 1892, on the other hand, Harry Fox found 'a certain degree of smartness in their appearance and movements'. As for their fighting abilities, the only evidence we have is the fact that when some 700–800 were deployed to Kiung-san and Cholla in 1894 to fight the Tonghak rebels, nearly half reputedly deserted en route and the rest were routed by the spear-armed Tonghaks (who, it should be remembered, vastly outnumbered them).

The reason for discrepancies in the reported strength of the central army during the 1890s was doubtless the continuing existence of an uncertain number of traditional, undrilled troops in Korea's provincial capitals, of whom the majority were stationed at Ping-Yang. These are said by Fox to have comprised some 2–3,000 men, while in 1891 A.E.J. Cavendish recorded the so-called 'Army of Ping-Yang' to have been between 1,200–1,500 strong, 'trained to fight after the native fashion with sword and gun'. He adds that 'part of it is invariably brought to the capital in case of any national danger', and it seems to have also been mustered in Seoul on the occasion of the grand reviews held once every 20–30 years. Curzon recorded the presence of 7–8,000 troops on one such occasion during his visit of either 1888 or 1892. His disparaging view of such 'purely native regiments' was that 'they are not a standing army but a standing joke'.

Most contemporary accounts record that Dye's troops were organised into three battalions, though Fox says two regiments each of three battalions of four companies, with each company consisting of a captain, a lieutenant, and 143 NCOs and men, making each regiment theoretically 1,740 strong. Referring, presumably, to its command cadre, Christopher Gardner (1895) reports that 'each battalion has a general, lieutenant-general, colonel, lieutenant-colonel, captain, sergeant.' It is apparent from the sources that a battalion's companies seldom served together, and each company in effect constituted an individual unit.

All of the officers continued to be provided by *yangban* appointed by the Board of War, so they were mostly of the same low quality as in the past. However, the lieutenants had generally passed through Dye's academy in addition to taking the traditional Korean examinations, and were consequently of a somewhat higher standard. Officers above that rank were 'practically useless,' according to Fox, 'as they have no training'. A later report describes them as 'entirely composed of men drawn from civil life, without any previous military knowledge or training, and suddenly appointed to be colonels or generals according to the influence they possess at court.' Curzon considered them 'beneath contempt'. Their duties were negligible, being summarised by Cavendish as 'nominally 48 hours in barracks or on guard, then 48 hours' leave, but practically they perform no duties at all, except to suit their own convenience.' The only times that they could be guaranteed to make an appearance were for official ceremonies and paydays.

With the arrival of the Japanese in 1894 Dye's military school was closed down and the army was reorganised under Japanese instructors. The Garrisons were replaced by four brigades referred to as the Royal Bodyguard Brigade, the Training Brigade, the Capital Defence Brigade, and the Infantry Brigade, all subdivided into battalions and companies. The Royal Bodyguard Brigade consisted of 700–800 American-trained troops – still 'advised', in a theoretically unofficial capacity, by

Dye (who had stayed on at King Kojong's special request following the Japanese takeover)[82] – while the Training Brigade or *Hullyondae*, more often referred to as the *Kunrentai*, was a new, two-battalion force of 800 men (later increased to 1,000) recruited amongst Korea's progressives and trained by the Japanese, who also provided its officers. The other two brigades were simply reconstituted from the residue of the pre-1894 Garrisons. The *Kunrentai* survived only until October 1895, when it was disbanded under pressure from Western diplomats following its involvement in the murder of Queen Min. It was at about this time that celebrated traveller Isabella Bird recorded the Korean army to comprise '4,300 men in Seoul, 800 of whom are drilled as a bodyguard for the king, and 1,200 in the provinces, in Japanese uniforms, and equipped (so far as they go) with 3,000 Berdan rifles presented by Russia.' Elsewhere she gives the strength of the Seoul units as 4,800, and even 6,000 (doubtless by adding the 4,800 figure to that of 1,200 provincial troops).

After King Kojong had taken shelter in the Russian Legation in February 1896 it became the Russians' turn to try their hand at modernising the Korean army. The only locally available officer, one Lieutenant Khmyeleff, got the ball rolling by beginning the instruction of 'a selected number of Korean officers [actually 33] in drill, with a view to their employment as instructors to the remainder at a later date'. A full-scale Russian military mission of three officers and ten or twelve NCOs arrived in October and was placed under the Legation military attaché, Colonel Poutiata, whose object was first and foremost the formation of an efficient unit of guards capable of protecting the king. This new unit, known simply as the Royal Bodyguard, was formed by collecting the army's best men together into a single regiment of five companies. Total strength as recorded by a British officer, Captain D. Mercer, consisted in June 1897 of 895 men, made up of 800 rank and file, 67 NCOs, 20 lieutenants, five captains, a paymaster, an adjutant, and a colonel, the officers being those trained by Khmyeleff. Two Russian instructors were appointed to each company, and all words of command were given in Russian, even after the eventual arrival of sufficient interpreters. The only interpreter available during the mission's first fortnight in the country was a Korean officer who 'knew only very little Russian'. He was subsequently joined by a Russian interpreter, a Russian-speaking Korean cadet and, later, several bilingual Russian Koreans recruited in Manchuria.

The so-called Training Brigade – usually referred to as the 'Korean Cadet Corps' – established by Khmyeleff, consisted of 37 men by 1897. It was probably the first Korean unit to be organised, uniformed, armed and trained along entirely Western lines. The intention was for its members 'to receive two years' military education from Russian officers'. As for the rest of the army, recorded by the Russian instructors to have comprised a mere 3,325 infantry and 85 cavalry at their arrival, this was gradually improved by the policy of periodically transferring a draft of men from the Bodyguard into one of the line regiments and filling their places with men drawn from the latter. Mercer reported that 'this policy has been steadily pursued, until there are now a good proportion of well-drilled troops scattered throughout the whole force'. A large number of the NCOs trained by the Russians were eventually promoted to the rank of lieutenant or captain, but their further advancement was obstructed by traditionalists within the military establishment.

A second party of Russian instructors arrived in 1897, bringing the strength of Poutiata's mission to six officers and 20 or 21 NCOs. Their intention was to start training a second battalion of 1,000 men, and Alexander Buller, visiting in January 1898, was told that the Russians were indeed 'actively engaged in drilling and organising two Korean regiments comprised of 1,000 men each'. In truth, however, what remained of the traditional army – from which the soldiers for the new battalion were to be selected – was found to be so destitute of men ('in consequence of the peculation which existed for the benefit of the authorities') that only 571 could be mustered. These were formed into three companies, which was the maximum strength attained by the new battalion, and a Russian report observed that training even this many additional men proved to be 'a further heavy blow to the pockets of the Korean Minister of War'. Despite such problems, Poutiata still hoped to eventually increase the army's strength to 6,000 trained men, under 160 Russian instructors – a modest ambition compared to the claim found in other sources that Russia's ultimate intention was to train up a Korean army of 250,000 men, doubtless as potential cannon-fodder for the increasingly inevitable war of supremacy between Russia and Japan.

Russia's plans came to naught when Emperor Kojong abruptly dismissed its instructors in March 1898 under pressure from the pro-Japanese *Tongnip Hyophoe* or 'Independence Club', a reform movement founded in 1896. The Club's clamorous objections were also responsible for Kojong's abandonment of his plans to form a foreign bodyguard in September the same year, obliging him to send home the 30 men who had already been recruited. Hired in Shanghai, these comprised 'a motley collection drawn mostly from the seafaring class ... composed of nine Americans, nine British, five Germans, five French, and two Russians'. The fact that they were employed at all is an interesting reflection on how little confidence the Emperor placed in his own people.

After the departure of the Russians the training of the Korean army reverted, by default, to the Japanese, who introduced instructors selected amongst exiled Korean radicals trained by the Japanese army. Organisation of the troops in the capital reverted to five units, consisting of two guard battalions and three line, each of four companies. Conscription was introduced in 1903, and by 1904 the army's strength had been increased to somewhere between 17–20,000 men in anticipation of the coming Russo-Japanese conflict. According to Vincent 8,000 of these were stationed in Seoul, 5,000 on the northern frontier, and the balance 'scattered about in the larger provincial towns'. They were organised into two guard battalions, eight line or garrison infantry battalions, one cavalry regiment (400 men), and an unrecorded number of small artillery and engineer units, plus service detachments.

Perhaps surprisingly, Korea remained neutral during the ensuing war, but nevertheless found itself occupied by Japanese forces. Once the fighting was over the country was declared a Japanese protectorate and its army was immediately reduced to six battalions and three companies, totalling about 8,500 men. King Kojong was obliged to abdicate in mid-1907 after voicing his objections to Japanese occupation, and on 31 July the Japanese forced his son and successor Sujong to terminate the Korean army's sorry existence by disbanding all but a single battalion of guards. It was armed resistance to this measure between 1907 and 1910 that finally persuaded Japan to annex the country outright.

Terms of service

Beyond the fact that it was invariably months in arrears, we know virtually nothing about Korean soldiers' pay before the 1880s, when it is said to have comprised about 8 cents and a ration of rice per diem. However, we are told that their duties were light, and that they served for at most only three days in every six, turn and turn about. As has already been mentioned, they also enjoyed numerous official privileges, in addition to which, as Gardner put it, 'as a rule, a soldier travelling enjoys free quarters at inns, free run of his teeth at restaurants, an unlimited supply of gratuitous tobacco and drinks, and occasional tips when on police duty.'

In 1892 Fox recorded that a soldier's monthly pay was 'one bag of rice, containing about 150 lbs, and (nominally) 900 *cash*', which he says was worth about 27 cents but which according to other sources would have been worth about 75 cents (there being roughly 1,200 Korean *cash* to a Mexican dollar at the end of the 1880s).[83] This figure is nevertheless low compared to pay in both 1883 (see above) and the 1890s (see below). Fox continues: 'This latter payment is usually in arrears. As a regular supply of rice is all the ordinary Korean lives for, the army offers great inducements to recruits; and they are, on the whole, well contented. There is no limit to service as long as they are able to carry arms. For the purpose of leave the garrison in Seoul is divided into three detachments – one-third guarding the palace for three days; one-third staying in barracks and drilling; one-third going home for three days. At the end of the month they are sent down the river in companies [to Chemulpo] to fetch their rice from the junks.'

By 1895 their pay had increased dramatically, to $5½ per month, equivalent at the time to about 11s 6d, or 57.5p (policemen received $8–$10). However, Captain Mercer, visiting in June 1897, observed that 'owing to the peculations of the officers they seldom receive more than $3' (their officers pocketing the rest), though each man received in addition a food allowance of 13 cents (3¼d, or 1.4p) per diem, this money being 'lumped together by each company, and the food is supplied by a contractor'. The staple food was still rice, but each man also got a ration of about half a pound (0.23 kg) of beef, and a supply of pickles (*kimchi*), cabbage, and bread. At the very end of the century soldiers were getting the equivalent of about 8s (40p) per month, lieutenants £2, captains £3, and generals £6.

WARFARE

Korea is a well-watered country of mountains and rice-fields, with hot, wet summers but long, cold winters, when temperatures can drop well below zero, especially in the north (where temperatures below –40°C were recorded during the Korean War of 1950–53). In the 19th century it was poorly provided with roads, bridges, or ferries, even the best roads being no more than unsurfaced tracks which were rarely passable for wagons or guns, especially during the rainy season (July–August). In the mountains these tracks generally dwindled to mere bridle paths, sometimes no more than a foot wide (about 0.3 m). It is hardly surprising, therefore, that contemporaries invariably described Korea as 'not a good country for cavalry or field artillery'.

Its policy of isolation meant that over the centuries Korea had evolved a sophisticated early warning system designed to forewarn local commanders of the approach of foreigners or enemies (fundamentally looked upon as one and the same thing). This comprised a complex network of nearly 700 beacon stations, principally following the north-eastern and south-eastern coastlines but also zigzagging cross-country in the south and the north-west. Each individual line of beacons invariably led to and from Seoul, enabling a signal from the most distant station, in Ham-kiung province, to be relayed the 300-plus miles (500 km) to Seoul – via 86 stations – in less than four hours, compared to the 15 days it would have taken a messenger by road. A typical station consisted of a low rampart enclosing a space about 20 yds (18 m) across, with a *pong dai* ('watch-tower') occupying most of the available space. The tower is described by E.W. Koons (1925) as resembling 'a truncated pyramid, built of rough stones, the top of it making a platform 20 feet higher than the ... ground ... Inside the pyramid is a chimney, four feet square, at the bottom of which is a horizontal flue that leads to the space inside the rampart.' Writing from personal experience in the 1860s, Ernest Oppert[84] tells us that 'when only one fire is lighted, the signal means "peace", or that nothing has come in sight, two fires means "war", and advise the approach of a ship near the coast'.

Where the beacon routes converged near the capital, however, the stations and signalling arrangements were, by necessity, more complicated, as is apparent from the following description by Lowell, dating to 1883/4. He tells us that the station on Nam San mountain near Seoul comprised five such towers (he calls them 'cairns'): 'In times of peace only four of these are lighted; and each of the four, respectively, represents two out of the eight provinces ... The danger signals are complicated ... An example or two will serve as a sufficient illustration. If, for instance, an enemy makes his appearance off ... Chullado [i.e., Cholla *do* or province], an extra bonfire is built close to the main one that represents the province of Chullado, and to its right, its left side being allotted to the use of the other province which it represents. Then, again, in times of danger other bonfires are lighted above the first in number, according to the imminence of danger – one when the enemy are observed off the coast or near the frontier, two when they are about to cross it or disembark, three when they have done so, and four when the fighting has actually begun.' An example of the network in practice is recorded by Winfield Schley, who noted that when the American flotilla arrived off Kangwha island in 1871 'on the same night that the squadron reached the anchorage beacon-fires were lighted on every hilltop visible'.

The 'Righteous Armies' that fought the Japanese after 1905 are reported by McKenzie to have used a similar 'elaborate system of mountain-top signalling' to avoid Japanese troops and to mount attacks on their outposts.

Korean soldiers saw little field service beyond what was necessitated by their more usual activities as tax-collectors and policemen, and they were said to be essentially non-violent. Fox, for instance, described them as 'peaceably disposed ... I have never seen them brawling or fighting, although they are very often drunk'. Nevertheless, Japanese officers placed in command of Korean detachments during the suppression of the Tonghak rebellion in 1894–95 reported them to be no less brave, efficient, or intelligent than their Japanese counterparts, while the Frenchmen and Americans who fought them in the 1860s and 1870s were impressed by their considerable courage. Schley, for instance, recorded that the Koreans defending Kwang-song fort in 1871 'died at their posts heroically and without fear. The men of no nation could have done more for home and country.' He adds that even after being subjected to a 30-minute hail of fire from both flanks, they did not give way 'until their men had been piled up after several bayonet charges and their quarters within the parapets had taken fire'. His view was that 'it is doubtful if better organised forces anywhere could have maintained a better morale after such sweeping defeats and destruction.' The general consensus was nevertheless that they would only usually offer such stout resistance when fighting from behind cover, William Griffis (1882) reflecting this view in his observation that they were 'poor soldiers in the open field ... but put the same men behind walls [and] they are more than brave, their courage is sublime, they fight to the last man'. Indeed, every 19th-century Korean battle that did not involve an ambush seems to have revolved around an attack on or the defence of a fortified position of some sort, be it a town, a fort, or a field entrenchment.

Despite this, Korean fortifications were not of a particularly high standard. The forts encountered by the Americans in 1871 were mere combinations of trenches, palisades, and uneven earth ramparts, while those defending the river approaches to Seoul were described in May 1894 as 'made of rough stones cemented together, breast high, about one yard thick, and pierced with loopholes about every five feet ... They were made in the days of bows and arrows, and would not resist the projectiles of modern ordnance unless well reinforced by earthworks.' Even city walls were generally insubstantial, White writing that they were nothing like those which surrounded Chinese cities, but were instead 'about six feet high, miserably constructed, of irregular and uneven stone blocks, and nearly every one of them would tumble down at the first shock of a ball fired from a modern gun.'

The assorted foreign military officers who visited the country in the 1890s considered Korean soldiers to be 'excellent guerrilla troops', from their ability to travel light, live off the land, and fight from concealment, which were their traditional strengths. Attempts by their foreign instructors to make them fight like Western soldiers were entirely unsuccessful when they were fielded against the Tonghak rebels, doubtless

Korean dead photographed by Felice Beato following the American assault on the entrenchments at Kwang-song ('Fort McKee') on 11 June 1871.

Another Beato photograph of the interior of Kwang-song fort following its bombardment. Note the breech-loading guns at lower left.

because their dislike of drilling meant that they lacked the necessary appreciation of discipline that would have enabled them to fight effectively in the open. This is precisely why the Japanese instructors introduced in 1894–96 abandoned the teaching of traditional Korean tactics – which, copied from those of the Chinese, were designed primarily to intimidate the enemy at as great a distance as possible by making a lot of noise and waving a lot of flags – in favour of the modern Western tactics which had been adopted in Japan.

Their effectiveness in such tactics, however, was compromised by their continuing lack of discipline and by the quality of their musketry. Even when using the most up-to-date Western firearms, this left a lot to be desired, largely, it would seem, through want of practice. Despite Cavendish's claim in 1891 that 'although they get no musketry instruction, they are very good shots up to 800 yards', at the beginning of 1897 their Russian instructors found that the troops they were given to train, though they were drawn from the central army, had never previously fired a gun and were found to be 'at first much frightened' by their rifles. Consequently their firing was 'very wild'. Though two months later their target practice is reported to have become 'satisfactory', this rather smacks of damning with faint praise. As late as 1902 it is recorded only that they were 'good shots' at up to 200 yds (180 m), which was the greatest range at which they practised.

DRESS AND APPEARANCE

Though 19th-century Koreans bore a closer resemblance to the Japanese than the Chinese, they were nevertheless significantly taller, stronger, and more sturdily built than the former, while having features described as 'even more pronouncedly Mongolian in type' than the latter. Their average height, as described by Western visitors, was between about 5 ft 4 ins (1.62 m) and 5 ft 6 ins (1.68 m). They had a tawny complexion said to have been neither as dark nor as yellow as that of the Chinese, and their hair was straight and usually black, though several sources mention that it often had a brown or reddish brown tinge – Isabella Bird, for instance, noted in 1895 that 'though the hair is dark, much of it is so distinctly a russet brown as to require the frequent application of lampblack and oil to bring it to a fashionable black'. Korean men did not shave and were noted to be on the whole distinctly more hirsute than their Chinese neighbours, many men having long moustaches and thick beards. Others, however, could only manage a very scanty growth – whence Gifford's claim that most had 'nothing or almost nothing on their faces to require the use of a razor', and Bird's observation that though some men had full moustaches and large goatees, 'on the faces of others a few carefully tended hairs, as in China, do duty for both'.

They wore their hair long, unmarried men parting it in the middle, gathering it behind, and wearing it in one or two long tails hanging down the back or on either side, usually plaited but sometimes left 'to stream in shaggy masses' – particularly amongst the lower working classes. Engaged and married men[85] instead wore it in a tight topknot (*sangtu*), just 2–3 inches tall and an inch in diameter, which was tied over (and completely concealed) a small tonsure and stood straight up from the crown of the head. It was usually secured by having a pin thrust through it. A tight-fitting, 1½–2 inch deep net band called a *manggon*, worn round the head above the ears and tied behind with a ribbon, kept stray hairs in place.

This came down well over the forehead and the base of the skull, and was bound on so tightly, says Bird, 'as to produce a permanent groove in the skin'. However, field-workers and labourers often made do instead with a strip of white cloth tied at the back of the head. In addition to the *manggon*, men of substance or rank wore a crownless, fine gauze skullcap over the topknot. Woven from horsehair and dyed a glossy black, this resembled a stiffened hairnet with a hole in the top.

The Japanese-inspired *Kabo* Reforms of 1895 attempted to abolish topknot and *manggon* alike because they were considered to epitomise Korea's links with its past, but following considerable unrest King Kojong rescinded the so-called 'Topknot Decree' in February 1896 (it was revived in 1902 and was this time enforced). By contrast, pro-Japanese reformers had already started to cut off their topknots and adopt Western hairstyles as early as the mid-1880s.

The most distinctive item of almost every Korean's dress was his hat (*kat*). Technically worn by all married men, this came in numerous shapes and sizes that could denote such things as the wearer's social class and occupation. The most common variety, however, worn by the majority of the middle and lower classes, was the *houkrip*, frequently and accurately described by visitors as 'shaped like a Welshwoman's' (though White rather nicely describes it as resembling 'a flowerpot inverted in the centre of a round table'). This had a high, flat-topped crown, a broad circular brim, and was made of either plaited horsehair or, among the better-off, plaited bamboo 'split to the fineness of a thread and woven so as to resemble horsehair'. The weaving of both varieties was so fine that the wearer's topknot could be clearly seen through it, and they were consequently very light. Such hats were almost invariably stained or lacquered glossy black, and were held in place by a black ribbon tied under the chin. However, hats worn during mourning were sometimes whitish-yellow.

The diameter of the brim varied according to social status, those of ordinary people measuring about 12–18 ins (0.3–0.45 m) while those of senior officials were commonly about 2 ft (0.6 m); an official seen in 1816, for example, is described as wearing 'an immense hat, not less than five or six feet round the brim'. The crown, by contrast, typically measured as little as 4–5 ins (100–125 mm) in diameter at the base, tapering to 3–4 ins (75–100 mm), and was usually between 4½–6 ins (115–150 mm) tall with a flat circular top. Labourers working in the sun wore a similar hat of uncoloured plaited bamboo with a crown up to 9 ins (225 mm) tall.

A Korean kept his hat on as a mark of respect, and, other than when he was working, when he was outdoors he only customarily removed it in the company of his closest friends. In wet weather he protected it from the rain with a shapeless oiled paper cover 'put over it like an extinguisher and tied under the chin' (see detail 132a), while in winter he wore a fur and/or wadded silk or cotton headdress under it for added warmth. For the hats of officials see the caption to Figures 104–107.

Though the cut of Korean dress was the same for every class, its colour and the material from which it was made were strictly regulated by sumptuary laws that had been in force since mediaeval times. These decreed that the lower and middle classes could only wear clothes made of cotton or hemp, while silk (either locally

One of the earliest known photographs of Koreans, taken in 1863. The man on the right is a yangban. All three wear typical dress of the period. (Wikipedia)

manufactured or imported from China) was the prerogative of officials and the upper classes. Cotton clothes predominated in the south, but were not much worn in the north, where the hemp variety generally replaced them. Those of ordinary Koreans were almost universally white, albeit often almost imperceptibly tinged with blue or less often green, and were very slightly glazed by means of rice starch, which gave them 'a fine silky gloss'. Foreigners considered that their white dress made the Koreans look darker-complexioned and taller than they really were (their height being further exaggerated by their tall black hats), but also noted that though they seemed 'snowy at a distance' their white clothes were often 'dingy and dirty' close up, especially amongst the labouring class.

Everyday dress consisted of a long robe with very wide sleeves, worn over two or more hip-length jackets and a pair of baggy trousers. The long robe, only worn by married men, could reach well below the knees but was vented almost to the armpits at the sides. It was tied by a single pair of tapes high up on the chest and secured by a cord belt or ribbon worn close under the armpits. The enormous baggy trousers were tied either round the waist or high up on the body, as well as being gathered below the knees, where they were folded and strapped close round the calves by means of cloth leggings tied at the ankles. Commoners' belts were blue-green, soldiers' black, minor officials' dark blue, higher officials' peach, and government ministers' maroon. The belt customarily supported a tobacco-pouch, the Koreans being enthusiastic pipe-smokers. Their pipes had a metal mouthpiece and bowl and a slender bamboo stem which could be up to 3 ft/0.9 m long (the greater the length, the higher the rank of the user).

Most working men went without the long robe and wore just the shorter jacket, belted round the waist, and closer-fitting trousers.

Footwear consisted of thickly wadded white socks and a pair of sandals, wooden clogs (substituted by the lower classes in wet weather), or Chinese-style shoes. The clogs were almost identical in shape to French *sabots*, while the sandals were either of leather, stout hemp twine 'with many strands woven over the top of the foot', or rice-straw, the last usually lasting for no more than a few days. The shoes, worn predominantly by the upper classes, are described as having 'the form of a slipper and the solidity of a boot', with leather or leather-lined cloth uppers, pointed toes, and rope or leather soles about a quarter of an inch (6 mm) thick. The leather is described by J.C. Hall (1882) as 'oxhide, not tanned into leather, but dried and stiffened into a substance as hard as horn', rendering such a shoe 'as harsh and uncomfortable ... as if it were made of iron. It would be altogether impossible to wear it but for the thick cotton-wadded bags in which the Koreans encase their feet by way of socks.' Lowell described this type of footwear as 'of Chinese origin ... less ornamental [and] also less solidly made, in spite of its unyielding rigidity. Its colour is black, varied now and again for officials by some passing fancy of temporary fashion' (in 1898, for instance, Arthur Diósy records the shoes of *yangban* being black or dark blue). The soles and heels of those intended for outdoor use were shod with nails, a custom hallowed by tradition and legislation following a victory once obtained by hobnailed Koreans in a battle fought against smooth-shod Chinese troops on the surface of a frozen river.

Winter clothes were also of cotton or hemp cloth, but padded with unspun cotton. Isabella Bird describes Korean men's winter dress as comprising 'white cotton sleeved robes, huge trousers, and socks; all wadded. On their heads were black silk wadded caps with pendant sides edged with black fur,' on top of which they wore the usual high-crowned, broad-brimmed *kat*. Edward Belcher (1845) similarly observed that in winter 'some of the lower orders wear huge fur caps, made of wolf or lynx skin; and the heads of others are covered with enormous brown or black sombreros, fashioned from a kind of felt, while many again affect huge cone-shaped hats, covered with painted oiled paper.' In place of cotton wadding *yangban* lined their winter garments with fur, most often sable.

On ceremonial occasions the upper classes dressed entirely in silk, but at other times they usually wore cotton inner jackets, cotton or silk trousers, and a long silk outer robe, buttoned on the chest. The middle class, made up predominantly of minor government officials, wore light blue outer coats, and were consequently nicknamed 'blue clouds'. Only the upper classes (i.e., senior officials) were permitted to use other colours, most wearing various shades of pink, red, green, and blue, though senior government officials generally wore a violet outer robe. After the 1860s such coloured clothes were always plain, never patterned. For fuller details of upper-class dress, see the caption to Figures 104–107.

From 1888 on there were Japanese-inspired moves to modernise Korean costume, including attempts to reduce the size of hat brims and the bagginess of sleeves, coats, and trousers. Korean progressives adopted Western costume in its entirety, but conservatives regarded such changes with ill-concealed abhorrence, considering Western dress to be 'uncultured'. As a result it was not until 1900 that the wearing of Western-style clothes by government officials became obligatory.

Uniforms

Until the introduction of foreign instructors began to influence military fashion in the 1880s, Korean uniforms comprised no more than a government-issue jacket and felt hat issued twice a year, one jacket being for summer wear and the other for winter, doubtless distinguished from one another by no more than the weight of the material from which they were manufactured. These jackets were worn over the soldier's own everyday clothes. The hat – which differed from the traditional *kat* only in having a rounded rather than a flat-topped crown – was supposed to be worn in place of its civilian counterpart, but it is apparent from pictorial sources that in practice many soldiers continued to wear the latter. Footwear usually consisted of white stockings and either straw sandals or low, black shoes with the pointed toes that, in Korea, were traditionally associated with soldiers. Some, however, went barefoot.

Whereas civilian hats were made of horsehair or crinoline, military hats were made of felt. They appear to have been as often brown as black during the first half of the century; in fact in the mid-1840s Belcher described them as being 'generally of a dirty brown felt', and as late as 1882 Griffis wrote that Korean soldiers wore 'large black or brown felt hats, resembling Mexican sombreros'. After about 1885, however, military hats were almost universally black, with a small, pointed brass finial, a narrow red or pink tape round the join between crown and brim, and a red or black ribbon which was tied beneath the chin. On ceremonial occasions until at least the mid-1890s, and sometimes on campaign too, a 'plaited string' with a long, red horsehair plume was suspended from the crown by means of a swivel button, to hang over the brim and down the back; fox-tails might be utilised in the same fashion. (Belcher records that officers substituted two or three peacock's feathers, which 'appended to a curved ivory ball on the pointed apex, hang gracefully over the capacious brim'.) Following the introduction of foreign instructors a small white metal badge denoting the wearer's regiment was sometimes added to the front of the crown just above the red tape, while in earlier times a considerably larger badge was sometimes worn (see Figure 116). During the last two decades of the century the diameter of the hat's brim progressively reduced to such an extent that Western visitors described it as resembling a Tyrolean hat.

Until at least the late 1880s the government-issue jacket provided to the majority of troops comprised a sleeved or sleeveless, usually knee-length (though sometimes longer) cotton coat referred to as an 'open surcoat' by Griffis. Bonar describes it as 'hanging in strips from the shoulders', an allusion to the fact that it was split not only at front and back but was also vented almost to the armpits at the sides. Among the army's

An 18th- or 19th-century Korean armour, described by Boots (1934) thus: 'Of coarse hemp cloth lined with blue cotton and covered on the outside with a formal flower design printed with wooden blocks. On the inside of the front and the back, there are cuir bouilli plates 2¾ by 3¾ ins, each the same size in 8 even rows, each fastened by two iron rivets, the rounded heads of which serve as a decoration on the outside; on the inside, the rivets are hammered over a rough hand-cut washer. The plates overlap from above downward and from right to left. The rivets pierce the centre of the plates, one at the top and one about halfway down, except those of the rows where the garment opens, which are riveted only at the edge. On the outside is an epauliere of heavy iron, hinged in three sections, below which is a group of 10 half-sized plates in 2 rows protecting the front of the shoulder. The open round neck is finished with white leather sewn with coarse thread. The casque ... is of conical shape, of 2 iron plates riveted together and banded on the outside. A visor of iron with silver inlay decoration is riveted on, and below it another piece of iron to protect the forehead. Ear protectors and couvrenuque [ie neckguard] plates, are riveted to the bottom of the helmet. They hang loose, to be tied with strings of the hemp cloth. The helmet is surmounted by an iron cap which held an iron trident and a tuft of red horsehair.'

foreign-drilled elements this long outer coat was subsequently relegated to ceremonial wear, and was replaced on all other occasions by a thigh-length (later hip-length) jacket with long baggy sleeves. This had its own white collar and cuffs sewn round the inside of the neck and sleeve ends. Both types of coat were similar in cut to those worn by civilians, and were tied and/or belted in the same way (see above).

The change from a long coat to a short one amongst Korea's drilled troops probably began with the appointment of Chinese instructors in 1882, several authorities alluding to the introduction of new 'Chinese-style' uniforms that year. Writing of soldiers of the 'king's bodyguard' (the *Changoyong* division) seen in March 1883, Bonar describes their 'semi-Chinese' uniforms as consisting of the usual Korean military hat plus a blue cotton jacket with bright red facings and 'a sort of apron in two parts coming down to the knees, of black velvet designs on a bright red cloth, and covering the ordinary Korean wide trousers.' This 'apron' was undoubtedly a pair of Chinese *chan chün*, or 'battle trousers'. Another Chinese feature which it is tempting to suppose was introduced at the same time was the white cloth disc sewn to the front and back of the jacket, on which were inscribed details of the soldier's unit, or according to some visitors the word 'valour' in Chinese characters. However, we know that these were already in use by the 1860s, and probably considerably earlier, though contemporary evidence demonstrates that they remained uncommon. Indeed, pictures showing such discs in use are few and far between. Regardless of when they were introduced, it seems likely that they disappeared as Chinese influence waned after 1884.

Though most Korean uniforms were dark blue throughout the century, artillerymen are recorded wearing red in the Taewongun's time and other colours are also occasionally met with. In November 1884, for instance, W.R. Carles saw a procession in Seoul that included matchlockmen in green uniforms (a traditional colour for Korean military dress in earlier times) and 'soldiers in crimson with gold trimmings, beating drums'. Since most such references date to the 1880s or later it seems likely that the introduction of alternative uniform colours was a further consequence of foreign influence – Chinese, Japanese, American, and Russian.

During the army's period under American instructors dark blue nevertheless remained the principal, though not the only, colour of Korean uniforms. Frank Carpenter, who first visited Korea in 1888 and was there again in 1894, tells us that Dye's attempts to Westernise, or at least modernise, the army's uniform had in fact been cautious and as non-intrusive as possible, since the existence of a strong anti-foreign faction obliged him 'to work very slowly, as this faction was opposed to any change in army matters'. He nevertheless 'at last got the sleeves made smaller, cut off the skirt so that it was made into a kind of blouse, and took out four-fifths of the cloth which the Korean soldiers had formerly worn in their pantaloons. He did not attempt to make them change their hats ... The colors used in the new Korean uniform are different from those of any of the armies of Christendom. The shirtlike waists are of purple cotton faced with red; the hats are black, and there is a bright red band about them. The pantaloons are purple, and the feet are swathed in great white boots of padded cotton.' Except in the colour of their coats, this basically tallies with a description of 'Royal troops' seen at Seoul by John Ford in May 1894, who wore blue coats, 'plum-coloured' trousers, black hats (with bright yellow rather than red tassels), and 'half-high boots'. Contemporary pictures show that at this date some military jackets were still edged in a contrasting colour, doubtless red.

When they imposed themselves upon Korea following the outbreak of war with China in 1894, the Japanese stated that uniforms would remain unaltered for the present but were likely to be 'changed gradually to the foreign style', which tends to confirm that earlier attempts to replace traditional dress had been less than successful. Isabella Bird records that the troops she saw in Seoul in 1895 wore 'rusty black', brown, or blue cotton jackets, leather belts, baggy trousers (which she describes as 'sometimes a foot too short, at others a foot too long'), wadded white socks, straw or twine sandals, and black felt hats 'of Tyrolese style, with pink ribbon round the crowns'. Fox, writing later the same year, describes the uniform of 'the Korean standing army' as comprising hat, dark green or black tunic, leather belt, and black or white baggy trousers, adding that each soldier still customarily received two uniforms a year 'one summer, one winter'. Provincial infantrymen seen by Bird at Yö Ju and Sun-chhön wore 'Tyrolese hats and coarse cotton uniforms in which blue predominated'.

Likewise writing of the 1890s, Underwood (1904) states that 'the dress of the common soldiers was intended to be an imitation of European military costume adapted to the ideas of the Koreans. The result was a hybrid which had neither the dignity nor the usefulness of the one or the other. It consisted of a loose blouse jacket, and badly fitting, baggy trousers, made of thin black cotton cloth, with scarlet trimmings. The jacket was belted in, and a black felt hat surmounted the top-knot, and was fastened insecurely beneath the chin by a narrow band.' Gilmore adds that the dye faded 'with all degrees of irregularity' and the cut of the cloth was 'decidedly *sui generis*'.

In June 1897 the Royal Bodyguard regiment (now under Russian instructors) wore a uniform which Mercer described as comprising 'a blue serge frock and trousers, with low shoes and white gaiters, coming well over the shoe, and reaching to just below the knee. The head dress consists of a very ugly blue felt hat, circular in shape, and about the height of an English infantry helmet. It is ornamented with a red band, and has a flat rim round the bottom. A new pattern cap has just been introduced similar to the old one, but flattened on the top. The pouches and belts are of brown leather, which is in very bad condition usually.' He adds that the blue jackets and trousers were replaced by white in summer. Another visitor (writing in 1896) tells us that the trousers were of Western cut, doubtless indicating that, with the exception of the traditional hat, this uniform was actually Japanese in style. Certainly when Isabella Bird returned to Korea in 1897 the soldiers she saw were clothed 'in Japanese uniforms'; and nothing could be more Japanese than the officers' uniforms seen by Mercer that year, which consisted of a blue-braided patrol jacket, blue trousers, jackboots, and 'a French kepi, ornamented with much gold lace and scarlet cloth'. Mercer removes all doubt regarding the origin of Korean uniforms at this date by stating categorically that 'all the clothing is at present obtained from Japan'. The uniforms of the central army continued to reflect Japanese influence thereafter until Korea's armed forces were disbanded in 1907.

For additional uniform details see the captions to Figures 113–129.

ARMS

The traditional armament of Korean soldiers comprised a mixture of spears, polearms, swords, bows, matchlocks, and jingalls, the last being the British name for large-calibre, long-barrelled matchlocks called 'thousand *po* guns' by the Koreans, which fired shot weighing from a few ounces up to a pound or more (about 0.1–0.5 kg). Most of their weapons were copied from Chinese and Japanese prototypes. Some shields also appear to have survived in use right up until the early years of the 20th century. Circular, and constructed from tightly woven rattan or bamboo, these doubtless bore a close resemblance to their Chinese counterparts, so that in all probability they were convex and averaged some 2–3 ft (0.6–0.9 m) in diameter.

Firearms were relatively uncommon in the earlier part of the century; amongst the soldiers seen on the island of Quelpart in 1845, for instance, Belcher noted numerous bows and spears but only 'a few rude matchlocks, constructed in the Chinese fashion', while Oppert records that in 1866 the troops he saw escorting a group of officials 'had not even matchlocks,[86] but only lances and bows, and no swords.' Claims that the French captured as many as 6,000 matchlocks during their operations round Kangwha the same year are extremely dubious, not least because Korean sources indicate that it was the awesome effectiveness of the enemy's massed firearms during the French and American attacks of 1866 and 1871 that was responsible for the Korean government's decision to issue matchlocks in greater numbers. Western firearms also began to be imported following these invasions. Nevertheless, even in 1879 John Ross claimed that scarcely 1% of Korean soldiers

Typical tortoise-shaped Korean powder flasks. They were carved from wood, and generally lacquered either black or red.

possessed firearms – clearly an exaggeration, but indicative of the fact that they remained in very short supply. There seem to have been roughly as many spears and polearms as firearms in most military parades seen by Westerners well into the 1880s. By the mid-1890s, however, the majority of Korean regular troops possessed a firearm of some description.

Although cannon had been originally introduced into Korea from China, handguns had come instead from Japan at the end of the 16th century. Korean matchlocks remained unchanged in general appearance thereafter right up until their eventual displacement by Western muskets and rifles, by which time they were largely of Chinese or local manufacture. Like their Chinese and Japanese counterparts, Korean matchlocks had a small butt which, if the weapon was not simply fired held out at arm's length, was pressed against the cheek rather than braced against the shoulder. They were fired by means of a slow-match gripped in a pivoting lever arrangement, the excess match being wrapped round the firer's right wrist. Most were loaded with perhaps three or more crudely shaped metal slugs or pellets (described by Bird as 'imperfectly rounded balls the size of a pea'), by means of a wooden rammer that was inserted into the stock beneath the barrel when not in use. American missionary John Boots (1931) tells us that the shot were 'carried in a small bag about one inch in diameter and four inches long, of coarse hemp cloth, attached at its open end to a horn of the Korean mountain goat ... This horn is about four inches long, split at its outer end to allow it to be used as a pair of pincers to hold the shot as it comes from the bag.' Powder was carried in a wooden flask generally carved to look like a turtle, while a smaller round container held the priming powder. The barrels of matchlocks issued to soldiers of the central army were stamped close to the breech end with the name of their respective Garrisons.

Although matchlocks remained in service until the 1890s, by the end of the 1880s they were far outnumbered by Western firearms, and had been displaced by these in units that had undergone any sort of foreign instruction, whether Japanese, Chinese, or American. However, some soldiers (described, significantly, as wear-ing traditional rather than Westernised uniforms) were still armed with matchlocks at least as late as 1895, and such weapons are recorded in limited use even in 1898.

There had been occasional small purchases of Western firearms during the 1870s, but the first sizeable quantity to be imported consisted of 2,000 obsolete weapons of mixed origins bought in from Japan in 1882, followed by a shipment of rifles from China in 1883, and 4,000 obsolete breechloaders from the United States in 1884. It was doubtless these assorted consignments which provided the Lefaucheaux muzzle-loading rifles – of French origin, but supplied by the Chinese – with which Bonar records '300 men of the King's bodyguard' being armed in April 1883; the Peabody-Martini rifles carried by some of the soldiers seen on parade by Carles in November 1884 (the rest still had matchlocks); and the Remingtons and Peabody-Martinis mentioned in an American report dating to 1885. Other weapons known to have been in service with the Korean army by much the same date included Martini-Henrys, Sniders, and the inevitable Brown Bess or Tower flintlock muskets that constituted the mainstay of most 19th-century Asian armies.

Just as in China, this diversity was the result of ignorance and the absence of a coherent or consistent purchasing policy. Most units consequently ended up with an exotic mix of weapons that must have rendered the provision of ammunition and spares a logistical nightmare, so it is hardly surprising that several visitors noted the poor state in which Korean firearms were maintained – Curzon, for instance, wrote that muskets which he examined in 1888 'were commonly destitute either of hammer, trigger, or plate, sometimes of all three, and were frequently only held together by string; while the bayonets were bent and rusty'.

This melange of weaponry never entirely disappeared during the 19th century, and continued even after the Japanese took over the administration of the country. Even the foreign-drilled elements of the army continued to be armed with what Curzon diplomatically described as 'rifles of great variety and pattern' (A.H. Savage Landor says 'guns of all sorts, ages, and descriptions, from old flintlocks to repeating breechloaders'), and as late as 1894 Gilmore wrote that it was still possible to find two soldiers side by side 'one armed with a repeating rifle of excellent make, with sabre-bayonet fixed, and the other bearing a native flintlock'. Nevertheless, there are numerous indications that within the next year or so Remingtons equipped with sabre-bayonets came to predominate, and that these were inspected once a month by the army's American instructors in an effort to ensure they remained serviceable. Efforts were also made to minimise the variety of weapons found within a single unit, probably meaning that such other firearms as remained in service were confined wherever possible to individual sub-units – Bird, for instance, noted an entire troop of soldiers armed with Sniders, while Gilmore (who mentions that 'several battalions have been armed with modern breech-loaders, and, I believe, some with magazine rifles') mentions seeing 'companies marching side by side, one carrying the old flint-locks, or match-locks fired with punk, and the other armed with breech-loaders and sabre bayonets.'

After King Kojong had placed himself under their protection in February 1896 the Russian government provided him with 3,000 Berdan rifles, and Captain Mercer records that towards the end of the same year 'the old Remingtons and other rifles' with which the Russian-trained Bodyguard had formerly been armed were discarded and the Berdans were 'served to the Bodyguard, and, as far as they would go, to the other troops.' However, most of the Berdans disappeared as swiftly as Russian influence, and though a few remained in service at the beginning of the 20th century the majority of Korean firearms by this time were provided by the Japanese, and comprised Muratas (probably a mixture of 1880 single-shot and 1889 magazine models), Model 1897 ('30th Year') Meiji magazine rifles, Martinis, obsolete single-shot Gras rifles (Model 1874), and assorted muzzle-loading smoothbores, with what B. Vincent (1904–5) describes as 'a sprinkling of Winchester and Colt carbines in the artillery and cavalry'.

Korean swords from a plate illustrating Boots' article. From left to right, they are a royal bodyguard's sword with silver and gold inlay; a sword with a bamboo scabbard and hilt and a Japanese-style guard; an officer's dress sword with a carved bamboo hilt; and a more traditional sword with a shagreen grip. All have brass guards.

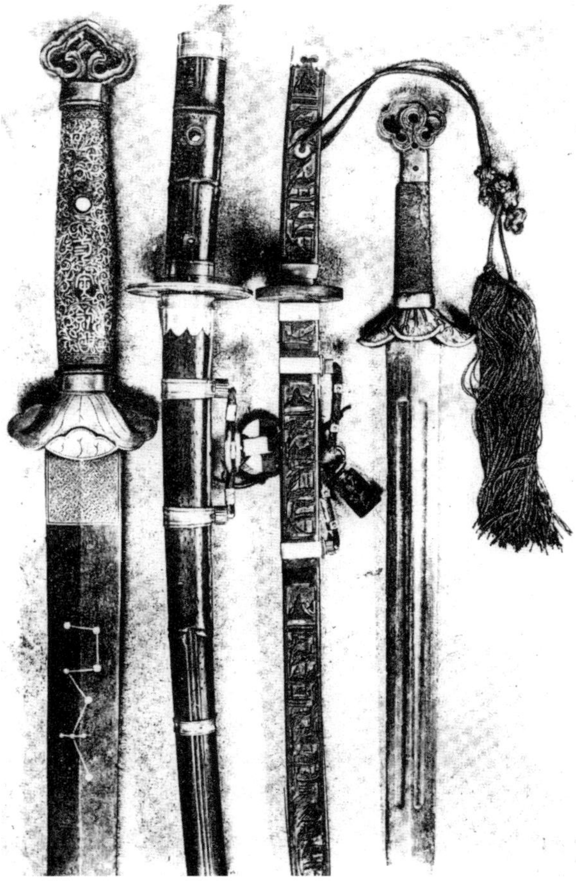

Regardless of weaponry, the quality of Korean musketry was not particularly high, because soldiers underwent little if any target practice. Cavendish reported in 1891 that it occurred only occasionally, while three years later Landor noted that though it 'amused and interested them much' practice seldom took place because of the expense of the ammunition, all of which had to be imported even after the construction of Korea's first ordnance factory in Seoul during the 1890s. (This could produce artillery shells and repair damaged rifles, but proved incapable of manufacturing new weapons or smallarm ammunition.)

Of the traditional weapons that remained in use alongside firearms for much of the century, those most frequently mentioned were spears, polearms, and bows. Spears remained in use until the very end of the century and were employed by some of the troops who fought against the Tonghaks in 1894. They were long, broad-bladed weapons, with their wooden or bamboo shafts often painted red, and usually with either a tuft of red-dyed horse or yak hair or else an animal tail attached to the socket. One elite unit raised by the Taewongun is recorded with tiger tails attached to its spears. Polearms consisted of tridents identical to those found in China and a variety of halberd called a 'reclining moon knife' (see Figure 110). Both weapons are known to have been used by horsemen as well as infantry. The trident was basically a three-pronged pitchfork, while the 'reclining moon knife' had a broad, curved, single-edged blade that somewhat resembled a cleaver or pruning hook. The blade itself was most often 2–2½ ft (0.61–0.76 m) long, while the shaft averaged about 4–4½ ft (1.22–1.37 m). A small curved protrusion was invariably found on the back of the blade, to which a tassel was sometimes attached by means of a metal ring.

Korean bows were composite weapons measuring from 3 ft up to about 4½ ft (0.9–1.3 m), with a twisted hemp string. They were fired using a thumb-draw. Carles records that some he saw at Seoul in 1884 (described as short weapons with 'a double curve like Cupid's') had a light pull but could nevertheless shoot at least 160 yds (146 m). He adds that 'a heavier bow was said to be used in war, while a bow only 18 to 20 inches long occasionally forms part of dress uniform, and is carried in what at first sight looks like holsters for a horse pistol.' Though references to bows occur less frequently as the century progresses, they are specifically recorded to have been used against the French in 1866 and the Americans in 1871, and in 1882 Griffis wrote that Korean soldiers still consisted almost entirely of archers, spearmen, and 'jingall-firers' (matchlockmen). As late as 1891, Cavendish records that provincial soldiers 'are trained to shoot with bows and arrows, and up to 120 yards they are for the most part very good archers. Nearly every prefectural town has its archery ground, on which, in former days, very frequently the Prefect would exercise his men, but now only very seldom does he do so.'

Bows were also used to shoot fire arrows. Referred to by the Koreans as 'dropping fire', these consisted of a ball of oil-soaked cotton attached to the head of an ordinary arrow. This was set alight immediately before the arrow was fired. The destructiveness of such fire arrows particularly impressed the Americans against whom they were employed in 1871.

19th-century Korean swords were of two types: a two-edged, straight-bladed variety of Chinese origin with a lotus-leaf shaped hilt, and a single-edged, curve-bladed Japanese type that was carried principally by officers. However, swords appear to have been relatively uncommon compared to other weapons, and according to Oppert they were hardly ever carried by 'common soldiers'. When they were, they were most often slung across the back in a wooden scabbard usually covered in either shagreen or black-lacquered or cloth-covered leather, with iron, copper, or brass fittings. The guard was of iron or brass. Most officials tended to be accompanied instead by a sword-bearer who carried their often rusty Japanese swords. These might be of considerable antiquity, some being trophies of Korea's wars against the Japanese in the 16th century.

For details of 19th-century Korean armour see the captions to Figures 108–110.

Artillery

The Koreans possessed sufficiently little artillery of any significant size that several foreign visitors felt justified in exaggeratedly stating that they had none at all. In reality, however, they had a considerable number of antiquated, small-calibre pieces of predominantly Chinese origin, which were employed in the defence of their towns and forts. Typical of these were the 80 or so bronze and iron pieces 'mostly of very small calibre' captured by the French at Kangwha in 1866, which 'had no carriages, but were fastened to logs or fixed platforms'; and the 454 2-pdrs and 4-pdrs which constituted the vast majority of the guns in the forts taken by the Americans in 1871. Schley describes how the Koreans fired these with wild abandon, regardless of whether their targets were within range, largely because most 'had a fixed range, the guns themselves being incapable of training, as they were crudely secured to the parapet, with their breech, in a number of instances, against trees to prevent recoil.' These small pieces resembled that depicted below. Griffis describes them as being breechloaders 'in that the powder, fixed in an iron cartridge, was introduced at the breech, while the ball seemed to be put in simultaneously at the muzzle.' Others resembled mediaeval organ-guns, comprising a row of barrels with 'several touch-holes in a row, the cannonier firing them by applying his match rapidly along the line of vents'.

As an indication of the relative proportions of such small-calibre pieces compared to larger guns, besides the 454 small guns mentioned above the Americans captured just eleven 32-pdrs, fourteen 24-pdrs, and two 20-pdrs in 1871. These and the handful of similar large pieces captured by the French in 1866 were apparently all copies of guns taken from the French warships *La Gloire* and *La Victorieuse* wrecked off the coast in 1847, and were cast in accordance with one of the few military reforms effected following China's defeat by the French and British in 1860.

The concept of field artillery seems to have remained unknown, or at least unexplored, until the 1880s, when it was introduced by the army's Japanese and Chinese instructors. It was also these two governments that provided the appropriate guns, though Korea never seems to have possessed more than a dozen such pieces. In April 1883, for instance, Bonar records the existence of a battery of five brass field-pieces thought to have been 9-pdrs; in 1891 Cavendish reports seeing a small number of 9-inch Krupp guns rusting away, their breech-blocks and sights stolen; and in 1895 Fox reports the army's single battery of Krupp field-guns (possibly the same guns as Cavendish saw) being rendered useless through lack of ammunition. By 1902 Korea's field-artillery is described as consisting of 'a few antiquated and worn out specimens bought at various times from Japan', plus eight 75 mm mountain-guns and four 75 mm field-guns purchased from the same country in 1901, which, Vincent tells us, were 'still in their packing cases because no-one knew how to use them.'

Surprisingly, the Koreans also possessed a number of machine guns. Six Gatlings had been imported before the end of 1884, and several foreign visitors observed these being dragged along during parades. H.N. Allen, for instance, recorded 'an artillery company dragging Gatling guns' in 1888, Curzon witnessed 'a small detachment of artillery, dragging after them two small Gatling guns' in either 1888 or 1892, and Bird saw 'two Gatling guns ... dragged by *yamen* runners' in 1895. In fact by 1891 the kingdom was the proud possessor of what Cavendish describes as 'two batteries of machine-guns – that is, it has 14 Gatling guns'. The *Korean Repository* records that in March 1892 Colonel Nienstead imported six more, and it would seem that by 1894 the army's two American-drilled regiments had as many as

Engraving dating to the 1880s of a breech-loading gun about 4 ft long, of an early type still in widespread use in Korea as late as the 1890s. The charge was contained in the separate metal breech, which locked into the rear of the barrel. Such guns usually had more than one breech element, which enabled several charges to be loaded in readiness, thereby facilitating a higher rate of fire than would otherwise have been possible.

Fig 104

Fig 105

Fig 106

Fig 107

30 Gatling guns between them, which they practised with regularly (because, says Gilmore, 'the noise is pleasing to His Majesty') and according to Fox they were 'able to work with some degree of proficiency'. At least some of these were deployed in readiness to defend the approaches to the capital during the Tonghak Rebellion, but it does not appear that they were ever fired in anger. The Gatlings were eventually replaced by Maxim guns, of which the first six were purchased in 1901.

There appears to have been no such thing as an artillery corps, and few men were trained in the use of guns. The few that were seem to have been posted largely in the forts guarding the coastline. The crews of Korea's handful of field-guns consisted of men drawn from the army's foreign-drilled infantry battalions and provided with special, but limited, training, and when not required for artillery duty they went back to serving as infantrymen.

FIGURES

104–107. OFFICIALS OR OFFICERS c.1800–1880s
As in China, the functions of government officials and military officers overlapped to such an extent that, for the greater part of the century, it was virtually impossible to distinguish military mandarins from their civilian counterparts. All were drawn from the privileged *yangban* class, and dressed in a manner befitting their elevated social status. In contrast to the generally white-clad lower classes, *yangban* invariably wore coloured outer garments which were light blue in the case of lower ranking mandarins; either pink, red, dark green, or dark blue amongst those of the middle and upper ranks (the different colours denoting seniority); and violet for those holding the most senior posts. Many of these gowns had bi-coloured sleeves, some having large red or green cuffs, while others had orange upper sleeves and red cuffs (Bonar describes 'the old military dress' of officers, still to be seen in 1883, as 'long robes with red sleeves'). Most of their gowns were of silk, and during the first half of the century they generally boasted floral patterns. However, revised sumptuary laws introduced by the Taewongun in the 1860s required that henceforth *yangban* robes should be unpatterned, and that their excessively baggy sleeves should be narrowed. Contemporary pictures seem to indicate that little attention was paid to the latter injunction.[87]

As in China, roughly 10-inch (250 mm) square decorated panels worn on the breast or back of the gown, or both, denoted a mandarin's specific status. Isabella Bird described in 1895 how these were 'embroidered in unique designs, representing birds and beasts, storks indicating civil, and tigers military, rank, while the number of birds or animals on the lozenges denoted the wearer's exact position' (Gilmore says that 'all officials below a certain grade may wear only one of these figures; all above that grade wear two'; he also describes the bird as a crane rather than a stork). However, such panels were probably worn principally on ceremonial occasions (Underwood says 'when in attendance at the palace'), and they do not appear in many 19th-century illustrations – none of the officers depicted here wear them, for example. Status was also denoted by a wand of office, consisting of a short length of black-lacquered bamboo inscribed with the bearer's rank and with a coloured silk ribbon twisted spirally round it.

The rest of a mandarin's costume comprised a white under-tunic; baggy white or coloured trousers which Belcher describes as hanging 'in a rather loose bag below the knee'; white linen socks; a buff-coloured leather belt or a wide, coloured silk waist-sash; leather shoes or low boots with pointed, turned-up toes; and the usual hat, but with a wider brim than those of the lower classes and with a long string of alternate amber and bamboo (or sometimes cornelian) beads in place of a chin-strap. The wearer's rank was also denoted by different ornaments on the crown, made of (in ascending order) silver, gold, or jade. On ceremonial occasions these took the form of different birds and animals (presumably denoting civil or military rank respectively, just like their gown chest-panels), rank being further denoted by 'a variety of small balls or buckles of amber, jadestone, or silver, used in securing the chinstrap above the ear.'

Officers' and officials' hats were of the finer

kind, constructed of a finely split bamboo 'skeleton' interwoven with black silk, and generally decorated with plumes. Sometimes the underside of the brim was lined with coloured silk. Lowell records that 'among the head-coverings of the officers decoration runs riot. Plumes of the gaudiest colours and brilliant ribbons vie with one another in spreading over the ample brim.' Carles describes the officers he saw in November 1884 as wearing 'hats decked with red plush and peacocks' feathers', and 'round-topped hats decorated with blue plush balls'.

Examples of *yangban* dress recorded by Western visitors include that of officers encountered by Basil Hall RN in 1816, who wore 'over a loose pink frock with wide sleeves ... another which fits closer, and is without sleeves, the corners being tucked up, like the skirts of some [European] military uniforms. Their hat is a broad flat cone made of thick grass, the under part being embossed with different coloured silks, and from a gilt ornament on the peak there hangs a tassel made of peacock's feathers, and another of hair dyed red; some are armed with bows and arrows, others with only a straight sword, having no guard for the hand.'

Officials seen by Isabella Bird participating in a parade in 1895 'wore black, high-crowned hats, with long crimson tassels behind, and heavy, black ostrich plumes falling over the brim in front, mazarine blue silk robes and most voluminous crimson trousers, loosely tied above the ankles with knots of sky blue ribbon, while streamers of ribbon fell from throats and girdles, and the hats were secured by throat lashes of large amber beads ... The sleeves were orange in the upper part and crimson in the lower, and very full.'

The first of the four figures depicted here is based on pictures of the officers encountered by Basil Hall. He wears a dark green gown with pink sleeves and red cuffs, a white under-tunic, white trousers and socks, and a black hat with peacock feather and red horsehair plumes and a blue-lined brim. Figures 105 and 106 are *tai tai-chyang* (colonels) from photographs dating to c.1887 and 1884 respectively (note the curled up brim of the latter's hat – photographs indicate that Korean hat brims often lost their pristine flatness after years of use). Figure 107 is from a Korean drawing of much the same date. He wears a red tunic over a gown of a nondescript dark colour, a white under-tunic, white trousers and socks, and a blue-edged black hat with peacock feathers on each side, a red plume at the back, and a chin-strap of red and white beads. On campaign all Korean officers appear to have been mounted and most wore armour.

108 & 109. MOUNTED OFFICERS OR CAVALRYMEN As has already been intimated, Korea possessed very few cavalry at any point during the 19th century. The attempts by American instructors to train up a unit of 500 'in foreign fashion' during the early 1890s enjoyed sufficiently little success that when Russian instructors took over the training of the army in 1896 they found just 85 cavalrymen in Seoul. In fact the largest number of cavalrymen seen in one place at one time during the entire century seems to have been a body of just 200 observed on Quelpart island – which was, significantly, an important horse-breeding centre – in 1888. Even as late as 1902, when the first Western-style cavalry unit was finally raised it consisted of just 200 men 'with no knowledge of horsemanship, and with no idea of their weapons or their duties.' Indeed, foreigners visiting during the 1890s record the Koreans being such poor

Fig 108 *Fig 109* *Fig 110*

horsemen that when their traditionally equipped cavalry paraded on ceremonial occasions they provided considerable entertainment for the crowd by constantly falling out of their saddles, despite their ponies being led by grooms and the riders being supported by a footman on either side. Gilmore records that even their mounted generals 'look ridiculously helpless, supported by their attendants, and they are said to go into battle held on their horses.'

Traditionally Korea's few cavalrymen had always been armoured, and this remained the case throughout the greater part of the 19th century. As can be seen from Figure 108 (based on pictures in a military manual of 1791, photographs taken in the 1880s, and surviving examples), Korean armour was very similar to that found in neighbouring China, albeit usually more heavily decorated, and had changed little since mediaeval times. Indeed, some of that which remained in use in the 19th century dated back to the 16th century at least, if not earlier (Charles Chaillé-Long – U.S. *chargé d'affaires* in Korea – was told that the armour worn by cavalrymen he saw on parade in Seoul in 1888 was 'the same as worn by the soldiers of the great Kublai Khan', and Curzon recorded the cavalry he saw as being clad in armour 'probably some 300 years old'). Its age was often reflected in its condition; several eyewitnesses record seeing numerous battered helmets and shabby, moth-eaten corselets even on important ceremonial occasions.

The armour of cavalrymen comprised a helmet and a short-sleeved, thickly wadded corselet, worn over a heavy, calf-length brocade coat divided at front, back, and sides. Though some lamellar and mail corselets also remained in use, by the 19th century most were of black leather, dyed hemp or cotton, or imported red or blue woollen cloth, all generally lined with, on average, about seven horizontal rows of fairly large, overlapping rectangular leather or metal plates, averaging about 10 cm or so long and 7.5 cm wide. These were secured in place by pairs of large brass- or copper-headed iron rivets through the surface of the fabric, which was more often than not covered all over with block-printed patterns that included birds' heads, floral designs, trees, arabesques, and sanskrit letters. Openings at the front and sides of the corselet were fastened by means of either laces or bone buttons and leather loops. (For further details of construction see the caption on page 128.)

Helmets could be of various materials, including iron, steel, copper, brass, tin, and black-lacquered leather. They had a conical crown, sometimes strengthened with vertical ribs and almost invariably surmounted by a spike or 'trident' boasting a red horsehair plume. Most were also provided with a sometimes plate-lined leather or padded cloth curtain (or sometimes three curtains, one at the back and one on each side) to protect the back and sides of the head. Where the crown of the helmet was not tall enough to accommodate a Korean's top-knot the hair seems to have been worn loose, Chaillé-Long recording that the hair of the cavalrymen seen on Quelpart in 1888 'straggled in disorder' from beneath their helmets.

Some, perhaps most, officers substituted imitation armours for the real thing, these having their outer surfaces studded with brass rivet heads though they lacked the plate lining. Doubtless such armour was originally intended to be worn only on ceremonial occasions, but once firearms had become widespread it was probably substituted for the real thing on campaign too, being infinitely more comfortable.

Figure 109 – from a photograph of a general taken in the 1880s – wears a corselet of red felt covered with overlapping, alternate red- and gold-coloured metal scales on the outside plus, presumably, the usual plate lining on the inside. His helmet is of moulded, black-lacquered leather with ornate gilt bronze decoration. A general seen on parade in November 1884 wore similar 'armour of crimson and gold', and another recorded in 1895 had 'a gleaming helmet and a splendid blue, crimson, and gold uniform'.

It was only in the mid-1890s that armour began to be abandoned, and uniforms similar to those of the infantry were slowly adopted by the cavalry. In 1894, for instance, Landor records the cavalrymen he saw as still being dressed in armour (albeit in conjunction with a traditional Korean hat rather than a helmet), whereas the following year Isabella Bird watched a parade in which horsemen in 'antique armour' were mixed with cavalry 'dressed and armed in European fashion'. She describes the uniforms of the latter as a loose, black (perhaps very dark blue) cotton coat and baggy trousers, white socks, a brown leather belt with a brass clasp, 'hempen shoes', and a black 'Tyrolese' hat (i.e., the narrower-brimmed variety of the traditional Korean *kat*) with a pink band.

Korean ponies were diminutive creatures standing 10–13 hands, the majority being about 11–11½ hands. Sure-footed though never shod, and strong and hardy despite their size, they were capable of bearing even a heavy man with ease. However, since they were never gelded they were notoriously bad-tempered, being described by James Gale in 1898 as capable of biting through six-inch plate armour at the slightest provocation. Bird records that they bit, kicked, and bucked, and were 'most desperate fighters, squealing and trumpeting on all occasions, attacking every pony they meet on the road.' The one that she rode was just 10 hands tall, but every time another pony came close it 'rushed upon them teeth and hoof, entirely oblivious of bit and rider.' Most were roan or grey, with long manes and shaggy coats, the manes of officers' horses often being dyed red.

The largest of them came from the north of the country and were more like Manchu ponies. The most typical and distinctly Korean variety came instead from Ham-kiung, Quelpart, and the islands off the west coast of Ping-Yang province. Larger Chinese and Japanese ponies had also been introduced by the 1890s at the latest, but they were not considered to be anywhere near as good as the native breed.

Bird records that cavalry ponies were 'showily caparisoned, the heads covered with blue, red, and yellow balls, and surmounted with great crimson silk pompons, the bridles a couple of crimson silk scarves, the saddles a sort of leather-covered padded pack saddle twelve inches above the animal's back, with wide, deep flaps of bright green silver-bossed leather hanging down on either side, the cruppers folded white silk, and the breastplate shields of gold embroidery. The rider ... stands erect in his stirrups with his feet not halfway down his pony's sides, his left hand clutching ... an arch placed for this purpose at the bow of the saddle.' Elsewhere she nevertheless writes that some ponies were so small that their riders' feet 'nearly touched the ground'. Their tall saddles (described by Curzon as 'pyramidal') are similarly mentioned and

Fig 111 Fig 112 Fig 113 Fig 114

criticised by other writers. Bonar observed that 'as they never ride fast, the saddle is more used as a chair on which they sit with folded arms, the animal being always led by the groom.' In conjunction with the temperamental nature of their ponies this explains not only why so many cavalrymen fell off their horses during parades, but also why Korean cavalry were of relative unimportance.

The traditional armament of cavalrymen was sword, composite bow, and spear or polearm, the last including halberds, flails, and tridents – competent use of such two-handed weapons on horseback had to be proved by men taking traditional military examinations even at the very end of the century (the long handle of a flail can be seen beneath the quiver of Figure 108). 19th-century Korean cavalry do not seem to have ever carried firearms. Even those retrained by the Americans at the beginning of the 1890s had 'sabres of German manufacture instead of guns'.

110–114. INFANTRYMEN c.1800–80 Though Korean authorities state that armour was worn only by officers and cavalrymen, Bird records 'footmen in armour bossed with large nails' participating in a parade in 1895, and both Stone's *Glossary* and Russell Robinson's *Oriental Armour* include pictures of a 19th-century infantryman's munition armour held by the Metropolitan Museum of Art in New York, comprising the quilted hemp cloth corselet, belt, and iron-reinforced helmet worn by Figure 110. Stone describes it as 'made of coarse brown cotton cloth padded to a thickness of about an inch and a half', with decorations and inscription stencilled in black. This is doubtless one of the theoretically bulletproof fabric armours introduced by the Taewongun following Admiral Roze's attack in 1866. It was initially intended that these should be made from 12 layers of cloth, but since it was found during testing that bullets only stopped when they had penetrated all the way to the eleventh layer a thirteenth was added as a safety measure. The end product, however, proved unpopular, being so bulky and heavy (the corselet and helmet together are reported to have weighed about 20 lbs/9 kg) that it restricted the wearer's movements, and hot enough in warm weather to induce heatstroke. Such armour was nevertheless worn by many of the Koreans who defended Kangwha Island against the Americans in 1871, a contemporary source recording that they were 'clad in long surtouts resembling heralds' tabards in shape, made of coarse cotton cloth and stuffed with many thicknesses of the same, which were found to be proof against both sword-cuts and musket-balls, although not impervious to rifle-shots.' An American officer records that the corselets of some men caught fire during the artillery barrage that preceded the American assault.

Needless to say, not all the Koreans encountered in 1871 were armoured, and many of those who were are reported to have discarded their uncomfortable corselets during the fighting. Figures 111 and 112, from pictures of prisoners taken on Kangwha, wear ordinary white civilian dress, as do the casualties in the photograph reproduced on p.124. The Koreans faced by Roze's expedition five years earlier were probably similarly attired. Only the tiger-hunters who formed a significant part of their strength may have been in any way distinctive, since they wore a particular variety of hat (a coarse black felt one with a conical crown, the usual broad brim and red tassels) and a dark blue coat, both of which were provided by the government annually. However, even this much uniform may only have been worn on parade. Certainly a photograph taken of tiger-hunters in the 1880s shows them wearing the usual white peasant dress, and Carles describes their costume as 'a short wadded jacket ... gathered in tight round the loins; the sleeves are bound round the arms over wadded cuffs which reach from the wrist to the elbow; in the same way the trousers are bound round the calf of the leg; a light straw sandal is worn over a long piece of cotton cloth strapped neatly over the foot and ankle. The supplementary portions of the dress are a cord, which serves as a slow match, wound round the left arm; a huge string bag slung over the back; a crane's bill or an antelope's horn slit in two to hold the bullets, which are kept in place by a ring; a tortoise-shaped case of oil-paper or leather for the powder; a flint bag; and lastly, a pipe and tobacco pouch.'

Most tiger-hunters had matchlocks or (by the 1890s) flintlocks, but some were still armed with bows at the time of the French attack, when Griffis records that every one of them 'was a dead shot either with bow or matchlock'. Writing of tiger-hunters that he saw in 1906, serving in one of the 'Righteous Armies', McKenzie says that 'their only weapon is an old-fashioned percussion gun, with long barrel and a brass trigger seven to eight inches in length. Many of them fire not from the shoulder, but hold their guns low. They never miss. They can only fire one charge in an attack, owing to the time required to load. They are trained to stalk the tiger, to come quite close to it, and then to kill it at one shot. No tiger-hunter in the field to-day has ever failed to hit his prey. The man who fails once dies; the tiger attends to that.'

Figures 113 and 114, dating to c.1800 and 1877 respectively, wear the government-issue 'uniform' – comprising no more than a round-crowned, broad-brimmed *kat* and a knee-length sleeveless jacket, worn over their own everyday clothes – issued to most Korean soldiers since at least the beginning of the 18th century. Both men's hats are provided with red horsehair plumes, suspended from a cord attached to a swivel button on the crown.

115–121. INFANTRYMEN 1880s–1890s Though infantrymen dressed like Figures 113 and 114 could still be found even at the end of the 1880s, the selection depicted here is more typical of the century's last two decades and includes several who have undergone foreign training. Figure 115, for instance, wears one of the Chinese-style uniforms introduced by Yüan Shih-k'ai in 1882. The characters painted on the circular panel on his chest (repeated on an identical panel on his back) read 'Left Body Guard', indicating him to be from the Left battalion of the Chinese-drilled *Changoyong* Guards. Note that he has rolled the long skirt of his jacket up round his hips.

Figures 116–118, from undated photographs and a drawing of c.1890, wear more typical Korean military dress of 1880–90, and except for the absence of chest panels (which, as has already been observed, rarely feature in contemporary pictures) accord well with Lowell's description of soldiers of this period, written in 1885: 'The costume of the soldiers is a dark blue for the greater part; in places it is crimson, with which ribbons effectively play their part. Over the breast is embroidered the character for valour ... They are a fine and quiet-looking lot, and absolutely need to be labelled dangerous to produce the proper military effect. The cut of the tunic is conventional, not to say odd. It is assumed that the waist lies on a line with the armpits ... Instead of meeting at an acute angle, the two folds of the tunic are cut around the neck so as to join in the form of an oval. Fitted on to the silk, on the inner side, is a white band of cotton. It represents the European collar'. Note the metal badge on the front of Figure 116's hat, which is unclear in the original photograph but may be the character for 'valour' or 'courage', as shown in the badge in detail 116b, from another source. (Korea at this time still used Chinese characters – *Hanja* – rather than the *Hangul* script used today, which though it hade been around for centuries was not adopted for official use until the mid-1890s). Note that even the most 'modern'-looking of these three soldiers (Figure 118) still wears his belt in its traditional place under the armpits rather than round the waist, and has padded socks and slippers rather than boots. The dimensions of his hat brim, however, have diminished considerably.

Soldiers dressed like Figures 116 and 118 continue to feature prominently in photographs taken during the first half of the 1890s. The more traditional dress of Figure 117, however, seems to disappear at about the end of the 1880s. Note his tatterdemalion appearance, which is confirmed by the observations of various foreign visitors – Bonar, for instance, says that Korean soldiers were 'mostly shabby-looking' and Alexis Krausse (1900) that they were generally 'badly clothed', while Bird

Fig 115

Fig 116

Fig 117

Fig 118

describes their uniforms as 'coarse and ragged'.

Figures 118, 119 (from a print depicting soldiers marching against the Tonghaks in 1894) and 120 (from photographs of a parade taken in May 1894) are all soldiers who have undergone foreign training under the auspices of General Dye, their partial Westernisation being apparent from the cut of their buttoned jackets, Figure 119's bugle, and Figure 120's ammunition pouches. However, note Figure 119's lack of a backpack, which tallies with Mercer's observation in June 1897 that Korean infantry 'have no marching order equipment, and if required to proceed to a distance, each man improvises the necessary gear, and carries his kit as seems most comfortable to himself' (as, for instance, in Figure 116). However, photographs of the 1890s occasionally show haversacks worn over one or other shoulder.

A British cigarette card published c.1895 depicts a soldier very much like Figure 120. His dress consists of a dark brown hat, a blue jacket with a white collar and a yellow panel round the neck which extends down the front behind the white metal buttons, plus blue trousers and short brown boots. A steel bayonet scabbard is suspended by a frog from his brown waistbelt. Mercer noted that most soldiers carried 'the old triangular bayonet', but a few had short sword-bayonets instead.

Some Japanese prints depicting the fighting between Japanese and Korean troops at Seoul in 1894 indicate that the hat was sometimes white or grey, but presumably only in the summertime (the fighting took place in July); even so, this would have been contradictory to traditional practice, since white hats were normally only worn when in mourning, so the depiction of white hats may simply be a mistake. These prints also confirm that swords were often still carried by Korean troops even at this late date, as one might have expected, worn across the back in a brown or black scabbard that was held in place by means of a sash, much as depicted in Figure 114.

Note the considerably smaller and flat-topped *kats* of Figures 118–121, which look very much like a fez with a brim. Judging by pictorial sources these seems to have displaced the older variety amongst the military during the second half of the 1890s.

122 & 123. WESTERNISED INFANTRYMEN 1895–97 Figure 122 depicts a soldier of the elite corps subjected to Russian training during the mid-1890s. This unit wore a Western-style black or very dark blue uniform comprising helmet, jacket, trousers, and black shoes. The trousers had red piping down the seam, the jacket had shoulder straps, a high collar and five white metal buttons down the front, and the helmet had leather peaks fore and aft plus a 'spike' and a wreathed, five-petalled Rose of Sharon badge. Korean written sources say that officers' trousers had a red stripe, while their jackets had four pockets, a five-pointed silver star badge on each side of the collar, plus one, two, or three narrow yellow bands (denoting company officers, field officers, and general officers respectively) round their jacket cuffs with, beneath them, one to three silver buttons bearing a yin-yang motif, to denote their specific rank, i.e. one button for a second lieutenant, two for a lieutenant, and three for a captain if a company officer; one for a major, two for a lieutenant-colonel, and three for a full colonel if a field officer; and so on. However, photographs show the officers wearing jackets with five rows of braid across the chest, plus a simple red cuff and a red band round the upper left arm, without any further rank insignia.

The jackets of other ranks in such photographs are slightly shorter than those of officers and lack the braid and cuffs, while their helmet badges are smaller. Armament consisted of a Berdan rifle. Belt and ammunition pouch (behind the left hip) were black leather. Isabella Bird, who saw such troops on parade in 1897, records that their smartness was compromised by their hair 'which had been cropped at the time of the abolition of the topknot, [but] had grown again, and hung in heavy shocks behind the ears'. Note that this man also wears traditional Korean padded socks, which are hanging down round his ankles.

It is apparent that this uniform was subsequently

Fig 119

Fig 120

Fig 121

Fig 122

Fig 123

Fig 124

Fig 125

Fig 126

adopted by at least some elements of the other troops trained by the Russians, since a visiting Royal Navy officer, T.T. Jeans, saw and sketched several soldiers like Figure 123 both guarding the king's palace and patrolling the streets of Seoul at about the beginning of 1898. Note the bayonet scabbard thrust through his belt, and the way in which this particular man has tied up his trousers in traditional Korean fashion. Front views show that, unlike Figure 122, his jacket is double-breasted.

124–127. INFANTRYMEN c.1898–1907 Unsurprisingly, Japanese ascendancy in Korea after 1898 was accompanied by the introduction of uniforms virtually identical to those worn by Japanese soldiers. These theoretically consisted of a single-breasted jacket, trousers, shoes, and a kepi, for which a soft peaked cap was substituted from 1906. The winter uniform was dark blue and the summer uniform white, eventually replaced by khaki in the very year of the army's disbandment, 1907. However, a variant of the helmet of Figure 122 – but now looking more like a cross between a bowler hat and a traditional Korean *kat* with cut-down brim – continued to be sometimes worn in place of the kepi until at least 1902 (Figure 124); and Vincent records at much the same date that, though canvas gaiters and Western-style shoes were worn in barracks, 'on the march both officers and men use the native padded stocking and straw sandals'.

Collars and shoulder straps in arm-of-service colours were also introduced. These, too, probably followed the Japanese system, which means that prior to 1905 they would have been yellow for infantry, red for Guards, green for cavalry, white for artillery, and dark red for engineers, probably changing thereafter to red for infantry, green for cavalry, yellow for artillery, and white for engineers. The cap-badge was a gilt-edged, red enamel Rose of Sharon (silver-edged gold for officers, with a gold wreath), the same device being embroidered in the same colours on the crown of officers' kepis, which were ornamented with much additional gold lace identical to that found on Japanese officers' headwear. As in the Japanese army, NCOs' ranks were denoted by one to three broad or narrow horizontal red stripes round the cuffs, the number and width of the stripes denoting the individual's specific status.

The four infantrymen depicted come from photographs taken at various times between about 1899 and 1905, Figure 124 (from a 1902 issue of *East of Asia Magazine*) being the earliest, and Figure 125 the latest. Figures 126 and 127 are from Vincent's article 'Notes on the Korean Army', published in 1904–5 but seemingly from material compiled two or three years earlier, probably c.1901/2. They are of particular interest in giving us some idea of how Korean soldiers of this period dressed in the depths of winter. Vincent records that they were issued with sheepskin collared coats (Figure 126), and for additional warmth generally wore white civilian clothes beneath their ill-fitting uniforms, giving them a bulged-out appearance. Sentries standing out in the cold in potentially sub-zero temperatures were provided with what he calls 'large blue padded cotton cloaks' (Figure 127's appears to be worn over a greatcoat, the hood of which can be seen on his shoulders).

128. OFFICER c.1898–1907 Officers' service dress comprised a black-braided, blue-black patrol jacket (possibly with coloured collar and cuffs), blue-black trousers with one or two red seam stripes of varying widths depending on rank, and knee-length black boots. The patrol jacket was replaced by a single-breasted and then a double-breasted jacket c.1900, which had red piping, a gold-embroidered red collar, pointed red cuffs, and one broad and up to nine narrow gold chevrons and an outline Rose of Sharon above the cuffs to denote the wearer's rank. Other rank insignia included gold epaulettes (fringed for general officers and, after 1899, colonels) with badges comprising a red and blue yin-yang device (mounted on a silver cartouche embossed with a silver wreath for officers above the rank of captain) with one or two silver arrows on either side, points upwards. Later changes included the substitution of stars for the arrows. The figure depicted represents a general officer of c.1900 in full dress, reconstructed from contemporary photographs and a surviving uniform. The feather plume

Fig 127

Fig 128

Fig 129

Fig 130

was white. Infantry officers of less elevated status resembled Figure 129, complete with red waist sash.

129. CAVALRYMAN 1902–7 This is a trooper of Korea's first modern cavalry unit, raised in 1902. These wore double-breasted scarlet tunics with two rows of seven gilt buttons, green piping, green collar and cuffs, red waistband, dark blue trousers with a green stripe, black boots, and a dark blue kepi with the usual Rose of Sharon badge plus a green arm of service band and a white plume. Though armed with sabres and a mixture of Colt and Winchester carbines, this was fundamentally a ceremonial guard unit.

130 & 131. TONGHAK REBELS Contemporary Korean prints show the Tonghaks to have worn the usual dress of the country's lower classes, albeit generally with a white scarf tied round the head in place of the more usual black hat. Many also had the character *Tong* ('Eastern') painted in dark red or black on the left breast of their jacket for identification. Figure 130's jacket is depicted a light blue-grey colour in the original source. Tonghak documents tell us that provisions were 'collected' from the wealthy, but that each man provided his own weapons. At first they had only cudgels, old swords, bamboo spears, polearms, and a handful of matchlocks, but these were quickly augmented by government rifles either taken in battle or looted from captured arsenals. Two Western field-guns also fell into their hands at the Battle of Changsong in May 1894, though it is unclear if, and probably unlikely that, these were ever used in action since their captors would not have known how to use them.

In battle, the Tonghaks depended principally on numbers and surprise for victory, but they were not lacking in courage and their spearmen appear to have successfully charged down firearm-equipped government troops on several occasions. However, Chon Pong-jun exhorted his followers not to take lives unless absolutely necessary ('Although you are obliged to fight, try to avoid injury to life'), which must have cramped their fighting style. For protection they carried slips of paper bearing written charms that they believed rendered them immune to firearms. Needless to say, the efficacy of such charms was found seriously wanting when the Tonghaks came face to face with Japanese troops in January 1895, and an anonymous contemporary records that as the Japanese bullets began to take deadly effect 'the rebels ... cried out to the leader in chief to use his magic. He replied that though he had now repeated those letters for ten years he knew of no better trick under such circumstances than to run.'

Tonghak organisation was very loose. The brethren of each province were under the orders of a provincial leader called a *toju*, under whom were a number of district leaders called *tojopchu*, and under them local leaders called *chopchu*, each in charge of a *p'o* or local group. All of these various grades of chief were genuine Tonghak brethren, but many of the men they led were simply what Chon Pongjun himself called 'patriotic and righteous persons'. The leaders were mounted on horses seized wherever they could be found, and most were accompanied by 'floating banners and rattling of drums and cymbals'.

132. COOLIE 1894 As was customary in the Far East, a Korean army on the march was accompanied by a sizeable baggage train of coolies, bullocks,[88] and ponies, but few carts (which were two-wheeled and drawn by bullocks). Using an A-shaped wooden frame called a *chigi*, Korean coolies could carry remarkably heavy loads of reputedly, but improbably, up to 400 lbs (180 kg), described by Bonar in 1883 as 'piled up five or six feet over their heads'. Isabella Bird records that they considered a load of 100 lbs (45 kg) to be 'a moderate one', and Vincent says that the average coolie would carry this much all day provided he got plenty to eat, being prepared to 'put up cheerfully with any other hardship except hunger'. Ponies, by contrast, could carry about 150–200 lbs (70–90 kg) for 30–35 miles (48–56 km) a day, 'week after week, on sorry food'. Bird tells us that baggage-ponies were all stallions, 10–12 hands tall, 'well formed, and singularly strong', but sufficiently ornery (see the caption to Figures 108 and 109) that each of them had to have its own *mapu* (handler). Bullocks could carry 300 lbs (135 kg) easily, for 20 miles (32 km) a day.

The Japanese made use of Korean coolies during the early stages of the Sino-Japanese War, to whom Bird says they paid 'enormous wages'. However, since the local population generally ran away at the approach of the Japanese it was frequently difficult for the latter to muster sufficient porters to meet its needs, and those who were coerced into serving usually fled at the first opportunity – often with the loads they were carrying or the ponies they were leading – for fear of being decapitated by their own countrymen as collaborators.

Detail 132a depicts one of the shapeless 'umbrella' wet-weather covers often worn over the *kat* by civilians and soldiers alike.

133 & 134. POLICEMEN The *keso* or police, often described as 'gendarmes' by Westerners, constituted a second armed force at the government's disposal. There are variously reported to have been between 1,200 and more than 2,000 in Seoul during the 1880s and 1890s, serving in a wide variety of capacities ranging from patrolmen to bodyguards for magistrates and government officials. Provincial governors and magistrates had their own units of such gendarmes, which constituted the so-called provincial 'armies' referred to in the section on organisation. In the closing years of the century Seoul's gendarmes are frequently recorded coming to blows with soldiers based in the capital, whose arrogance they strongly resented.

The traditional attire of policemen differed little from that worn by soldiers, and followed the same slow course of evolution, and pictures dating to the period up to the 1880s show that most policemen were dressed like Figure 117. The jacket was dark blue, though some pictures show it with different-coloured sleeves, while the hat, called a *sansoutol tenrip*, was fundamentally the same shape as a soldier's but was red rather than black and crowned with a white metal ball rather than a brass finial. Oppert, however, describes a policeman he saw in 1866 as wearing a once red jacket that had faded to yellow, and 'a Korean black felt soldier's hat, broad-brimmed, and with a pointed top, which was ornamented with a fox-tail and a red cock's feather'. Several sources mention policemen carrying a bow and a quiver of arrows, for which Figure 133 – who comes from a picture of a 'City Gendarme' reproduced in the *Illustrated London News* of 10 May 1890 – substitutes a rifle.

Under Japanese influence the Seoul police were reconstituted along Western lines in 1895, and were provided with new dark blue uniforms such as that depicted in Figure 134, from Isabella Bird's *Korea and Her Neighbors*. But note that traditional footwear still prevailed. A kepi was subsequently substituted for the helmet. They were armed with a sword in a nickel-plated scabbard.

135. FLAGS As in China, Korean armies were provided with a superabundance of flags in the belief that it would deceive an enemy into believing their strength to be greater than it actually was. Curzon exaggeratedly claims that some units had almost as many flags as men, while Oppert more realistically states that one flag was carried per section of ten or a dozen men. Certainly the capture of five forts by the Americans in 1871 netted 50–60 flags, and a parade of just 300 men of the King's bodyguard in April 1883 included as many as 22. Even in 1895 infantry units seen on parade in Seoul were still accompanied by 'innumerable standards', so modernisation of the army clearly had little effect on this particular tradition.

Military flags came in sundry colours and sizes, could be rectangular, square, or triangular, and were

Fig 131

Fig 132

132a

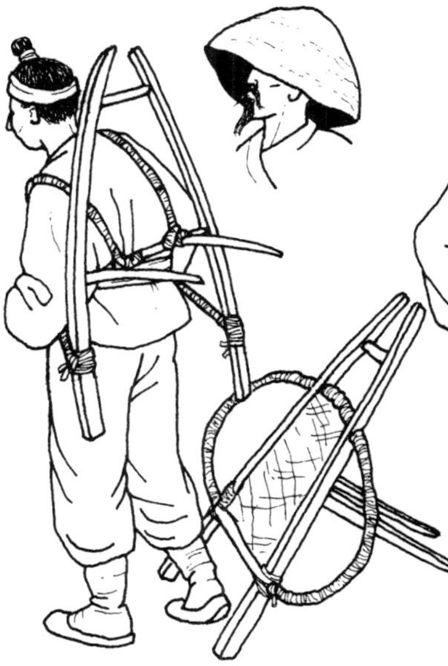

Fig 133

Fig 134

usually decorated with a pictorial motif and/or an inscription. Oppert describes those he saw as being dark blue and square shaped, 'with black or white characters, stating the name and number of the troop'. However, those accompanying the King's guardsmen in 1883 were triangular, with pink, white, and black stripes and green edging. Several visitors record seeing blue and yellow flags, while Curzon saw 'banners of yellow, red, and green, with a tuft of pheasant-feathers at the top'. Bird similarly observes that the staffs of Korean military flags were customarily 'crested with a tuft of pheasant's feathers', while pictures show some soldiers carrying feather-crested staffs that have no flag at all.

Amongst the flags captured by the Americans in 1871 was the huge yellow one depicted in 135a. Judging from photos, this was about 15 ft (4.5 m) long, and was made of 12 horizontal strips of cotton. This sort of flag accompanied each army commander; the black inscription says *shui*, which roughly translates as 'leader'. For other flags captured on this occasion see the pictures on p.114.

There was no Korean national flag until 1882–83, when that depicted in 135b was adopted and subsequently used until 1910. This comprised a *t'aeguk* (Chinese *tai chi*) device, representing the interaction between good and evil, on a white field, with the central yin-yang device blue and red rather than the more usual black and red, apparently as a mark of respect towards China, and the *kwae* devices in the corners in blue rather than the black used today. 135c, one of six such flags which a contemporary print shows at the head of a column of troops marching against the Tonghaks, has only the yin-yang device, while 135d, brought back from Korea by victorious Japanese troops in 1894/5 (and therefore just possibly a Chinese rather than a Korean flag) has additional decoration at the corners.

135e appears to be a company flag, from a print dating to the 1870s or 1880s. About a metre square, it is red with a white border and black device. Note the small red-edged white pennon at the top of the staff.

135f is a typical Tonghak flag. Though most of these appear to have been yellow, a declaration of May 1894 describes each Tonghak 'battalion' as having 'a flag of five colours, on which is written in large characters "The great manifestation of righteousness for the protection of the State and the pacification of the people".' The one depicted here is plain white with a dark red inscription.

NOTES

67 Some estimates are considerably higher. However, all figures quoted for Korea's population in the 19th century are unreliable guesses. It seems to have stood at about 7.5 million at the beginning of the century but had declined to 6.7 million by 1837. Though one Korean source claims that it stood at 28 million in the 1880s – a figure twice as large as most Western estimates of the same date – official censuses recorded just 6.8 million in about 1882 and 14.5 million in 1910. As much as 10% (one source says 20%) consisted of the hereditary official class or nobility, the *yangban*.

68 Two of the gunboats were named *Le Brethon* and *Tardif*, after

Fig 135

135a *135b* *135c* *135d* *135e* *135f*

Lieutenant de vaisseau Le Brethon de Caligny and *Capitaine* Tardif de Moidrey, the French officers who had commanded, respectively, the Ever-Triumphant Army and the Sikkaway Force in China during the mid-1860s. (For these units see volume 2 of this series, *China*, pp.93–4.) The other vessels were the frigate *La Guerrière*, the corvettes *Primauguet* and *Laplace*, and the gunboats *Kien-chan* and *Déroulède*.

69 This was the same vessel as had smuggled the American adventurer Henry Andrea Burgevine, sometime commander of the Ever-Victorious Army, back into China from Formosa in 1865 (see volume 2 of this series, *China*, p.149; and see also note 33 on p.105 above).

70 President of the Chinese Republic in 1912–16 before becoming, briefly, the self-proclaimed – and last – Emperor of China in 1916.

71 China had withdrawn the rest of its troops in June, for service in its war against the French. Li Hung-chang even gave fleeting consideration to the possibility of sending a Korean contingent to fight in Vietnam, and funds intended to finance Korea's internal reforms were surreptitiously diverted to 'war-like preparations' by pro-Chinese Min officials. The French, meanwhile, had already suggested to Japan that its military assistance in the conflict with China would be most welcome – which conjures up an almost surreal 'what if?' scenario in which Sino-Korean and Franco-Japanese armies battle for possession of Tonkin. For the Sino-French conflict, see volume 4 of this series, *Burma and Indo-China*, pp.168–70.

72 It has been suggested that the Taewongun – who, released from China in 1885, had been reinstated by the Japanese as prime minister following their seizure of power in July 1894 – secretly encouraged the Tonghaks to resume their military activities. This was doubtless one of the main reasons why the Japanese (who had soon found that his only interests were 'clinging to power and removing his opponents') forcibly retired him in October.

73 Despite being rarely armed with anything better than spears, swords, and rusty, antiquated firearms, the Righteous Armies maintained the unequal struggle against the Japanese until as late as 1911 within Korea itself, and until 1915 along the border with Manchuria.

74 The coup was said to have been hatched between the Japanese Minister, Miura Goro, and that arch-intriguer the Taewongun. This was his final piece of skulduggery before his death in 1898.

75 Needless to say, Britain was unhappy at the progress of Russian influence in Korea, about which she had been becoming steadily more concerned since the 1870s, fearing that it posed a threat to the growth of British trade in eastern Asia. Eventually, in April 1885, following unsubstantiated (and, as it turned out, inaccurate) rumours of Russian attempts to establish one or more colonies on the Korean coast, and the signing of a Russo-Korean treaty in July 1884 (never subsequently ratified), Britain had occupied the Korean island of Komundo ('Port Hamilton') as an advanced naval base intended to frustrate Russian designs. Korean protests at this seizure of its sovereign territory were met with an offer to pay rent for the island. The British only finally withdrew in February 1887 on receiving Russia's less than truthful promise that it had no intention of occupying any part of Korea. Continuing British distrust of Russia's intentions would eventually lead to the signing of an Anglo-Japanese treaty of alliance in 1902.

76 In theory, but not in practice, each province also had its own navy, but by the 1860s Korea's naval potential had dwindled to 'a few rotten junks at anchor near the capital'. Despite the existence of several admirals (uncharitably described by Henry Norman as knowing 'no more about a ship than a Hindu knows about skates'), in 1891 Korea's fleets were still non-existent save for two 800-ton steamers used for trade. By 1894 a naval academy established on Kangwha island the previous year by a retired British naval officer had trained some 200–300 men, but the king's two merchant steamers remained the only ships available.

77 The practice of buying admission into the army continued until at least the mid-1890s, when Russian instructors found that 'every soldier [had] to pay as much as $12 on joining, whereas NCOs have to pay more, as their duties are extremely light'. NCOs consequently tended to be older men, 'having saved more than younger ones'.

78 Hundreds of Koreans are said to have been killed by tigers every year during the 19th century, so that the government actively encouraged tiger-hunting. However, the generic term 'tiger-hunters' actually denoted all Koreans who earned a living by hunting. A.E.J. Cavendish observed in 1894 that 'in every province there are "hunters", men who ... receive a small allowance of money, powder, and bullets from [the king]; they are supposed to repay him by the skins and bodies of the game they slay ... They are liable to be called out for war, and in battle are selected to bear the brunt of the fighting; but preference is shown for those in the two Northern provinces, as being more inured to hardships and fatigue, and of better physique than those of the more Southern provinces, where the conditions of life are less rigorous.' The 800 who served against the French in 1866 were drawn from Ping-Yang province.

79 For the organisation of a *ying* see volume 2 of this series, *China*, p.19.

80 More may have been subsequently sent to study in Japan, since one account states that 20 cadets trained in Tokyo participated in the *Kapsin* coup of December 1884; other sources, however, mention just 12.

81 Cadets returning from Japan in autumn 1884 after being trained at Toyama had been similarly refused military posts by the conservative faction on the grounds that they had not taken the required traditional examinations.

82 Dye's involvement with Kojong's bodyguard continued until 1897 (he finally returned home in 1899). He seems to have been assisted by at least one other American. This was William H. Young, who, in a report of his death in 1899 (he was mortally wounded while serving as a civilian scout in the Philippines), is described as having previously been 'Captain of the King's bodyguard' in Korea.

83 Reflecting earlier Spanish influence in the region, Mexican coinage was in wide circulation throughout the Pacific and was utilised as a general currency of exchange.

84 Oppert was a German naturalised as an American citizen. He visited the west coast of Korea in March and August 1866 and spring 1868, his intention on the last occasion being to dig up the 'coffin of gold' containing the remains of the Taewongun's father, Prince Namyongun, believing that 'apart from its value as bullion, the possession of this treasure would insure the consent of the Koreans ... to any demands that might be made upon them' – specifically, the opening up of Korea to foreign trade. To this end he and another American named Jenkins assembled a motley gang of cut-throats consisting of a Frenchman, 10–12 other Europeans, 25 Filipinos, about a hundred Chinese, and an unknown number of Korean Christians. Claiming that they were Russian soldiers, the buccaneering expedition was able to land and capture the town of Toksan, and even reached Prince Namyongun's tomb, but the approach of the local magistrate with a detachment of soldiers or constabulary interrupted their digging and they beat a hasty retreat. They subsequently attempted to force their way into the walled town of Yongjong, but were beaten back from the walls by gunfire, two Filipinos being killed.

85 Many Koreans were already engaged at the age of 9–10, and most got married when they were 14–18.

86 He adds that 'one man alone, in the immediate neighbourhood of the chief official, had a peculiarly-shaped kind of firearm ... [which] consisted of three barrels, soldered together, and joined to a short round butt-end, and had the appearance of a very old-fashioned revolver. The barrels, about one foot and a half long, threw a good-sized jingall-ball, and as the soldier held a burning match in his hand, the weapon had probably been loaded. It must have been of a very venerable age, and to judge from the thick rusty crust which covered it ... it [must have] been taken for the occasion out of some old lumber-room'. John Boots (1931) suggests that such multi-barrelled handguns – which had appeared in Korea by the 16th century – were used for unspecified signalling purposes. However, since we know that Europeans used almost identical weapons in combat during the 15th century there is no especially good reason to suppose that the Koreans didn't too. Belcher's assumption that the one he saw was a relic of earlier times is nevertheless probably correct, since by the 19th century firearms of this type were decidedly primitive.

87 Pak Chehyong (died c.1884) records other *yangban* dress reforms introduced by the Taewongun as follows: 'Hats were reduced in size and jacket sleeves were narrowed. White leather shoes and brocade shoes were forbidden, leaving only black leather shoes for everyone's use. Court officials in the past had worn bead strings on their hats to be tied on the left cheek; the hat strings were now cut in length and were to be tied under the chin. Literati and commoners were allowed to use hat strings decorated with lacquered bamboo pieces or tree nuts, and the use of silk material was banned. The official attire in the past included flat-soled wooden shoes with painted toes, but they were replaced by pointed shoes resembling soldiers' footwear.'

88 Infantrymen sometimes rode the bullocks when on the march, a practice recorded by Carles in 1884.

BIBLIOGRAPHY

Abel, Laszlo. 'Japanese Military Modernization and the French Connection' *Japan Martial Arts Society Newsletter* 3, June 1985.

Addis, C.S. 'Corea under the Russians' *United Service Magazine* New Series XV, 1897.

Akamatsu, Paul. *Meiji 1868: Revolution and Counter-Revolution in Japan*, 1972.

Alcock, Rutherford. *The Capital of the Tycoon* (2 vols), 1863.

Allen, H.N. *Korean Tales*, 1889.

Anderson, L.J. *Japanese Armour*, 1968.

Asada, Sadao. *Japan and the World 1853–1952*, 1989.

Asakawa, K. 'Some Aspects of Japanese Feudal Institutions' *Transactions of the Asiatic Society of Japan* XLVI, 1918.

Aston, W.G. 'Russian Descents in Saghalien and Itorup in the Years 1806 & 1807' *Transactions of the Asiatic Society of Japan* I, 1874.

— 'The "Hi No Maru", or National Flag of Japan' *Transactions of the Asiatic Society of Japan* XXII, 1894.

Barrow, E.G. 'Military Japan' *United Service Magazine* New Series VII, 1893.

Bax, B.W. *The Eastern Seas (The Cruise of the Dwarf)*, 1875.

Batchelor, John. 'Notes on the Ainu' *Transactions of the Asiatic Society of Japan* X, 1882.

— *The Ainu of Japan*, 1892.

— *The Ainu and their Folk-Lore*, 1901.

— *Ainu Life and Lore*, 1971.

Baxter, E.H. *National Flags*, 1934.

Bekmann, George M. *The Modernization of China and Japan*, 1962.

Belcher, Edward. *Narrative of the Voyage of HMS Samarang during the Years 1843–46* vol.II, 1848.

Bennett, Terry. *Korea: Caught in Time*, 1989.

Bickmore, Albert S. 'The Ainos, or Hairy Men of Yesso' *American Journal of Science and Arts* 2nd Series XLV, 1868.

— 'The Ainos, or Hairy Men, of Saghalien and the Kurile Islands' *American Journal of Science and Arts* 2nd Series XLV, 1868.

Bird, Isabella L. *Unbeaten Tracks in Japan* (2 vols), 1880.

— *Korea and Her Neighbours*, 1897.

Bird, W.D. *Lectures on the Strategy of the Russo-Japanese War*, 1909.

Bishop, Donald M. 'Shared Failure: American Military Advisors in Korea, 1888–1896' *Transactions of the Royal Asiatic Society Korea Branch* LVIII, 1983.

Black, John R. *Young Japan* (2 vols), 1883.

Bonar, H.A.C. 'Notes on the Capital of Korea' *Transactions of the Asiatic Society of Japan* XI, 1883.

Boots, John L. 'Korean Weapons and Armor' *Transactions of the Korea Branch of the Royal Asiatic Society* XXIII, 1934.

Borton, Hugh. 'Peasant Uprisings in Japan of the Tokugawa Period' *Transactions of the Asiatic Society of Japan* XVI, 1938.

— *Japan's Modern Century: From Perry to 1970*, 1970.

Bottomley, Ian, and Hopson, Anthony. *Arms and Armour of the Samurai*, 1990.

Boxer, C.R. 'Notes on Early European Military Influences in Japan, 1543–1853' *Transactions of the Asiatic Society of Japan* VIII, 1931.

Brinkley, F. *A History of the Japanese People*, 1914.

Brown, Frederick. *From Tientsin to Peking with the Allied Forces*, 1902.

Brown, R. *Peoples of the World* vol.II, 1900.

Brunker, H.M.E. *Story of the Russo-Japanese War, 1904–05* (2 vols), 1909–11.

Buck, James H. 'The Satsuma Rebellion of 1877: From Kagoshima through the Siege of Kumamoto Castle' *Monumenta Nipponica* XXVIII, 1973.

Cable, E.M. 'United States-Korean Relations 1866–1871' *Transactions of the Korea Branch of the Royal Asiatic Society* XXVIII, 1938.

Carey, Jacqui. *Samurai Undressed*, 1995.

Carles, W.R. *Life in Corea*, 1888.

Carpenter, Frank G. 'Korea and its Army' in Martha Luther Lane (ed.) *Towards the Rising Sun: Sketches of Life in Eastern Lands*, 1902.

Cavendish, A.E.J. *Korea and the Sacred White Mountain*, 1894.

— 'Two Months in Korea' *Scottish Geographical Magazine* X, 1894.

Cenni, Quinto. *Gli Eserciti di Asia, Africa, America, Oceania*, 1986.

Chaillé-Long, Charles. 'La Corée ou Tchösen' *Annales du Musée Guimet* XXVI, 1894.

— *My Life in Four Continents* vol.II, 1912.

Chamberlain, Basil Hall. *Things Japanese*, 1890.

Chevalier, Henri. 'Les Coiffures Coréennes' *Internationales Archiv für Ethnographie* XII, 1899.

Choe, Ching Young. *The Rule of the Taewon'gun, 1864–1873*, 1972.

Chung, To-Woong. 'The Opening of Korea and her Military Reform in the Late Nineteenth Century' *Revue Internationale d'Histoire Militaire* 70, 1988.

Clement, Ernest W. 'The Saga and Satsuma Rebellions' *Transactions of the Asiatic Society of Japan* L, 1922.

Clyde, Paul H., and Beers, Burton F. *The Far East: A History of Western Impacts and Eastern Responses, 1830–1975*, 1975.

Collache, Eugène. 'Une Aventure au Japon' *Le Tour du Monde* LXXVII, 1874.

Conder, Josiah. 'The History of Japanese Costume: II Armour' *Transactions of the Asiatic Society of Japan* IX, 1881.

Conlan, Thomas D. *Weapons and Fighting Techniques of the Samurai Warrior 1200–1877 AD*, 2008.

Conroy, Hilary. *The Japanese Seizure of Korea: 1868–1910*, 1960.

'Corea' *The Edinburgh Review* CXXXVI, 1872.

Corput, Jeannette C. van der, and Wilson, Robert A. (ed. and trans.). *Henry Heusken: Japan Journal 1855–1861*, 1964

Cortazzi, Hugh (ed.). *Mitford's Japan*, 1985.

Cox, H.V. 'The Foreign Contingents in China' *Journal of the United Service Institution of India* XXXIII, 1902.

Craig, Albert M. *Choshu in the Meiji Restoration*, 1961.

Curey, M.C. (trans. by A.H.C. Phillpotts). 'Japanese Field and Mountain Artillery' *Proceedings of the Royal Artillery Institution* XXXI, 1904–5.

— (trans. by A.H.C. Phillpotts). 'The Japanese Artillery' *Journal of the Royal Artillery* XXXII, 1905–6.

Curzon, George N. *Problems of the Far East*, 1894.

Daniels, Gordon. 'The Japanese Civil War (1868) – A British View' *Modern Asian Studies* I, 1967.

Davidson, James W. *The Island of Formosa Past and Present*,

1903.
de Fonblanque, Edward Barrington. *Niphon and Pe-che-li*, 1862.
Dennett, Tyler. *Americans in Eastern Asia*, 1922.
Deuchler, Martina. *Confucian Gentlemen and Barbarian Envoys: The Opening of Korea, 1875–1885*, 1977.
Dickins, F.V., and Lane-Poole, S. *The Life of Sir Harry Parkes* vol.II, 1894.
Diósy, Arthur. *The New Far East*, 1900.
— 'The Spirit of the Armed Forces of Japan' *Journal of the Royal Artillery* XXXII, 1905–6.
Dix, C.C. *The World's Navies in the Boxer Rebellion*, 1905.
Dobree, A. 'Japanese Swords' *Archaeological Journal* LXII, 1905.
Drea, Edward. 'The Imperial Japanese Army (1868–1945): Origins, Evolution, Legacy' in Jeremy Black (ed.) *War in the Modern World Since 1815*, 2003.
du Boulay, N.W.H. *An Epitome of the Chino-Japanese War, 1894–95*, 1896.
— 'The Chino-Japanese War' *Proceedings of the Royal Artillery Institution* XXIII, 1896.
Duus, Peter. *The Abacus and the Sword: The Japanese Penetration of Korea, 1895–1910*, 1995.
Earl, G.W. *The Eastern Seas*, 1837.
Eastlake, F. Warrington, and Yamada Yoshi-aki. *Heroic Japan: A History of the War Between China & Japan*, 1897.
Edgerton, Robert B. *Warriors of the Rising Sun*, 1997.
Edwardes, Michael. *The West in Asia 1850–1914*, 1967.
Eunson, Roby. *100 Years: The Amazing Development of Japan since 1860*, 1965.
Fairbank, John K.; Reischauer, Edwin O.; and Craig, Albert M. *East Asia: Tradition & Transformation*, 1989.
Ford, John D. *An American Cruiser in the East*, 1898.
Fox, Harry H. 'The Corean Army' *Report of the 6th Meeting of the Australasian Association for the Advancement of Science*, 1895.
Fukushima Shingo. 'The Building of a National Army' *Developing Economies* 3, 1965.
Fuller, Richard, and Gregory, Ron. *Japanese Military and Civil Swords and Dirks*, 1996.
Gale, James S. *Korean Sketches*, 1898.
Garbutt, Matthew. 'Japanese Armour from the Inside' *Transactions & Proceedings of the Japan Society* XI, 1912–13.
Gardner, Christopher Thomas. 'Constitution and Government of Corea' *Report of the 6th Meeting of the Australasian Association for the Advancement of Science*, 1895.
General Staff, War Office. *The Russo-Japanese War: Part I*, 1906.
Gifford, Daniel L. *Every-day Life in Korea*, 1898.
Gilbertson, Edward. 'Japanese Archery and Archers' *Transactions & Proceedings of the Japan Society* IV, 1900.
Gilmore, G.W. *Corea of To-day*, 1894.
Goedertier, Joseph M. *A Dictionary of Japanese History*, 1968.
Goldman, Emily O. 'The Spread of Western Military Models to Ottoman Turkey and Meiji Japan' in Theo Farrell and Terry Terriff (eds.) *The Sources of Military Change: Culture, Politics, Technology*, 2002.
Golownin, Vasilii. *Memoirs of a Captivity in Japan during the Years 1811, 1812, and 1813* vol.III, 1824.
Grew, E. Sharpe. *War in the East* vol.I, 1905.
Grierson, J.M. *The Armed Strength of Japan*, 1886.
Griffis, William Eliot. *Corea: The Hermit Nation*, 1882.
— *The Mikado's Empire* (2 vols), 1903.
Gubbins, J.H. *The Progress of Japan 1853–1871*, 1911.
— *The Making of Modern Japan*, 1922.
Hacker, Barton C. 'The Weapons of the West: Military Technology and Modernization in 19th-century China and Japan' *Technology and Culture* 18, 1977.
Hackett, Roger F. 'The Military: Japan' in Robert E. Ward and Dankwart A. Rustow (eds.) *Political Modernization in Japan and Turkey*, 1964.
Hall, Basil. *Account of a Voyage of Discovery to the West Coast of Corea*, 1818.
Hall, J.C. 'A Visit to West Coast and Capital of Korea' *Transactions of the Asiatic Society of Japan* XI, 1883.
Hamilton, Angus. *Korea*, 1904.
Hammerton, J.A. (ed.). *Peoples of All Nations* vol.V, 1922.
Hane, Mikiso. *Peasants, Rebels and Outcastes*, 1982.
— *Premodern Japan: A Historical Survey*, 1991.
Hardy, Arthur Sherburne. 'The Army of Japan' *The Cosmopolitan* X, 1890.
Harries, Merion and Susie. *Soldiers of the Sun: The Rise and Fall of the Imperial Japanese Army 1868–1945*, 1991.
Hasunuma Keisuke. 'Nishi Amane and G.H. Lewes' *Kobe University Law Review* 15, 1981.
Hilger, M. Inez. *Together with the Ainu*, 1971.
Hillsborough, Romulus. *Samurai Sketches: From the Bloody Final Years of the Shogun*, 2001.
— *Shinsengumi: The Shogun's Last Samurai Corps*, 2005.
Hitchcock, Romyn. 'The Ainos of Yezo, Japan' *Report of the U.S. National Museum 1890*, 1891.
Honeycutt, Fred L., and Anthony, F. Patt. *Military Rifles of Japan* 5th edition, 1996.
House, Edward H. *The Japanese Expedition to Formosa*, 1875.
Hulbert, Homer B. *The History of Korea* vol.II, 1905.
— *The Passing of Korea*, 1906.
Humbert, Aimé. *Japan and the Japanese Illustrated*, 1874.
Inagaki, Manjro. *Japan and the Pacific*, 1890.
'The Island of Saghalin' *Scottish Geographical Magazine* X, 1894.
James, David H. *The Rise and Fall of the Japanese Empire*, 1951.
Jansen, Marius B. *Japan and China: From War to Peace 1894–1972*, 1975.
— (ed.). *The Cambridge History of Japan, vol.5: The Nineteenth Century*, 1989.
Jintaro, Fujii (ed.). *Outline of Japanese History in the Meiji Era*, 1958.
Joe, Wanne J. *Traditional Korea: A Cultural History*, 1972.
Kane, Daniel C. 'Bellonet and Roze: Overzealous Servants of Empire and the 1866 French Attack on Korea' *Korean Studies* 23, 1999.
Kearsey, A. *A Study of the Strategy and Tactics of the Russo-Japanese War, 1904, up to 24th August*, 1935.
Kelly, W. Hyde. 'The Japanese Attack on Port Arthur, November, 1894' *United Service Magazine* New Series XXIX, 1904.
Kim, C.I. Eugene, and Kim, Han-kyo. *Korea and the Politics of Imperialism 1876–1910*, 1968.
Knollys, Henry. *Sketches of Life in Japan*, 1887.
Knötel, Herbert, and Sieg, Herbert (trans. by Ronald G. Ball). *Uniforms of the World*, 1980.
Kodama, Sakuzaemon. *Ainu Historical and Anthropological Studies*, 1970.
Koons, E.W. 'Beacon-Fires of Old Korea' *Transactions of the Korea Branch of the Royal Asiatic Society* XVI, 1925.
Koop, A.J. 'The Use of Leather in Japanese Military Equipment' *Transactions & Proceedings of the Japan*

Society XIV, 1915–16.
Korea: Its People and Culture, 1970.
Korea Past and Present, 1972.
Korean Repository I–V, 1891–98.
Krausse, Alexis. *The Far East: Its History and Its Question*, 1900.
Kublin, Hyman. 'The "Modern" Army of Early Meiji Japan' *Far Eastern Quarterly* IX, 1949–50.
Kuno, Yoshi S. *Japanese Expansion on the Asiatic Continent* vol.2, 1940.
Kyu-tae, Yi. *Modern Transformation of Korea*, 1970.
Landor, A. Henry Savage. *Alone with the Hairy Ainu*, 1893.
— 'A Visit to Corea' *Fortnightly Review* LVI, 1894.
Laufer, Berthold. *Chinese Clay Figures, Part I: Prolegomena on the History of Defensive Armor*, 1914.
Leader, John. 'The Japanese Army' *United Service Magazine* New Series XXVI, 1903.
Lebon, F.E.B. 'The Origins of the Japanese Army' *Proceedings of the Royal Artillery Institution* XXV, 1898.
Lee, Ki-baik. *A New History of Korea*, 1984.
Lee, Peter H. *Sourcebook of Korean Civilization* vol.II, 1996.
Lehautcourt, Pierre. 'The Army and Navy of Japan' *Journal of the Royal United Service Institution* XXXVII, 1893.
Lehmann, Jean-Pierre. 'The French Military Mission to Japan, 1866–1868, and Bakumatsu Politics' *Proceedings of the British Association for Japanese Studies* I, 1976.
Leroi-Gourhan, Arlotte and André. *Un Voyage Chez les Aïnous*, 1989.
Lew Young Ick. 'American Advisers in Korea 1885–1894: Anatomy of Failure' in Andrew Nahm (ed.) *The United States and Korea: American-Korean Relations 1866–1976*, 1979.
Lone, Stewart. *Japan's First Modern War: Army and Society in the Conflict with China, 1894–95*, 1994.
— and McCormack, Gaven. *Korea Since 1850*, 1993.
Lowell, Percival. *Chosön: The Land of the Morning Calm*, 1885.
Maruyama Nobuhiko. *Clothes of Samurai Warriors*, 1994.
Maxwell, William. *From the Yalu to Port Arthur*, 1906.
McClatchie, Thomas R.H. 'Japanese Heraldry' *Transactions of the Asiatic Society of Japan* V, 1877.
McEvedy, Colin. *The Penguin Historical Atlas of the Pacific*, 1998.
McKenzie, F.A. *The Tragedy of Korea*, 1908.
M'Leod, John. *Narrative of a Voyage in His Majesty's Ship Alceste to the Yellow Sea*, 1818.
Medzini, Meron. *French Policy in Japan during the Closing Years of the Tokugawa Regime*, 1971.
Merson, John. *Roads to Xanadu: East and West in the Making of the Modern World*, 1989.
'Military Notes' *Journal of the Royal United Service Institution* XXXIX–XLIX, 1895–1905.
Miln, Louise Jordan. *Quaint Korea*, 1895.
Minnich, Helen Benton. *Japanese Costume*, 1963.
Montgomery, H.B. *The Empire of the East*, 1908.
Morris, J. *Advance Japan*, 1895.
Mossman, Samuel. *New Japan*, 1873.
Mounsey, Augustus H. *The Satsuma Rebellion*, 1879.
Mullaly, B.R. 'The Evolution of the Japanese Army' *Army Quarterly* XVI, 1928.
Murdoch, James (ed. by Joseph H. Longford). *A History of Japan* vol.III, 1926.
Nahm, Andrew C. *Korea: Tradition and Transformation*, 1988.
— *A Panorama of 5000 Years: Korean History*, 1989.
— (ed.). *The United States and Korea: American-Korean Relations 1866–1976*, 1979.
Nakanishi, Ritta. *Japanese Military Uniforms 1841–1929: From the Fall of the Shogunate to the Russo-Japanese War*, 2001.
Nakata, Tadao. *Imperial Japanese Army and Navy Uniforms & Insignia*, 1987.
Nish, Ian (ed.). *British Documents on Foreign Affairs*, part I, series E, vols.2–7, 1989.
Nock, Elizabeth Tripler. 'The Satsuma Rebellion of 1877' *Far Eastern Quarterly* VII, 1947–48.
Norman, E. Herbert. *Japan's Emergence as a Modern State*, 1940.
— *Soldier and Peasant in Japan: The Origins of Conscription*, 1943.
Norman, F.J. *The Fighting Man of Japan*, 1905.
Norman, Henry. *The Real Japan*, 1892.
— *The Peoples and Politics of the Far East*, 1895.
Okamoto, Shumpei. *Impressions of the Front: Woodcuts of the Sino-Japanese War, 1894–95*, 1983.
Okuda, T. (trans. C.H.N. James). 'The Bombardment of Kagoshima by the British Fleet, August 1863' *Journal of the Royal United Service Institution* LVII, 1913.
Okuma Shigenobu (trans. by Marcus Huish). *Fifty Years of New Japan* (2 vols), 1909.
Oppert, Ernest. *A Forbidden Land: Voyages to the Corea*, 1880.
Pack-Beresford, A.W. 'The Artillery of Japan' *Proceedings of the Royal Artillery Institution* XXIV, 1897.
Paine, S. *The Sino-Japanese War of 1894–1895: Perceptions, Power and Primacy*, 2005.
Perkins, Dorothy. *Japan Goes to War: A Chronology of Japanese Military Expansion from the Meiji Era to the Attack on Pearl Harbor, 1868–1941*, 1997.
Perrin, Noel. *Giving Up the Gun: Japan's Reversion to the Sword, 1543–1879*, 1979.
Preble, George Henry (ed. by Boleslaw Szczesniak). *The Opening of Japan*, 1962.
Presseisen, Ernst L. *Before Aggression: Europeans Prepare the Japanese Army*, 1965.
Ralston, David B. *Importing the European Army: The Introduction of European Military Techniques and Institutions into the Extra-European World, 1600–1914*, 1990.
Ravina, Mark J. *The Last Samurai: The Life and Battles of Saigo Takamori*, 2004.
— 'The Apocryphal Suicide of Saigo Takamori: Samurai, *Seppuku*, and the Politics of Legend' *Journal of Asian Studies* 69, 2010.
Recent Progress in Korea, 1910.
Rein, J.J. *Japan: Travels and Researches*, 1884.
Rennie, D.F. *The British Arms in North China and Japan*, 1864.
'Reorganisation of the Japanese Army' *The Phoenix* II, 1871–72.
Rhee, M.J. *The Doomed Empire: Japan in Colonial Korea*, 1997.
Robinson, H. Russell. *A Short History of Japanese Armour*, 1965.
— *Oriental Armour*, 1967.
Ross, John. *History of Corea*, 1879.
Ruhl, Moritz (ed. Bruce Bassett-Powell and Philip Cranz). *The Imperial Japanese Army 1896*, 2008.
Ruschenberger, W.S.W. *Narrative of a Voyage Round the World During the Years 1835, 36, and 37* (2 vols), 1838.
St.John, H.C. 'The Ainos: Aborigines of Yeso' *Journal of the Anthropological Institute of Great Britain and Ireland* II, 1873.

Sakai, Robert K. 'Feudal Society and Modern Leadership in Satsuma-han' *Journal of Asian Studies* XVI, 1956–57.
Sakata, Yoshio, and Hall, John Whitney. 'The Motivation of Political Leadership in the Meiji Restoration' *Journal of Asian Studies* XVI, 1956.
Salwey, Charlotte M. *The Island Dependencies of Japan*, 1913.
Sansom, George B. *The Western World and Japan*, 1950.
Satow, Ernest Mason. *A Diplomat in Japan*, 1921.
— (trans.). *Japan 1853–1864, or Genj Yume Monogatari*, 1905.
Saunderson, H.S. 'Notes on Corea and its People' *Journal of the Anthropological Institute* XXIV, 1895.
Schley, Winfield Scott. *Forty-Five Years Under the Flag*, 1904.
Sedgwick, F.R. *The Russo-Japanese War on Land*, 1908.
'Seven Months Among the Tong Haks' *Korean Repository* II, 1895.
Shoberl, Frederic (ed.). *The World in Miniature: Japan*, 1823.
Sinclaire, Clive. *Samurai: The Weapons and Spirit of the Japanese Warrior*, 2001.
Singleton, Esther (ed. and trans.). *Japan as Seen and Described by Famous Writers*, 1905.
Smith, Bradley. *Japan: A History in Art*, 1972.
Smith, George. *Ten Weeks in Japan*, 1861.
Smith, W. Richmond. *The Siege and Fall of Port Arthur*, 1905.
Sonoda, Hidehiro. 'The Decline of the Japanese Warrior Class, 1840–1880' *Japan Review* I, 1990.
Stead, Alfred (ed.). *Japan by the Japanese*, 1904.
Stephan, John J. 'Saigo Takamori and the Satsuma Rebellion' *Papers on Japan* 3, 1965.
— *The Kuril Islands: Russo-Japanese Frontier in the Pacific*, 1974.
Stone, George Cameron. *A Glossary of the Construction, Decoration and Use of Arms and Armor in all Countries and in all Times*, 1934.
Summers, James. 'On Recent Changes in Japan' *The Phoenix* I, 1870–71.
Takata, Y., and Ogawa, Gotaro. *Conscription System in Japan*, 1921.
Taylor, Bayard. *A Visit to India, China & Japan*, 1860.
Taylor, W. 'The Medico-Military Arrangements of the Japanese Army in the Field' *Aldershot Military Society Journal*, 1895.
Tennant, Roger. *A History of Korea*, 1996.
Tilley, Henry Arthur. *Japan, the Amoor, and the Pacific*, 1861.
Totman, Conrad. *The Collapse of the Tokugawa Bakufu 1862–1868*, 1980.
Trewartha, Glenn Thomas. *Japan: A Physical, Cultural & Regional Geography*, 1945.
Turnbull, Stephen R. *The Samurai: A Military History*, 1977.
— *The Book of the Samurai: The Warrior Class of Japan*, 1982.
— *Samurai Warfare*, 1996.
— *Samurai: The Warrior Tradition*, 1996.
Underwood, L.H. *Fifteen Years Among the Top-Knots, or Life in Korea*, 1904.
Upton, Emory. *The Armies of Europe & Asia*, 1878.
Vincent, B. 'The Japanese Field and Mountain Artillery' *Proceedings of the Royal Artillery Institution* XXXI, 1904–5.
— 'Notes on the Korean Army' *Proceedings of the Royal Artillery Institution* XXXI, 1904–5.
Walder, David. *The Short Victorious War: The Russo-Japanese Conflict 1904–5*, 1974.
The War in the Far East 1904–1905, 1905.
Weems, Benjamin B. *Reform, Rebellion and the Heavenly Way*, 1964.
Westney, D. Eleanor. 'The Military' in Marius B. Jansen and Gilbert Rozman (eds.) *Japan in Transition: From Tokugawa to Meiji*, 1986.
White, Trumbull. *The War in the East: Japan, China, and Corea*, 1895.
Wigmore, John Henry. 'Administrative and Commercial Institutions of Old Japan' *Transactions of the Asiatic Society of Japan* XX, 1893.
Williams, S. Wells. 'A Journal of the Perry Expedition to Japan (1853–1854)' *Transactions of the Asiatic Society of Japan* XXXVII, 1910.
Williamson, Alexander. *Journeys in North China, Manchuria, and Eastern Mongolia, with some Account of Corea*, 1870.
Woo-Keun, Han. *The History of Korea*, 1970.
Wood, W. Martin. 'The Hairy Men of Yesso' *Transactions of the Ethnological Society of London* IV, 1866.
Woodward, David. *Armies of the World 1854–1914*, 1978.
Wright, Diana E. 'Female Combatants and Japan's Meiji Restoration: The Case of Aizu' *War in History* 8, 2001.
Yanaga, Chitoshi. *Japan Since Perry*, 1949.
Yashi, Shozan (trans. by Ernest Mason Satow). *Kinse Shiriaku, a History of Japan (1853–69)*, 1906.
Younghusband, G.J. *On Short Leave to Japan*, 1894.

INDEX to volumes 1–5

Square bracketed numbers 1–5 refer to volume number. Dates in parentheses refer to either (a) the date of a military engagement or treaty; (b) the duration of a war or an individual's reign; or (c) the date of an individual's death (denoted by 'd.').

The letter 'n' signifies a note – e.g., 28n56 = page 28 note 56.

NB There is often more than one reference to a subject on a page.

Risings and Rebellions 1919-39

Interwar Colonial Campaigns in Africa, Asia and the Americas

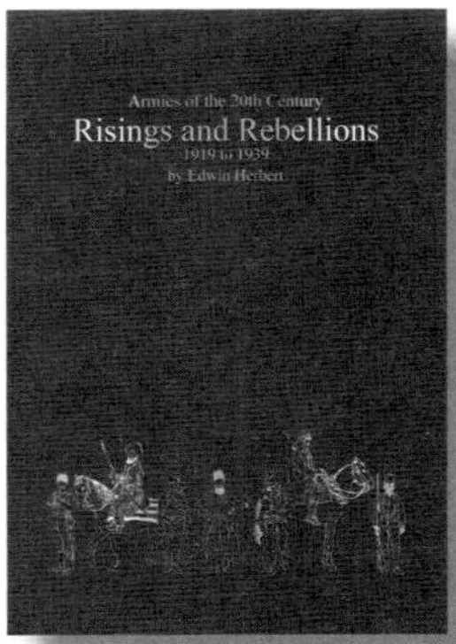

Following on from the author's highly-acclaimed Small Wars and Skirmishes, this volume covers the most significant 'small wars' of the interwar period up to the Italian occupation of Abyssinia in 1935–36. The author illustrates the main types of campaign involved, the organisation of forces, the effects of new weaponry, and the tactics that the indigenous peoples adopted to counter the technology of the colonial invaders. A4 sized hardback with traditional linen and glittering gilt binding, 192 pages. Illustrations include 137 drawings of soldiers, 50 other illustrations and maps.

India's North-East Frontier

The Abors, the Akas, Assam, Cachar, the Chin-Lushai, the Daflas, the Garos, the Khamtis, the Khasis, Manipur, the Mikirs, the Mishmis, the Nagas, the Singhpos and Tripura.

This is the first ever in-depth study of one of the most remote and neglected theatres of 19th-century colonial conflict, where for decades British and Indian troops fought a forgotten war against merciless warbands of head-hunters and slave-raiders. The greater part of the information contained in this book will be entirely new to readers, and is here made available to a wider audience for the very first time. Illustrations include 125 drawings of warriors, 53 other illustrations, and nine maps.

Burma and Indo-China

The Kingdom of Ava, The Kachins, The Karens, The Shan States, The Wa, Cambodia, The Lao States, Siam & Vietnam

This volume covers a region which witnessed fierce competition between Britain and France during the 19th century, as each sought to establish a southern trade route into China while at the same time continuing the vigorous jockeying for local political pre-eminence. A4 sized hardback with traditional linen and glittering gilt binding. 207 pages, over 60 pictures and maps, over 160 line illustrations.

China

19th Century Imperial China

The Celestial Empire's traditional distrust of all foreigners, exacerbated by misunderstandings guaranteed that relations between the Empire and the Western world would lead to war. This book is an illustrated study of the Empire's armed forces during this turbulent period, its organisational structure, arms, uniforms, and tactics. Such foreign-officered units as the Ever-Victorious Army are also covered, as are the armies of the many revolutionary movements, including the Taipings, Boxers, Panthays, Miao, Tungans, and Nien. A4 sized hardback with traditional linen and glittering gilt binding. 174 pages, illustrations include 183 drawings of warriors and soldiers, 39 other illustrations, and six maps.

Central Asia and the Himalayan Kingdoms

This volume is the first to examine the military history of this remote region, wedged uncomfortably between the British, Russian, and Chinese empires: Central Asia's long-established Uzbek states of Bokhara, Kokhand, and Khiva were all destined to submit to the expanding Russian Empire in the 1870s, while the ancient kingdoms of the Himalayas would be contested between the vigorous British Empire and ailing China, before mostly ending up in British hands A4 hardback with traditional linen and gilt binding. 133 drawings of warriors and soldiers, 41 other illustrations, and 12 maps.

The African Knights

Armies of the 19th Century Eastern African Savannah

The Armies of Sokoto, Bornu and Bagirmi in the Nineteenth Century. This book provides a description of what was, in the 19th century, one of the most neglected parts of the African continent, but was at the same time, without doubt, one of the most culturally sophisticated — the eastern Savannah, an area now divided between the modern countries of Nigeria, Niger, Mali, and Cameroon. It begins with the Sokoto jihad and ends with the conquest of the Savannah states by Europeans. A4 softback with colour covers, 64 pages illustrated throughout with black and white contemporary photographs and engravings.

NAPOLEON

Rules for Battles of the Napoleonic Wars

Napoleon contains a unique set of entertaining rules that are flexible enough to be used with almost any basing conventions. It also includes many army lists for the most popular Napoleonic armies, plus advanced rules covering such diverse subjects as pontoon bridges, grand battery fire, ground conditions, setting fire to buildings, friendly fire and ambulances! Napoleon also features articles on painting and collecting Napoleonic models plus many other sections detailing uniforms and historical background. For the miniature painters and collectors, Kevin Dallimore has added his own article on painting Napoleonic models. 232 pages full colour, A4 sized hardback, over 400 colour photographs and illustrations, including many Knotël prints, numerous diagrams, maps and other illustrations.

Medieval Warfare

Rules for Medieval Battles 450-1515 AD

Terry's long awaited, definitive and detailed set of wargame rules for the Medieval period. An A4 hardback with 168 pages, lavishly illustrated throughout in black and white with colour sections. Special illustrations by Peter Denis with cover illustrations by Chris Collingwood. Spanning everything from the Late Romans to the beginning of the sixteenth century; with these rules you can command and fight against some of the most exciting armies ever to stride the battlefields of Europe and the Middle East. More than 80 colour illustrations, over 172 black and white illustrations, 36 diagrams and maps.

The Foundry Compendium

Pirates to Darkest Africa

The Foundry Compendium is packed with rules, painting advice and ideas for making great-looking terrain. It will appeal to anyone interested in playing games such as exploration in Darkest Africa, fighting for survival and glory in Rome's gladiatorial arenas and plundering the West African coast with your band of cutthroat pirates. Themed to concentrate on Pirates and Darkest Africa, but covering other historical periods too; Aztecs, Gladiators, Greeks and Romans. 96 pages, lavishly illustrated in full colour throughout. A4 Softback.

The Rules With No Name

Rules for the Old West

The Rules With No Name are a straightforward set of rules for gunfights in the age of the Cowboy and the Indian, the Lawman and the Outlaw. Classic encounters are played out using 28mm miniatures in an easy-to-learn game full of subtle complexity. The innovative Fate Deck introduces a fun and realistic element of chance while simple rules for movement, shooting and fighting allow for quick, friendly games in which players will find themselves presented with a deceptively challenging set of tactical choices from one turn to the next. This book contains all the rules you will need to play. 136 pages, lavishly illustrated in full colour throughout.

KEVIN DALLIMORE'S
Painting & Modelling Guide
MASTER CLASS

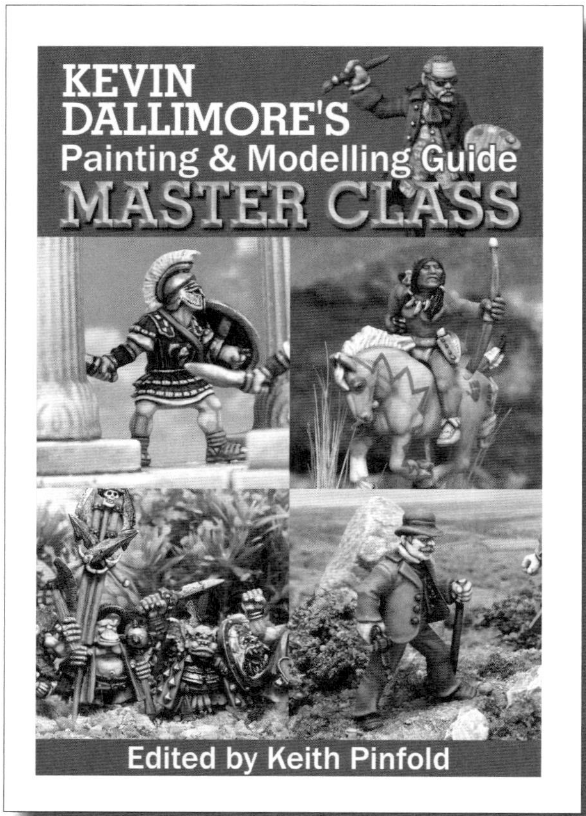

Everything you ever wanted to know about painting miniatures and models to a professional standard is contained in this 308 page book.

Kevin Dallimore and over twenty five other renowned and respected painters and modellers reveal the techniques they use to give their miniatures and models that great professional finish; techniques such as varnishing, dry brushing, non metallic metal, shading, highlighting, blending, textured leather and the use of diluted washes are all discussed in depth together with many modelling ideas too; ideas for doing conversions, creating dioramas, making and painting scenery, vehicles and many more. All of the processes described in the many different articles are fully detailed and coupled with photographs of each important stage.

Initially, Kevin goes quickly through the all important basics before clearly detailing all of the advanced techniques that he and his fellow painters use to produce great looking models. There then follow many articles where guest painters and modellers share their thoughts and ideas on particular techniques when painting historical, fantasy and sci-fi models: Old West, Napoleonic, Ancients, Romans,Swashbucklers,WW2, Goblins, Orcs, Beastmen, Trolls, Judge Dredd and lots more.

By copying the methods and techniques in this book and with a little determination and practice, everyone will be able to produce painted miniatures and models to a standard that previously they had only dreamed of.